AIRCRAFT ANATOMY OF WORLD WAR II

AIRCRAFT ANATOMY OF WORLD WAR II

TECHNICAL DRAWINGS OF KEY AIRCRAFT 1939–1945

GENERAL EDITORS: PAUL E. EDEN AND SOPH MOENG

This edition first published in 2007 by
Amber Books Ltd
Bradley's Close
74–77 White Lion Street
London N1 9PF
United Kingdom
www.amberbooks.co.uk

Reprinted in 2009

ISBN: 978-1-905704-32-3

Printed in Thailand

Contents

Bombers and Dive Bombers

Arado Ar 234

Above: This captured aircraft is an example of the major production model, the Ar 234B-2. The projection above the cockpit is a periscope sight which could serve the two optional 0.79in (20-mm) rear-firing cannon, or give the pilot his only view aft of the aircraft.

Arado Ar234

Cutaway key

1 Port elevator hinge
2 Tailplane skinning
3 Port elevator
4 Tab actuating rod
5 Elevator trim tab
6 Geared rudder tab (upper)
7 Rudder hinges
8 Tail navigation light
9 Plywood fin leading edge
10 T-aerial
11 Re-transmission aerial
12 Aerial matching unit
13 Tailfin structure
14 Rudder construction
15 Rudder post
16 Rudder tab (lower)
17 Lower rudder hinge
18 Rudder actuating rods
19 Parachute cable
20 Cable anchor point/tailskid
21 Starboard elevator tab
22 Elevator construction
23 Tailplane construction
24 Elevator control linkage
25 Tailplane attachment points
26 Elevator rod
27 Port side control runs
28 Internal mass balance
29 Parachute release mechanism
30 Main FuG 16zy panel (BZA computer)
31 Brake parachute container
32 Starboard MG 151 cannon muzzle
33 Brake chute door (open)
34 Mauser MG 151/20 cannon (rearward firing)
35 Cannon support yoke

36 Spent cartridge chute
37 Access panel (lowered)
38 Ammunition feed chute
39 Tail surface control rods (starboard)
40 Ammunition box
41 Bulkhead
42 Fuel vent pipe
43 Fuel pumps
44 Fuel lever gauge
45 Rear fuel cell (2000-litre –440-Imp gal capacity)
46 Fuselage frames
47 Fuel filler point
48 Fuel lines
49 Inner flap construction
50 Exhaust cone
51 Nacelle support fairing
52 RATO exhaust
53 Outer flap section
54 Aileron tab

55 Tab actuating rod
56 Port aileron
57 Port navigation light
58 Aileron control linkage
59 Pitot tube
60 Front spar
61 Outer flap control linkage
62 Wing construction
63 Nacelle attachment points (front and rear spar)
64 Detachable nacelle cowling
65 FuG 25a IFF unit
66 Inner flap control linkage
67 Control rods and hydraulic activating rod
68 Rear spar
69 Hydraulic fluid tank (18-litre – 4-Imp gal capacity)
70 Centre section box

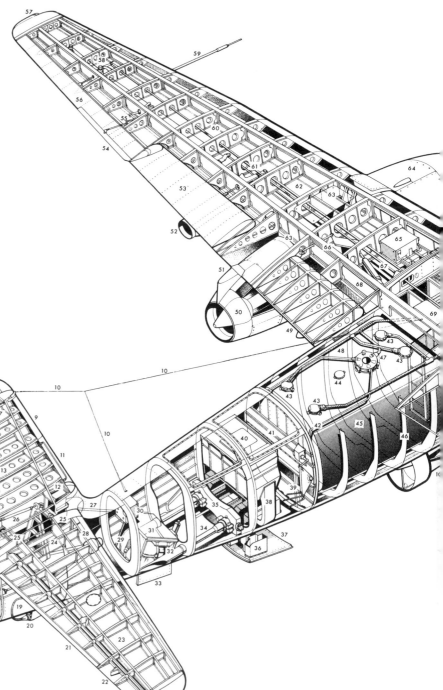

SPECIFICATION		
Arado Ar 234B-2 Blitz		
Type		**Weights**
Single-seat multi-role warplane		Empty 11,464 lb (5200 kg); maximum take-off 21,715 lb (9850 kg)
Powerplant		**Dimensions**
Two Junkers Jumo 004B turbojet engines each rated at 1,962 lb st (8.73 kN)		Wing span 46 ft 3½ in (14.10 m); length 41 ft 5½ in (12.64 m); height 14 ft 11½ in (4.30 m); wing area 284.18 sq ft (26.40 m2)
Performance		
Maximum speed 460 mph (740 km/h) at 19,685 ft (6000 m); climb to 19,685 ft (6000 m) in 17 minutes 30 seconds with 3,307-lb (1500-kg) bombload; service ceiling 32,810 ft (10000 m); range 1,013 miles (1630 km)		

*The Ar 234B-2 was far more versatile than its predecessor, the Ar 234B-1, being capable of bombing, pathfinding or reconnaissance missions. This model is equipped with **Rauchgeräte** take-off assistance rockets outboard of the engine nacelles.*

71 FuG 25a ring antenna
72 Suppressed D/F antenna
73 Fuel pumps
74 Fuel level gauge
75 Fuel filler point
76 Fuel lines
77 Bulkhead
78 Port control console (throttle quadrant)
79 Pilot entry hatch (hinged to starboard)
80 Periscopic sight
81 Periscopic head (rearview mirror/gunsight)
82 Clear vision cockpit glazing
83 Instrument panel
84 Rudder pedal
85 Swivel-mounted control stick
86 Lotfo 7K tachometric bombsight mounting
87 Pilot's seat
88 Starboard control console (oil/temperature gauges)
89 Radio panel (FuG 16zy behind pilot's seat)
90 Oxygen bottles
91 Nosewheel door
92 Nosewheel fork
93 Rearward-retracting Nosewheel
94 Nosewheel well centre section
95 Fuselage frames
96 Forward fuel cell (1800-litre – 385-Imp gal capacity)
97 Bulkhead
98 Mainwheel door
99 Starboard mainwheel well
100 Mainwheel leg door
101 Starboard mainwheel leg
102 Forward-retracting mainwheel
103 SC 1000 "Hermann" bomb beneath fuselage
104 Engine exhaust
105 Auxiliary cooling intakes
106 Starboard Jumo 004B turbojet
107 Annular oil tank
108 Riedel starter motor on nose cone
109 Auxiliary tank (300 litre/66 Imp gal) beneath nacelle (not carried with SC 1000 bomb)
110 Flat outer section construction
111 Walter HWK 500A-1 RATO unit
112 RATO recovery parachute pack
113 Aileron tab
114 Starboard aileron construction
115 Wing skin stiffeners
116 Starboard navigation light

Arado 234s line up awaiting another mission during the Ardennes counter-offensive of December 1944–January 1945. The Ar 234s were used for pinpoint attacks on the advancing Allied positions.

Arado Ar 234

This aircraft bears the markings of the 9th Staffel, III Gruppe, Kampfgeschwader (KG) 76. This unit was equipped with Ar 234s in January 1945, and was heavily involved in the attacks on Remagen bridge. KG 76 flew its first sorties with the Ar 234 during the Ardennes offensive in January, although the sortie rate was strictly limited through shortage of fuel. During the second week of February, the Kampfgeschwader was heavily engaged in an attempt to relieve the Allied pressure on Kleve. By the end of March 1945, sorties by KG 76 had virtually ceased.

Periscope

The persicope mounted above the cockpit for use in dive-bombing attacks could also be turned rearwards in the Ar 234C variant and used to aim the rearward-firing fixed cannon. Considering the radical nature of the aircraft, development flying proceeded very smoothly, with one or two of the numerous development aircraft being allocated to test the various systems. The only serious accident occurred when the last A-series development aircaft, the Ar 234V-7, suffered an engine fire in flight; the control rods in the port wing burned through and the aircraft crashed as its pilot was trying to land it.

Cockpit

The pilot sat on a primitive ejection seat, with armour platting behind his headrest. The bomber was equipped with a Patin PDS three-axes autopilot with LKS 7D-15 overriding control, enabling the pilot to swing the control column clear so that he could use the Lofte 7K tachometric bomb sight, which was mounted beneath his feet. For shallow dive-bombing a BZA bombing computer was used in conjunction with an RF2C periscopic sight; steep dives were strictly forbidden because of jet surge and the sensitivity of the lateral trim.

Armament

The Ar 234C-1 variant was intended to be fitted with two fixed rearward-firing 0.79in (20mm) MG 151/20 cannon mounted in the underside of the rear fuselage to protect against attack from astern. In addition, two similar weapons were to be installed beneath the nose. Several night fighter versions of the Ar 234 were proposed; the Ar 234C-7, for example, had a crew of two seated side by side and was dsigned to have the FuG 245 Bremen O centimetric radar with a scanner installed in the nose. Some night fighter sorties were flown by two converted Ar 234s at the end of the war.

Bomber and reconnaissance variants

The Ar 234B had a maximum bomb load of 3307lb (1500kg). Its usual bomb load was three 1102lb (500kg) bombs mounted in nacelles under each engine and the fuselage. Larger single bombs could be carried under the fuselage alone. Several sub-variants were produced, including the B-2/b reconnaissance aircraft, the B 2/1 pathfinder and the B 2/r, which was equipped with auxiliary fuel tanks. All aircraft were fitted with braking parachutes, but these were rarely used operationally. The final proposed bomber version was the Ar 234B-3, which was abandoned in favour of the Ar 234C.

Powerplant

The Ar 234 was powered by a pair of Junkers Jumo 004B-1 Orkan axial flow turbojets, which gave the aircraft a top speed of some 742km/h (461mph) when flying 'clean', without external stores. Some of the development Ar 234s were fitted with the BMW 003A-1 engine, but a great deal of trouble was experienced with the thrust control of this powerplant, which also proved difficult to restart after a flamout during flight. The problem of thrust regulation was solved by the use of the Jumo 004 system. The turbojets had a life of only about 25 hours.

Avro Lancaster

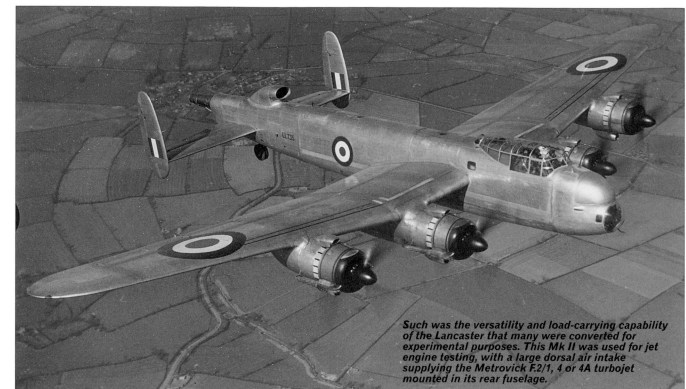

Such was the versatility and load-carrying capability of the Lancaster that many were converted for experimental purposes. This Mk II was used for jet engine testing, with a large dorsal air intake supplying the Metrovick F.2/1, 4 or 4A turbojet mounted in its rear fuselage.

Lancaster B.Mk III

Cutaway key

1 Two 0.303-in (7.7-mm) Browning machine-guns
2 Fraser-Nash power-operated nose turret
3 Nose blister
4 Bomb-aimer's panel (optically flat)
5 Bomb-aimer's control panel
6 Side windows
7 External air temperature thermometer
8 Pitot head
9 Bomb-aimer's chest support
10 Fire extinguisher
11 Parachute emergency exit
12 F24 camera
13 Glycol tank/step
14 Ventilator fairing
15 Bomb-bay doors forward actuating jacks
16 Bomb-bay doors forward bulkhead
17 Control linkage
18 Rudder pedals
19 Instrument panel
20 Windscreen sprays
21 Windscreen
22 Dimmer switches
23 Flight engineer's folding seat
24 Flight engineer's control panel
25 Pilot's seat
26 Flight-deck floor level
27 Elevator and rudder control rods (under floor)
28 Trim tab control cables
29 Main floor/bomb-bay support longeron
30 Fire extinguisher
31 Wireless installation
32 Navigator's seat
33 Canopy rear/down-view blister
34 Pilot's head armour
35 Cockpit canopy emergency escape hatch
36 D/F loop
37 Aerial mast support
38 Electrical services panel
39 Navigator's compartment window
40 Navigator's desk
41 Aircraft and radio compass receiver
42 Wireless operator's desk
43 Wireless operator's seat
44 Wireless operator's compartment window
45 Front spar carry-through/fuselage frame
46 Astrodome
47 Inboard section wing ribs
48 Spar join
49 Aerial mast
50 Starboard inboard engine nacelle
51 Spinner
52 Three-bladed de Havilland constant-speed propellers
53 Oil cooler intake
54 Oil cooler radiator
55 Carburettor air intake
56 Radiator shutter
57 Engine bearer frame
58 Exhaust flame damper shroud
59 Packard-built Rolls-Royce Merlin 28 liquid-cooled engine
60 Nacelle/wing fairing
61 Fuel tank bearer ribs
62 Intermediate ribs
63 Leading-edge structure
64 Wing stringers
65 Wingtip skinning
66 Starboard navigation light
67 Starboard formation light
68 Aileron hinge fairings
69 Wing rear spar
70 Starboard aileron
71 Aileron balance tab
72 Balance tab control rod
73 Aileron trim tab
74 HF aerial
75 Split trailing-edge flap (outboard section)
76 Emergency (ditching) exit
77 Crash axe stowage
78 Fire extinguisher
79 Hydraulic reservoir
80 Signal/flare pistol stowage
81 Parachute stowage box/spar step
82 Rear spar carry-through
83 Bunk backrest
84 Rear spar fuselage frame
85 Emergency packs
86 Roof light
87 Dinghy manual release cable (dinghy stowage in starboard wingroot)
88 Mid-gunner's parachute stowage
89 Tail turret ammunition box
90 Ammunition feed track
91 Emergency (ditching) exit
92 Flame floats stowage
93 Sea markers stowage
94 Roof light
95 Dorsal turret fairing
96 Fraser-Nash power-operated dorsal turret
97 Two 0.303-in (7.7-mm) Browning machine-guns
98 Turret mounting ring
99 Turret mechanism
100 Ammunition track cover plate
101 Turret step
bracket
102 Header tank
103 Oxygen cylinder
104 Fire extinguisher
105 DR compass housing
106 Handrail
107 Crew entry door (starboard)
108 Parachute stowage
109 First-aid pack

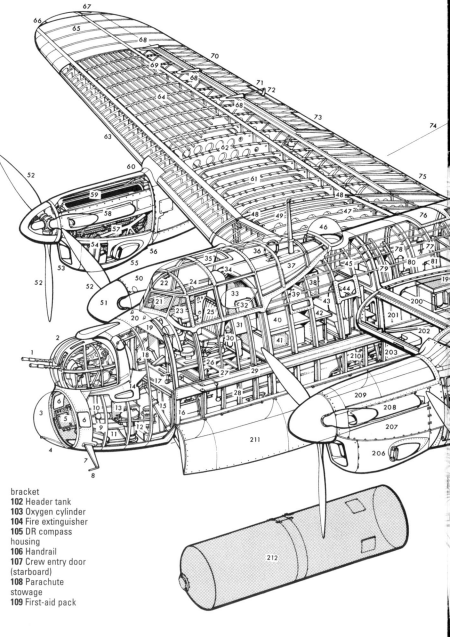

A single Lancaster is maintained in flying condition by the Royal Air Force's Battle of Britain Memorial Flight. Based at RAF Coningsby in Lincolnshire, the aircraft wears its true serial number PA474, but has appeared in a variety of colour schemes since it joined the Flight in 1973.

SPECIFICATION

Lancaster Mk I

Dimensions

Length: tail up 69 ft 6 in (21.28 m); tail down 68 ft 10 in (20.98 m)
Wingspan: 102 ft (31.09 m)
Wing area: 1,300 sq ft (120.77 m²)
Total flap area: 146 sq ft (13.56 m²)
Total aileron area: 85.5 sq ft (26.06 m²)
Total fin and rudder area: 111.4 sq ft (10.35 m²)
Rudder area: 20.06 sq ft (1.86 m²)
Tailplane area (including elevators): 237 sq ft (22.02 m²)
Total elevator area: 87.5 sq ft (8.13 m²)
Height: tail up 20 ft 6 in (6.25 m); tail down 20 ft 4 in (6.20 m)
Undercarriage track: 23 ft 9 in (7.24 m)
Wing section: NACA 23018

Powerplant

Four 1,280-hp (955-kW) Rolls-Royce Merlin XX, or 1,460-hp (1089-kW) Merlin 22, or 1,640-hp (1223-kW) Merlin 24 liquid cooled, 12 cylinder, single-stage supercharged, Vee-type piston engines
Propellers: four de Havilland Type 5140 or Nash Kelvinator A5/138 Hydromatic three-bladed, feathering/constant-speed propellers

Weights

Empty: 37,000 lb (16783 kg)
Empty equipped: 41,000 lb (18614 kg)

Maximum take-off: 68,000 lb (30845 kg)

Fuel and load

Total internal fuel: 2,154 Imp gal (9792 litres)
Maximum bombload: 22,000 lb (9979 kg)

Performance

Maximum speed: 275 mph (442 km/h) at 15,000 ft (4570 m)
Cruising speed: 200 mph (322 km/h) at 15,000 ft (4570 m)
Climb rate: climb to 20,000 ft (6100 m) in 41 minutes 36 seconds
Service ceiling: 20,000 ft (6100 m) at maximum weight
Take-off run (to 50 ft/15 m): 4,649 ft (1417 m)
Landing run (from 50 ft/15 m): 3,002 ft (915 m)

Range

Range (with one auxiliary fuel tank and 7,000-lb/3175-kg payload): 2,530 miles (4072 km)
Range (with standard fuel and 10,000-lb/4540-kg payload): 1,040 miles (1673 km)

Defensive armament

Early production model: nine 0.303 in (7.7 mm) Browning machine guns (one in F.N.64 ventral, two each in F.N.5 nose and F.N.50 dorsal, and four in F.N.20 tail turrets)

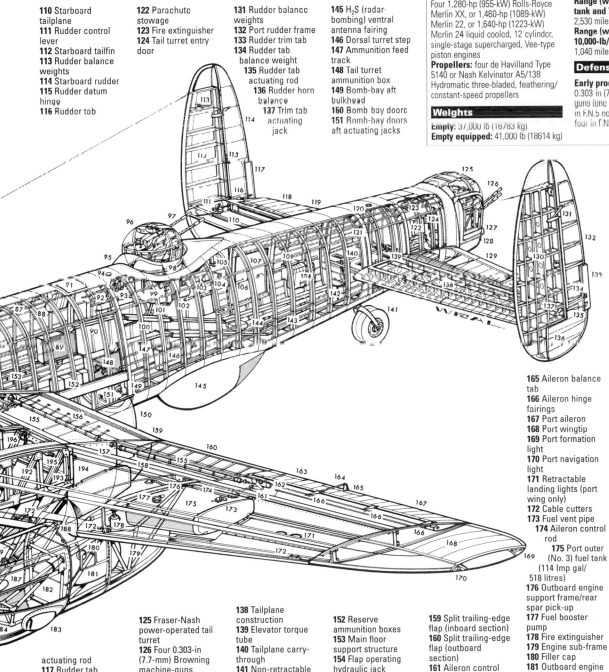

110 Starboard tailplane
111 Rudder control lever
112 Starboard tailfin
113 Rudder balance weights
114 Starboard rudder
115 Rudder datum hinge
116 Rudder tab
117 Rudder tab
118 Starboard elevator
119 Elevator balance tab
120 Roof light
121 Tail main frame
122 Parachute stowage
123 Fire extinguisher
124 Tail turret entry door
125 Fraser-Nash power-operated tail turret
126 Four 0.303-in (7.7-mm) Browning machine-guns
127 Cartridge case ejection chutes
128 Rear navigation light
129 Elevator trim tab
130 Fin construction
131 Rudder balance weights
132 Port rudder frame
133 Rudder trim tab
134 Rudder tab balance weight
135 Rudder tab actuating rod
136 Rudder horn balance
137 Trim tab actuating jack
138 Tailplane construction
139 Elevator torque tube
140 Tailplane carry-through
141 Non-retractable tailwheel
142 Elsan closet
143 Ammunition track cover plate
144 Elevator and rudder control rods
145 H₂S (radar-bombing) ventral antenna fairing
146 Dorsal turret step
147 Ammunition feed track
148 Tail turret ammunition box
149 Bomb-bay aft bulkhead
150 Bomb bay doors
151 Bomb-bay doors aft actuating jacks
152 Reserve ammunition boxes
153 Main floor support structure
154 Flap operating hydraulic jack
155 Flap operating tube
156 Flap toggle links
157 Flap tube connecting link
158 Rear spar
159 Split trailing-edge flap (inboard section)
160 Split trailing-edge flap (outboard section)
161 Aileron control lever
162 Aileron trim tab control cable linkage
163 Aileron trim tab
164 Aileron balance tab control rod
165 Aileron balance tab
166 Aileron hinge fairings
167 Port aileron
168 Port wingtip
169 Port formation light
170 Port navigation light
171 Retractable landing lights (port wing only)
172 Cable cutters
173 Fuel vent pipe
174 Aileron control rod
175 Port outer (No. 3) fuel tank (114 Imp gal/518 litres)
176 Outboard engine support frame/rear spar pick-up
177 Fuel booster pump
178 Fire extinguisher
179 Engine sub-frame
180 Filler cap
181 Outboard engine oil tank
182 Firewall/bulkhead
183 Carburettor air intake
184 Outboard engine support frame
185 Port mainwheel
186 Undercarriage oleo struts
187 Flame-damper shroud
188 Outboard engine support frame/main spar pick-up
189 Undercarriage retraction jacks
190 Oleo strut attachment pin
191 Undercarriage support beam (light-alloy casting)
192 Centre-section outer rib/undercarriage support
193 Location of port intermediate (No. 2) fuel tank (383 Imp gal/1741 litres)
194 Main wheel well
195 Emergency retraction air valve
196 Retraction cylinder attachment
197 Port inner (No. 1) fuel tank (580 Imp gal/2637 litres)
198 Oxygen bottle stowage
199 Rest bunk
200 Main spar
201 Hinged inboard leading edge
202 Cabin heater installation
203 Air intake
204 Inboard engine support frame
205 Inboard engine oil tank
206 Carburettor intake anti-ice guard
207 Port inner nacelle
208 Flame-damper shroud
209 Detachable cowling panels
210 Bomb shackles
211 Bomb-bay doors (open)
212 8,000-lb (3632-kg) bomb

Lancaster B.Mk I (Special)

This specially-modified aircraft spent its entire operational career with the RAF's No. 9 Squadron. It is illustrated here dropping a 12,000-lb (5443-kg) 'Tallboy' bomb on the German navy U-boat pens at Bergen, Norway during a raid on the night of 11/12 January 1945. This particular mission involved a total of 32 Lancasters and one Mosquito, drawn from Nos 9 and 617 Squadrons, both units being experienced in the use of the 'Tallboy'. Contemporary reports record that three 'Tallboys' caused serious damage to the U-boat pens after penetrating their 11½-ft (3.5-m) thick concrete roof. In addition, two U-boats suffered minor damage, while a cargo ship was seriously damaged and a minesweeper sunk. The accuracy of the raid prevented any repetition of the civilian casualties that had been suffered during two earlier missions, but four Lancasters were lost, one from No. 9 and the others from No. 617 Squadron.

Crew

In regular operational Bomber Command service, the Lancaster was normally crewed by seven men. The flight crew consisted of a pilot, flight engineer, navigator and wireless operator. No second pilot was carried, but most pilots trained the flight engineer in the art of keeping the aircraft straight and level so that the crew could bale out if the pilot was incapacitated. In aircraft fitted with a mid-upper turret, the additional crew members consisted of a tail gunner, mid-upper gunner and a nose gunner who doubled as the bomb-aimer. Aircraft without mid-upper turrets (like that illustrated) still carried two dedicated gunners, one in the tail position and the second in the nose turret. This configuration left the bomb-aimer free to concentrate on just this one task. A crew rest-bunk was provided in the form of a foldaway padded couch aft of the wireless operator's station.

Nose art

In common with many other Bomber Command Lancasters, WS-Y wears colourful nose art. From its mission tally, the aircraft is engaged on its 41st successful mission, 39 of its previous sorties being conventional bombing raids and the 40th an anti-shipping strike. *GETTING YOUNGER EVERY DAY* uses its code letter 'Y' to allude to Youngers brewery and features a character synonymous with that company's beer. Another famous Lancaster of No. 9 Sqn, W4964/WS-J, with the radio call sign 'J-Johnny', received the slogan *Still Going Strong* and the Johnny Walker figure from the whisky brand. 'J-Johnny' accumulated an impressive total of 106 missions, including a 'Tallboy' attack on the *Tirpitz*.

12,000-lb (5443-kg) 'Tallboy'

Having already designed the revolutionary 'bouncing bomb', Barnes Wallis turned his design genius to the creation of the devastating 'Tallboy'. The weapon was first used in action by No. 617 Sqn on the night of 8/9 June 1944 against the Saumur railway tunnel, which was being used by German reinforcements moving towards Normandy.

Twin-fins standard

With the need to get the first Manchester Mk III (soon to be known officially as the Lancaster) into the air as soon as possible, Avro decided to use as many standard Manchester components as was practical. Thus, the first Lancaster prototype featured a central tail fin, an item which was to be replaced by a twin-finned empennage, with fins of greatly increased height, on all production machines. Such was the commonality between the Manchester and Lancaster – around 70 per cent of the components were common – that the first 43 Lancasters were modified from Manchester airframes already on the production line.

Fuel capacity

Normal maximum fuel capacity was 2,154 Imp gal (9792 litres). Each wing accommodated one outer tank of 114-Imp gal (518-litre) capacity, one 383-Imp gal (1741-litre) intermediate tank and one 580-Imp gal (2637-litre) inboard tank. For ferry operations, a further 800 Imp gal (3637 litres) of fuel could be carried in two auxiliary bomb bay fuel tanks. From 1943, the possibility emerged of operating Lancasters in the Middle or Far East and Avro designed a 1,200-Imp gal (5455-litre) auxiliary tank which fitted over the fuselage for use on such deployments. The Lancaster was never deployed operationally to either theatre, however.

Merlin power

All Lancasters – with the exception of the Hercules-engined Mk II and the two-stage Merlin 85-engined Mk VI– were powered by Rolls-Royce Merlin XX-series engines, or their Packard-built equivalents. The use of an engine which was also in great demand for both the Halifax, Hurricane and Spitfire, among several other lesser types, placed a great strain on Britain's aero-engine manufacturing industry. The Merlin XX as used in the earliest Lancasters used a single-stage supercharger and was designed for a maximum power output of 1,390 hp (1036 kW). Rolls-Royce built 3,391 Merlin XXs at Crewe, 2,592 at Derby and 9,500 at Glasgow, while Ford built a further 12,538. Total production was 28,021 between 1940 and 1944.

Boeing B-17

Sentimental Journey, N9323Z, an ex-DB-17P and fire-bomber, operates with the Confederate Air Force at Mesa, Arizona. This is one of only 43 B-17s that survive in some form around the world. Of these, 13 are capable of flight and all were original B-17Gs or their derivatives.

Boeing B-17F

Cutaway key
1 Rudder construction
2 Rudder tab
3 Rudder tab actuation
4 Tail gunner's station
5 Gunsight
6 Twin 0.5-in (12.7-mm) machine-guns
7 Tailcone
8 Tail gunner's seat
9 Ammunition troughs
10 Elevator trim tab
11 Starboard elevator
12 Tailplane structure
13 Tailplane front spar
14 Tailplane/fuselage attachment
15 Control cables
16 Elevator control mechanism
17 Rudder control linkage
18 Rudder post
19 Rudder centre hinge
20 Fin structure
21 Rudder upper hinge
22 Fin skinning
23 Aerial attachment
24 Aerials
25 Fin leading-edge de-icing boot
26 Port elevator
27 Port tailplane
28 Tailplane leading-edge de-icing boot
29 Dorsal fin structure
30 Fuselage frame
31 Tailwheel actuation
32 Toilet
33 Tailwheel (retracted) fairing
34 Fully-swivelling retractable tailwheel
35 Crew entry door
36 Control cables
37 Starboard waist hatch
38 Starboard waist 0.5-in (12.7-mm) machine-gun
39 Gun support frame
40 Ammunition box
41 Ventral aerial
42 Waist gunners' positions
43 Port waist 0.5-in (12.7-mm) machine-gun
44 Ceiling control cable runs
45 Dorsal aerial mast
46 Ball turret stanchion support
47 Ball turret stanchion

48 Ball turret actuation mechanism
49 Support frame
50 Ball turret roof
51 Twin 0.5-in (12.7-mm) machine-guns
52 Ventral ball turret
53 Wingroot fillet
54 Bulkhead
55 Radio operator's compartment
56 Camera access hatch
57 Radio compartment windows (port and starboard)
58 Ammunition boxes
59 Single 0.3-in (7.62-mm) dorsal machine-gun
60 Radio compartment roof glazing
61 Radio compartment/bomb-bay bulkhead

62 Fire extinguisher
63 Radio operator's station (port side)
64 Handrail links
65 Bulkhead step
66 Wing rear spar/fuselage attachment
67 Wingroot profile
68 Bomb-bay central catwalk
69 Vertical bomb stowage racks (starboard installation shown)
70 Horizontal bomb stowage (port side shown)
71 Dinghy stowage
72 Twin 0.5-in (12.7-mm) machine-guns
73 Dorsal turret
74 Port wing flaps
75 Cooling air slots
76 Aileron tab (port only)
77 Port aileron
78 Port navigation light
79 Wing skinning
80 Wing leading-edge de-icing boot
81 Port landing light

82 Wing corrugated inner skin
83 Port outer wing fuel tank (nine inter-rib cells)
84 No. 1 engine nacelle
85 Cooling gills
86 Three-bladed propellers
87 No. 2 engine nacelle
88 Wing leading-edge de-icing boot
89 Port mid-wing (self-sealing) fuel tanks
90 Flight deck upper glazing
91 Flight deck/bomb-bay bulkhead

92 Oxygen cylinders
93 Co-pilot's seat
94 Co-pilot's control column
95 Headrest/armour
96 Compass installation
97 Pilot's seat
98 Windscreen
99 Central control console pedestal
100 Side windows
101 Navigation equipment

102 Navigator's compartment upper window (subsequently replaced by ceiling astrodome)
103 Navigator's table
104 Side gun mounting
105 Enlarged cheek windows (flush)

106 Ammunition box
107 Bombardier's panel
108 Norden bombsight installation
109 Plexiglass frameless nosecone

110 Single 0.5-in (12.7-mm) nose machine-gun
111 Optically-flat bomb-aiming panel
112 Pitot head fairing (port and starboard)
113 D/F loop bullet fairing
114 Port mainwheel

A 1,000-lb (454-kg) bomb is hoisted off its bomb truck ready to be loaded into the bomb bay of a waiting B-17G of the 8th Air Force on the night prior to a mission on 6 June 1944. 2,000-pounders were the largest bombs carried by B-17s; standard weaponload was usually 500-lb (227-kg) or 1,000-lb (908-kg) bombs.

SPECIFICATION

B-17F-25-BO Flying Fortress

Dimensions

Length overall: 74 ft 9 in (22.80 m)
Wingspan: 103 ft 9 in (32.60 m)
Wing area: 1,420 sq ft (131.92 m²)
Height: 19 ft 2 in (5.85 m)
Propeller diameter: 11 ft 7 in (3.54 m)

Powerplant

Four Wright R-1820-97 Cyclone radial piston engines each rated at 1.200 hp (895 kW) at 25,000 ft (7620 m)

Weights

Empty (typical): 34,000 lb (15422 kg)
Loaded (normal): 56,500 lb (25628 kg)
War overload from 1943: 72,000 lb (32660 kg)

Fuel load

Maximum fuel capacity: 1,700 US gal (6435 litres)

Performance

Maximum speed: 299 mph (481 km/h)
Cruising speed: 160 mph (257.5 km/h)

Initial climb rate: 900 ft (274 m) per minute
Service ceiling: 36,000 ft (10975 m)
Combat radius with 5,000-lb (2270-kg) bombload: 800 miles (1287 km)

Crew

Normal complement of nine, but more could be carried. Crew included: bomb-aimer, pilot, co-pilot, upper turret gunner, radio operator, two waist gunners, ball turret gunner and tail gunner.

Armament

Maximum bombload 9,600 lb (4355 kg), later increased to 17,600 lb (7983 kg); defensive firepower normally 10-12 0.5-in (12.7-mm) guns: two cheek-mounted guns, two on top of fuselage, one above radio operator's compartment, two in 'ball' turret below fuselage, two on hand-operated mountings firing through side ports and two in the extreme tail. The G-variant could carry 1-13 guns, the most notable being two chin-mounted .50-cal machine-guns.

115 Flight deck underfloor control linkage
116 Wingroot/fuselage fairing
117 Wing front spar/fuselage attachment
118 Battery access panels (wingroot leading edge)
119 No. 3 engine nacelle spar bulkhead

120 Intercooler pressure duct
121 Mainwheel well
122 Oil tank (nacelle inboard wall)
123 Nacelle structure
124 Exhaust
125 Retracted mainwheel (semi recessed)
126 Firewall
127 Cooling gills

128 Exhaust collector ring assembly
129 Three-bladed propellers
130 Undercarriage retraction struts
131 Starboard mainwheel

132 Axle
133 Mainwheel oleo leg

155 Landing flap profile
156 Cooling air slots
157 Starboard outer wing fuel tank (in inter-rib cut-outs)
158 Flap structure
159 Starboard aileron
160 Outboard wing ribs
161 Spar assembly
162 Wing leading-edge de-icing boot
163 Aileron control linkage
164 Wing corrugated inner skin
165 Wingtip structure
166 Starboard navigation light

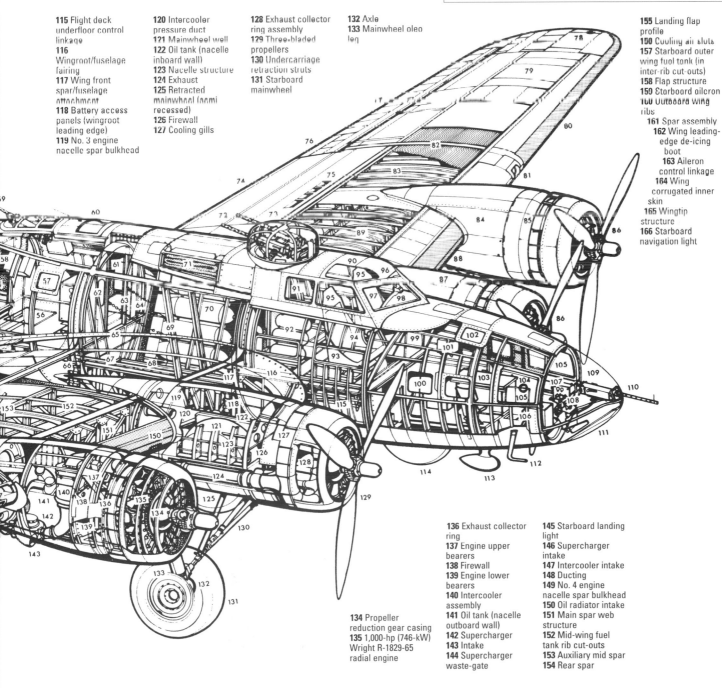

136 Exhaust collector ring
137 Engine upper bearers
138 Firewall
139 Engine lower bearers
140 Intercooler assembly
141 Oil tank (nacelle outboard wall)
142 Supercharger
143 Intake
144 Supercharger waste-gate

134 Propeller reduction gear casing
135 1,000-hp (746-kW) Wright R-1829-65 radial engine

145 Starboard landing light
146 Supercharger intake
147 Intercooler intake
148 Ducting
149 No. 4 engine nacelle spar bulkhead
150 Oil radiator intake
151 Main spar web structure
152 Mid-wing fuel tank rib cut-outs
153 Auxiliary mid spar
154 Rear spar

B-17G-15-BO

Chow-hound, the Boeing-built B-17G 42-31367, was so named by its first crew, entering combat with the 322nd Bomb Squadron of the 91st BG on 29 January 1944. Shortly afterwards, the Group artist, Tony Starcer, added to the nose a painting of Disney's Pluto the dog. By 12 March 1944, *Chow-hound* had completed 15 missions and had been credited with 19 aerial victories. The aircraft went on to fly 26 missions with all of its original engines, one being changed at this point, and the other three 'retired' after 30 'trips'. The last captain of the aircraft was First Lieutenant Jack Thompson, whose crew was flying its 13th mission over Caen on 8 August 1944 when the aircraft was cut in half by flak. Thompson was the only crew member who escaped to become a prisoner of war. *Chow-hound*, like the majority of B-17s delivered to the ETO (European Theatre of Operations), wore the standard Olive Drab (OD) over Neutral Gray scheme introduced at the outbreak of the war. The centre-section of the fin was often painted in medium-green and remained so on most aircraft until the advent of colourful group markings from July 1944 which extended to large areas of the fin. As well as applying colour to the centre of the fin, as in this case, the 91st BG also added red to fixed portions of the horizontal tail surfaces. From February 1944, replacement aircraft arrived with all camouflage paint removed.

Cockpit

The cockpit of the B-17 was typically spacious and well laid out, as were those of many American warplanes of the period. The pilot was the aircraft commander and sat in the right-hand seat, which was armoured unlike that of the co-pilot. Like all crew positions, the pilots could communicate with each other by interphone, but it usually proved easier for the two men to wear their inboard headphones askew and communicate by shouting. It has been said that one could always differentiate between ex-B-17 pilots and co-pilots by determining in which ear they were deaf! Each pilot shared the flying (which could be of eight hours' duration in close formation), but the co-pilot was responsible for the landing gear, flaps, the starting-up of the engine and power monitoring.

Engines

The B-17G was powered by four nine-cylinder Wright R-1820-98 Cyclone engines, each producing 1,380 hp (1030 kW). From October 1943, B-17Gs were produced with new Honeywell electric turbo-supercharger regulators. They allowed for the simultaneous control of engine boost without the problems associated with the operation of hydraulic controls at altitude. The result of this was to reduce the proportion of aborted missions and to relieve pilot fatigue brought about by the constant need to monitor the hydraulics of each supercharger. Although a reliable powerplant, the Cyclone ran less smoothly than the R-1830 of the B-24, and many crews wondered why the Pratt & Whitney engine was never fitted to the B-17.

Radio room

The radio operator sat in a compartment between the bomb bay and the waist. Unlike the radio operators on RAF heavy bombers, who operated under virtual radio silence, the B-17's radio-man made relatively frequent transmissions, including obtaining 'fixes' to aid the navigator and giving a bombing accuracy report (in the lead aircraft) as the group left the target. The radio operator was always on the alert for recall signals from base or diversions from the primary target that might be called by the group or wing leader in flight. Another duty of the radio operator was to operate the vertical strike camera that recorded bombing results. The single 0.50-in (12.7-mm) gun fitted in the radio room hatch did little more than give the radio operator something to do during fighter attacks, and, with its limited field of fire, sometimes did more damage to the B-17 than to the enemy. The gun was originally fired through the open hatch, but later aircraft had a mount fitted in a closed hatch cover. By the end of the war, most B-17 groups had dispensed with the radio room gun altogether, and the mount was deleted from production.

Top turret

The power-operated top turret was manned by the flight engineer, who was responsible for managing fuel consumption as well as performing a general trouble-shooting role. He had the skills to repair the airframe and engines if away from base, and the weapons, oxygen and radio systems in flight. The engineer sat in a canvas sling (or, if above average height, stood up and used it as a backrest) and operated the turret motion and firing with two levers (twisting the right-hand lever operated the rangefinder for the K-3 computing gunsight). Following trials with a captured B-17, Luftwaffe Me 262 pilots were encouraged to make diving attacks from above because the top turret sight could not calculate quickly enough to track the attacking aircraft. There were two types of Sperry top turret fitted to the B-17G: a low profile early type with large areas of metal sheeting; and the taller (by 6 in/15 cm) later model, as fitted to *Chow hound*, which had larger glazed areas.

Tail gun position

The tail gunner on the B-17 did not have a proper seat, only a bicycle-type saddle with padded knee rests. With his upper body exposed to the sunlight through the armoured glass sighting screen and Plexiglass side panels, and his lower body in the shade, the gunner could be subjected simultaneously to extremes of temperatures. The wearing of a flak suit as well as a parachute in the confined space was impossible, and gunners had to choose between them, a process made easier by the progressive elimination of armour plating from the turret. On the original type of B-17G tail turret, such as that on *Chowhound*, the sighting of the guns was done with a ring and post system which moved with the guns through a bell crank. The United Airlines Modification Centre at Cheyenne, Wyoming developed an improved turret with enlarged glazed areas, and that replaced the original canvas boot from which the guns protruded with a swivelling dome, giving a much improved field of fire and better air-sealing for the gunner. 'Cheyenne' turrets began to arrive in the ETO on new-build Fortresses from June 1944, although some had been fitted at depot level to a number of B-17Gs that had lost their tail turrets in combat. Some B-17s, particularly in the 15th AF, were field modified with a single 20 mm weapon, although this was not fitted to any production aircraft.

Bombload

The theoretical maximum bombload for a B-17G was 13,600 lb (6170 kg), but for actual operations over Europe, loads of more than 4,000 lb (1815 kg) were seldom carried, and often as little as 2,000 lb (907 kg). The bombs available for use by the 8th Air Force ranged from 2-lb (0.9-kg) incendiaries (bundled in clusters of up to 250) to 2,000-lb (907-kg) demolition bombs, of which only one could practically be carried in the restricted space of the B-17 bomb bay. The small size of the bomb bay was a limiting factor in the utility of the B-17. A pair of external bomb racks with a capacity of 1,000 lb (454 kg) each was used on occasion, including trials with glide bombs and 'Disney' rocket bombs, although the use of these racks adversely affected aircraft performance.

Waist guns

The waist guns on the earliest B-17Gs were fired through completely open windows, as on the B-17F. In order to reduce the cold and discomfort felt by the gunners, closed Plexiglass windows were added. Initially, this was a framed three-piece unit as seen here but, later, an improved single-piece clear-vision item was introduced, with the gun mounted on the lower sill rather than on a swivel post. It was not until Boeing and Vega -50, and Douglas -25, series aircraft that the problem of gunners obstructing each other in combat was solved by the introduction of staggered waist gun positions. Due to the infrequency of beam attacks in actual combat and the limited field of fire of the guns, the waist position was one of the least effective defensive stations, and also statistically one of the most dangerous due to its exposed nature. Towards the end of the war, many 8th Air Force B-17s carried only one gunner, and the 91st BG flew without either gun in March 1945 as part of a 1st AD (Air Division) experiment.

Boeing B-29 Superfortress

The B-29 was the first of the true 'very heavy' bombers to enter service and its appearance in the Pacific theatre revolutionised the way the war was fought there. Now, American bombers could cross the vast distances of the Pacific and strike the increasingly vulnerable Japanese home islands.

B-29 Superfortress

Cutaway key
1 Temperature probe
2 Nose glazing
3 Optically-flat bomb-aiming panel
4 Bombsight
5 Windscreen panels
6 Forward gun sight
7 Bombardier's seat
8 Pilot's instrument console
9 Control column
10 Co-pilot's seat
11 Pilot's seat
12 Side console panel
13 Cockpit heating duct
14 Nose undercarriage leg strut
15 Steering control
16 Twin nosewheels
17 Retraction struts
18 Nosewheel doors
19 Underfloor control cable runs
20 Pilot's back armour
21 Flight engineer's station
22 Forward upper gun turret, four 0.5-in (12.7-mm) machine-guns, 500 rpg
23 Radio operator's station
24 Chart table
25 Navigator's instrument rack
26 Fire extinguisher bottle
27 Forward lower gun turret, two 0.5-in (12.7-mm) machine-guns, 500 rpg
28 Ventral aerial
29 Navigator's seat
30 Hydraulic system servicing point
31 Access ladder
32 Forward cabin rear pressure bulkhead
33 Armoured bulkhead
34 Pressurised tunnel connecting front and rear cabins
35 Astrodome observation hatch
36 Forward bomb racks
37 Bomb-hoisting winches
38 Catwalk
39 Bomb rack mounting beam

40 Pressurised tunnel internal crawlway
41 D/F loop aerial
42 Radio communications aerials
43 Starboard main undercarriage wheel bay
44 Wing inboard fuel tanks, 1,415 US gal (5356 litres)
45 Starboard inner-engine nacelle
46 Intercooler exhaust flap
47 Engine-cooling air outlet flaps
48 Engine cowling panels
49 Hamilton Standard four-bladed, constant-speed propellers, 16-ft 7-in (5.05-m) diameter
50 Propeller hub pitch change mechanism
51 Starboard outer engine nacelle
52 Exhaust stub
53 Wing outboard fuel tanks, 1,320 US gal (4991 litres), maximum internal fuel load 9,363 US gal (35443 litres) including bomb bay ferry tanks
54 Wing bottom skin stringers
55 Leading-edge de-icing boots
56 Starboard navigation light
57 Fabric-covered aileron
58 Aileron tab
59 Flap guide rails
60 Starboard Fowler-type flap
61 Flap rib construction
62 Inboard nacelle tail fairing
63 Life raft stowage
64 Wing panel centreline joint
65 Wing/fuselage attachment mainframes
66 Pressurisation ducting
67 Heat exchanger
68 Centre-section fuel tank, 1,333 US gal (5046 litres)
69 Cabin heater

70 Pressurisation control valve
71 Fuselage framing
72 Rear bomb bay, 4 x 2000-lb (907-kg) bombs shown
73 Bomb rack
74 Access door
75 Rear cabin front pressure bulkhead
76 Radio aerial mast
77 Upper gun turret sighting hatch
78 Upper gunner's seat
79 Remote gun controller
80 Radio and electronics racks
81 Upper gun turret, two 0.5-in (12.7-mm) machine-guns, 500 rpg
82 Rear pressure bulkhead
83 Finroot fillet
84 Starboard tailplane
85 Starboard elevator
86 Leading-edge de-icing boot
87 Tailfin construction
88 HF aerial cable
89 Fintip fairing
90 Fabric-covered rudder construction

Designed to rectify the problem of the slow rate of fuel transfer with the hose refuelling system, a single KB-29M was converted to a three-hose tanker that could refuel three fighters simultaneously. The aircraft received the new designation YKB-29T and is seen here refuelling three RAF Gloster Meteors. One hose was installed in the tail, while the other two were installed on reels mounted in pods under the wingtips. Since later jet fighters and bombers did not have slow-flight characteristics that were compatible with the obsolete B-29, the triple-hose arrangement was used on jet-assisted B-50 tankers.

SPECIFICATION	
B-29 Superfortress	

Dimensions

Length: 99 ft (30.18 m)
Height: 29 ft 7 in (9.02 m)
Wingspan: 141 ft 3 in (43.05 m)
Wing area: 1,736 sq ft (161.27 m²)

Powerplant

Four 2,200-hp (1641-kW) Wright R-3350-23 Cyclone 18 turbocharged radial piston engines

Weights

Empty: 70,140 lb (31815 kg)
Maximum take off: 124,000 lb (56245 kg)

Performance

Maximum speed at 25,000 ft (7620 m): 358 mph (576 km/h)
Cruising speed: 230 mph (370 km/h)
Service ceiling: 31,850 ft (9710 m)
Range: 3,250 miles (5230 km)

Armament

Two 0.5-in (12.7-mm) guns each in four remotely-controlled, power-operated turrets, and three 0.50-in (12.7-mm) guns or two 0.50-in (12.7-mm) guns and one 20-mm cannon in the tail turret, plus a bombload of up to 20,000 lb (9072 kg) which could consist of incendiaries, conventional munitions or nuclear weapons

On 14 March 1947, the US Navy took over four B-29-BWs for long-range search missions and assigned them the designation P2B-1S. One aircraft (illustrated) was modified for USN tests of the D-558-II high-speed research aircraft which was carried by the bomber for drop-launching.

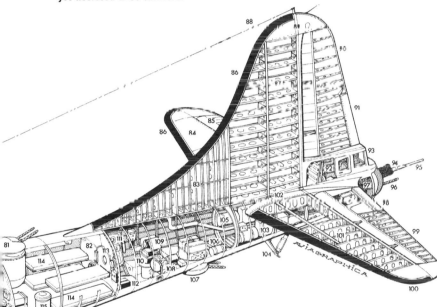

91 Rudder tab
92 Pressurised tail gunner's compartment
93 Armoured-glass window panels
94 Tail gun camera
95 20-mm cannon, 100 rounds
96 Twin 0.5-in (12.7-mm) machine-guns, 500 rpg
97 Remotely-controlled ball turret
98 Elevator tab
99 Port fabric-covered elevator construction
100 Tailplane leading-edge de-icing boot
101 Tailplane construction
102 Fin/tailplane attachment joints
103 Tail turret ammunition boxes
104 Retractable tail bumper
105 Oxygen bottles
106 APU fuel tank
107 Rear ventral turret, two 0.5-in (12.7-mm) machine-guns, 500 rpg
108 Auxiliary power unit (APU)
109 Oblique camera
110 Vertical camera
111 Crew entry door
112 Batteries
113 Pressure bulkhead access door
114 Crew rest bunks
115 Toilet
116 Radio communications tuning units
117 Remote gun sight
118 Gun aiming blister
119 Gunner's seat, port and starboard
120 Voltage regulator
121 Bomb door hydraulic jacks
122 Rear bomb bay doors
123 Port Fowler flap
124 Flap shroud ribs
125 Rear spar
126 Outer wing panel joint
127 Aileron tab
128 Fabric-covered aileron construction
129 Wingtip fairing
130 Port navigation light
131 Wing stringers
132 Outer wing panel ribs
133 Front spar
134 Leading-edge nose ribs
135 Leading-edge de-icing boots
136 Port wing fuel tank bays
137 Engine nacelle firewall
138 Nacelle construction
139 Engine mounting frame
140 Twin mainwheels
141 Main undercarriage leg strut
142 Mainwheel leg pivot mounting
143 Port mainwheel bay
144 Hydraulic retraction jack
145 Nacelle tail fairing
146 Self-sealing oil tank, 85 US gal (322 litres)
147 Hydraulic reservoir
148 Mainwheel doors
149 Exhaust stub
150 Exhaust-driven turbo-supercharger
151 Intercooler
152 Engine-cooling air exit flaps
153 Exhaust collector ring
154 Wright Cyclone R-3350-23 18-cylinder, two-row radial engine
155 Engine intake ducting
156 Forward bomb bay doors
157 20 x 500-lb (227-kg) bombs, maximum bombload 20,000 lb (9072 kg)

To meet post-war British long-range bomber requirements until the Avro Lincoln could be delivered in sufficient quantity, 87 standard B-29s were loaned to the RAF, which named them Washington. The loan period lasted from March 1950 to 1955.

B-29 Superfortress

The 504th Bombardment Group (Very Heavy) was activated on 11 May 1944. Initially equipped with B-17s, it later received B-29s and was assigned to the 313th Bombardment Wing, 20th Air Force. Combat operations commenced out of the Marianas Islands from January 1945 and the first heavy attacks were made against Japanese airfields and other installations on Maug and Iwo Jima and in the Truk Islands. Throughout 1945, attacks were made against the Japanese home islands, most notably in May 1945 when the Group received a Distinguished Unit Citation for striking the industrial centre at Yokohama. Following this, incendiary raids across Japan and mining operations against enemy shipping resulted in more awards for the Group. After the cessation of hostilities, the B-29s dropped food for POWs and flew over Japan to evaluate damage inflicted by bombardment operations.

Powerplant
Power for the Superfortress came from four Wright R-3350-23 Duplex Cyclones, each with two General Electric turbochargers. Developing 2,200 hp (1641 kW) for take-off, the massive engine drove an equally huge, 16-ft 7-in (5.05-m) diameter four-bladed Hamilton Standard propeller. Throughout the aircraft's early career, the R-3350 proved prone to engine fires, although the powerplant was retained throughout the bomber's life.

Pressurisation
The B-29 was the world's first pressurised bomber. the aircraft had two separate pressure cabins for the crew, fore and aft, connected by a sealed tunnel that bypassed the unpressurised bomb bays. The large forward cabin provided accommodation for seven of the crew: the pilot, co-pilot, bombardier (who sat in the extreme nose), navigator, flight engineer and two radar operators. The rear fuselage was pressurised between the rear of the bomb bay and a point roughly level with the start of the dorsal fin. In addition to the four gunners' positions, four bunks were provided to enable the crew to rest during long flights, or for relief crews.

Bombs
This aircraft is depicted dropping M47 incendiary bombs 'in train' from both bomb bays. The small incendiaries were tied together in bundles for loading, breaking free from each other in the airstream. Incendiary bombs were widely used against Japanese cities during the last months of the war, causing almost total destruction amid the wooden buildings and enormous casualties. Two vast weapon bays were located either side of the immensely strong wing carry-through structure. Bomb-hoisting winches inside the bomb bays facilitated loading. Up to 20,000 lb (9072 kg) of bombs could be carried internally.

Wing

The slender wing was designed to take a massive loading and bestowed excellent cruise performance, but posed lift problems at low speeds. Powerful Fowler flaps offset this disadvantage, adding 21 per cent to the area of the wing when deployed. Fuel was housed mostly within the wing structure, between the two main spars. Tanks ran through the centre-section out to a point level with the flap/aileron break. For ferry flights, additional fuel could be carried in the bomb bays.

Radar

Often retouched out of wartime-era photographs, the B-29 featured a bombing radar located between the bomb bays. This was the AN/APQ-13 system, developed by Massachusetts Institute of Technology (MIT) and Bell Telephone Labs. It had a 30-in (0.76-m) diameter dish mounted within the radome.

Colour scheme

Although the early B-29s flew with Olive Drab over Neutral Gray camouflage, most served unpainted to reduce weight. The fuselage stripes on this aircraft identified it as a lead-ship, performing the main navigation tasks for the following bomber formation, and supplying bomb-drop information.

Defensive armament

Two turrets were mounted on the forward fuselage, one above and one below. Each had two 0.50-in (12.7-mm) Browning machine-guns, although the upper unit later had four guns. The pressurised cabin made the use of conventional manned turrets impossible. Further twin 50-calibre gun turrets were mounted above and below the rear fuselage, aimed remotely by the three gunners in the rear cabin. Three glazed blisters above and to the sides allowed ample visibility for the gunners. The central gunner was seated on a raised seat which swivelled through 360°. A potent sting in the tail of the Superfortress was provided by a pair of 50-calibre machine-guns and a 20-mm cannon, aimed by a gunner sitting in a pressurised turret with armoured windscreens. Mounted above the cannon was a camera to record firing. A fire control system used an analog computer. The system was normally set up so that the central (upper) gunner controlled both upper turrets, the left and the right gunners shared the lower rear turret, while the bombardier operated the lower forward turret. However, any turret could be overridden to suit individual requirements.

Bristol Blenheim

The two flying 'Blenheims' to survive and all but one of the static exhibits are Bolingbroke Mk IV-Ts. Painstakingly restored from various Bolingbroke Mk IV-T components, this machine flies from Duxford, UK as a fitting tribute to the many aircrew who flew the Blenheim into battle.

Blenheim Mk IV

Cutaway key
1 Starboard navigation light
2 Starboard formation light
3 Wing rib construction
4 Aileron control rod
5 Starboard aileron
6 Aileron tab
7 Starboard outer flap
8 Outboard, long-range fuel tank, capacity 94 Imp gal (427 litres)
9 Fuel tank filler cap
10 Starboard nacelle fairing
11 Main inboard fuel tank, capacity 140 Imp gal (636 litres)
12 Oil tank, capacity 11.5 Imp gal (52 litres)
13 Engine bearers
14 Oil cooler exhaust duct
15 Engine cooling flaps
16 Cowling blister fairings
17 Bristol Mercury XV nine-cylinder radial engine
18 Oil cooler ram air intakes
19 Propeller hub mechanism
20 De Havilland three-bladed propeller
21 Nose compartment glazing
22 Cabin air intake
23 Navigator/bombardier's instrument panel
24 Bomb-aiming windows
25 Pitot tube
26 Rearward-firing, ventral machine-gun cupola
27 Browning 0.303-in (7.7-mm) machine-gun
28 Fireman's axe
29 Nose compartment escape hatch
30 Fire extinguisher
31 Chart table
32 Fixed foresight
33 Back of instrument panel
34 Foot boards
35 Rudder pedals
36 Compass
37 Control column
38 Windscreen panels
39 Pilot's gunsight
40 Navigator/bombardier's seat
41 Pilot's seat
42 Engine throttles
43 Venturi tube
44 Pilot's blister observation window
45 Armoured headrest
46 Cockpit roof sliding hatch
47 Parachute stowage
48 Wing centre-section construction
49 Sliding hatch rails
50 Aerial mast
51 Parachute stowage
52 Wing centre-section attachment frame
53 Pneumatic system compressed air bottle
54 Three-man dinghy
55 First-aid box
56 Fuselage double frame
57 Rear gunner's entry/emergency escape hatch
58 Rear gunner's seat
59 Gun turret
60 Two Browning 0.303-in (7.7-mm) machine-guns
61 Aerial cable
62 Fuselage skin plating
63 Starboard tailplane
64 Starboard elevator
65 Fin construction
66 Rudder balance
67 Fabric-covered rudder construction
68 Rudder tab
69 Tail navigation lights
70 Elevator tab
71 Fabric-covered elevator construction
72 Elevator balance
73 Port tailplane
74 Rudder cables
75 Elevator hinge control
76 Tailwheel shock absorber
77 Tailwheel
78 Control cable cross shaft
79 Tail assembly joint ring
80 Rear fuselage frames
81 Fuselage stringer construction
82 Control cables
83 Access steps
84 Two 4FL flares
85 Trailing-edge flap shroud construction
86 Flap jack
87 Inboard split trailing-edge flap
88 Outer wing spar attachment joint
89 Flap lever mechanism
90 Outboard split trailing-edge flap
91 Rear spar
92 Aileron hinge control
93 Aileron tab
94 Fabric-covered aileron construction
95 Port formation light
96 Wingtip construction
97 Port navigation light
98 Landing and taxiing lamps
99 Wing rib construction
100 Front spar
101 Aileron control rod
102 Leading-edge ribs
103 Ammunition tank
104 Fixed Browning 0.303-in (7.7-mm) machine-gun
105 Outboard, long-range fuel tank, capacity 94 Imp gal (427 litres)
106 Fuel tank filler cap
107 Main wheel well
108 Auxiliary oil tank, capacity 2.5 Imp gal (11 litres)

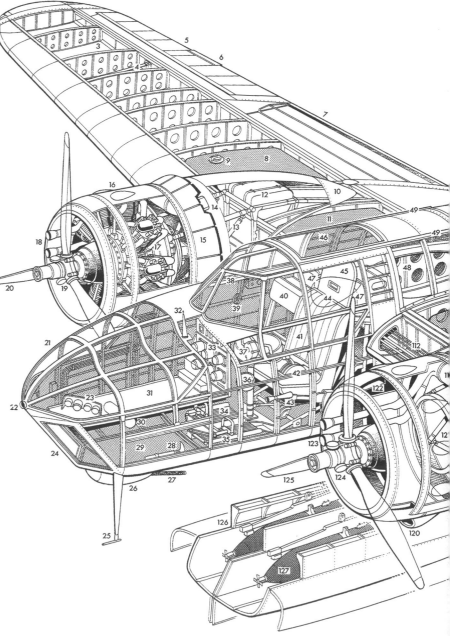

SPECIFICATION

Blenheim Mk IV

Dimensions

Wingspan: 56 ft 4 in (17.17 m)
Length: 42 ft 7 in (12.98 m)
Height: 9 ft 10 in (3.00 m)
Wing area: 469 sq ft (43.57 m²)

Powerplant

Two 905-hp (675-kW) Bristol Mercury XV radial piston engines

Weights

Empty: 9,790 lb (4441 kg)
Maximum take-off: 14,400 lb (6532 kg)

Performance

Maximum speed at 11,800 ft (3595 m): 266 mph (428 km/h)
Cruising speed: 198 mph (319 km/h)
Service ceiling: 27,260 ft (8310 m)
Maximum range: 1,460 miles (2350 km)

Armament

Four 0.303-in (7.7-mm) machine-guns (one forward-firing in port wing, two in power-operated dorsal turret, and one remotely-controlled in mounting beneath nose and firing aft), plus up to 1,000 lb (434 kg) of bombs internally and 320 lb (145 kg) of bombs externally

Finland ordered 18 Blenheim Mk Is in October 1936, and these aircraft were modified to carry Swedish-built bombs. The Blenheims were used for bombing and reconnaissance and were supplemented by a further 24 examples. In addition, Valtion Lentokonetehdas of Finland built a total of 55 Mk IIs and Mk IVs. Finnish Blenheims saw action in both the Winter and Continuation Wars against the Soviet Union, and then against German forces in the Lapland War. This Blenheim Mk I is seen in 1944, shortly after transfer to a bomber training unit.

109 Main oil tank, capacity 11.5 Imp gal (52 litres)
110 Nacelle fairing
111 Inboard main fuel tank, capacity 140 Imp gal (636 litres)
112 Control runs
113 Oil cooler
114 Engine cooling flaps
115 Main undercarriage retraction jack
116 Main wheel leg
117 Rear strut
118 Port mainwheel
119 Leg fairing door
120 Carburettor air intake
121 Engine bearer
122 Exhaust collector ring
123 Oil cooler ram air intakes
124 Propeller hub mechanism
125 De Havilland three-bladed propeller
126 Two cell bomb bay
127 250-lb (113.5-kg) HE bombs

Blenheim Mk IV

The RAF's No. 88 Squadron only operated the Blenheim for a short while, with the first Mk IVs arriving in July 1941 and departing in November of that year, to be replaced by Douglas Bostons. During the period that the unit operated the Blenheim, it was involved in Circus operations over northern France and Operation Channel Stop. The Blenheim suffered mixed fortunes in RAF service: while it was able to operate at some risk in daylight raids over Occupied Europe, it never possessed the armour, armament or bombload that would have made it an outstanding aircraft.

Cockpit
The nose of the Blenheim Mk IV was redesigned to bring the windscreen closer to the pilot. The scalloping (on the port side only – where the pilot sat) gave him a better view, but gave the nose a characteristic asymmetric appearance. Several Blenheim units in North Africa fixed 'banshees' (hardwood sirens) under the nose which could be turned across the air stream, causing them to emit a blood-curdling wail. This banshee, like the Ju 87's 'Trumpet of Jericho' siren, had the effect of scaring inexperienced troops at a critical time, but proved to have no long-lasting value.

Fuselage
As a direct derivative of the Type 142, the Blenheim was of all-metal construction, albeit with fabric-covered, cable-operated flying controls. The mid-set cantilever wing (raised by about 16 in/40 cm compared to the Type 142 to allow an internal bomb bay to be provided) had mass-balanced Frise ailerons and trailing-edge split flaps, while the tailplane (with no dihedral) was similarly raised, and was increased in span. Unlike the 142's variable-incidence tailplane, that of the 142M was fixed and provided with longer-chord, trim-tabbed elevators. The raised wing also raised the engine nacelles, which now almost entirely robbed the pilot of any view directly out to the sides. This peculiarity remained a feature of all Blenheim variants, and was the price imposed by the Blenheim's unbroken internal bomb bay, although the later Beaufort and Beaufighter restored the pilot's view by slinging their engine nacelles below the wings.

Armament

Early Blenheims were fitted with the B.I Mks I and II turrets with single Lewis guns, but these were soon superseded by the B.I Mk III with a Vickers 'K' gun. The turret was then modified to mount two 'K' guns, becoming the B.I Mk IIIA, which was then modified again, as supplies permitted, to B.I Mk IV standard, which incorporated two Browning guns with continuous belt feed and an improved rate of fire. The increased firepower of the Mk IV turret enabled Blenheims to better hold their own in many encounters against superior enemy forces and there were several occasions when single Blenheims fought off several Bf 109s and managed to escape into cloudbanks. In general, however, hard manouvering and optimal use of cloud cover were the Blenheim's best chance of survival if attacked by fighters.

Crew access

The gunner accessed his station through a dorsal hatch immediately forward of the turret. The pilot and navigator climbed up over the wing and entered the cockpit through a sliding roof panel. A bail-out hatch was located below the cockpit.

Undercarriage

The fixed tailwheel was originally designed to be retractable, but this offered no notable increase in performance. As operations were mainly from grass airfields, the tailwheel was fitted with a strong shock absorber. The single mainwheels were mounted on sturdy twin-strut units, retracting backwards to lie semi-recessed in the rear of the engine nacelles.

Performance

The Blenheim Mk IV's two 905-hp (675-kW) Bristol Mercury XV engines allowed the aircraft to reach a maximum speed of 266 mph (428 km/h) which made it, at the time, the fastest bomber in the world. However, this speed was rarely attained, especially when the aircraft was bomb-laden; more emphasis had been placed on field performance than on flat-out speed. Aircraft like the Ju 88 and Do 17 – or the Baltimore, Boston, Maryland and Ventura – showed what was possible by using massive two-row radial engines and by accepting longer take-off and landing distances and the need for concrete runways. All these aircraft made the Blenheim look unimpressive and, furthermore, they could all carry much heavier bombloads over larger distances at greater speed.

Consolidated B-24 Liberator

A B-24H of the 453rd BG (part of the Eighth Air Force) returns home after attacking a Nazi air base on 21 February 1944. The contrails that criss-cross the sky belong to the attendant fighters patrolling the skies in search of potential interceptors.

B-24J Liberator

Cutaway key

1 Rudder trim tab
2 Fabric-covered rudder
3 Rudder hinges (metal leading edge)
4 Starboard tailfin
5 Leading-edge de-icing boot
6 Starboard rudder horn
7 Rudder push-pull tube
8 Rear navigation light
9 Tailplane stringers
10 Consolidated (or Motor Products) two-gun electrically-operated tail turret (0.5 in/12.7 mm)
11 Elevator torque tube
12 Elevator trim tab
13 Elevator frame (fabric-covered)
14 Rudder trim tab
15 Tab control linkage
16 Rudder post
17 Light alloy rudder frame
18 HF aerial
19 Tailfin construction
20 Metal-covered fixed surfaces
21 Tailplane front spar
22 Port elevator push/pull tube
23 Elevator drive quadrant
24 Elevator servo unit
25 Rudder servo unit
26 Ammunition feed track (tail turret)
27 Fuselage aft main frame
28 Walkway
29 Signal cartridges
30 Longitudinal 'Z' section stringers
31 Control cables
32 Fuselage intermediate secondary frames
33 Ammunition box
34 Aft fuselage camera installation
35 Lower windows

36 Waist gun support mounting
37 Starboard manually operated waist gun (0.5 in/ 12.7 mm)
38 Waist position (open)
39 Wind deflector plate
40 Waist position hinged cover
41 Port manually-operated 'waist' gun (0.5 in/12.7 mm)
42 Dorsal aerial
43 Ball-turret stanchion support beam
44 Ammunition box
45 Ball-turret stanchion
46 Midships window
47 Turret well
48 Cabin floor
49 Tail-bumper operating jack
50 Tailbumper fairing
51 Briggs-Sperry two-gun electrically-operated ball-turret (0.5 in/12.7 mm)
52 Turret actuation mechanism
53 Bomb-door actuation sprocket (hydraulically-operated)
54 Bomb-door corrugated inner skin
55 Bomb-bay catwalk (box keel)
56 Bomb-bay catwalk vertical channel support members (bomb release solenoids)
57 Bomb-door actuation track and rollers
58 Wing rear spar
59 Bomb-bay access tunnel
60 Fuselage main frame/bulkhead
61 D/F loop housing
62 Whip antenna
63 Oxygen cylinders
64 Aileron cable drum
65 Starboard flap extension cable
66 Wing rib cut-outs

67 Wing centre section carry-through
68 Two 5-man inflatable dinghies
69 Flap hydraulic jack
70 Flap/cable attachments
71 Hydraulically-operated Fowler flap
72 Wing rear spar
73 Port mainwheel well and rear fairing
74 Engine supercharger waste gate
75 Three auxiliary self-sealing fuel cells (port and starboard)
76 Wing outer section
77 Aileron gear boxes
78 Flush riveted smooth metal wing skinning
79 Port statically-balanced aileron (fabric-covered)
80 Port wingtip
81 Port navigation light
82 Wing leading-edge de-icing boot
83 Hopper-type self-sealing oil tank (32.9 US gal/125 litres)
84 Engine nacelle
85 1,200-hp (895-kW) Pratt & Whitney Twin Wasp R-1830-65 14-cylinder two-row radial engine
86 Hamilton Standard Hydromatic constant-speed airscrew (11-ft 7-in/3.53-m diameter)
87 Landing/taxiing light
88 Nacelle structure
89 Supercharger ducting
90 12 self-sealing inter-rib fuel cells (wing centre section)
91 Martin two-gun electrically-operated dorsal turret (0.5 in/12.7 mm)
92 Turret mechanism
93 Fuselage main frame/bulkhead
94 Radio compartment starboard window

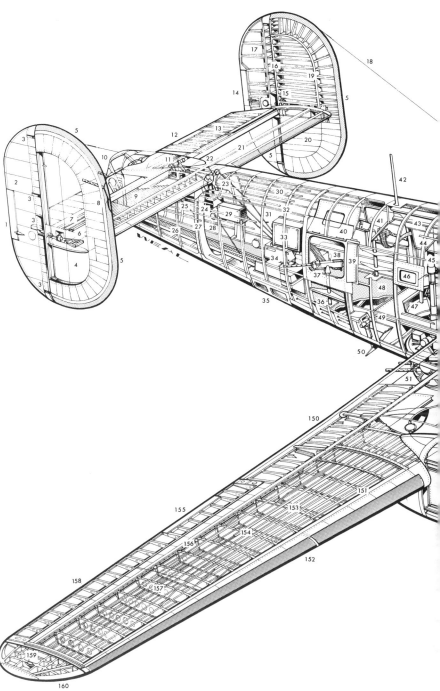

Diamond Lil *can be seen here in 1980 as part of the* **Confederate Air Force.** *The windows under the outboard engine and forward of the insignia stem from the days when the aircraft operated as a* **C-87 Liberator Express.** *Today, it is still flying with the CAF and is based at Midland, TX. Several B-24s still exist in flying condition and many more have been placed in museums and collections around the world.*

SPECIFICATION

B-24J Liberator

Dimensions

Length: 67 ft 2 in (20.47 m)
Height: 18 ft (5.48 m)
Wing span: 110 ft (33.52 m)
Wing area: 1,048 sq ft (319.4m²)

Powerplant

Four Pratt & Whitney R-1830-65 14-cylinder air-cooled radial engines with General Electric B-22 exhaust-driven turbo-chargers, each delivering 1,200 hp (895 kW) at take-off and maintaining this power at a military rating up to 31,800 ft (9692 m)

Weights

Empty: 38,000 lb (17236 kg)
Combat: 56,000 lb (25401 kg)
Maximum overload: 71,200 lb (32295 kg)
Maximum bombload: 12,800 lb (5806 kg)

Performance

Maximum speed at 30,000 ft: 300 mph (483 km/h)
Maximum speed at 20,000 ft: 277 mph (445 km/h)
Maximum continuous speed at 25,000 ft: 278 mph (447 km/h)
Initial climb rate: 1,025 ft (312.42 m) per minute
Service ceiling: 28,000 ft (8534 m)

Range and endurance

Range with 5,000-lb (2268-kg) bombload: 1,700 miles (2735 km) in 7.3 hours at 25,000 ft (7620 m)

Armament

Ten 0.5-in (12.7-mm) Browning machine guns in nose, upper, ventral, ball and tail turrets and in waist positions, with a total of 4,716 rounds. Maximum short-range bomb load was 12,800 lb (5806 kg), while normal offensive load was 5,000 lb (2268 kg)

---

95 Bomb-bay catwalk access trap
96 Radio-operator's position
97 Sound-insulation wall padding
98 Emergency escape hatch
99 Pilot's seat
100 Co-pilot's seat
101 Co-pilot's rudder pedals
102 Instrument panel
103 Windscreen panels
104 Compass housing
105 Control wheel
106 Control wheel mounting
107 Control linkage chain
108 Fuselage forward main frame bulkhead
109 Pitot heads
110 Navigator's chart table
111 Navigator's compartment starboard window
112 Chart table lighting
113 Astro-dome
114 Consolidated (or Emerson) two-gun electrically-operated nose turret (0.5 in/12.7 mm)
115 Turret seating
116 Optically-flat bomb-aiming panel
117 Nose side-glazing
118 Bombardier's prone couch
119 Ammunition boxes
120 Navigator's swivel seat
121 Navigator's compartment entry hatch (via nosewheel well)
122 Nosewheel well
123 Nosewheel door
124 Forward-retracting free-swivelling nosewheel (self-aligning)
125 Mudguard
126 Torque links
127 Nosewheel oleo strut
128 Angled bulkhead
129 Cockpit floor support structure

130 Nosewheel retraction jack
131 Smooth-stressed Alclad fuselage skinning
132 Underfloor electrics bay
133 Roll top desk-type bomb-bay doors (four)
134 Supercharger nacelle cheek intakes
135 Ventral aerial (beneath bomb-bay catwalk)
136 Nacelle/wing attachment cut-out
137 Wing front spar nacelle support
138 Undercarriage front pivoting shaft
139 Drag strut
140 Bendix scissors
141 Internal bomb load (max 8,000 lb/3629 kg)
142 Starboard mainwheel
143 Engine-mounting ring
144 Firewall
145 Monocoque oil tank
146 Mainwheel oleo (Bendix pneudraulic strut)
147 Side brace (jointed)
148 Undercarriage actuating cylinder
149 Starboard mainwheel well and rear fairing
150 Fowler flap structure
151 Wing front spar
152 Wing leading-edge de-icing boot
153 All-metal wing structure
154 Spanwise wing stringers
155 Aileron trim tab (starboard only)
156 Wing rear spar
157 Wing ribs (pressed and built-up former)
158 Statically-balanced aileron (metal frame)
159 Starboard navigation light
160 Wingtip structure

B-24H Liberator

This Liberator, 42-7697, *The Stork*, belongs to the 726th Bombardment Squadron of the 451st Bombardment Group which was part of the 15th Air Force, based in Italy. Within each bomb group, several aircraft had additional patches of colour on the tail and fuselage to identify them as lead ships. In early 1944, B-24s of the 451st carried red discs (as did all those of the 49th BW) as a means of identification.

Crew
The normal crew of a USAAF B-24 was 10 men. This comprised a pilot/aircraft commander and co-pilot seated side by side in a cockpit fitted with dual controls, a bombardier in the lower nose, a nose gunner, a navigator in the forward fuselage, a radio operator in a compartment with a gun turret in the roof, two beam gunners, a ventral 'ball turret' gunner and a tail gunner. The navigator's station had a transparent dome above it to allow him to take sextant readings. Small windows either side gave him some measure of outside visibility. Just aft on either side were mounted the pitot probes.

Bombs and the bomb bay
The central bomb bay was divided into front and rear segments divided by a catwalk which was also the fuselage keel beam. The B-25H's maximum bombload of 12,800 lb (5806 kg) was stowed vertically in racks. These could accommodate bombs from 100 to 1,600 lb (45 to 726 kg) although 2,000-lb (907-kg) bombs could be carried on special rack adaptors. Some Liberators could carry a 4,000-lb (1814-kg) bomb on a rack installed under each wing. The unique roller-type bomb doors retracted upwards into the fuselage sides when opened, offering considerably reduced drag compared to the standard outward-hinging doors. The bombs depicted here are standard high-explosive (HE) weapons, although incendiaries were also carried. A wind-driven vane on the front of each bomb armed the fuse as it fell into the slipstream, a safety measure to prevent bombs from being armed in the aircraft itself.

Camouflage and serial numbers

This Liberator is painted in the standard bomber scheme of Olive Drab upper surfaces and Neutral Gray undersides, the two colours demarcated along the lower fuselage by a wavy line. As weight became more crucial than camouflage, many USAAF bombers were stripped of paint as the war progressed, as a weight-saving measure. Presented in abbreviated form on the fin, the serial number identified this aircraft as one of 1,580 B-24H Liberators built by Ford at Willow Run, Michigan. The factory also built the E, J, L, and M variants.

Powerplant

The prototype XB-24 was originally conceived with Pratt & Whitney R-1830-33 Twin-Wasp 14-cylinder two-row air-cooled radial engines. These were changed during construction for 1,200-hp (895-kW) turbo-supercharged R-1830-43s, with oil coolers mounted on the sides of the engine, giving the aircraft its unmistakable elliptical engine cowlings. The major production variant, the B-24J, was fitted with R-1830-65 engines able to deliver the same power, 1,200 hp (895 kW) at a height of up to 31,800 ft (9692 m). Each engine drove a three-bladed Hamilton Standard Hydromatic constant-speed fully-feathering propeller of 11ft 7-in (3.53-m) diameter.

Armament

Early models of the B-24 had provision for relatively few hand-held (0.3-in/7.62-mm) machine-guns – one installed in the glazed nose together with others which could be fired through apertures in the roof, floor and each side of the fuselage. The fully-developed B-24H sported 10 Browning 0.5-in (12.7-mm) machine-guns installed in electrically-actuated twin-gun nose, upper, ventral and tail turrets, and single-gun waist 'positions' on each side of the fuselage.

Wings

The B-24 was designed around a high-aspect ratio wing employing a 'Davis' high-lift section, so named after an eminent NACA wing designer. This aerofoil was claimed to offer 25 per cent less drag at low speeds and 10 per cent less at higher speeds than other more conventional wing profiles. The use of heavy box spars resulted in a stiff wing structure allowing maximum space for fuel tanks. The wing itself, spanning 110 ft (33.53 m) was shoulder-mounted on the fuselage in order to accommodate a large bomb bay and facilitate bomb-loading.

Most of the trailing edge of the wing was taken up by the sizeable flaps (inboard) and ailerons (outboard), the latter incorporating a trim tab on the starboard side only. The leading edges of the wings, fins and tailplanes were all de-iced by pneumatic rubber boots.

Curtiss SB2C Helldiver

A group of Helldivers heads out on another mission over the Pacific, with F6F Hellcats flying top cover. Though unpopular with pilots, the SB2C was the most successful Allied dive-bomber of World War II.

SB2C Helldiver

Cutaway key
1 Curtiss Electric four-bladed constant-speed propeller
2 Spinner
3 Propeller hub mechanism
4 Spinner backplate
5 Propeller reduction gearbox
6 Carburettor intake
7 Intake ducting
8 Warm air filters
9 Engine cowling ring
10 Oil cooler intake
11 Engine cowlings
12 Wright R-2600-20 Cyclone 14 radial engine
13 Cooling air exit louvres
14 Exhaust collector
15 Exhaust pipe fairing
16 Oil cooler
17 Engine accessories
18 Hydraulic pressure accumulator
19 Boarding step
20 Cabin combustion heater
21 Engine oil tank (25 US gal/94.6 litre capacity)
22 Engine bearer struts
23 Hydraulic fluid tank
24 Fireproof engine compartment bulkhead
25 Aerial mast
26 Starboard wing fold hinges
27 Wing fold hydraulic jack
28 Gun camera
29 Rocket projectiles (4.5-in/11.43-cm)
30 Starboard leading edge slat (open)
31 Slat roller tracks
32 Slat operating cables
33 Starboard navigation light
34 Formation light
35 Starboard aileron
36 Aileron aluminium top skins
37 Aileron control mechanism
38 Starboard dive brake (open position)
39 Windshield

40 Bullet proof internal windscreen
41 Reflector gunsight
42 Instrument panel shroud
43 Cockpit coaming
44 De-icing fluid tank
45 Instrument panel
46 Pilot's pull-out chart board
47 Rudder pedals
48 Control column
49 Cockpit floor level
50 Engine throttle controls
51 Pilot's seat
52 Oxygen bottle
53 Safety harness
54 Armoured seat back
55 Headrest
56 Pilot's sliding cockpit canopy cover
57 Jury strut
58 Wing folded position
59 Fixed bridge section between cockpits
60 Fuel tank filler cap
61 Fuselage fuel tank (110 US gal/416 litre capacity)
62 Fuselage main longeron
63 Handhold
64 Fuselage frame and stringer construction
65 Autopilot controls
66 Sliding canopy rail
67 Aerial lead-in
68 Radio equipment bay
69 Life raft stowage
70 APG-4 low-level bombing radar
71 Gunner's forward sliding canopy cover
72 Gun mounting ring
73 Gunner's seat
74 Footrests
75 Ammunition boxes
76 Armour plate
77 Wind deflector
78 Twin 0.3-in (7.62-mm) machine-guns
79 Retractable turtle decking
80 Gun rest mounting
81 Folding side panels
82 Upper formation light
83 Fin root fillet
84 Starboard tailplane
85 Deck handling handhold

86 Fabric-covered elevator
87 Remote compass transmitter
88 Tailfin construction
89 Aerial cable
90 Sternpost
91 Rudder construction
92 Fabric skin covering
93 Trim tab
94 Balance tab
95 Elevator trim tab
96 Elevator construction
97 Tailplane construction
98 Tailplane spar root fixing
99 Deck arrester hook
100 Arrester hook damper
101 Tail navigation light
102 Tailwheel leg strut
103 Solid tyre tailwheel
104 Leg fairing
105 Rear fuselage frames
106 Tailplane control cables
107 Lifting bar
108 Gunner's floor level
109 Wing root trailing edge fillet
110 Aft end of bomb bay
111 Rear spar centre section fixing
112 Wing walkway
113 Port upper surface flap dive brake
114 Rear spar hinge joint
115 Split trailing edge flaps
116 Balance tab
117 Aileron hinge control
118 Aileron trim tab
119 Lower surface fabric skinning
120 Wing rib construction
121 Wing tip construction

122 Port navigation light
123 Pitot tube
124 Automatic leading edge slat (opens with undercarriage operation)
125 Slat riblets
126 Slat operating cables
127 Main spar
128 Leading edge nose ribs

129 500-lb (226.8-kg) bomb
130 Rocket projectiles (4.5-in/11.43-cm)
131 Drop tank (58 US gal/219.5 litre capacity)
132 Wing fold joint line

133 Main undercarriage leg fairing doors
134 Drag strut
135 Port mainwheel
136 Shock absorber leg strut
137 20-mm wing cannon
138 Cannon barrel fairing

Curtiss SB2C Helldiver

Type

Two-seat carrierborne and land-based scout-bomber

Powerplant

One Wright R-2600-20 Cyclone 14 radial piston engine rated at 1,900 hp (1417 kW)

Performance

Maximum speed 260 mph (418 km/h) at 16,100 ft (4910 m); cruising speed 148 mph (238 km/h) at optimum altitude; climb to 10,000 ft (3050 m) in 8 minutes 54 seconds; service ceiling 26,400 ft (8045 m); range 1,805 miles (2905 km)

Weights

Empty 10,580 lb (4799 kg); maximum take-off 15,918 lb (7220 kg) in the scout role with maximum fuel

Dimensions

Wingspan 49 ft 8⅝ in (15.15 m); length 36 ft 8 in (11.18 m); height 13 ft 11½ in (4.01 m); wing area 422.00 sq ft (39.20 m2)

Armament

Two 20-mm M2 fixed forward-firing cannon in the leading edges of the wing and two 0.3-in (7.62-mm) Browning trainable rearward-firing machine-guns in the rear of the cockpit, plus up to 2,000 lb (907 kg) of bombs or one torpedo in the lower-fuselage weapons bay and on underwing racks

The XSB2C-1 prototype (BuNo. 1758) is seen here having sustained damage in an accident during test-flying in wintry conditions in February 1941. Although it was repaired, the aircraft was never tested by the US Navy before being destroyed after suffering an in-flight wing failure on 21 December 1941.

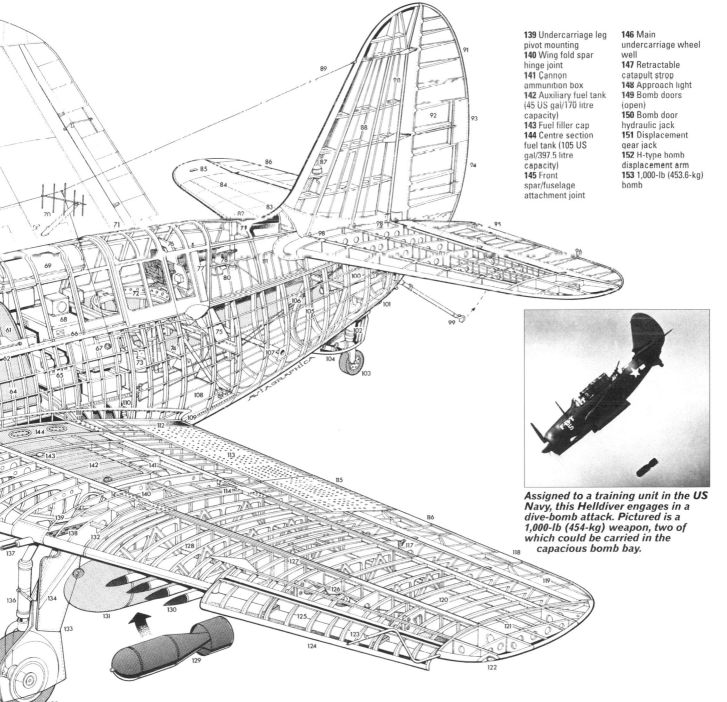

139 Undercarriage leg pivot mounting
140 Wing fold spar hinge joint
141 Cannon ammunition box
142 Auxiliary fuel tank (45 US gal/170 litre capacity)
143 Fuel filler cap
144 Centre section fuel tank (105 US gal/397.5 litre capacity)
145 Front spar/fuselage attachment joint

146 Main undercarriage wheel well
147 Retractable catapult strop
148 Approach light
149 Bomb doors (open)
150 Bomb door hydraulic jack
151 Displacement gear jack
152 H-type bomb displacement arm
153 1,000-lb (453.6-kg) bomb

Assigned to a training unit in the US Navy, this Helldiver engages in a dive-bomb attack. Pictured is a 1,000-lb (454-kg) weapon, two of which could be carried in the capacious bomb bay.

De Havilland Mosquito

Pioneer of unescorted high-speed day bombing raids over Germany, the Mosquito B.Mk IV series II was given a tremendously enthusiastic reception by the squadrons to which it was allocated. First among these was No. 105, to which these aircraft belong.

Mosquito B.XVI

Cutaway key

1 Three-bladed de Havilland type 5000 hydromatic propeller
2 Spinner
3 Starboard engine cowling panels, Merlin 73 engine
4 Exhaust stubs
5 Starboard oil radiator
6 Coolant radiator
7 Radiator air intake
8 Carburettor air intake and guard
9 Fuselage nose skinning
10 Windscreen de-icing fluid nozzle
11 Instrument panel
12 Parachute stowage
13 Junction box
14 Fire axe
15 SYKO apparatus stowage
16 Nose compartment side windows
17 Portable oxygen bottles
18 Mk XIV bombsight
19 Nose glazing
20 Forward navigation/identification light
21 Temperature probe
22 Windscreen de-icing fluid nozzle
23 Optically flat bomb-aiming window
24 Bombsight mounting
25 Bomb selector switches
26 Camera remote control box
27 Bomb aimer's kneeling cushion
28 Signal pistol cartridge racks
29 Rudder pedals
30 Compass
31 Control linkages
32 Oxygen system economiser units
33 Elevator trim handwheel
34 Port radiator ram air intake
35 Oil and coolant radiators
36 Engine throttle levers
37 Ventral entry hatch
38 Control column handwheel
39 Folding chart table
40 Windscreen panels
41 Trailing aerial winch
42 Cockpit roof escape hatch
43 Seat back armour plate
44 Navigator/bombardier's seat
45 Rearward vision blister fairing
46 Pilot's seat
47 Intercom socket
48 Portable fire extinguisher
49 Cabin pressurisation and heating air ducts
50 Non-return air valve
51 Engine control runs
52 Wingroot rib
53 Centre section fuel tanks (two), capacity 68 Imp gal (309 litres) each; 46 Imp gal (209 litres) port and 47.5 Imp gal (216 litres) starboard with 4000-lb (1814-kg) bombload
54 Wing upper surface attachment joint
55 Centre fuel tank filler cap
56 ARI-5083 receiver
57 IFF transmitter/receiver
58 Signal pistol aperture
59 Cockpit aft glazing
60 Rear pressure bulkhead
61 Starboard inboard fuel tanks, capacity 78 Imp gal (355 litres) inner and 66 Imp gal (298 litres) outer
62 Fuel filler cap
63 Nacelle fairing

SPECIFICATION	
Mosquito B.IV series II	**Mosquito PR.Mk 34**
Dimensions	**Dimensions**
Length: 40 ft 9½ in (12.43 m) **Height:** 15 ft 3 in (4.65 m) **Wingspan:** 54 ft 2 in (16.51 m) **Wing area:** 454 sq ft (42.18 m²)	**Length:** 41 ft 6 in (12.65 m) **Height:** 15 ft 3 in (4.65 m) **Wingspan:** 54 ft 2 in (16.51 m) **Wing area:** 454 sq ft (42.18 m²)
Powerplant	**Powerplant**
Two 1,230-hp (918-kW) Rolls-Royce Merlin 21 inline piston engines	Two 1,710-hp (1276-kW) Rolls-Royce Merlin 113/114 inline piston engines
Weights	**Weights**
Empty: 13,100 lb (5942 kg) **Maximum take-off:** 22,380 lb (10152 kg)	**Empty:** 16,631 lb (7544 kg) **Maximum take-off:** 25,500 lb (11567 kg)
Performance	**Performance**
Maximum speed: 380 mph (612 km/h) at 21,000 ft (6400 m) **Cruising speed:** 265 mph (426 km/h) **Initial climb rate:** 2,500 ft (762 m) per minute **Service ceiling:** 34,000 ft (10363 m) **Range:** 2,040 miles (3283 km)	**Maximum speed:** 425 mph (684 km/h) at 30,500 ft (9295 m) **Cruising speed:** 300 mph (483 km/h) **Initial climb rate:** 2,000 ft (609 m) per minute **Service ceiling:** 43,000 ft (13106 m) **Range:** 3,340 miles (5375 km)
Armament	**Armament**
Normal internal bombload: 2,000 lb (907 kg)	None

Coastal Command wreaked havoc on German shipping throughout the war, attacking vessels in the open sea and in their docks. As many as 34 Mosquitoes would attack a single target. A Mosquito FB.Mk VI of No. 143 Sqn is illustrated, unleashing a cannon and rocket attack on shipping in Sande Fjord, Norway, on 4 April 1945. During this strike, five enemy ships were left burning.

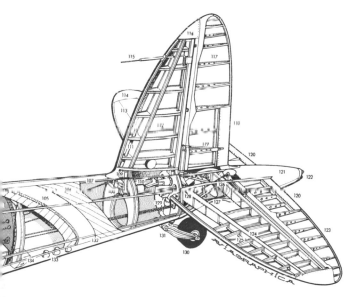

103 Fuselage stringers, between inner and outer skin laminations
104 Heat-conserving canvas bulkhead cover
105 Fuselage half shell sandwich skin construction (plywood/balsa/plywood)
106 Diagonal graining pattern
107 Centreline fuselage half shell joint strip
108 Rudder control linkage
109 Fin attachment bulkhead
110 Rudder mass balance weight
111 Ferrite aerial rod
112 Tailfin construction
113 Starboard tailplane
114 Elevator horn balance
115 Pitot tube
116 Rudder horn balance
117 Fabric-covered rudder construction
118 Rudder tab
119 Tab operating rod
120 Elevator tab
121 Tailcone
122 Tail navigation lights
123 Fabric-covered elevator construction
124 Tailplane construction
125 Ferrite aerial rod
126 Elevator operating linkage
127 Tailwheel housing
128 Tailplane spar attachment joint
129 Tailwheel leg strut
130 Retracting tailwheel

131 Levered suspension tailwheel forks
132 Fuselage skin fabric covering
133 Identification code lights, white, amber and green
134 Beam approach aerial
135 Camera mounting
136 F.24 camera
137 Tailplane control cables
138 Rear fuselage entry hatch
139 Crew equipment stowage bag
140 Bulged bomb bay tail fairing
141 Bomb door hydraulic jacks
142 Beam approach receiver
143 Oxygen bottles
144 Flap shroud ribs
145 Inboard fuel tank bay ventral access panel
146 Bomb carriers
147 500-lb (227-kg) short-finned HE bombs (four)
148 Port engine nacelle top fairing
149 Main undercarriage hydraulic retraction jack
150 Undercarriage leg rear strut mounting
151 Flap hydraulic jack
152 Nacelle tail fairing
153 Short plain flap segments
154 All-wooden flap construction
155 Port outer fuel tanks
156 Fuel filler cap
157 Retractable landing lamp

158 Aileron tab control linkage
159 Rear spar
160 Aileron hinge control
161 Aileron tab
162 Aluminium aileron construction
163 Resin lamp
164 Port formation lamp
165 Detachable wingtip fairing
166 Port navigation light
167 Leading-edge nose ribs
168 Front spar, box beam construction
169 Wing lower surface single skin/stringer panel
170 Wingrib construction
171 Plywood leading-edge skinning, fabric-covered
172 Port auxiliary fuel tank, capacity 50 Imp gal (227 litres)
173 Fuel filler cap
174 Main undercarriage rear strut
175 Mudguard
176 Mainwheel doors
177 Port mainwheel
178 Mainwheel leg strut
179 Pneumatic brake disc
180 Rubber compression block shock absorber
181 Spring-loaded door guides
182 Main undercarriage pivot fixing
183 Engine oil tank, capacity 16 Imp gal (73 litres)
184 Cabin heater
185 Fireproof bulkhead

186 Two stage supercharger
187 Intercooler
188 Heywood compressor
189 Rolls-Royce Merlin 72 liquid cooled 12-cylinder Vee engine
190 Exhaust ports
191 Alternator
192 Engine bearers
193 Carburettor air intake duct
194 Intake guard
195 Intercooler radiator exhaust
196 Intercooler radiator
197 Engine mounting block
198 Coolant header tank
199 Spinner armoured backplate
200 Propeller hub pitch change mechanism
201 Spinner
202 Intercooler radiator intake
203 Port three-bladed de Havilland hydromatic propeller
204 4000-lb (1814 kg) HC bomb

64 Starboard main undercarriage bay
65 Hydraulic retraction jack
66 Outboard fuel tanks, capacity 34 Imp gal (155 litres) inner and 24 Imp gal (109 litres) outer
67 Wing stringers
68 Starboard auxiliary fuel tank, capacity 50 Imp gal (227 litres)
69 Fuel filler cap
70 Plywood leading-edge skinning
71 Wing top skin panelling, double plywood sandwich construction
72 Starboard navigation light
73 Wingtip fairing
74 Formation light
75 Resin light
76 Starboard aileron

77 Aileron hinge control
78 Mass balance weights
79 Aileron tab
80 Underside view showing bulged (increased volume) bomb-bay doors
81 Ventral entry hatch with drift sight aperture
82 Trailing aerial fairing
83 Starboard outer plain flap segment
84 Flap hydraulic jack
85 Nacelle tail fairing
86 Flap inboard segment
87 Oil filler cap
88 Dinghy access panel
89 Two-man dinghy stowage compartment

90 Wing fixing bearer
91 Rear fuselage equipment heater air ducting
92 Long-range oil tank, capacity 10 Imp gal (46 litres)
93 Hydraulic reservoir
94 TR1143 transmitter/ receiver
95 Mk XIV bomb sight computer
96 Batteries
97 Hydraulic and pneumatic systems servicing panel
98 Pneumatic system air bottle
99 De-icing fluid reservoir
100 Picketing equipment stowage
101 Camera motor
102 TR1143 aerial

Mosquito PR.Mk 34A

The ultimate photo-reconnaissance (PR) version of the Mosquito developed during World War II was the PR.Mk 34/34A. Developed specifically for Far East service with the South East Asia Command, the size of the wing tanks was doubled, and a large overload fuel tank was installed in the bomb bay, which allowed for a range of over 3,500 miles (5632 km). Powered by a Merlin 113 and 114 and equipped with two F.52 vertical cameras and one F.24 oblique camera, the first production PR.Mk 34 flew on 4 December 1944 and 50 were built at Luton by Percival Aircraft Ltd, before contracts were cancelled at the end of the war. Mosquito PR.Mk 34/34As saw post-war service with the RAF – this aircraft served with No. 81 Squadron, operating alongside photo-reconnaissance Spitfires. The squadron was the RAF's Far East Air Force's reconnaissance unit for many years. The Mosquitoes saw action during the Malayan campaign in 1949 and undertook significant mapping surveys of Malaya, Java and Thailand. No. 81 Squadron had the distinction of flying the RAF's last operational Mosquito sortie, with PR.Mk 34A serial RG314, in December 1955. Prior to that it had also flown the last Spitfire mission, and subsequently it would be responsible for the last operational flight of an RAF Meteor.

Colour scheme
This PR.Mk 34A carried the standard post-war reconnaissance colour scheme of a Medium Sea Grey upper fuselage, with peacetime roundels. The undersides were Cerulean, more commonly known as PRU Blue. The same scheme also appeared on Spitfire PR.Mk XIXs, Meteors and early Canberras.

Cockpit and crew
The two-man side-by-side cockpit, the layout of which was improved over that of the PR.Mk 34, accommodated the pilot in the left-hand seat. The seat backs were both armoured and the canopy sides were bulged outwards to aid the crew's rearward vision. The bulletproof flat glass windscreen was fitted with an electric wiper and de-icing spray. The cockpit glazing featured a welded steel framework and was fitted with a jettisonable escape hatch. Like the majority of photo-Mosquitoes, PR.Mk 34As were fitted with a bulged perspex astrodome – used for taking navigational sextant readings – above the navigator's seat. Positioned directly behind the canopy on the top of the fuselage was an equipment hatch, giving access to the rear fuselage, where radio equipment was housed. A two-man dinghy was also carried.

Engines and intakes
The PR.Mk 34A differed primarily from the PR.Mk 34 in its engines. The conversion work was undertaken by Marshalls of Cambridge and the aircraft was fitted with Rolls-Royce Merlin 114A two-stage supercharged piston engines, mounted on steel-tube frames attached to the main spar. The PR.Mk 34 was fitted with a Merlin 113 on the starboard side, with a Merlin 114 opposite, the latter driving the cabin supercharger. Each engine was protected by an automatic Graviner fire extinguisher, which could also be operated from the cockpit. The intakes beneath the engines were for the carburettor and were covered with an anti-ice guard. The wingroots housed the intakes for the engine oil and coolant radiators. Coolant temperature was maintained by electro-pneumatic ram-controlled flaps in the radiator duct exits.

Fuselage and fuel load

The Mosquito's unique wooden fuselage had an oval tapering cross-section and was made of balsa, sandwiched between plywood sheeting. This structure was braced internally with several wooden bulkheads. At first, the Air Ministry was unenthusiastic about the de Havilland Company's proposal for such an aircraft and refused to believe that it could be of any value. By the end of the war, 7,781 Mosquitoes of 43 different marks had been built. The Mosquito PR.Mk 34 was fitted with a bulged bomb bay which allowed space for extra fuel tankage. While the bomb bay was still potentially able to accommodate a 4,000-lb (1814-kg) bomb, such a weapon was never used by photo Mosquitoes. A total of 1,524 US gal (5769 litres) of fuel was carried, making the PR.Mk 34/34A the heaviest of all the Mosquitoes, with a loaded weight of 25,500 lb (11567 kg).

Reconnaissance missions

For normal vertical photography, the standard bomb sight was used to align the cameras and was operated by the observer, kneeling in the nose. When the oblique cameras were needed, it was the pilot's responsibility to sight the cameras, so calibration marks were provided on the port-side panels of the cockpit and along the wing.

Tail

The tailplane and fin were cantilever one-piece wooden structures, with two box spars covered by a stressed plywood skin. Like the ailerons, the elevator and rudder were made from Alclad, though the rudder was fabric covered.

RG177

Fuel tanks and undercarriage

The PR.Mk 34A was fitted with a pair of underwing fuel tanks which were significantly larger than those fitted to any other version. The two slip tanks housed an extra 400 US gal (1818 litres). Quite often, these would not be carried operationally due to the weight penalties and resultant drag, but they were extremely useful for long-range ferry flights. The main landing gear comprised two interchangeable single wheel units which retracted backwards into their nacelles under the engines. Two Dunlop pneumatic brakes were used per wheel and the shock absorbers were of the rubber-block compression type. An armoured oil tank was also located in each wheel bay.

Wing and antennas

The slender one-piece cantilever wing, with an aspect ratio of 7:1, had a wooden-ply skin stretched over two main spars with inter-connecting spruce stringers. The upper skin was double the thickness of the lower, and was exceptionally strong. Ten self-sealing fuel tanks were housed within. The ailerons were made from aluminium and the leading edge, while still of wooden construction, was covered in fabric. The PR.Mk 34 and PR.Mk 34A had six aerials on each wingtip, dedicated to the Identification Friend or Foe (IFF) transmitter/receiver.

Douglas A-26 Invader

USAF 64-17640 was the first of On Mark Engineering's 40 'production' B-26K Counter Invaders. The aircraft has a solid 'gun nose', eight underwing hardpoints and wingtip fuel tanks.

A-26 Invader

Cutaway key
1 Starboard wing tip
2 Starboard navigation light
3 Water tank
4 Water tank filler cap
5 Aileron hinge control
6 Starboard aileron
7 Aileron tab
8 Landing and taxiing light
9 Control cables
10 Bombardier nose configuration, A-26C
11 Optically flat bomb sight window
12 Bomb bay doors
13 Ventral periscope gunsight
14 Ventral turret
15 Starboard outboard flap
16 Wing access panels
17 Chordwise stiffeners
18 Double slotted flap segments
19 Oil cooler radiator
20 Cooler intake ducting
21 Ram air intake to oil cooler
22 Nacelle fuel tank, capacity 300 US gal (1136 litres)
23 Wing inboard fuel tank, capacity 100 US gal (379 litres)
24 Control runs
25 Oil tank filler

26 Oil tank
27 Carburettor intake ducting
28 Exhaust stubs
29 Cowling air flaps
30 Pratt & Whitney R-2800-27 Double Wasp, two-row 18-cylinder radial engine
31 Carburettor ram air intake
32 Propeller reduction gearbox
33 Propeller hub mechanism
34 Three-bladed propeller
35 Detachable engine cowlings
36 General purpose nose configuration, A-26B
37 Machine-gun barrels
38 Four 0.5-in (12.7-mm) machine-guns, starboard side
39 Spent cartridge case chutes
40 Gun bay bracing strut
41 Two 0.5-in (12.7-mm) machine-guns, port side
42 Ammunition feed chutes
43 Ammunition boxes
44 Pitot tube
45 Nosewheel torque scissors
46 Rearward retracting nosewheel
47 Shock absorber leg strut
48 Nosewheel doors

49 Nosewheel bay/flight deck floor support construction
50 Rudder pedals
51 Interchangeable nose joint bulkhead
52 Autopilot controls
53 Back of instrument panel
54 Fixed foresight
55 Windscreen panels
56 Instrument panel shroud
57 Reflector sight
58 Clear vision panel
59 Control column
60 Pilot's seat
61 Pilot's side window panel/entry hatch
62 Bomb release controls
63 Bombardier/navigator's seat
64 Canopy hatch handles
65 Bombardier/navigator's side canopy/entry hatch
66 Oxygen regulator
67 Radio racks
68 Radio receivers and transmitters
69 Bomb-bay armoured roof panel
70 Wing root fillet
71 Armoured wing spar bulkhead
72 Hydraulic accumulators
73 Air filter
74 De-icing valve

75 Aerial mast
76 Double slotted flap inboard section
77 Wing de-icing fluid reservoir
78 De-icing fluid pump
79 Starboard bomb rack, five 100-lb (45-kg) HE bombs
80 Port bomb rack, five 100-lb (45-kg) HE bombs
81 Bomb launcher rails
82 Rear wing spar bulkhead
83 Turret drive motor
84 Upper remotely controlled gun turret
85 Two 0.5-in (12.6-mm) machine-guns
86 Turret mechanism
87 Ammunition boxes
88 Port aft bomb rack, three 100-lb (45-kg) HE bombs
89 Inboard double slotted flap
90 Gunner's bomb bay entry hatch

The Invader was first blooded during 1944, the 386th Bomb Group operating A-26Cs (nearest the camera, with gun packs beneath its wings) and A-26Bs against targets on the Continent. 'RU'-coded aircraft belonged to the 554th BS.

SPECIFICATION

Douglas A-26B-15 Invader

Type

Three-seat light attack bomber

Powerplant

Two Pratt & Whitney R-2800-27 or -79 radial piston engines each rated at 2,000 hp (1491 kW)

Performance

Maximum speed 355 mph (571 km/h) at 15,000 ft (4570 m); cruising speed 284 mph (457 km/h) at optimum altitude; climb to 10,000 ft (3050 m) in 8 minutes 6 seconds; service ceiling 22,100 ft (6735 m); range 1,400 miles (2253 km) with standard fuel and warload

Weights

Empty 22,370 lb (10147 kg); maximum take-off 35,000 lb (15876 kg)

Dimensions

Wingspan 70 ft (21.34 m); length 50 ft (15.24 m); height 18 ft 6 in (5.64 m); wing area 540.00 sq ft (50.17 m2)

Armament

Six 0.5-in (12.7-mm) Browning M2 fixed forward-firing machine-guns in the forward fuselage, two 0.5-in (12.7-mm) Browning M2 trainable machine-guns in the dorsal barbette that could be locked to fire directly forward under pilot control, two 0.5-in (12.7-mm) Browning M2 trainable rearward-firing machine-guns in the optional ventral barbette, and provision for eight 0.5-in (12.7-mm) Browning M2 fixed forward-firing machine-guns installed in four two-gun packs under the outboard wing panels, plus up to 6,000 lb (2722 kg) of disposable stores carried in two lower-fuselage weapons bays and on four underwing hardpoints

91 Oxygen cylinders
92 Life raft
93 Gunner's canopy cover
94 Ditching hatch
95 Upper periscope sight
96 Periscope eyepiece
97 Turret controls
98 Oxygen bottles
99 Gunner's armoured bulkhead
100 Ventral turret ammunition
101 Cabin heater
102 D/F loop antenna fairing
103 Fin root fillet
104 Tailplane control cables
105 Cable pulleys
106 Fin rib construction
107 Starboard tailplane
108 Starboard elevator
109 Fin leading edge
110 Aerial cables
111 Fin tip fairing
112 Fabric covered rudder construction
113 Rudder tab
114 Trim tab control
115 Rudder hinge post
116 Tail navigation lights
117 Elevator tab
118 Port elevator
119 Port tailplane construction

France made good use of the B-26 in colonial wars in Indo-China and Algeria. The firepower housed in the nose of a B-26B – eight 0.5-in (12.7-mm) machine-guns – was ideal for ground strafing.

120 Elevator control horns
121 Tailplane root fillet
122 Fin/tailplane fixing frame
123 Rear fuselage construction
124 Oxygen bottles
125 Rear fuselage construction joint bulkhead
126 Turret control amplifier
127 Turret covers
128 Ventral turret control mechanism
129 Two 0.5-in (12.7-mm) machine-guns
130 Port nacelle tailcone
131 Aft nacelle construction
132 Engine fire extinguishers
133 Main undercarriage wheel well
134 Outboard double slotted flaps
135 Flap hinge links
136 Wing rear spar
137 Aileron tab
138 Port aileron
139 Fabric covered aileron construction
140 Port wing tip

141 Port navigation light
142 Wing rib construction
143 Leading edge stiffeners
144 Aileron hinge control
145 Landing and taxiing lamp housing
146 Wing front spar
147 Fluid de-iced leading edge
148 Mainwheel doors
149 Main undercarriage door link mechanism
150 Retraction jack
151 Main undercarriage leg
152 Rearward retracting mainwheel
153 Access panel
154 Nacelle fuel tank, capacity 300 US gal (1136 litres)
155 Oil cooler ram air intake
156 Oil tank filler cap
157 Engine compartment bulkhead/firewall
158 Engine mounting struts
159 Exhaust ducts
160 Cowling cooling air flaps

161 Engine mounting bulkhead
162 Carburettor intake ducting
163 Cowling construction
164 Propeller hub mechanism
165 Three bladed propeller

Douglas DB-7/A-20/P-70 Havoc/Boston

After France's capitulation in 1940, large numbers of DB-7s, -7As and -73s were delivered to the RAF. AL399 is one of the latter, so-designated to avoid confusion with similar DB-7Bs ordered directly by the British. Both the DB-7B and DB-73 were known locally as the Boston Mk III and were the first aircraft in the A-20 family to see service in their intended role.

Boston Mk III
Cutaway key
1 Starboard fabric covered elevator
2 Starboard tailplane
3 Elevator tab
4 Tail navigation and signal lights
5 Tailcone
6 Ruddertab
7 Fabric-covered rudder construction
8 Rudder hinges
9 Pitot tube
10 Fin tip fairing
11 Aerial cable
12 Port elevator
13 Port tailplane
14 Fin leading edge
15 Tail fin construction
16 Elevator hinge control
17 Rudder hinge control
18 Fin attachment joints
19 Tailplane stub attachment
20 Tailplane root fillet
21 Tail bumper
22 Tailcone construction
23 Rear fuselage/tailcone joint frame
24 Fin root fillet
25 Flare launcher tube
26 Reconnaissance flares
27 Ventral hatch cover, open
28 Rear gunner's side window
29 Reconnaissance camera
30 Vickers 0.303-in (7.7-mm) ventral machine-gun
31 Spare ammunition containers
32 Map case
33 Upper identification light
34 Dorsal gun stowage doors
35 Dorsal gun mounting ring
36 Twin Browning 0.303-in (7.7-mm) machine-guns
37 Armour plated screen
38 Rear gunner's cockpit enclosure

39 Gunner's seat
40 Rear emergency control column
41 Trailing aerial reel
42 Wing root trailing-edge fillet
43 Starboard inboard flap
44 Rear spar attachment joint
45 Radio racks
46 Rear gunner's canopy cover, open position
47 Radio receiver
48 Cabin heater pack
49 Propeller de-icing fluid tank
50 D/F loop aerial
51 Aerial mast
52 Radio transmitters

53 Main spar attachment joint
54 Inboard wing panel construction
55 Main undercarriage wheel well housing
56 Hydraulic flap jack
57 Nacelle tail fairing
58 Outer flap construction
59 Main spar
60 Outer wing panel attachment point
61 Wing ribs
62 Aileron tab
63 Fabric covered aileron construction
64 Formation light
65 Starboard navigation light
66 Leading-edge nose ribs
67 Wing stringer construction
68 Main wheel doors

69 Starboard mainwheel
70 Undercarriage leg strut
71 Mainwheel pivot mounting struts
72 Hydraulic retraction jack
73 Engine exhaust
74 Sloping fireproof bulkhead
75 Engine bearer struts
76 Cooling air exit flaps
77 Exhaust collector ring
78 Detachable engine cowlings

79 Hamilton Standard three-bladed, constant speed propeller, 11-ft 3-in (3.43-m) diameter
80 Propeller hub pitch change mechanism

81 Propeller reduction gearbox
82 Wright GR-2600-A5B Cyclone, two-row radial engine
83 Upper cooling air duct
84 Carburettor air intake

85 Starboard oil tank, 19-Imp gal (86-litre) capacity
86 Fuel filler cap
87 Inboard main fuel tank, 110-Imp gal (500-litre) capacity
88 Bomb door central hydraulic jack
89 Wing root fillet
90 Cockpit heater duct

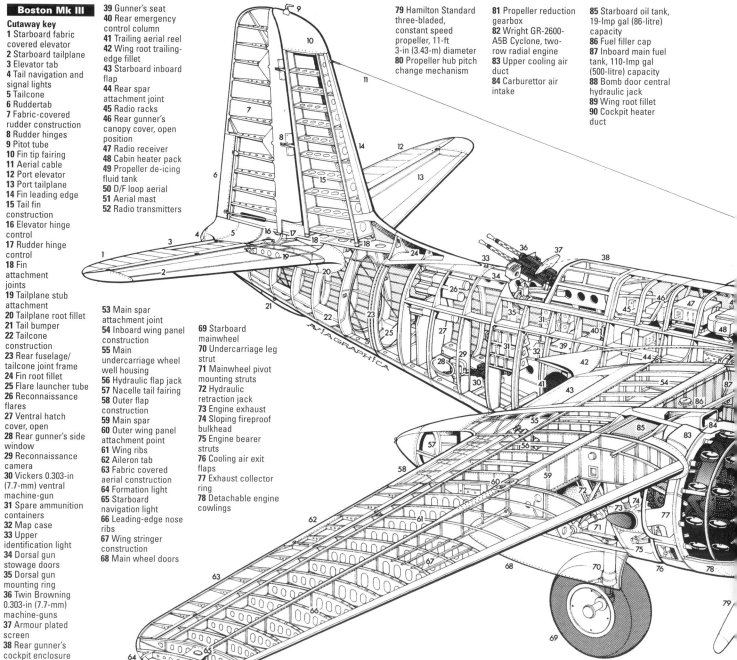

DB-7 (early production)	A-20G-20 Havoc
Dimensions	**Dimensions**
Length: 46 ft 11¾ in (14.32 m) **Height:** 15 ft 10 in (4.83 m) **Wingspan:** 61 ft 3 in (18.67 m) **Wing area:** 465.00 sq ft (43.20 m²)	**Length:** 47 ft 11⅞ in (14.63 m) **Height:** 17 ft 7 in (5.36 m) **Wingspan:** 61 ft 4 in (18.69 m) **Wing area:** 465.00 sq ft (43.20 m²)
Powerplant	**Powerplant**
Two Pratt & Whitney R-1830-SC3-G 14-cylinder air-cooled radial piston engines each delivering 1,000 hp (746 kW)	Two Wright R-2600-23 14-cylinder air-cooled radial piston engines each delivering 1,600 hp (1193 kW)
Weights	**Weights**
Empty: 11,400 lb (5171 kg) **Gross:** 19,040 lb (8636 kg)	**Empty:** 16,993 lb (7708 kg) **Gross:** 24,127 lb (10964 kg)
Performance	**Performance**
Maximum speed at 13,000 ft (3960 m): 295 mph (475 km/h) **Climb to 12,000 ft (3658 m):** 8 minutes **Service ceiling:** 25,800 ft (7835 m) **Combat range:** 996 miles (1603 km)	**Maximum speed at 10,700 ft (3260 m):** 317 mph (510 km/h) **Cruising speed:** 256 mph (412 km/h) **Climb to 10,000 ft (3048 m):** 8 minutes 48 seconds **Service ceiling:** 23,700 ft (7225 m) **Combat range:** 945 miles (1521 km)
Armament	**Armament**
Four 0.295 in (7.5 mm) fixed forward-firing machine-guns, plus single similar weapons on flexible mount in dorsal and ventral positions; plus up to 1,764 lb (800 kg) of bombs could be carried in the internal bomb bay	Six 0.5-in (12.7-mm) Browning M2 fixed forward-firing machine guns, plus two similar weapons in a power-operated Martin dorsal turret, and one rearward-firing on a flexible mount in the ventral tunnel position; plus up to 4,000 lb (18184 kg) of bombs could be carried in the internal bomb bay, with an extra 2,000 lb (907 kg) on underwing racks

Though the XP-70 was finished in matt black, production P-70 Nighthawks often retained the standard Olive Drab/Neutral Gray scheme applied to A-20s. In general, the P-70 was bereft of markings.

91 Bomb doors
92 Forward pair of 500-lb (227-kg) bombs; maximum bomb load 2,000 lb (907 kg)
93 Lower fuselage box beam construction
94 Bomb carrier
95 Bomb hoist winches
96 Bomb bay top decking
97 Cockpit entry hatch aft extenstion
98 Port inboard main fuel tank, 110-Imp gal (500-litre) capacity

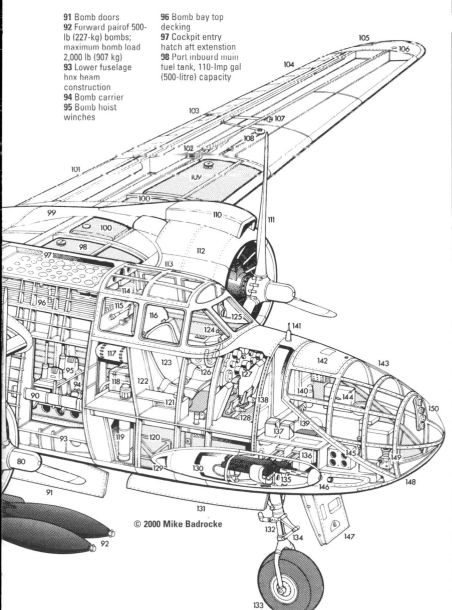

© 2000 Mike Badrocke

Another new A-20 is run-up prior to a test flight after completion. Douglas built Havocs and Bostons at Long Beach and Santa Monica; small batches were also built by Boeing.

99 Engine nacelle fairing
100 Port oil tank, 19-Imp gal (86-litre) capacity
101 Port outer flap
102 Outer wing panel joint
103 Aileron trim tab
104 Port aileron
105 Formation light
106 Port navigation light
107 Trim tab screw jack
108 Aileron hinge control
109 Port outer auxiliary fuel tank, 51-Imp gal (232-litre) capacity
110 Carburettor intake tropical air filter housing
111 Port propeller
112 Port engine nacelle
113 Cockpit roof entry hatch
114 Emergency equipment packs
115 Crash axe
116 Pilot's folding

head armour
117 Hydraulic reservoir
118 Batteries
119 Signal flare chute
120 Nose undercarriage wheel bay
121 Trim tab control handwheels
122 Cockpit sloping bulkhead
123 Pilot's seat
124 Engine throttle and propeller controls
125 Armoured windscreen
126 Control column handwheel
127 Instrument panel
128 Rudder pedals
129 Gun gas exhaust vent
130 Fixed forward gun blister fairing
131 Nosewheel doors
132 Nose undercarriage leg strut
133 Nosewheel
134 Torque scissor links

135 Twin fixed Browning 0.303-in (7.7-mm) machine-guns
136 Ammunition boxes
137 First aid and emergency ration packs
138 Nose compartment joint frame
139 Observer's seat
140 Vacuum flask
141 Pilot's fixed gunsight
142 Observer's ditching hatch
143 Nose compartment glazing
144 Map case
145 Bomb electrical switches and release control
146 Fixed gun muzzles
147 Observer's entry hatch
148 Bomb aiming window
149 Drift sight
150 Observer's instrument panel

A-20G Havoc

A-20G-35-DO 43-10181 *'Joker'* wears the markings of the 647th Bomb Sqn (Light), 410th Bomb Group (Light) around the time of the Allied invasion of Europe in June 1944 – Operation Overlord. The 410th was formed in July 1943 and trained on the A-20 before departing for England, where it joined the 9th Air Force. Entering combat in May 1944, the group's four squadrons of A-20s attacked targets in France in preparation for the invasion, and after D-Day concentrated on lines of communication. The group moved to France in September.

Forward-firing armament

Forward-firing nose-mounted gun armament was a feature of the Havoc's predecessor, the Model 7B, and some form of fixed forward-firing armament was installed in virtually all A-20/Boston variants, with the exception of the F-3A reconnaissance aircraft. French DB-7s and DB-7As carried a pair of 0.295-in (7.5-mm) machine-guns on the fuselage, either side of their nose glazing, while in the DB-7Cs built for the Dutch Koninklijke Marine four 0.303-in (7.7-mm) guns were substituted. Subsequent aircraft in the early batches built for the USAAC (A-20, A-20A, A-20C, A-20E) had four 0.3-in (7.62-mm) guns as standard and it was not until the A-20J and K entered production that 0.5-in (12.7-mm) guns replaced the quartet of '30-calibers'. Nose armament was introduced in USAAF aircraft in the field; A-20As, Bs and Cs were modified with a battery of six 0.5-in (12.7-mm) guns in faired-over glazed noses. The first members of the Havoc/Boston family delivered with factory-installed 'gun noses' were A-20Gs, which were initially fitted with four 20-mm cannon in a solid nose, but were mostly equipped with six 0.5-in (12.7-mm) machine-guns. (The A-20G had no fuselage-mounted forward-firing guns.) The A-20H, which only differed from the A-20G in being powered by different engines, was also equipped with six '50-calibers'. RAF Bostons generally had four 0.303-in (7.7-mm) fuselage-mounted guns; RAF Havoc Mk I night-fighters had an additional four mounted in their noses, while the Havoc Mk II dispensed with the fuselage-mounted guns and boasted 12 nose-mounted 'three-oh-threes'.

Bomb load

An A-20G was able to carry 4,000 lb (1814 kg) of bombs in an internal bay – twice the load of the A-20C; late production aircraft were additionally able to carry a pair of 500-lb (227-kg) bombs on racks beneath each outer wing. Extra armour added further to the variant's overall weight and performance suffered accordingly.

Defensive armament

Dorsal and ventral gun positions were available in most Havocs/Bostons, though the armament fitted varied considerably. French DB-7s were able to carry a single 0.295-in (7.5-mm) machine-gun on a flexible mount in both positions. The DB-7A followed the same pattern, though the original French specifciation called for a single gun to be mounted in the rear of each of the aircraft's engine nacelles, for rearward defence! American aircraft, starting with the A-20, had a pair of flexible 0.3-in (7.62-mm) machine-guns in the open dorsal position and a single 0.3-in (7.62-mm) gun in the ventral position. In the A-20B the twin '30-calibers' were replaced by a single 0.5-in (12.7-mm) gun, this arrangement remaining standard until the 751st A-20G was completed. This and subsequent aircraft had a Martin dorsal turret, with 'twin 50s' installed.

Colours and markings

This A-20G is finished in the Olive Drab upper surfaces that were standard on Ninth Air Force Havocs from their introduction in the ETO. Small patches of disruptive Medium Green were applied to the leading edges of the flying surfaces and the undersides were Neutral Gray. Note the black and white so-called 'invasion stripes' applied for the D-Day landings as an Allied identification feature. The black and white rudder stripes were a 410th Bomb Group marking; the yellow nose cone and propeller hubs signified the 647th Bomb Squadron.

Powerplant

Like the Douglas Model 7B before it, the DB-7 was powered by a pair of Pratt & Whitney R-1830-SC3-G 14-cylinder radials rated at 1,000 hp (746 kW) and equipped with a single-speed supercharger. After 100 of the 270 DB-7s ordered by the French had been completed, a pair of 1,100-hp (820-kW) R-1830-S3C4-Gs, with two-speed superchargers, was substituted. A follow-on order for 100 DB-7As brought a complete change of powerplant, in a further effort to improve performance. The Wright R-2600-A5B 14-cylinder supercharged radials installed were rated at 1,600 hp (1193 kW). The R-2600 remained the powerplant of the US Army's A-20, though in turbocharged form to improve altitude performance. However, the 1,700-hp (1268-kW) R-2600-7 proved troublesome and turbocharging was abandoned. After all, the A-20 was expected to operate at low and medium altitudes, rendering turbocharging unnecessary; all subsequent Havoc variants were powered by supercharged R-2600s. Somewhat ironically, the P-70 interim night-fighters were converted from the original batch of A-20s that should have been powered by turbocharged Wright R-2600-7 engines. Re-engined with R-2600-11s, they were soon found wanting as they were unable to reach the altitudes at which Japanese bombers generally operated.

Douglas SBD Dauntless

SBD-3 Dauntless

Cutaway key
1 Aerial stub
2 Rudder balance
3 Rudder upper hinge
4 Rudder frame
5 Rudder tab
6 Rudder lower hinge
7 Tailfin structure
8 Port elevator
9 Port tailplane
10 Tailfin root fillet
11 Frame
12 Fuselage frame/tailfin pick-up
13 Tailplane spar attachment
14 Tailplane structure
15 Elevator torque tube
16 Tail navigation light
17 Elevator tab hinge fairing
18 Elevator hinge
19 Elevator tab
20 Elevator frame
21 Elevator outer hinge
22 Tailplane forward spar
23 Fixed tailwheel (pneumatic tyre on A-24 versions)
24 Arresting hook uplock
25 Fuselage frame
26 Lift point
27 Arresting hook (extended)
28 Tie-down ring
29 Arresting hook pivot
30 Control cables
31 Fuselage structure
32 Bulkhead
33 Section light
34 Radio bay
35 Radio bay access door
36 Wingroot fairing frame
37 Stringers
38 Life-raft cylindrical stowage (access door portside)
39 Dorsal armament stowage
40 Hinged doors
41 Aerial
42 Twin 0.30-in (7.62-mm) Browning machine-guns
43 Gunner's face armour
44 Canopy aft-sliding section (open)

45 Gun mounting
46 Ammunition feed
47 Canopy aft-sliding section (closed)
48 Ammunition box
49 Oxygen cylinder
50 Oxygen rebreather
51 Oxygen spare cylinder
52 Entry hand/foothold
53 Aft cockpit floor
54 Radio controls
55 Gunner's position
56 Gun mounting
57 Canopy fixed centre-section
58 Wind deflector
59 Armoured centre bulkhead

60 Angled support frame
61 Gunner's emergency flight controls
62 Control direct linkage
63 Hydraulics controls
64 Entry hand/foothold
65 Oxygen rebreather
66 Map case
67 Pilot's seat and harness
68 Back armour
69 Catapult headrest
70 Canopy forward-sliding section
71 Compass
72 Perforated dive flap
73 Aerial mast
74 Aileron tab
75 Port aileron
76 Aileron tab control linkage
77 Port formation light
78 Port navigation light
79 Pitot head
80 Fixed wing slots
81 Wing skinning

82 Underwing ASB radar antenna (retrofit)
83 Port outer wing fuel tank (55 US-gal/208-litre capacity)
84 Aileron control rod
85 Telescopic sight
86 Windscreen
87 Armoured inner panel
88 Instrument panel shroud
89 Two 0.50-in (12.7-mm) machine-guns
90 Control column
91 Switch panel

SPECIFICATION

SBD-5 Dauntless

Dimensions

Wingspan: 41 ft 7 in (12.67 m)
Length: 33 ft 2 in (10.10 m)
Height: 13 ft 7 in (4.14 m)
Wing area: 325 sq ft (30.19 m²)

Powerplant

One 1,200-hp (895-kW) Wright
R-1820-60 Cyclone radial piston
engine

Weights

Empty: 6,533 lb (2963 kg)
Loaded: 9,359 lb (4245 kg)
Maximum take-off: 10,700 lb
(4854 kg)

Performance

**Maximum speed at 10,000 ft
(3050 m):** 252 mph (406 km/h)
Service ceiling: 25,200 ft (7681 m)
Normal range: 773 miles (1244 km)
Maximum range: 1,370 miles
(2205 km)

Armament

Two 0.5-in (12.7-mm) fixed machine-
guns in the nose and two 0.3-in
(7.62 mm) trainable machine-guns in
the rear crewman's position, plus up
to 1,600 lb (726 kg) of bombs under
the fuselage and 650 lb (295 kg) of
bombs under the wings

*Above: About 20 Dauntlesses currently exist in museums or private
collections. However, only one example is currently airworthy, owned by
the Confederate Air Force in Texas. Marked as 2-B-4, the aircraft was built
as a USAAF A-24 and then operated by a Mexican photographic service. It
was purchased in 1970 and is now painted as a US Navy SBD-3.*

*Left: The A-24's career was a short one – the USAAF found the Douglas
bomber too slow and unpopular with crews and it was quickly relegated to
second-line duties in the US. Here, the A-24 found a new lease of life, being
used for crew training and ancillary duties. A number of A-24s, or F-24s as
they were redesignated, was still in the USAF inventory some two and a half
years after the inception of that service in 1947.*

*Marine Corps Scout Squadron VMS-3 is shown in
echelon formation, one favoured for approaching a
dive-bombing target. The aircraft are SBD-5s, and the
Gull Gray and off-white colour scheme was adopted in
early 1944 for the North Atlantic theatre (this unit was
based in the Caribbean, however).*

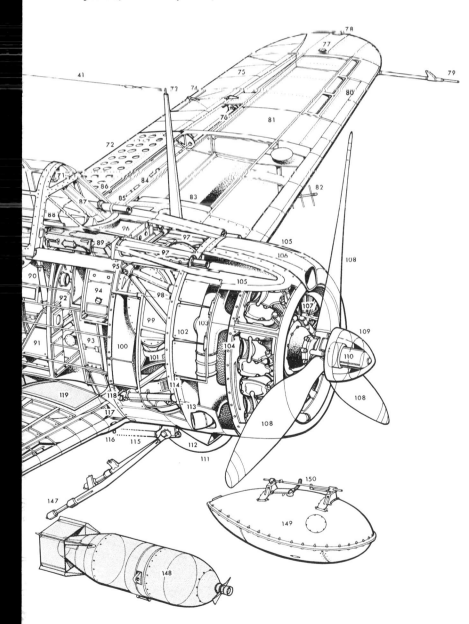

92 Instrument panel
93 Case ejection
chute
94 Ammunition box
95 Engine bearer
upper attachment
96 Armoured
deflection plate
97 Machine-gun
barrel shrouds
98 Engine bearers
99 Oil tank
100 Exhaust slot
101 Oil cooler
102 Cooling gills
103 Exhaust manifold
104 Engine cowling
ring
105 Machine-gun
troughs
106 Carburettor air
intake duct
107 Wright R-1820-52
Cyclone radial engine
108 Three-bladed
propeller
109 Spinner
110 Propeller hub
111 Port mainwheel
112 Oil cooler intake
113 Exhaust outlet
114 Engine bearers
115 Bomb
displacement crutch
(in-flight position)
116 Hydraulics vent
117 Case ejection
chute outlet
118 Engine bearer
lower attachment

119 Starboard
mainwheel well
120 Wingroot
walkway
121 Starboard inner
wing fuel tank (75-US
gal/284-litre capacity)
122 Centre-section
dive flap (lower)
123 Wing outer-
section attachment
plate fairing
124 Starboard outer
wing fuel tank (55-US
gal/208-litre capacity)
125 Mainwheel leg
pivot
126 Mainwheel leg
door actuation
127 Wing nose ribs
128 Multi-spar wing
structure
129 Wing ribs
130 Stiffeners
131 Perforated dive
flaps
132 Aileron inner
hinge
133 Starboard aileron
frame
134 Aileron outer
hinge **135** Starboard
navigation light
136 Starboard
formation light
137 Wingtip structure
138 Fixed wing slots
139 Wing leading
edge

140 Underwing radar
antenna (retrofit)
141 Underwing stores
pylon
142 100-lb (45-kg)
bomb
143 Mainwheel leg
door
144 Starboard
mainwheel
145 Mainwheel axle
146 Mainwheel leg
147 Bomb
displacement crutch
148 500-lb (227-kg)
bomb
149 Aluminium drop
tank (58-US gal/
220-litre capacity)
150 Underwing
shackles/fuel line

SBD-1 Dauntless

Seen during peacetime, this SBD wears the bright colours that typified between-the-wars US Navy and US Marine Corps aircraft. It is the personal aircraft of the commanding officer of VMB-1, the second unit to receive the Dauntless (after VMB-2), and was based at Quantico, Virginia in early 1941 (the unit was renumbered VMSB-132 later that year). It was VMB-2 (later VMSB-232) that received its baptism of fire on the opening day of the war when a number of SBD-2s was surprised during a flight between the USS *Enterprise* and Pearl Harbor, while other SBD-1s of VMB-2 were caught on the ground at Ewa, Hawaii. However, the losses of 7 December 1941 were promptly avenged when Dauntlesses from the USS *Enterprise* contributed to the first sinking of a Japanese submarine.

Powerplant
Power for the SBD-1 came in the form of a Wright R-1820-32 Cyclone. This produced 1,000 hp (746 kW) for take-off, and had a normal rating of 950 hp (709 kW) at 2,300 rpm between sea level and 5,000 ft (1524 m). The large intake on top of the NACA engine cowl fed air to the carburettor.

Bombs
Small pylons underwing could carry a 100-lb (45-kg) bomb each; standard box-fin bombs were the usual ordnance dropped. The main weapon was carried under the centre-section, the maximum weight being 1,600 lb (725 kg). The central bomb was held in a special cradle which swung forward to ensure that the bomb cleared the propeller on release during dive attacks. For level bombing, as here, the cradle was not required.

Pilot

The pilot enjoyed an excellent view from the high-set cockpit, protected to the rear by an armoured backplate, although a bulletproof windscreen was not fitted to this variant. A three-power telescopic sight was provided, which protruded though the windscreen, used for both bomb- and gun-aiming. Immediately ahead of the pilot was a pair of 0.5-in (12.7-mm) Browning machine-guns, each armed with 360 rounds of ammunition, fed from containers behind the fireproof engine bulkhead. The breeches projected into the cockpit, allowing the pilot to clear blockages and recock the guns if there was a stoppage.

Observer/gunner

The observer/gunner sat in the rear cockpit, facing rearwards. The aft section of cockpit slid forwards over him to allow relatively unobstructed firing over the rear hemisphere. A single 0.3-in (7.62-mm) drum-fed machine gun was provided, with 600 rounds. This was stowed in a compartment in the rear fuselage when not in use, covered by folding doors. Two belt-fed guns were fitted to later variants.

Fin

The fin was built integrally with the fuselage and, like the tailplane, employed stressed-skin construction. Both the elevators and rudder were metal-framed with fabric covering. Tabs were built into all the tail control surfaces. Standard radio communications were provided, with a wire aerial running between the fintip and a prominent mast offset to port. The equipment was housed in the rear fuselage, with a rapid-access hatch.

Dive flaps

Much of the trailing edge of the SBD's wing was taken up with perforated split dive flaps. Both upper and lower halves were hinged, the lower operating as conventional flaps during landing and take-off, but both halves operating in unison as dive brakes. To prevent tail buffet, the flaps were perforated with 1.75-in (44.50-mm) holes.

Wing structure

The 'multi-cellular' construction was pioneered by John K. Northrop, the Dauntless's designer. Around two main spars was a Duralumin structure with stressed skin. The centre-section was a rectangular box, while the dihedral outer panels tapered in both plan and section. Surprisingly, no wing-fold was incorporated. An unusual feature of the SBD was the incorporation of three 'letter-box' slots in the wing, forward of the ailerons, in order to maintain aileron control at slow speeds.

Fairey Swordfish

Swordfish prepare for take-off from the flight deck of HMS Eagle off Mombasa in April 1941. The aircraft are from Nos 813 and 824 Squadrons, which carried out anti-submarine patrols. On 6 June 1941, Swordfish from these squadrons found and sank the U-boat supply ship, Elbe.

Fairey Swordfish

Cutaway key

1 Rudder structure
2 Rudder upper hinge
3 Diagonal brace
4 External bracing wires
5 Rudder hinge
6 Elevator control horn
7 Tail navigation light
8 Elevator structure
9 Fixed tab
10 Elevator balance
11 Elevator hinge
12 Starboard Tailplane
13 Tailplane struts
14 Lashing down shackle
15 Trestling foot
16 Rear wedge
17 Rudder lower hinge
18 Tailplane adjustment screw
19 Elevator control cable
20 External bracing wires
21 Elevator fixed tab
22 Tailfin structure
23 Bracing wire attachment
24 Aerial stub
25 Bracing wires
26 Port elevator
27 Port Tailplane
28 Tailplane support struts
29 Dinghy external release cord
30 Tailwheel oleo shock absorber
31 Non-retractable Dunlop tailwheel
32 Fuselage framework
33 Arrester hook housing
34 Control cable fairleads
35 Dorsal decking
36 Rod aerial
37 Lewis gun stowage trough
38 Aerial
39 Flexible 0.303-in (7.7-mm) Lewis machine gun

40 Fairey high-speed flexible gun mounting
41 Type O-3 compass mounting points
42 Aft cockpit coaming
43 Aft cockpit
44 Lewis drum magazine stowage
45 Radio installation
46 Ballast weights
47 Arrester hook pivot

48 Fuselage lower longeron
49 Arrester hook (part extended)
50 Aileron hinge
51 Fixed tab
52 Starboard upper aileron
53 Rear spar
54 Wing ribs
55 Starboard formation light
56 Starboard navigation light
57 Aileron connect strut
58 Interplane struts
59 Bracing wires
60 Starboard lower aileron
61 Aileron hinge
62 Aileron balance
63 Rear spar
64 Wing ribs
65 Aileron outer hinge
66 Deck-handling/lashing grips
67 Front spar
68 Interplane strut attachments
69 Wing internal diagonal bracing wires
70 Flying wires
71 Wing skinning
72 Additional support wire (fitted when underwing stores carried)

SPECIFICATION

Type

Two/three-seat carrierborne and land-based torpedo bomber and reconnaissance aircraft

Powerplant

One Bristol Pegasus IIIM radial piston engine rated at 690 hp (515 kW)

Performance

Maximum speed 139 mph (224 km/h) at 4,750 ft (1450 m); cruising speed 128 mph (206 km/h) at 5,000 ft (1525 m); climb to 5,000 ft (1525 m) in 10 minutes 30 seconds; service ceiling 12,400 ft (3780 m); range 1,030 miles (1657 km) with auxiliary fuel and 546 miles (878 km) with a 1,500-lb (680-kg) bombload

Weights

Empty 5,200 lb (2359 kg); maximum take-off 9,250 lb (4196 kg)

Dimensions

Wingspan 45 ft 6 in (13.87 m); length 36 ft 1 in (11.00 m) with the tail down; height 12 ft 10 1/2 in (3.92 m) with the tail down; wing area 607.00 sq ft (56.39 m2)

Armament

One 0.303-in (7.7-mm) Vickers Mk V fixed forward-firing machine-gun in the starboard side of the forward fuselage and one 0.303-in (7.7-mm) Vickers 'K' or Lewis trainable rearward-firing machine-gun in the rear cockpit, plus up to 1,610 lb (739 kg) of disposable stores carried on one underfuselage and eight underwing hardpoints, and generally comprising one 1,610-lb (739-kg) 18-in (457-mm) torpedo or one 1,500-lb (680-kg) mine carried under the fuselage, or up to 1,500 lb (680 kg) of weapons, including 500-lb (227-kg), 250-lb (113-kg) and 20-lb (9-kg) bombs, carried under the fuselage and lower wing

Seen overflying the newly-commissioned HMS Ark Royal in early 1939, this Swordfish Mk I is from No. 820 Squadron. The unit had become the first squadron to deploy aboard the carrier in January of that year.

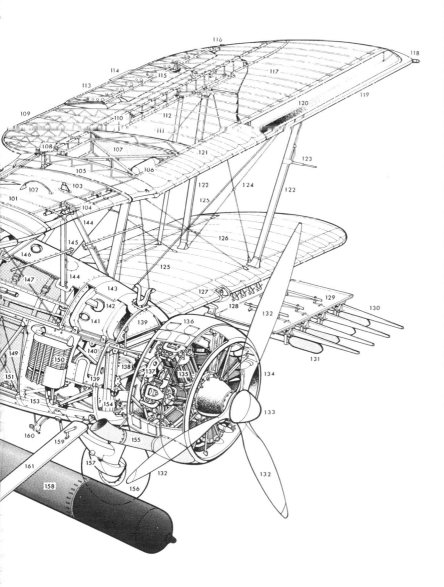

73 Wing fold hinge
74 Inboard interplane struts
75 Stub plane end rib
76 Wing locking handle
77 Stub plane structure
78 Intake slot
79 Side window
80 Catapult spool
81 Drag struts
82 Cockpit sloping floor
83 Fixed 0.303-in (7.7-mm) Vickers gun (deleted from some aircraft)
84 Case ejection chute
85 Access panel
86 Camera mounting bracket
87 Sliding bomb-aiming hatch
88 Zip inspection flap
89 Fuselage upper longeron
90 Centre cockpit
91 Inter-cockpit fairing
92 Upper wing aerial mast
93 Pilot's headrest
94 Pilot's seat and harness
95 Bulkhead
96 Vickers gun fairing
97 Fuel gravity tank (12.5 Imp gal/57 litre capacity)
98 Windscreen
99 Handholds
100 Flap control handwheel and rocking head assembly
101 Wing centre section
102 Dinghy release cord handle
103 Identification light
104 Centre section pyramid strut attachment
105 Diagonal strengtheners

106 Dinghy inflation cylinder
107 Type C dinghy stowage well
108 Aileron control linkage
109 Trailing edge rib sections
110 Rear spar
111 Wing rib stations
112 Aileron connect strut
113 Port upper aileron
114 Fixed tab
115 Aileron hinge
116 Port formation light
117 Wing skinning
118 Port navigation light
119 Leading-edge slot
120 Front spar
121 Nose ribs
122 Interplane struts
123 Pitot head
124 Bracing wires
125 Flying wires
126 Port lower mainplane
127 Landing lamp
128 Underwing bomb shackles
129 Underwing strengthening plate
130 Rocket-launching rails
131 Four 60-lb (27-g) anti-shipping rocket projectiles
132 Three-blade fixed-pitch Fairey-Reed metal propeller
133 Spinner
134 Townend ring
135 Bristol Pegasus IIIM3 (or Mk 30) radial engine
136 Cowling clips
137 Engine mounting ring
138 Engine support bearers
139 Firewall bulkhead
140 Engine controls
141 Oil tank immersion heater socket
142 Filler cap

143 Oil tank (13.75 Imp gal/62.5 litre capacity)
144 Centre section pyramid struts
145 External torpedo sight bars
146 Fuel filler cap
147 Main fuel tank (155 Imp gal/705 litre capacity)
148 Vickers gun trough
149 Fuselage forward frame
150 Oil cooler
151 Fuel filter
152 Stub plane/fuselage attachment
153 Fuel feed lines
154 Dinghy immersion switch
155 Exhaust
156 Port Dunlop mainwheel
157 Jacking foot
158 1,610-lb (730-kg) 18-in (45.7-cm) torpedo

159 Access/servicing footholds
160 Torpedo forward crutch
161 Radius rod fairing
162 Undercarriage axle tube fairing
163 Undercarriage oleo leg fairing
164 Starboard mainwheel
165 Hub cover
166 Underwing bombs
167 Underwing outboard shackles
168 Depth-charge
169 250-lb (113-kg) bomb
170 Anti-shipping flares

Grumman TBF/TBM Avenger

The Confederate Air Force is one of numerous warbird operators to display the Avenger. A dozen or so examples are currently flying in the US, with others in Australia, Canada and Europe while further Avengers await restoration. Many survivors are former fire-fighters.

TBM-1C Avengers

Cutaway key

1 Starboard elevator
2 Fabric-covered aileron construction
3 Elevator trim tab
4 Elevator horn balance
5 Tailplane construction
6 Rudder tab
7 Trim tab control jack
8 Tail navigation light
9 Fabric-covered rudder construction
10 Aerial cable rear mounting
11 Fin construction
12 Port elevator
13 Port tailplane
14 Elevator hinge controls
15 Tailplane support frames
16 Deck arrester hook (lowered)
17 Arrester hook guide rails
18 Rudder hinge control
19 Rear fuselage frames
20 Flush-riveted aluminium skin covering
21 Finroot fairing
22 Tailplane control cables
23 Arrester hook retraction drive motor
24 Lifting tube
25 Rear fuselage frame and stringer construction
26 Tailwheel shock-absorber strut
27 Catapult 'hold-back' shackle
28 Retractable tailwheel
29 Crew compartment rear bulkhead
30 Search flares
31 Parachute flare launch tube
32 Ventral gun turret
33 Ammunition magazine
34 Browning 0.3-in (7.62-mm) machine-gun
35 Machine-gun mounting
36 Gun camera switch box
37 Crew door
38 Parachute stowage
39 Rear fuselage production break point
40 Spare coil stowage rack
41 Bombardier's side window
42 Upper turret spare ammunition magazines
43 Bombardier's folding seat
44 Gun turret mounting ring
45 Gun elevating mechanism
46 Ammunition feed chute
47 Browning 0.5-in (12.7-mm) machine-gun
48 Upper rotating gun turret
49 Bulletproof windscreen
50 Gunner's armoured seat back
51 Aerial cable
52 Port wing, folded position
53 Canopy aft glazing
54 Emergency life raft stowage
55 Hydraulic reservoir
56 Radio communications equipment
57 ASB weapons aiming controller
58 Bomb release levers
59 Cabin heater duct
60 Aft end of bomb bay
61 Fixed wing, root construction
62 Wing fold joint line
63 Browning 0.5-in (12.7-mm)/fixed machine-gun
64 Ammunition feed chute
65 Ammunition magazine (320 rounds)
66 Trailing-edge flap shroud construction
67 Lattice wing ribs
68 Starboard, fabric-covered aileron construction
69 Aileron hinge control
70 Aileron trim tab
71 Starboard wingtip
72 Starboard navigation light
73 Leading-edge ribs
74 Fixed leading-edge slot
75 ASB aerial
76 RT-5/APS-4 search radar pod
77 Radar mounting sway braces
78 Rocket-launching pylons
79 Jettisonable fuel tank
80 Main undercarriage wheel well
81 Sloping main spar
82 Wing fold hinge axis
83 Twin hydraulic folding jacks
84 Machine-gun blast tube
85 Starboard main fuel tank
86 Centre-section main spar
87 Oxygen bottle
88 Autopilot controls
89 Rear cockpit entry hatch

In Fleet Air Arm service the Avenger was initially known as the Tarpon. This flight of Tarpon TR.Mk 1s of No. 846 Squadron was photographed on 10 December 1943. The squadron was then at Macrihanish, and embarked on HMS Tracker in January 1944, transferring to Trumpeter in July 1944 for operations off Norway and in Arctic waters until April 1945. Fleet Air Arm Tarpon crews received their initial training and commissioning at NAS Squantum, Massachusetts in July 1943.

SPECIFICATION

TBF-1C Avenger

Dimensions

Length: 40 ft (12.19 m)
Wingspan: 54 ft 2 in (16.51 m)
Wingspan (folded): 19 ft (5.79 m)
Wing area: 490 sq ft (45.52 m²)
Height: 16 ft 5 in (5.00 m)

Powerplant

One 1,700-hp (1268-kW) Wright R-2600-8 Cyclone 14-cylinder two-row radial piston engine

Weight

Empty: 10,555 lb (4788 kg)
Normal, loaded: 16,412 lb (7444 kg)
Maximum take-off: 17,364 lb (7876 kg)

Performance

Maximum speed: 257 mph (414 km/h) at 12,000 ft (3660 m)
Cruising speed: 153 mph (246 km/h)
Climb to 10,000 ft (3048 m): 13 minutes
Climb rate: 768 ft (234 m) per minute
Service ceiling: 21,400 ft (6525 m)
Range with torpedo: 1,105 miles (1780 km)
Range as scout: 2,335 miles (3755 km)

Armament

Two 0.5-in/12.7-mm machine-guns firing ahead (in TBF-1 one 0.3-in/7.62-mm forward-firing machine-gun); one 0.5-in (12.7-mm) machine-gun in dorsal turret and one 0.3-in (7.62-mm) machine-gun in lower rear position; internal weapons bay for one 22.4-in (56.9-in) torpedo or up to 2,000 lb (907 kg) of other stores

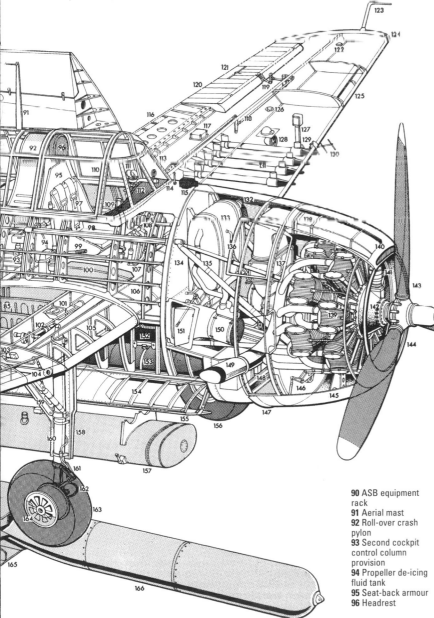

90 ASB equipment rack
91 Aerial mast
92 Roll-over crash pylon
93 Second cockpit control column provision
94 Propeller de-icing fluid tank
95 Seat-back armour
96 Headrest
97 Safety harness
98 Pilot's seat
99 Emergency hydraulic handpump
100 Centre main fuel tank
101 Fuel tank filler cap
102 Main undercarriage retraction jack
103 Wing fold locking cylinder
104 Machine-gun muzzle
105 Centre section leading-edge construction
106 Front fuselage frames
107 Rudder pedals
108 Back of instrument panel
109 Control column
110 Pilot's sliding entry hatch
111 Illuminated torpedo sight
112 Instrument panel shroud
113 Windscreen panels
114 Ring-and-bead gunsight
115 Gun camera
116 Port split trailing-edge flaps
117 Remote compass transmitter
118 Aileron control rods
119 Aileron hinge control
120 Fabric-covered port aileron
121 Aileron trim tab
122 Formation light
123 Pitot tube
124 Port navigation light
125 Fixed leading-edge slot
126 Wing 'tie-down' shackle
127 ASB aerial mounting
128 Retractable landing lamp
129 Red, white and green approach lights
130 Port ASB aerial
131 Ground attack rockets
132 Oil tank filler cap
133 Engine oil tank 13 US gal (49 litres)
134 Engine compartment bulkhead
135 Engine mounting struts
136 Cowling air exit flap
137 Twin carburettors
138 Carburettor air trunking
139 Wright-cyclone, 14-cylinder, two-row radial engine
140 Carburettor air intake
141 Propeller governor
142 Reduction gearbox
143 Hamilton Standard three-bladed propeller
144 Engine cooling intake
145 Engine cowlings
146 Cowling air flap control lever
147 Lower cowling air flap
148 Batteries
149 Starboard exhaust pipe
150 Oil cooler
151 Oil cooler air exit flap
152 Bomb release shackle
153 500-lb (227-kg) bombs
154 Bomb bay door construction
155 Bomb doors (open)
156 Port mainwheel
157 Bomb bay fuel tank (270-US gal/1022-litre capacity)
158 Main undercarriage leg door
159 Retraction strut
160 Shock absorber leg strut
161 Torque scissor links
162 Hydraulic brake pipe
163 Starboard mainwheel
164 Removable wheel disc cover
165 Torpedo stabilising vanes
166 Mk XIII-2 torpedo

The loss of five Fort Lauderdale-based TBM Avengers and their 14 crewmen in the Bermuda Triangle area remains an enduring aviation mystery. In the mid-1980s some wreckage was recovered, but it was not from the missing flight.

TBM-3 Avenger

A TBM-3 built by Eastern Aircraft, this Avenger served with Torpedo Squadron 4 (VT-4), Air Group 4 (CVG-4), aboard USS *Essex* and is seen as it appeared on 12 January 1945. VT-4 was established on 10 January 1942, aboard the deck of USS *Ranger* (CV-4) while it was in Bermuda. Operations began with the Douglas TBD-1 Devastator, before transition to the TBF-1 Avenger in August 1942. VT-4's Avengers saw action in October 1943 when *Ranger* was deployed as part of Operation Leader, and VT-4 Avengers attacked German shipping along the Norwegian coast in the first US Navy carrier strike in northern Europe. In July 1944 Air Group 4 (including VT-4) moved to the Pacific, entering combat on 11 November 1944 in support of General MacArthur's return to the Philippines, from the deck of *Bunker Hill* (CV-17). In the ensuing days the squadron's Avengers struck targets at Ormoc Bay, Cavite and Clark Field. In late November 1944 the Avengers of VT-4 transferred to USS *Essex* (CV-9) which was promptly damaged by a kamikaze attack off the Philippines before the Avengers had seen action from their new carrier. In January 1945 the repaired carrier received VT-4's TBM-3 Avenger in time for a series of strikes against Western Pacific and Indochinese targets.

Powerplant

Although consideration was given to fitting a 2,000-hp (1491-kW) Pratt & Whitney R-2800 Double Wasp to the TBM-3, Wright's R-2600-20 Cyclone 14, rated at 1,900 hp (1417 kW), was chosen instead, replacing the 1,600-hp (1193-kW) R-2600-8 of the previous production variant, the TBM-1C. A new engine was necessary to counter the marginal performance of the aircraft at normal gross weights, especially when operating from the small decks of escort carriers. The increased cooling requirements of the new variant necessitated some redesign of its cowling: multiple cowl flaps and an oil cooler intake on the lower lip were new features.
The R-2600 – a 14-cylinder, twin-bank derivative of Wright's 1920s-vintage nine-cylinder R-1750/-1820 Cyclone – also powered the Curtiss SB2C Helldiver and, as such, is often described as one of America's 'war-winning' powerplant designs. More than 50,000 were built at Wright's Cincinnati plant.

Torpedo

The Mk XIII 'ring-tailed' torpedo was developed by modifying the standard Mk XIII-1A with a 10-in (25.4-cm) steel band welded around the fins. These were first used in August 1944 by VT-13 from aboard USS *Franklin*, west of Iwo Jima. Compared to the unmodified torpedoes, which had to be dropped within a speed range of 115-126 mph (185-204 km/h), and a height of 100 ft (30.50 m), the 'ring tails' could be released from as high as 800 ft (244 m) and as fast as 321 mph (519 km/h). The Mk XIII was designed for aircraft use in about 1938. It had a greater diameter (22.4 in/56.9 cm) than the standard 21-in (53.3-cm) naval torpedo, a steam turbine engine producing 95 bhp (71 kW), a weight of 3,050 lb (1383 kg), and a theoretical maximum speed and range of 53 mph (85 km/h) and 9,000 yd (8230 m), respectively.

Crew

Three crew manned a typical TBM-3: a pilot, radio operator and bombardier. The pilot was housed in a separate cockpit, while the rear portion of the 'glasshouse' contained the radioman and his Grumman 150SE turret, with a 0.50-in (12.7-mm) machine gun. The rest of the crew compartment consisted of the so-called 'tunnel' in which the bombardier manned a 0.30-in (7.62-mm) machine-gun in the ventral 'stinger' position. The bombardier's main piece of equipment was a Norden bombsight, fitted to early Avengers in an unusual position, sighted through a transparency aft of the weapons bay. He also had a scope for the aircraft's Air-to-Surface Type B (ASB) radar set, the moveable receivers for which (Yagi antennas) were fitted beneath each wing.

The bombsight was deleted in late-production TBM-3s as horizontal bombing was found to be ineffective against manoeuvring ships and less accurate than glide-bombing when attacking smaller land targets and ships at anchor. The radioman then manned the 'stinger' gun, while a dedicated gunner operated the turret. The pilot was able to use a 0.50-in (12.7-mm) machine-gun in each wing to strafe targets.

12 January 1945

On 12 January 1945, 12 TBM-3s, loaded with torpedoes, roared off *Essex*'s flight deck with the mission of attacking shipping on the Saigon River near Cap St Jacques. Among the pilots was Ensign William H. Cannady, a relatively new pilot to VT-4, flying aircraft number '131' (TBM-3 BuNo. 68417). On this occasion, he shared his aircraft with just one other crew member, Aviation Radioman Third Class (ARM3c) J. C. Gerke.

The 'torpeckers' encountered a convoy of merchantmen and their escorts which, along with the shore installations, began filling the sky with intense anti-aircraft fire. Jinking as they approached the release point at an altitude of 250 ft (76 m), the VT-4 Avengers dropped their weapons. Cannady's torpedo combined with those of two of his squadron mates to finish off a merchant vessel.

Bombloads

As a glide- or skip-bomber, the Avenger carried a variety of weapons according to mission, but typical stores included one 2,000-lb (907-kg) general-purpose (GP), one 1,600-lb (726-kg) armour-piercing (AP), two 1,000-lb (454-kg) GP, four 500-lb (227-kg) GP, 12 100-lb (45-kg) GP or four 350-lb (159-kg) depth bombs. The latter was the primary anti-submarine weapon used by the Avenger, along with newly developed aircraft rockets. Rockets were introduced in late 1943, initially in 3.5-in (8.8-cm) form and later with 5-in (12.7-cm) calibre warheads. In early 1944, the first 5-in (12.7-cm) High Velocity Aircraft Rockets (HVARs) were used in combat, nicknamed 'Holy Moses'.

Handley Page Halifax

With dorsal and tail turrets removed and faired over, the Halifax C.Mk VIII was developed from the B.Mk VI as a dedicated transport aircraft. A detachable underfuselage pannier for up to 8,000 lb (3636 kg) of freight could be fitted, and freight, passengers, paratroops or stretcher cases could be carried within the fuselage.

Halifax B.Mk III

Cutaway key
1 Starboard navigation light
2 Formation light
3 Aileron balance weight
4 Wing skinning
5 Starboard aileron
6 Aileron servo tab
7 Trim tab
8 Wing stringer construction
9 Landing/taxiing lamp
10 Carburettor air intake duct
11 Exhaust collector ring
12 Propeller hub pitch change mechanism
13 de Havilland three-bladed propellers
14 Bristol Hercules XVI radial engine
15 Oil cooler intake
16 Cowling air outlet flaps
17 No. 6 fuel tank, capacity 123 Imp gal (559 litres)
18 No. 5 fuel tank, capacity 122 Imp gal (555 litres)
19 Leading-edge oil tank
20 No. 4 fuel tank, capacity 161 Imp gal (732 litres)
21 No. 3 fuel tank, capacity 188 Imp gal (855 litres)
22 Fuel tank breather
23 No. 1 fuel tank, capacity 247 Imp gal (1123 litres)
24 Trailing-edge ribs
25 Starboard flap construction
26 Fuel jettison pipes
27 Starboard main undercarriage wheel bay

28 Inboard wing section bombcells
29 Starboard inner engine cowlings
30 Asymmetric
windscreen
31 Nose skinning
32 De-icing fluid tank
33 Nose section frames
34 Spare ammunition drums
35 Bomb aimer's control panel
36 Nose glazing
37 0 303-in (7.7-mm) Vickers 'K' gun
38 Bomb-aiming panels, optically flat
39 Bomb sight
40 Bomb aimer's prone position couch
41 Pitot tube
42 Parachute stowage
43 Navigator's folding seat
44 Chart table
45 Ventral escape hatch
46 Camera
47 Aerial rail
48 Radio transmitters and receivers
49 Radio operator's control panel
50 Rudder pedals
51 Instrument panel

52 Co-pilot's and engineer's folding seats
53 Control column
54 Pilot's seat

55 Cockpit floor level
56 Cabin side windows
57 Radio operator's seat
58 Trailing aerial winch

59 Bomb bay doors (open)
60 Bomb door operating jacks
61 Main floor/bomb bay support longeron
62 Oxygen bottles
63 Parachute stowage
64 Front fuselage diagonal bracing strut

65 Engineer's control panel
66 Astrodome
67 Fuselage skin plating
68 Hydraulic accumulator
69 Batteries
70 D/F loop aerial fairing
71 Nose/centre section joint frame

72 Cabin roof escape hatch
73 Heater duct
74 Rest bunks, port and starboard
75 Hydraulic accumulators
76 Escape ladder
77 Fuselage/rear spar joint
78 Rear escape hatch
79 Fuselage upper longeron

After lying beneath the water of Lake Hoklingen in Norway for 31 years, Halifax Mk II W1048 'S for Sugar' was recovered in 1973 and is now displayed at the RAF Museum, Hendon. The aircraft belonged to No. 35 Squadron and was one of 11 Halifaxes which departed RAF Kinloss for a low-level attack on the German battleship, Tirpitz. The aircraft was downed by anti-aircraft fire and crash-landed on the frozen lake.

SPECIFICATION

Halifax B.Mk III

Dimensions

Wingspan: 98 ft 10 in (30.20 m) or later aircraft 104 ft 2 in (31.75 m)
Length: 70 ft 1 in (21.36 m)
Height: 20 ft 9 in (6.32 m)
Wing area: 1,275 sq ft (118.45 m²)

Powerplant

Four 1,615-hp (1204-kW) Bristol Hercules XVI 14-cylinder radial piston engines

Weights

Empty: 38,240 lb (17345 kg)
Maximum take-off: 65,000 lb (29484 kg)
Maximum landing: 55,000 lb (24947 kg)

Fuel capacity

Normal: 1,806 Imp gal (8210 litre) in 12 fuel tanks

Long-range: 2,688 Imp gal (12220 litre) in 17 fuel tanks

Performance

Maximum speed at 13,500 ft (4115 m): 282 mph (454 km/h)
Long-range cruising speed at 20,000 ft (6095 m): 215 mph (346 km/h)
Service ceiling: 24,000 ft (7315 m)
Range with maximum bombload: 1,030 miles (1658 km)
Maximum range: 950 miles (1529 km)

Armament

Four 0.303-in (7.7-mm) Browning machine-guns in Boulton Paul E.Mk I tail turret, four 0.303-in (7.7-mm) machine-guns in Boulton Paul A.Mk VIII dorsal turret and one 0.303-in (7.7-mm) Vickers 'K' machine-gun on trainable mount in nose position plus up to 13,000 lb (5897 kg) of bombs

80 Upper turret ladder
81 Flare stowage
82 Sea marker stowage
83 Turret mounting ring
84 Boulton Paul A.Mk.III mid upper gun turret
85 Four 0.303-in (7.7 mm) Browning machine-guns
86 Tail gun turret ammunition boxes
87 Rear fuselage frame construction
88 Ammunition feed tracks
89 Tail fuselage joint frame
90 Tail gunner's access door
91 Tailplane mounting
92 Starboard tailplane construction
101 Boulton Paul Type E tail gun turret
102 Four 0.303-in (7.7-mm) Browning machine-guns
103 Turret sliding doors
104 Port elevator
105 Port tailfin construction
112 Rudder and elevator control hinges
113 Tailwheel strut
114 Semi-retractable tailwheel
115 Rear fuselage bulkhead
116 ARI 5122 radar bombing control units
117 Tailplane control rods
118 Master compass
119 Toilet
120 Crew entry door, opens inward and upward
121 Flare launch tubes
122 Main fuse
123 H₂S radar bombing antenna fairing
124 Port inner flap
125 Flap jack
126 Dinghy stowage
127 Flap control rods
128 Rear spar inboard section attachment joints
129 Port outer flap
130 Fuel jettison pipes
131 Rear spar outer panel attachment joint
132 Trim tab controls
133 Aileron hinge control
134 Trim tab
135 Aileron servo tab
136 Port aileron
137 Aileron balance weight
138 Formation light
139 Port navigation light
140 Wingrib construction
141 Front spar
142 Leading-edge nose ribs
143 Armoured leading edge
144 Cable-cutters
145 Retractable landing/taxiing lamps
146 Lamp operating jack
147 Outer engine mounting ribs
148 Engine bearer struts
149 Engine mounting ring
150 Flame suppressor exhaust pipe
151 Exhaust collector ring
152 Carburettor intake duct
153 Outer wing panel joint
154 Port wing fuel tanks
155 Main undercarriage jacks
156 Port main wheel bay
157 Inner wing panel front spar joint
158 Wing bomb-cell long-range fuel tank, capacity 96 Imp gal (436 litres)
159 Front spar girder construction
160 Leading-edge No. 2 fuel tank, capacity 62 Imp gal (282 litres)
161 Engine control runs
162 Port inner Bristol Hercules XVI engine
163 Oil cooler air intake
164 Inboard engine bearers
165 Main undercarriage hinge mounting
166 Messier main undercarriage leg
167 Port mainwheel
168 Tyre guard
169 Folding retraction strut
170 Mainwheel door

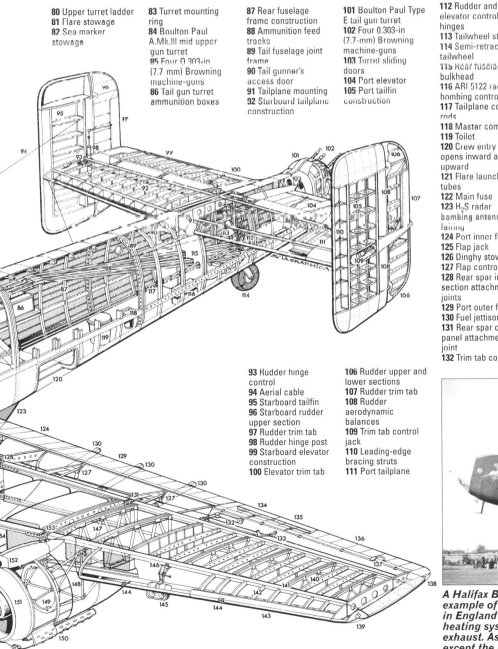

93 Rudder hinge control
94 Aerial cable
95 Starboard tailfin
96 Starboard rudder upper section
97 Rudder trim tab
98 Rudder hinge post
99 Starboard elevator construction
100 Elevator trim tab
106 Rudder upper and lower sections
107 Rudder trim tab
108 Rudder aerodynamic balances
109 Trim tab control jack
110 Leading-edge bracing struts
111 Port tailplane

A Halifax B.Mk VI displaying a relatively subtle example of nose art runs up at an airfield 'somewhere in England'. Piping for the aircraft's Graveley cabin heating system can be seen at the rear of the engine exhaust. As on the Halifax B.Mk III, all of the engines, except the port outer unit, exhausted to starboard. The flame-damping exhausts of the Hercules-engined aircraft are also illustrated to good effect.

Halifax B.Mk VII

This particular B.Mk VII served with No. 408 ('Goose') Squadron of the Royal Canadian Air Force at RAF Linton-on-Ouse, Yorkshire. The unit was formed at RAF Lindholme in June 1941 as one of the many RCAF squadrons operating as part of the RAF's war effort. It initially flew Hampdens before transferring to Halifaxes, then Lancasters, then back to Halifaxes again. The name of the unit came from its badge, which featured a Canada Goose. Graphic nose art such as *Vicky the Vicious Virgin* was very rare on RAF aircraft, but the Canadian squadrons were less strict. The nicknames of the crew were also applied near their positions.

Navigation equipment

The Halifax was equipped with a direction-finding loop in a teardrop radome above the fuselage, which also served as a mast for wire aerials leading back to the fintips. Some Halifaxes were fitted with 'Mandrel' and 'Airborne Cigar' jamming equipment for special radio countermeasures missions.

Accommodation

The Halifax had a crew of seven, comprising the pilot on the flight deck, bomb aimer/gunner in the nose (lying prone on a couch and peering through an optically-flat pane), navigator and wireless operator on the lower deck beneath the pilot, flight engineer on the upper deck behind the pilot and the two gunners in the mid-upper and rear turrets. A co-pilot's seat was next to that of the pilot, although no such dedicated crew member was carried. Above the engineer's station was an astrodome for sextant navigation. The crew entered the aircraft through a hatch which opened upwards and inwards.

Bristol power

The B.Mk VII featured the same Bristol Hercules XVI engines as the B.Mk III. These were 14-cylinder two-row sleeve-valve radials, each rated at 1,615 hp (1204 kW) for take-off, 1,675 hp (1249 kW) in 'M' gear at 4,500 ft (1372 m) and 1,455 hp (1085 kW) in 'S' gear at 12,000 ft (3658 m). Each engine drove a de Havilland constant-speed three-bladed propeller. The large intakes above the engines admitted air for the carburettor, while those underneath were for the oil cooler. Engine cooling was by the airflow, which was increased at slow speed by the use of cooling gills around the rear of the cowling. One of the more distinctive features of Hercules-powered Halifax variants was the large flame damper on the exhaust. The cowlings were inherited from the Beaufighter night-fighter.

Tail unit

Throughout its early career, the Halifax suffered from rudder overbalance, which could lead to the aircraft entering a spin in an asymmetric flight condition, such as two unserviceable engines on one side. The Type D fin (out of several different shapes trialled) was introduced to the later variants, curing the problem.

Dorsal and rear turrets

This B.Mk VII is fitted with a Type D tail turret with twin 0.5-in (12.7-mm) machine-guns. Ammunition was stored just aft of the mid-upper turret and fed by tracks to the rear position. Upper protection for the Halifax came courtesy of a Boulton Paul A.Mk VIII mid-upper turret, with a permanent gunner. The four Browning 0.303-in (7.7-mm) machine-guns had 1,160 rounds each. Aircraft which did not have H_2S radar had a Preston-Green ventral gun mounting.

Finding the target

The large radome under the rear fuselage housed the H_2S bombing radar, displacing the ventral gun turret of earlier aircraft. The Halifax was instrumental in the development of this pinpoint bombing aid, and along with the Stirling was responsible for its introduction into service on the night of 30/31 January 1943. Most sets were of 3-cm wavelength, and used the magnetron valve. The large bomb bay could accommodate up to 13,000 lb (5897 kg) of bombs, but in practice space limitations restricted this to one 8,000-lb (3629-kg) weapon, two 4,000-lb (1814-kg) bombs, or six 1,000-lb (454-kg) and two 2,000-lb (907-kg) bombs.

Wing structure

The wing was built around two spars, which carried through the centre-section. The outer wing was made up of two sections, one join being just inboard of the outer engine, and the other being outboard of the inner engine. From the B.Mk III, subsequent Halifax bomber variants had extended rounded wingtips, which had originally been proposed for high-altitude versions. These raised the wing span to 104 ft 2 in (31.75 m) and allowed a substantial increase in maximum take-off weight.

Heinkel He 111

Above: A classic Battle of Britain image of a classic Battle of Britain bomber. This KG 1 He 111 was photographed over West India Docks, London on 7 September 1940.

He 111H-3

Cutaway key
1 Starboard navigation light
2 Starboard aileron
3 Wing ribs
4 Forward spar
5 Rear spar
6 Aileron tab
7 Starboard flap
8 Fuel tank access panel
9 Wing centre section/outer panel break line
10 Inboard fuel tank (154-Imp gal/700-litre capacity) position between nacelle and fuselage
11 Oil tank cooling louvres
12 Oil cooler air intake
13 Supercharger air intake
14 Three-bladed VDM airscrew
15 Airscrew pitch-change mechanism
16 Junkers Jumo 211D-1 12-cylinder, inverted-vee, liquid-cooled engine
17 Exhaust manifold
18 Nose-mounted 0.31-in (7.9-mm) MG 15 machine-gun
19 Ikaria ball-and-socket gun mounting (offset to starboard)
20 Bomb sight housing (offset to starboard)
21 Starboard mainwheel
22 Rudder pedals
23 Bomb aimer's horizontal pad
24 Additional 0.31-in (7.9-mm) MG-15 machine-gun (fitted by forward maintenance units)
25 Repeater compass
26 Bomb aimer's folding seat
27 Control column
28 Throttles
29 Pilot's seat

30 Retractable auxiliary windscreen (for use when pilot's seat in elevated position)
31 Sliding entry panel
32 Forward fuselage bulkhead
33 Double-frame station
34 Port ESAC bomb bay (vertical stowage)
35 Fuselage windows (blanked)
36 Central gangway between bomb bays
37 Double-frame station
38 Direction finder
39 Dorsal gunner's (forward) sliding canopy
40 Dorsal 0.31-in (7.9-mm) MG 15 machine-gun
41 Dorsal gunner's cradle seat
42 FuG 10 radio equipment
43 Fuselage window
44 Armoured bulkhead (8-mm)
45 Aerial mast
46 Bomb flares
47 Unarmoured bulkhead
48 Rear fuselage access cut-out
49 Port 0.31-in (7.9-mm) beam MG 15 machine-gun
50 Dinghy stowage
51 Fuselage frames
52 Stringers
53 Starboard tailplane
54 Aerial
55 Starboard elevator
56 Tailfin forward spar

57 Tailfin structure
58 Rudder balance
59 Tailfin rear spar/rudder post
60 Rudder construction
61 Rudder tab
62 Tab actuator (starboard surface)
63 Remotely-controlled 0.31-in (7.9-mm) MG 17 machine-gun in tail cone (fitted to some aircraft only)
64 Rear navigation light
65 Elevator tab
66 Elevator structure
67 Elevator hinge line
68 Tailplane front spar
69 Semi-retractable tailwheel

70 Tailwheel shock-absorber
71 Tail surface control linkage
72 Fuselage/tailfin frame
73 Control pulley
74 Push-pull control rods
75 Master compass
76 Observation window fairing
77 Glazed observation window in floor
78 Ventral-aft firing 0.31-in (7.9-mm) MG 15 machine gun in tail of *Sterberbett* (death bed) gondola

79 Ventral gondola entry hatch
80 Ventral gunner's horizontal pad
81 Forward-firing 20-mm (Oerlikon) MG FF cannon (for anti-shipping operations)
82 Rear spar carry-through
83 Forward spar carry-through
84 Oil cooler
85 Anti-vibration engine mount
86 Oil tank
87 Engine bearer
88 Exhaust flame-damper shroud
89 Radiator air intake
90 Radiator bath
91 Port mainwheel
92 Mainwheel leg

SPECIFICATION

He 111H-16

Dimensions

Length: 53 ft 9½ in
Height: 13 ft 1¼ in
Wingspan: 74 ft 1¾ in
Wing area: 931.10 sq ft (16.40 m²)

Powerplant

Two Junkers Jumo 211F-2 inline piston engines, each rated at 1,350 hp (1006 kW) for take off

Weights

Empty: 19,136 lb (8680 kg)
Maximum take-off: 30,864 lb (14000 kg)

Performance

Never-exceed speed: 298 mph (480 km/h)
Maximum speed at maximum take-off weight at sea level: 217 mph (349 km/h)

Maximum speed at maximum take-off weight at 13,120 ft (4000 m): 252 mph (406 km/h)
Normal range with maximum bomb load at sea level: 1,212 miles (1950 km)
Climb to 13,120 ft (4000 m) at maximum take-off weight: 23 minutes 30 seconds
Service ceiling at maximum take-off weight: 21,980 ft (6700 m)
g limits at 24,251 lb (11000 kg): 2.7

Armament

One 20-mm MG FF cannon in the nose, one 0.51-in (13-mm) MG 131 machine-gun in the dorsal position, two 0.31-in (7.9-mm) MG 81 machine-guns in the rear of the ventral gondola and one or two 0.31-in (7.9-mm) MG 15 or MG 81 machine-guns in each of the beam positions, plus up to 5,512 lb (2500 kg) of bombs, torpedoes or other stores

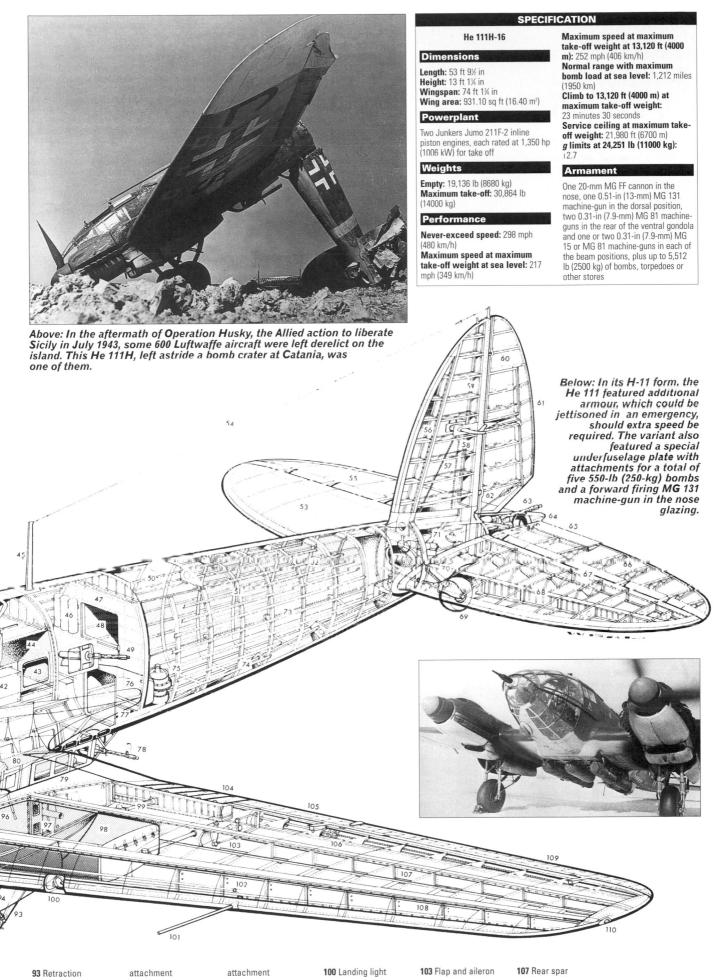

Above: In the aftermath of Operation Husky, the Allied action to liberate Sicily in July 1943, some 600 Luftwaffe aircraft were left derelict on the island. This He 111H, left astride a bomb crater at Catania, was one of them.

Below: In its H-11 form, the He 111 featured additional armour, which could be jettisoned in an emergency, should extra speed be required. The variant also featured a special underfuselage plate with attachments for a total of five 550-lb (250-kg) bombs and a forward firing MG 131 machine-gun in the nose glazing.

93 Retraction mechanism
94 Mainwheel door (outer)
95 Multi-screw wing
    attachment
96 Trailing-aerial tube (to starboard of ventral gondola)
97 Rear spar
    attachment
98 Port outboard fuel tank (220-Imp gal/1000-litre capacity)
99 Flap control rod
100 Landing light
101 Pitot head
102 Pitot head heater/ wing leading-edge de-icer
103 Flap and aileron coupling
104 Flap structure
105 Aileron tab
106 Tab actuator
107 Rear spar
108 Forward spar
109 Port aileron
110 Port navigation light

He 111H-22

This aircraft is illustrated as it appeared on the strength of III Kampfgeschwader 3 based at Venlo in Holland in the late summer of 1944. The unit was tasked with the continuation of Operation Rumpelkammer, the Fi 103 (V1) missile offensive against the UK. III./KG 3 employed He 111H-22s alongside converted H-16s and H-20s to air-launch the missiles. In September 1944, KG 53 was withdrawn from the Eastern Front, the crews of I./KG 53 then being absorbed into II. and III./KG 53 and III./KG 3 being redesignated as an all-new I./KG 53. By November 1944 the II. Gruppe of KG 53 had joined I. Gruppe in making Fi 103 attacks, but operating from the Oldenburg and Bremen areas of Germany. Meanwhile, I./KG 53 itself had been forced out of its Dutch base by the advancing Allied armies and had also been forced to withdraw to Germany. KG 27 probably provided veteran crews to KG 53, although itself disbanded between January and April 1945, at which point its III. Gruppe was probably training for the Fi 103 mission.

Wing, tail and rear fuselage

The all-metal wing was constructed around a two-spar structure, with the spars continuing through the fuselage forward and aft of the bomb bay. At its inboard trailing edges on both sides, the wing carried hydraulically-operated slotted flaps, while outboard of these were ailerons equipped with two-section trim tabs. In the landing sequence, the selection of flaps automatically deflected the ailerons downwards, providing greater lift at this critical stage than the flaps alone would have achieved and apparently not affecting the aircraft's trim. The tailplane could be adjusted on the ground through a range of 3° 12' into three separate positions for trimming purposes, while the rudder was the only control surface activated by the autopilot. With the automatic pilot engaged, three different rates of turn could be selected via a switch on the control column. To the rear of the crew compartment, aft of the cabin bulkhead, the fuselage was more-or-less empty, although it did provide accommodation for the emergency dinghy, master compass and tail control cable runs. A hatch in the bulkhead allowed the crew to access the rear fuselage for reasons of maintenance.

Fi 103 launches

With the withdrawal of conventional V-1 launch sites into central Holland, the UK, specifically London, fell out of the missile's range, hence the switch to airborne launching. The air-launched Fi 103 was normally sent on its way by an He 111 flying at around 1,500 ft (457 m) at night over the North Sea. The missiles were carried on special pylons under the wing root and could be launched from either port or starboard, although only one missile was ever carried at a time. The first air-launched Fi 103s were sent against Southampton on 7 July 1944, with minimal results. Nevertheless, by the end of August some 90 missiles had been fired at the town, with another 300 being aimed at London and 20 at Gloucester. By mid-December a further 865 missiles had been expended, but the cost in terms of aircraft and crews was high. When operations ceased on 14 January 1945, KG 53 had lost 77 He 111s, 12 of them when their missiles detonated immediately after take off.

Defensive armament

On the He 111H-22 defensive weapons were usually reduced to just two (as here) or three guns. The dorsal turret mounted a 0.51-in (13-mm) MG 131 machine-gun with 1,000 rounds of ammunition. A vane protruding from the rear of the turret, inline with the gun, offset the aerodynamic drag caused by the weapon's barrel as the turret rotated. A 20-mm MG FF cannon with 180 rounds was mounted in the extreme nose, while a 0.31-in (7.9-mm) MG 15 could be fixed on an Ikaria universal mounting to fire through the foremost upper glazed panel to the right of the cockpit area.

Fuel system

Fuel was contained in two tanks in each wing, positioned between the wing spars. A 154-Imp gal (700-litre) capacity main fuel tank was fitted between each engine nacelle and the fuselage, while 220-Imp gal (1000-litre) reserve tanks were fitted immediately outboard of the nacelles. The engines took fuel from the main tanks first, fuel being automatically moved from the reserve to the main tanks by electric transfer pumps when the main tanks were down to 44 Imp gal (200 litres) of fuel remaining.

Jumo powerplant

Since the He 111H-22s were modified from H-21 airframes on the production line, they retained the Jumo 213E-1 engines of the night-bomber variant. These delivered 1,750 hp (1305 kW) for take-off and 1,320 hp (985 kW) at 32,000 ft (9753 m). V1-carriers converted from H-16 bomber and H-20 multi-role glider tug/transport airframes retained the Jumo 211F-2 engines of these variants, producing just 1,350 hp (1007 kW) on take off and as little as 1,060 hp (791 kW) at 17,390 ft (5300 m).

Fieseler Fi 103

With a typical launch weight of 4,806 lb (2180 kg), the Fi 103 was better known as the V-1 (Vergeltungswaffe Eins – Reprisal Weapon One). At launch, it was simply aimed in the direction of its target, the chances of hitting a city-sized area in this manner being fairly high. The weapon was powered by a 661-lb st (2.94-kN) Argus-Schmidt As 014 pulse-jet which operated at 47 Hz to produce the distinctive sound of the 'buzz-bomb'. An autopilot kept the weapon on course during its 32-minute flight and maximum range was in excess of 150 miles (240 km). The Amatol warhead weighed 1,874 lb (850 kg) and was detonated by an impact fuse in the missile's nose.

Heinkel He 115

The He 115 was fitted with a permanent ladder to allow crew access via the floats. The ladder is clearly visible in this wartime colour photograph.

He 115

Cutaway key

1 7.9-mm MG 15 machine-gun
2 Gunsights
3 Ikaria nose mounting
4 Cartridge collector chute
5 Nose ring
6 Entry/escape hatch
7 Nose glazing
8 Bomb/torpedo-sight
9 Selector panel
10 Handhold
11 Bombardier's kneeling-pad
12 Ventral glazing
13 Bombardier's/navigator's hinged seat
14 Duplicate throttle controls
15 Duplicate control column
16 Instrument panel
17 Nose compartment windscreen
18 Fixed glazing
19 Electrics panel
20 Batteries
21 Cockpit/nose access
22 Smoke floats
24 Fuselage frame
25 Cockpit floor
26 Rudder pedals
27 Throttles
28 Control column
29 Instrument panel
30 Windscreen
31 Starboard nacelle oil tank location
32 Engine bearer supports
33 Cooling gills
34 Starboard BMW 132K nine-cylinder radial engine
35 Nacelle nose ring
36 Propeller hub
37 Spinner
38 VDM three-bladed metal propeller of 10.83-ft (3.30-m) diameter
39 Nacelle hinged access/maintenance panels
40 Leading-edge hinged access/servicing panel
41 Starboard outer main fuel tank
42 Leading-edge tank (provision)
43 Wing structure
44 Front spar
45 Starboard navigation light
46 Starboard outer rib
47 Aileron outer hinge
48 Starboard aileron
49 Aileron tabs
50 Rear spar
51 Aileron tab hinge fairing
52 Control linkage
53 Flap outer section
54 Aileron profile
55 Starboard flap
56 Canopy hinged section
57 Fixed section
58 Cockpit rear-sliding canopy
59 Pilot's seat
60 Leading-edge inboard hinged access/servicing panel
61 Front spar carry-through
62 Fuselage/spar main frame
63 Front spar
64 Port inner main fuel tank
65 Filler cap
66 Fuselage centre bay
67 Wireless installation
68 Aerial mast
69 Dorsal identification light
70 Rear spar carry-through
71 Wireless operator's position
72 Flare stowage
73 Pistol flare port
74 Wireless operator/gunner's swivel seat
75 Cockpit coaming
76 Canopy fixed section
77 Gunner's hinged canopy section
78 Dorsal 7.9-mm MG 15 machine-gun
79 Ammunition magazine stowage (1,500 rounds)
80 Cockpit warm air
81 Wing upper surface walkway
82 Rescue dinghy stowage
83 Port flap inner section
84 Trailing-edge flap
85 Crew entry ladder (port and starboard)
86 Ladder attachments
87 Handholds
88 Fuselage frame
89 Dorsal skinning
90 Semi-monocoque fuselage structure
91 Control runs
92 Compass installation
93 Stringers
94 Fuselage aft frame
95 Port tailplane forward attachment
96 Tailfin leading edge
97 Starboard tailplane
98 Starboard elevator mass balances
99 Tailplane spar
100 Aerial
101 Elevator outer hinge
102 Starboard elevator tab
103 Aerial attachment
104 Rudder upper hinge
105 Tailfin structure
106 Front spar
107 Rudder mass balances
108 Starboard tailplane lower brace strut
109 Port tailplane aft attachment
110 Rudder tab hinge fairing
111 Rudder
112 Rudder tab upper section
113 Rudder tab lower section
114 Elevator tab
115 Port elevator upper mass balance
116 Tab hinge fairing
117 Port elevator
118 Elevator outer hinge
119 Port elevator lower mass balance
120 Port tailplane lower brace strut
121 Tailplane front spar
122 Mooring attachment
123 Brace strut/fuselage fairings
124 Fuselage aft main frame
125 Ventral skinning
126 Wing construction break-point
127 Rib strap joint
128 Port flap outer section
129 Aileron control linkage
130 Rear spar
131 Aileron tab hinge fairing
132 Aileron tab
133 Outer hinge
134 Port aileron
135 Port wingtip
136 Port navigation light
137 Outer rib
138 Wing structure
139 Front spar
140 Pitot head
141 Wing leading edge
142 Landing lamp
143 Port float aft section
144 Float sternpost
145 Mooring bollard
146 Spar section
147 Ladder/float attachment
148 Port outer main fuel tank
149 Filler cap

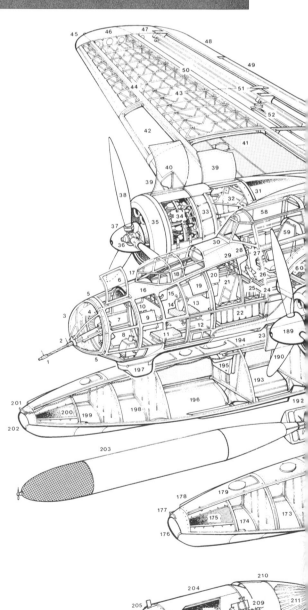

SPECIFICATION

Type
Three-seat coastal general-purpose and torpedo bomber floatplane

Powerplant
Two BMW 132K radial piston engines each rated at 960 hp (716 kW)

Performance
Maximum speed 186 mph (300 km/h) at 3,280 ft (1000 m); cruising speed 180 mph (290 km/h) at 6,560 ft (2000 m); climb to 9,845 ft (3000 m) in 22 minutes 18 seconds; service ceiling 16,950 ft (5165 m); range 1,740 miles (2800 km) with maximum fuel

Weights
Empty 15,146 lb (6870 kg); normal take-off 23,545 lb (10680 kg)

Dimensions
Wingspan 73 ft 1 in (22.28 m); length 56 ft 9 in (17.30 m); height 21 ft 7¾ in (6.60 m); wing area 933.23 sq ft (86.70 m2)

Armament
One 15-mm MG 151 fixed forward-firing cannon on the lower port side of the nose, one 0.31-in (7.92-mm) MG 17 fixed rearward-firing machine-gun in the rear of each engine nacelle, one 0.31-in (7.92-mm) MG 15 trainable forward-firing machine gun in the nose position and one 0.31-in (7.92-mm) MG 15 trainable rearward-firing machine-gun in the dorsal position, plus up to 2,205 lb (1000 kg) of disposable stores carried in a lower-fuselage weapons bay and on two underwing hardpoints

Norway became an important area of operations for He 115 seaplanes during World War II. Ironically, Norway's Marinens Flyvevåben also operated the type, and a few enemy He 115s were captured by both sides during the fighting. Six Norwegian-flown He 115s bombed German positions during the battle for Narvik.

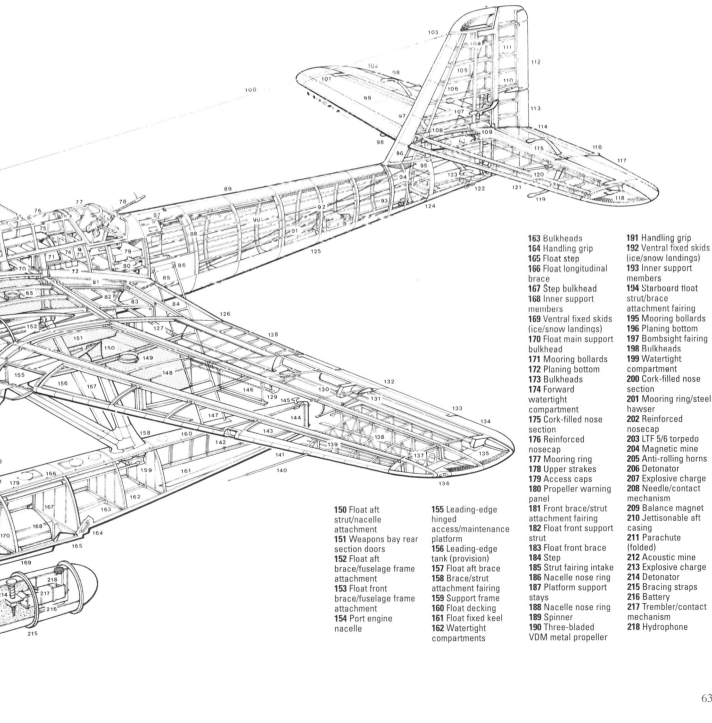

150 Float aft strut/nacelle attachment
151 Weapons bay rear section doors
152 Float aft brace/fuselage frame attachment
153 Float front brace/fuselage frame attachment
154 Port engine nacelle
155 Leading-edge hinged access/maintenance platform
156 Leading-edge tank (provision)
157 Float aft brace
158 Brace/strut attachment fairing
159 Support frame
160 Float decking
161 Float fixed keel
162 Watertight compartments
163 Bulkheads
164 Handling grip
165 Float step
166 Float longitudinal brace
167 Step bulkhead
168 Inner support members
169 Ventral fixed skids (ice/snow landings)
170 Float main support bulkhead
171 Mooring bollards
172 Planing bottom
173 Bulkheads
174 Forward watertight compartment
175 Cork-filled nose section
176 Reinforced nosecap
177 Mooring ring
178 Upper strakes
179 Access caps
180 Propeller warning panel
181 Front brace/strut attachment fairing
182 Float front support strut
183 Float front brace
184 Step
185 Strut fairing intake
186 Nacelle nose ring
187 Platform support stays
188 Nacelle nose ring
189 Spinner
190 Three-bladed VDM metal propeller
191 Handling grip
192 Ventral fixed skids (ice/snow landings)
193 Inner support members
194 Starboard float strut/brace attachment fairing
195 Mooring bollards
196 Planing bottom
197 Bombsight fairing
198 Bulkheads
199 Watertight compartment
200 Cork-filled nose section
201 Mooring ring/steel hawser
202 Reinforced nosecap
203 LTF 5/6 torpedo
204 Magnetic mine
205 Anti-rolling horns
206 Detonator
207 Explosive charge
208 Needle/contact mechanism
209 Balance magnet
210 Jettisonable aft casing
211 Parachute (folded)
212 Acoustic mine
213 Explosive charge
214 Detonator
215 Bracing straps
216 Battery
217 Trembler/contact mechanism
218 Hydrophone

Heinkel He 177

An audacious British operation saw this He 177A-5/R6 being taken from the Luftwaffe airfield at Blagnac. The machine was tested in autumn 1944 and into 1945. Officially named Grief (Griffon), the He 177 proved almost as dangerous to its crews as it did to the enemy, and it was generally considered a poor machine by its British test pilots.

Ju 87D-3

Cutaway key

1 Starboard navigation light
2 Detachable wingtip
3 FuG 101 radio altimeter (FM)
4 Aileron control runs
5 Starboard aileron
6 Aileron trim tab
7 Spring-loaded geared tab
8 Aileron counter-balance
9 FuG 102 radio altimeter (pulsed)
10 Tab mechanism
11 Fowler flap outboard track
12 Fowler flap position (extended)
13 Aileron tab control linkage
14 Flap actuating cylinder (hydraulic)
15 Control cables
16 Main spar (outboard section)
17 Wing ribs
18 Auxiliary front spar
19 Heated leading edge
20 Oil radiator intake
21 Starboard Hs 293 radio-controlled glide-bomb
22 Starboard outer mainwheel door (open position)
23 Starboard outer mainwheel well
24 Balloon cable-cutter in leading edge
25 Starboard ETC weapons rack
26 Radiator outlet flap
27 Radiator outlet flap
28 Hot-air ducting
29 Mainwheel door actuating cylinder
30 No. 8 (starboard outer) fuel tank of 1,120 litre/246.5 Imp gal capacity (flexible bag)
31 Fuel filler cap
32 Fowler flap outer section
33 auxiliary rear spar
34 Wing dihedral break point
35 Fowler flap track
36 Starboard fuel starting tank (9 litre/2 gal capacity)
37 Starboard oil tanks

38 Main hydraulic tank (starboard only) (32 litre/7 gal capacity)
39 Fuel filler cap
40 No. 3 (starboard inner) fuel tank of 621 litre/136.5 Imp gal capacity (metal/self sealing)
41 Fowler flap inner section
42 Main spar (inboard section)
43 Starboard inner mainwheel well
44 Engine supercharger
45 Nacelle fairing
46 Wing spar attachment point and fairing
47 Engine accessories
48 Daimler-Benz DB 610A-1 24-cylinder liquid-cooled engine
49 Anti-vibration side-mounting pad
50 Supercharger and wing de-icing intakes
51 Nacelle former
52 Coolant vents
53 Engine forward mounting
54 Cooling gills
55 Double-gear crank casing
56 Single propeller shaft
57 Propeller de-icing saddle tank
58 Nacelle cooling profile
59 Propeller variable-pitch mechanism
60 Propeller boss
61 Blade cuffs
62 VDM four-bladed propeller (right-handed)
63 Chin intake
64 Flame damper exhaust
65 Starboard outer mainwheel leg
66 Starboard inner mainwheel leg
67 Starboard outer mainwheel
68 D/F loop in dorsal blister
69 Emergency hydraulic tank (25 litre/5.5 Imp gal)
70 No. 7 fuselage frame

71 C-Stand ammunition tank (1,000 rounds)
72 Dorsal barbette remote drive motor
73 Revi gunsight with slotted 10-mm armour protection
74 Remote control sighting cupola
75 Barbette traverse control handle
76 Barbette elevation control handle
77 Main radio panel (FuG 10P; general-purpose set) (FuG17Z: VHF communication and homing) (FuG BL 2F: Blind-approach)
78 First-aid pack
79 Navigator's take-off/landing station
80 Window
81 Gunner's seat
82 Emergency jettison panels (port and starboard)
83 Bomb aimer's seat (raised)
84 External rear-view mirror
85 Engine control panel (starboard)
86 Internal rear-view mirror
87 Offset ring-and-bead gunsight
88 MG 81 7.9-mm machine-gun (A1-Stand)
89 Circular gun mounting
90 Balloon cable-cutters in nose horizontal frames
91 Ammunition feed
92 A1-Stand ammunition tank (1,000 rounds)
93 Hinged window panel (port and starboard)
94 Pilot's seat (armour plate: 9-mm back, 6-mm seat)
95 Rudder pedals
96 Cockpit hot-air
97 Lower glazed section often overpainted/armoured
98 Lotfe 7D bombsight fairing
99 'Boxed' gunsight
100 MG 151 20-mm cannon (A2-Stand)
101 Bullet-proof glass in nose of 'bola'
102 De-icing intake

103 Ventral crew entry hatch
104 Telescopic ladder
105 Actuating arm

106 MG 161 20-mm cannon ammunition feed
107 De-icing air heater/blower
108 A2-Stand ammunition tank (300 rounds)
109 Toilet installation
110 C-Stand ammunition feed
111 Thermos flasks
112 Circular vision port
113 MG 131 13-mm machine gun (C-Stand) at rear of 'bola'
114 'Fritz X' (Kramer X-1) radio-controlled bomb
115 Cruciform main fins
116 SAP warhead
117 Tail fin structure
118 Air-brake attachment
119 Ventral bomb rack (only fitted if forward bomb bay blanked off)
120 Forward-bomb bay (often blanked off)
121 Fuel tank retaining strap lugs
122 Internal bomb shackle
123 Bomb bay central partition
124 No. 4 (fuselage) fuel tank (1520 litre/334 Imp gal)
125 Fuel filler cap

126 Barbette remote drive cooling duct and linkage
127 Remote control dorsal barbette (B1-Stand)
128 Twin 10-mm MG 131 guns
129 No. 13 fuselage frame
130 Barbette structure
131 B1-Stand double ammunition tank (1,000 rounds per gun)
132 Central bomb bay (often blanked off)

133 Bomb bay door (outer section)
134 Port inner mainwheel well
135 No. 5 (fuselage) fuel tank (1520 litre/334 Imp gal) (Replaced by 3450 litre/759 Imp gal tank if bomb bay blanked off) (metal/self sealing)
136 Fuel filler cap
137 No. 19 fuselage frame

SPECIFICATION

Type
Five-seat heavy bomber and missile-carrier

Powerplant
Two Daimler-Benz DB 610A-1/B-1 24-cylinder inverted-Vee piston engines each rated at 2,950 hp (2200 kW)

Performance
Maximum speed 304 mph (490 km/h) at 19,685 ft (6000 m); cruising speed 258 mph (415 km/h) at 19,685 ft (6000 m); initial climb rate 623 ft (190 m) per minute; service ceiling 26,245 ft (8000 m); range 3,417 miles (5500 km) with two Hs 293 missiles

Weights
Empty 37,038 lb (16800 kg); max take-off 68,343 lb (31000 kg)

Dimensions
Wingspan 103 ft 13/4 in (31.44 m); length 66 ft 111/4 in (20.40 m); height 20 ft 113/4 in (6.39 m); wing area 1,097.95 sq ft (102.00 m2)

Armament
One 0.31-in (7.92-mm) MG 81J trainable forward-firing machine-gun in the nose position, one 20-mm MG 151/20 trainable forward-firing cannon in the ventral gondola, two 0.31-in (7.92-mm) MG 81 trainable rearward-firing machine-guns in the ventral gondola, two 0.51-in (13-mm) MG 131 trainable machine-guns in the remotely controlled power-operated dorsal barbette, one 0.51-in (13-mm) MG 131 trainable machine-gun in the power-operated dorsal turret and one 20-mm MG 151/20 trainable rearward-firing cannon in the tail position, plus up to 13,228 lb (6000 kg) of disposable stores carried in a lower-fuselage weapons bay and on underwing hardpoints

During Operation Steinbock, experienced He 177 crews found that by entering enemy airspace at 29,527 ft (9000 m), and attacking at full power and in a shallow dive at about 435 mph (700 km/h), they stood a chance of avoiding interception.

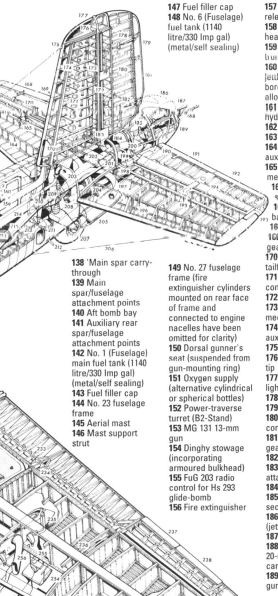

147 Fuel filler cap
148 No. 6 (Fuselage) fuel tank (1140 litre/330 Imp gal) (metal/self sealing)
149 No. 27 fuselage frame (fire extinguisher cylinders mounted on rear face of frame and connected to engine nacelles have been omitted for clarity)
150 Dorsal gunner's seat (suspended from gun-mounting ring)
151 Oxygen supply (alternative cylindrical or spherical bottles)
152 Power-traverse turret (B2-Stand)
153 MG 131 13-mm gun
154 Dinghy stowage (incorporating armoured bulkhead)
155 FuG 203 radio control for Hs 293 glide-bomb
156 Fire extinguisher
157 Dinghy manual release
158 De-icing air heater/blower
159 De-icing intake trunking
160 Starboard fuel jettison pipe (large-bore seamed light alloy)
161 Tailwheel hydraulic lines
162 Fuselage skinning
163 Short-wave aerial
164 Tailplane forward auxiliary spar
165 Tailplane tab mechanism
166 Tailplane main spar
167 Elevator balance
168 Elevator trim tab
169 Spring loaded geared tab
170 De-icing intake in tailfin root
171 Tailfin construction
172 Tailfin main spar
173 Rudder hinge mechanism
174 Tailfin forward auxiliary spar
175 Aerial attachment
176 Detachable tailfin tip
177 Rear navigation light
178 Tab mechanism
179 Rudder trim tab
180 Rudder construction
181 Spring-loaded geared tab
182 Tab mechanism
183 Tailfin/fuselage attachment point
184 Tail gunner's seat
185 Fixed canopy section
186 Hinged (jettisonable) hood
187 'Coned' gunsight
188 Gimbal-mounted 20-mm MG 151 cannon (H-Stand)
189 18-mm armoured gun mounting
190 Tab hinge
191 Spring-loaded geared tab
192 Elevator trim tab
193 Elevator balance
194 Elevator construction
195 Tailplane construction
196 Heated leading edge
197 Hot-air ducting
198 Tailplane/fuselage attachment points
199 H-Stand ammunition feed motor
200 Tail position hot-air
201 First-aid pack
202 Continuous main spar carry-through
203 No. 44 fuselage frame
204 Tailplane auxiliary spar/fuselage attachment points
205 Hinged tailwheel doors
206 FuG 203 aerial (Hs 293 control)
207 Tailwheel
208 Port fuel jettisonable pipe (large-bore seamed light alloy)
209 Tailwheel leg
210 Retraction mechanism
211 Rectangular vision port
212 Trailing aerial lead-in and matching unit
213 Trailing aerial winch
214 Main hot-air duct
215 H-Stand ammunition feed
216 Master compass
217 Semi-monocoque fuselage construction
218 Dorsal turret hot-air
219 Jettisonable floor/entry escape hatch
220 H-Stand ammunition tank (800 rounds)
221 B2-Stand ammunition tank (1,000 rounds)
222 Ammunition feed
223 Flexible chute
224 Empty belt link and cartridge collector box
225 Aft bomb bay door (outer section)
226 No. 2 (port inner) fuel tank (621 litre/136.5 Imp gal) (metal/self sealing)
227 Port oil tanks
228 Auxiliary rear spar
229 Fowler flap construction (inner section)
230 Port fuel starting tank (9 litre/2 gal)
231 No. 7 (port outer) fuel tank 1120 litre/246 Imp gal) (flexible bag)
232 Fuel filler cap
233 Fowler flap construction (outer section)
234 Flap hinge fairing
235 ETC rack hot air
236 Fowler flap track attachment
237 Spring-loaded geared tab
238 Aileron trim tab
239 Port aileron construction
240 Tab mechanism
241 Aileron mechanism
242 Wingtip attachment bolts
243 Port navigation light
244 Detachable wingtip
245 Wing undersurface access/inspection panels
246 Pitot head
247 Heated leading edge
248 Main spar (outboard section)
249 Auxiliary front spar
250 Hs 293 radio-controlled glider-bomb
251 590-kg (1,300-lb) thrust rocket motor housing
252 500-kg (1,100-lb) warhead
253 Wing control surfaces
254 Tail-mounted aerial masts (radio signal receivers)
255 Tracking flare installation
256 Outboard leading-edge hot air
257 Port ETC weapons rack
258 Oil radiator outlet flap
259 Twin oil radiators (port engines)
260 Searchlight/landing light
261 Port outer mainwheel door (open position)
262 Oil radiator intake
263 Port outer mainwheel well
264 Mainwheel door actuating cylinder
265 Hot air ducting
266 Wing spar attachment point and fairing
267 Individual undercarriage/main spar attachment
268 Engine bearer ball socket
269 Hydraulic retracting jack attachment
270 Upper engine bearer
271 Coolant tanks
272 Engine support strut
273 Mainwheel oleo leg pivot points
274 Supercharger and wing de-icing intakes
275 Cooling gills
276 Engine forward mounting
277 Segmented annular radiator
278 VDM four-bladed propeller (left-handed)
279 Blade cuffs
280 Propeller boss
281 Chin intake
282 Flame damper exhaust
283 Port inboard mainwheel oleo leg (inward retracting)
284 Port outboard mainwheel oleo leg (outward retracting)
285 Mainwheel axle
286 Port outer mainwheel
287 Port inner mainwheel

138 'Main spar carry-through
139 Main spar/fuselage attachment points
140 Aft bomb bay
141 Auxiliary rear spar/fuselage attachment points
142 No. 1 (Fuselage) main fuel tank (1140 litre/330 Imp gal) (metal/self sealing)
143 Fuel filler cap
144 No. 23 fuselage frame
145 Aerial mast
146 Mast support strut

Junkers Ju 87

No aircraft in history was ever as effective (when unopposed) as the infamous 'Stuka', nor so vulnerable when it encountered opposition. Its devastating effects in the early months of the war were only equalled by its dismal failure when it met the RAF over England a few weeks later.

Ju 87D-3

Cutaway key
1 Spinner
2 Pitch-change mechanism housing
3 Blade hub
4 Junkers VS 11 constant speed airscrew
5 Anti-vibration engine mounting attachments
6 Oil filler point and marker
7 Auxiliary oil tank (5.9-Imp gal/26.8-litre capacity)
8 Junkers Jumo 211J-1 12-cylinder inverted-Vee liquid-cooled engine
9 Magnesium alloy forged engine mount
10 Coolant (Glysantin-water) header tank
11 Ejector exhaust stubs
12 Fuel injection unit housing
13 Induction air cooler
14 Armoured radiator
15 Inertia starter cranking point
16 Ball joint bulkhead fixing (lower)
17 Tubular steel mount support strut
18 Ventral armour (0.315 in/8 mm)
19 Main oil tank (9.9-Imp gal/45-litre capacity)
20 Oil filling point
21 Transverse support frame
22 Rudder pedals
23 Control column
24 Heating point
25 Auxiliary air intake
26 Ball joint bulkhead fixing (upper)
27 Bulkhead
28 Oil tank (6.8-Imp gal/ 31-litre capacity)
29 Oil filler point and marker (Intava 100)

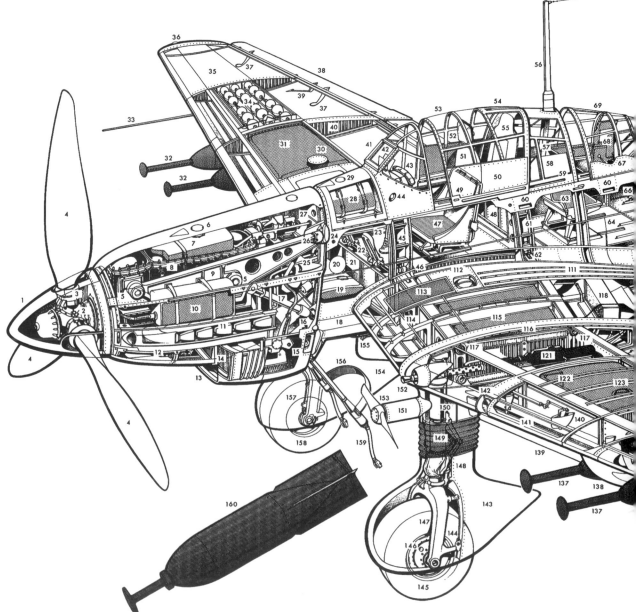

The Battle of Kursk saw the Stuka reach the end of its career as a successful dive-bomber – it was at this battle that Germany mounted its last, ultimately unsuccessful, great armoured offensive. The Ju 87 was no longer regarded as a 'terror weapon' and ground commanders had learned how to keep the number of casualties to a minimum. Evidence of this altered perspective of the Stuka can be seen in the omission of the propeller sirens from the aircraft.

63 Radio operator/ gunner's seat (folding)
64 Floor armour (0.2 in/ 5 mm)
65 Armoured bulkhead (0.315 in/8 mm)
66 Ammunition magazine
67 Additional (external) side armour with cut-out for hand grip
68 Internal side and head armour
69 Sliding canopy section (shown part open)
70 Ring and bead gunsights

71 Twin 0.311-in/7.9-mm Mauser MG 81Z machine-gun on GSK-K 81 mount
72 Canopy track fairing
73 Peil G IV D/F equipment
74 Circular plexiglass access panel
75 Back-to-back L-section stringers (fuselage horizontal break)
76 First-aid stowage
77 Z-section fuselage frames
78 Radio aerial
79 Faired elevator mass balance
80 Starboard elevator
81 Tailplane structure
82 Tailplane brace/spar attachment point
83 Tailplane bracing strut
84 Fuselage skinning
85 Control runs
86 Tailfin attachment fairing
87 Tailfin structure
88 Rudder horn balance
89 Rudder
90 Rudder trim tab controls
91 Rudder trim tab
92 Rudder control linkage

93 Rudder post
94 Rear navigation light
95 Elevator tab
96 Port elevator
97 Faired elevator mass balance
98 Tailplane front spar
99 Control pulley circular access panels
100 Rudder lower hinge fairing
101 Tailplane bracing strut
102 Emergency tailskid
103 Tailwheel
104 Tailwheel leg
105 Jacking point
106 Fuselage stringers
107 Master compass
108 Crew entry step (port and starboard)
109 Entry step support (with control run cut-outs)
110 Wingroot fairing
111 Non-slip walkway (aft section external metal strakes)
112 Fuel filler point
113 Non-slip walkway (forward section composite surface)
114 Leading-edge structure
115 Self-sealing port inner wing fuel tank (52.8-Imp gal/240-litre capacity)
116 Wing-joint external cover strip
117 Ball-and-socket wing attachment points
118 Armoured coolant radiator (port and starboard)
119 Inboard flap structure
120 Flap hinge
121 Rheinmetall-Borsig MG 17 machine-gun of 0.312-in/7.92-mm calibre (port and starboard)
122 Ammunition tank (1,000 rounds capacity) inboard of rib
123 Port outer self-sealing fuel tank (33-Imp gal/150-litre capacity)
124 Corrugated wing rib
125 ETC bomb rack support bar
126 ETC bomb rack underwing fairing
127 Port outboard flap
128 Port aileron

129 Aileron mass balance
130 Rear spar
131 Wing rib
132 Port navigation light
133 Front spar
134 Wing leading edge
135 Underwing bombload (two 110-lb/ 50 kg bombs) on multi-purpose carrier
136 Bomb shackles
137 Dienartstab percussion rod attachments
138 ETC 50/VIII fairing
139 Air brake (extended)
140 Air brake activating mechanism
141 Airbrake (retracted)
142 Landing lamp
143 Wheel spat
144 Fork/spat attachment
145 Port mainwheel
146 Brake reservoir filler port
147 Cantilever fork
148 Leather shroud
149 Oleo-pneumatic shock absorber
150 Mainwheel leg
151 Siren fairing
152 Barrel of MG 17 machine-gun
153 Wind-driven siren
154 Starboard wheel spat
155 PVC ventral bomb rack
156 Bomb cradle
157 Starboard wheelfork
158 Starboard mainwheel
159 Bomb release trapeze
160 551-lb (250-kg) bomb with Dienartstab attachment

30 Fuel filler cap
31 Self-sealing starboard outer fuel tank (33-Imp gal/ 150-litre capacity)
32 Underwing bombs with Dienartsab percussion rods
33 Signal flare tube
34 Spherical oxygen bottles
35 Wing skinning

36 Starboard navigation light
37 Aileron mass balance
38 'Double wing' aileron and flap (starboard outer)
39 Aileron hinge
40 Corrugated wing rib station
41 Reinforced armoured windscreen
42 Reflector sight
43 Padded crash bar
44 Signal flare tune
45 Braced fuselage mainframe
46 Front spar/fuselage attachment point

47 Pilot's seat (reinforced with 0.158-in/ 4-mm side armour and 0.315-in/8-mm rear armour)
48 Inter-cockpit bulkhead
49 Sliding canopy handgrip
50 External side armour
51 Pilot's back armour (0.315 in/8 mm)
52 Headrest
53 Aft-sliding cockpit canopy (shown part open)
54 Radio mast cut-out
55 Anti-crash hoop (magnesium casting)
56 Radio mast
57 Radio equipment (FuGe 16) compartment
58 Additional (internal) side armour
59 Canopy track
60 Handholds/footrests
61 Braced fuselage mainframe
62 Rear spar/fuselage attachment point

Ju 87B-2

Stuka-(Sturzkampfflugzeug)-geschwader 77 was involved in the Ju 87's main operations throughout the war, elements of its complement taking part in the Polish campaign. Following the successful march through northern Europe, the unit then faced the fighters of the RAF in the Battle of Britain, and suffered accordingly. A successful campaign in Greece and the Balkans followed, before the Stukageschwader turned its attentions to the Eastern Front, where it fought until late 1943. By this time, the unit had been redesignated Schlachtgeschwader and was transitioning to the more powerful Fw 190.

Powerplant

The Ju 87B was powered by a Junkers Jumo 211Da 12-cylinder liquid-cooled engine. This unit was rated at 1,200 hp (900 kW) for take-off (2,400 rpm) and 1,100 hp (825 kW) at 4,920 ft (1500 m). The increase in power offered by this engine over the earlier Jumo 210 of the A-series enabled a greater bombload to be carried. The radiator was housed in an armoured 'bath' beneath the engine. Hydraulically-operated cooling gills immediately behind the radiator increased airflow through the engine at low speeds. The Ju 87B-1 model featured simple port exhausts, but the B-2 introduced ejector-type stubs behind an aerodynamic fairing. Angled back, these provided a small but useful amount of thrust. The Ju 87D offered more power, with a Jumo 211J-1 rated at up to 1,410 hp (1050 kW) with an induction air cooler and a strengthened crankshaft.

Fuel

Fuel was carried in two large tanks mounted in the inboard (anhedral) wing sections. The Ju 87R and later variants introduced additional fuel in the outboard wing sections.

Undercarriage

The immensely sturdy main undercarriage was shrouded by large trouser fairings around the legs, with spats around the wheels. This arrangement replaced the braced and trousered main gear of the Ju 87A. On the Eastern Front in the winter, many Ju 87s operated with their spats removed, since mud quickly accumulated and clogged the wheels.

Entry steps

On either side of the rear fuselage were mounted permanent steps, just aft of the wing trailing edge. Both crew entered the aircraft by climbing up these steps on to the wing and thence to their respective cockpits via hand/footholds.

Cockpit
The Ju 87 featured a crew of two, although Bs were often flown as single-seaters. Both pilot and radio operator/gunner sat under separate sliding canopies, the latter facing to the rear. Armour was provided where possible.

Control balances
A pair of large weights projecting from the underside of the wing balanced each aileron. The elevators had faired mass balances, resulting in the distinctive surfaces at the tips, while the rudder had a slim horn balance at the fintip. Two sections of trim tabs were incorporated in the elevators, while the rudder had a one-piece tab running virtually the full height of the fin.

Rear gun
To provide a limited measure of protection for the woefully vulnerable Ju 87, a single MG 15 0.312-in (7.92-mm) machine-gun was placed on a flexible mount in the rear of the cockpit, aimed by the radio operator. Later variants introduced the more potent Mauser MG 81Z twin-gun mount.

Tailplane
The strong tailplane was a two-spar structure. On the Ju 87B it was externally braced by two struts; on the refined Ju 87D these struts were formed into one aerodynamic strut. The elevators were not large, but provided enough authority to pull the aircraft out of a 90° dive with ease.

Wings
The characteristic inverted gull wings of the Ju 87 were built around a two-spar structure with closely-spaced ribs. The centre-section was integral with the fuselage. The cranked wing proved immensely strong, and kept the length of the fixed undercarriage short; the classic Junkers 'double wing' arrangement was used. The inboard surfaces (two sections) acted as flaps, while the outboard surfaces provided roll control.

Junkers Ju 88

Ju 88A-5 (M2-MK), of Küstenfliegergruppe 106, tasked with attacking shipping in the Irish Sea on 26 November 1941, landed by miscalculation at RAF Chivenor. After a wheels-down landing, the aircraft was flown to Duxford, with a Hudson escort, to join No. 1426 (Enemy Aircraft) Flight. The machine later starred in the film 'In Which We Serve'.

Ju 88G-1

Cutaway key
1 Starboard navigation light
2 Wingtip profile
3 FuG 227 Flensburg radar receiver antenna
4 Starboard aileron
5 Aileron control runs
6 Starboard flaps
7 Flap-fairing strip

8 Wing ribs
9 Starboard outer fuel tank (91-Imp gal/ 415-litre capacity)
10 Fuel filler cap
11 Leading-edge structure
12 Annular exhaust slot
13 Cylinder head fairings

14 Adjustable nacelle nose ring
15 Twelve-bladed cooling fan
16 Propeller boss
17 Variable-pitch VS 111 wooden propeller
18 Leading-edge radar array
19 FuG 220 Lichtenstein SN-2 intercept radar array
20 Nose cone
21 Forward armoured bulkhead

22 Gyrocompass
23 Instrument panel
24 Armoured glass windscreen
25 Folding seat
26 Control column
27 Rudder pedal/brake cylinder
28 Control runs
29 Pilot's armoured seat
30 Sliding window section
31 Headrest
32 Jettisonable canopy roof section
33 Gun restraint

34 Wireless-operator/ gunner's seat
35 Rheinmetall Borsig MG 131 machine-gun (0.51-in/13-mm calibre)
36 Radio equipment (FuG 10P HF, FuG 16ZY VHF, FuG 25 IFF)
37 Ammunition box (500 rounds of 0.51-in/ 13-mm)
38 FuG 220 Lichtenstein SN-2 indicator box
39 FuG 227 Flensburg indicator box

40 Control linkage
41 Bulkhead
42 Armoured gunmount
43 Aerial post traverse check
44 Fuel filler cap
45 Whip aerial
46 Forward fuselage fuel tank (105-Imp gal/ 480-litre capacity)

47 Fuselage horizontal construction joint
48 Bulkhead
49 Fuel filler cap
50 Aft fuselage fuel tank (230-Imp gal/1045-litre capacity)

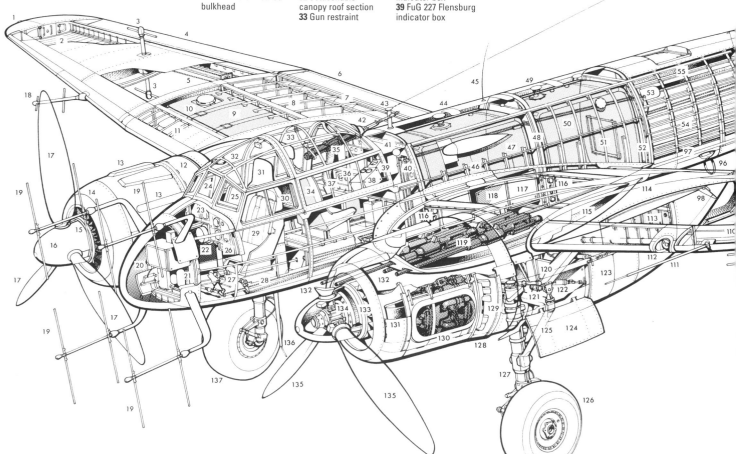

*Illustrated is a **Ju 88A-1** (or perhaps an A-5) of **KG 30**, the first operational Ju 88 unit. Operating initially in the anti-shipping role from bases around Scandinavia, Germany, and the Netherlands, the Gruppe was initially known as I./KG 25, prior to a change of designation in September 1939. KG 30's first major mission came on 26 September 1939, when aircraft struck British shipping, although damage was limited due to the fact that the SC 500 bombs of the Ju 88A-1s and A-0s failed to detonate. On 9 October two KG 30 Ju 88A-1s were shot down – the first combat losses of the type.*

SPECIFICATION

Ju 88A-4

Dimensions

Length: 47 ft 2¾ in (14.40 m)
Height: 15 ft 11 in (4.85 m)
Wingspan: 65 ft 7½ in (20.00 m)
Wing area: 586.63 sq ft (54.50 m²)
Wing loading: 41.8-46.9 lb/sq ft (204-229 kg/m²)

Powerplant

Two liquid-cooled Junkers Jumo 211J-1 or J-2 12-cylinder inline piston engines each rated at 1,340-hp (999-kW)

Weights

Empty: 21,737 lb (9860 kg)
Normal loaded: 26,686 lb (12105 kg)
Maximum loaded: 30,865 lb (14000 kg)

Performance

Maximum speed at 17,390 ft (5300 m): 292 mph (470 km/h) at 27,557 lb (12500 kg)
Climb to 16,405 ft (5000 m): 18 mins
Climb to 17,716 ft (5400 m): 23 mins
Economical cruising speed: 230 mph (370 km/h) at 17,390 ft (5300 m)

Maximum cruising speed: 248 mph (399 km/h) at 16,405 ft (5000 m)
Service ceiling: 26,900 ft (8199 m)
Range: 1,112 miles (1789 km) with 637 Imp gal (2896 litres) of fuel
Maximum range: 1,696 miles (2730 km) with 886 Imp gal (4028 litres) of fuel
Take-off speed: 115 mph (185 km/h)
Approach speed: 155 mph (250 km/h)

Armament

Defensive: one fixed or free-mounted forward-firing 0.31-in (7.92-mm) MG 81 machine-gun and one free-mounted forward-firing 0.51-in (13-mm) MG 131 or two 0.31-in (7.92-mm) MG 81 machine-guns, plus two 0.31-in (7.92-mm) MG 81 machine-guns firing aft above the fuselage, and one 0.51-in (13-mm) MG 131 machine-gun or two 0.31-in (7.92-mm) MG 81 machine-guns firing aft below the fuselage
Offensive: ten 50-kg (110-lb) SC 50 bombs internally, and four 250-kg (551-lb) SC 250 or two 500-kg (1,105-lb) SC 500 bombs externally, or four 500-kg (1,105-lb) SC 500 bombs externally

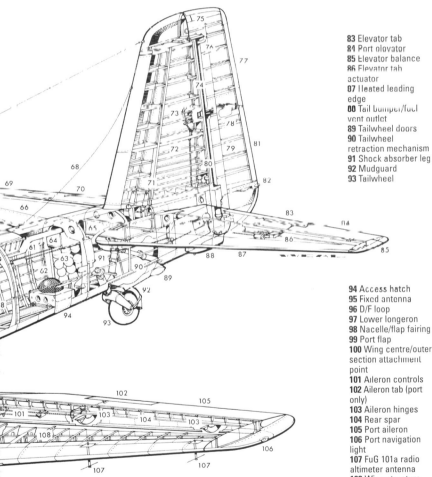

83 Elevator tab
84 Port elevator
85 Elevator balance
86 Elevator tab actuator
87 Heated leading edge
88 Tail bumper/fuel vent outlet
89 Tailwheel doors
90 Tailwheel retraction mechanism
91 Shock absorber leg
92 Mudguard
93 Tailwheel

94 Access hatch
95 Fixed antenna
96 D/F loop
97 Lower longeron
98 Nacelle/flap fairing
99 Port flap
100 Wing centre/outer section attachment point
101 Aileron controls
102 Aileron tab (port only)
103 Aileron hinges
104 Rear spar
105 Port aileron
106 Port navigation light
107 FuG 101a radio altimeter antenna
108 Wing structure
109 Leading-edge radar array
110 Forward spar
111 Pitot head
112 Landing lamp
113 Mainwheel well rear bulkhead
114 Port outer fuel tank location (91-Imp gal/ 415-litre capacity)
115 Ventral gunpack (offset to port)
116 Ball-and-socket fuselage/wing attachment points
117 Port inner fuel tank location (934-Imp gal/ 425-litre capacity)

118 Ammunition boxes for MG 151 cannon (200 rpg)
119 Mauser MG 151/20 cannon (four) of 20-mm calibre
120 Mainwheel leg retraction yoke
121 Leg pivot member
122 Mainwheel door actuating jack
123 Mainwheel door (rear section)
124 Mainwheel door (forward section)
125 Leg support strut
126 Port mainwheel

127 Mainwheel leg
128 Annular exhaust slot
129 Exhaust stubs (internal)
130 BMW 801D air-cooled radial engine (partly omitted for clarity)
131 Annular oil tank
132 Cannon muzzles (depressed 5°)
133 Twelve-bladed cooling fan
134 Propeller mechanism

135 Variable-pitch wooden VS 111 propeller
136 FuG 167 antenna
137 Starboard mainwheel

51 Access hatch
52 Bulkhead
53 Control linkage access plate
54 Fuselage stringers
55 Upper longeron
56 Maintenance walkway
57 Control linkage
58 Horizontal construction joint
59 Z-section fuselage frames
60 Dinghy stowage
61 Fuel vent pipe
62 Master compass

63 Spherical oxygen bottles
64 Accumulator
65 Tailplane centre section carry-through
66 Starboard tailplane
67 Elevator balance
68 Aerial
69 Starboard elevator
70 Elevator tab
71 Tailfin forward spar/ fuselage attachment
72 Tailfin structure
73 Rudder actuator
74 Rudder post

75 Rudder mass balance
76 Rudder upper hinge
77 Rudder tab (upper section)
78 Inspection/ maintenance handhold
79 Rudder structure
80 Tailfin aft spar/ fuselage attachment
81 Rudder tab (lower section)
82 Rear navigation light

Lt Johannes Geismann of I. Gruppe/KG 77 poses in front of the impressive kill tally on the rudder of his Ju 88. KG 77 transferred from the Russian Front to Sicily in the early summer of 1942, from where it was primarily engaged in attacks against Allied shipping involved in supplying Malta and North Africa.

Ju 88A-5

This Junkers Ju 88 wears the codes of KG 30, whose I. Gruppe was the first Luftwaffe unit to employ the Ju 88 in combat when, on 26 September 1939, it undertook a mission attacking British warships in the Firth of Forth. Based initially at Westerland-Sylt with Ju 88A-1s, the geschwader quickly re-located to Denmark, Norway and, as depicted here, the Netherlands, by which time the unit had re-equipped with the improved Ju 88A-5 model. During the Battle of Britain, KG 30 was heavily involved in raids over the British Isles, suffering heavy losses. For much of the remainder of the conflict, the unit was preoccupied with anti-shipping missions in the North Sea, ranging from convoy attacks off the Norwegian coast to high-speed raids on naval vessels based in British harbours.

Cockpit

The four-man crew sat close together in the forward fuselage. The pilot sat in the front of the upper cockpit, offset to port, while below him and to starboard sat the bombardier/second pilot, who had access to the glazed nose. In the rear of the upper cabin sat the flight engineer, facing to the rear to operate the gun in the back of the canopy. Alongside him, slightly below, sat the radio operator, who had access to the ventral gondola to operate the rear-facing lower gun. A prominent mast from the cockpit roof held a single wire aerial running back to the tail.

Bombload

Two fuselage bomb bays were provided, carrying a maximum of 28 50-kg (110-lb) SC 50 bombs. Four external racks were fitted under the inner wings which could carry a 500-kg (1,102-lb) SC 500 bomb or a similar weapon, while the A-4/A-5 introduced the provision for a further bomb rack under each outer wing. As illustrated, the Ju 88 could also carry the Luftminen Type B (LM-B) mine. Due to the low level from which the weapon was dropped, parachute retarding was required either to break the fall of the mine when used at sea, or to delay the detonation when used as a bomb over land. The rear of the mine was released on dropping to allow the parachute to deploy.

Wing structure

The dihedral wing was of stressed-skin construction around a strong two-spar box. The A-4/A-5 introduced a new wing with extended tips which allowed operations at higher weights. For divebombing, slatted divebrakes were fitted underneath the wing leading edge, swinging forward into the airflow when deployed. Metal-skinned ailerons replaced the fabric-covered units of earlier variants and drooped in concert with the flaps to provide additional lift at low speeds. The leading edges of the wings could be de-iced by hot air bled from the engines.

Powerplant

The Junkers Ju 88A-5 preceded the A-4 on the production lines due to development delays with the latter's Jumo 211J engines. The A-5 had the A-4's new wing but retained the Jumo 211G-1 engines of the A-1/A-2 models. These were 12-cylinder liquid-cooled units which produced 1,200 hp (894 kW) each at take-off settings. The circular engine cowlings of the Ju 88 were deceiving, for the engines carried within were actually inline units. The circular cross-section section allowed the use of annular radiators and oil coolers.

Rear fuselage

Oxygen bottles and the radio equipment were mounted in the rear fuselage just forward of the tail. A hatch in the rear wall of the aft bomb bay allowed maintenance personnel access to the rear fuselage, with a walkway provided back to the equipment. At the very rear of the fuselage, fuel could be rapidly jettisoned in flight through a fairing situated beneath the tail. Forward of this fairing was the fully-retracting tailwheel which was enclosed, when retracted, by bulged doors.

Armament

Early Ju 88 variants had the standard defensive armament of three 0.311-in (7.9-mm) MG 15 machine-guns. One was fired by the pilot from the windscreen while two faced aft, one from the rear of the canopy (fired by the flight engineer) and one from the rear of the ventral gondola (fired by the radio operator). Cockpit weapons were all operated through separate ball/socket mountings. This armament generally proved to be insufficient, and aircraft were steadily improved with additional lateral-firing weapons and guns in the nose panel. Other alterations included the substitution of the MG 15 machine-gun for the far superior MG 81 and 0.51-in (13-mm) MG 131. The bombardier was provided with a bombsight in the extreme nose for conventional bombing. For dive-bombing attacks, the pilot had a sight mounted on the cockpit ceiling, which could be swung sideways when not in use. In all, there were at least 40 different armament schemes employed by the Ju 88.

Junkers Ju188

A line-up of Ju 188D-2s of 1.(F)/FAGr 124 at Kirkenes, Norway. The Ju 188D-2 was intended primarily for the maritime strike and reconnaissance roles, and usually carried FuG 200 Hohentwiel radar.

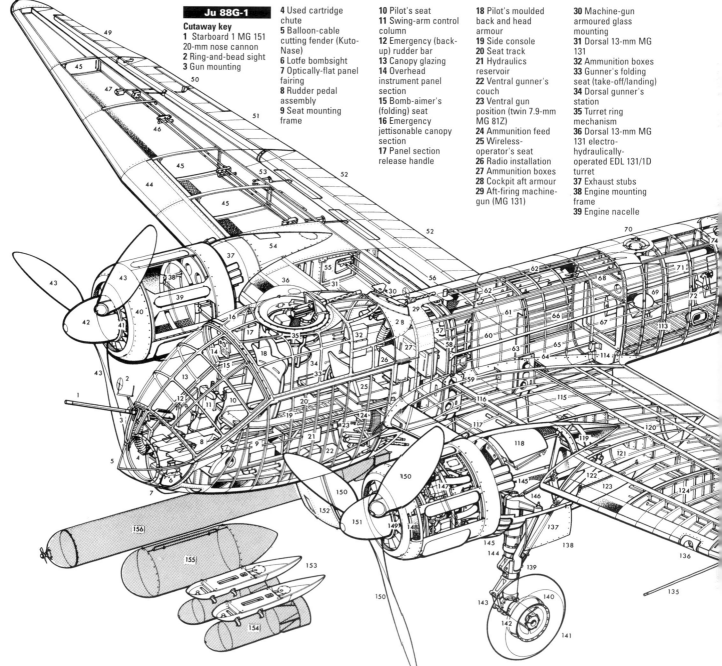

Ju 88G-1

Cutaway key
1 Starboard 1 MG 151 20-mm nose cannon
2 Ring-and-bead sight
3 Gun mounting
4 Used cartridge chute
5 Balloon-cable cutting fender (Kuto-Nase)
6 Lotfe bombsight
7 Optically-flat panel fairing
8 Rudder pedal assembly
9 Seat mounting frame
10 Pilot's seat
11 Swing-arm control column
12 Emergency (back-up) rudder bar
13 Canopy glazing
14 Overhead instrument panel section
15 Bomb-aimer's (folding) seat
16 Emergency jettisonable canopy section
17 Panel section release handle
18 Pilot's moulded back and head armour
19 Side console
20 Seat track
21 Hydraulics reservoir
22 Ventral gunner's couch
23 Ventral gun position (twin 7.9-mm MG 81Z)
24 Ammunition feed
25 Wireless-operator's seat
26 Radio installation
27 Ammunition boxes
28 Cockpit aft armour
29 Aft-firing machine-gun (MG 131)
30 Machine-gun armoured glass mounting
31 Dorsal 13-mm MG 131
32 Ammunition boxes
33 Gunner's folding seat (take-off/landing)
34 Dorsal gunner's station
35 Turret ring mechanism
36 Dorsal 13-mm MG 131 electro-hydraulically-operated EDL 131/1D turret
37 Exhaust stubs
38 Engine mounting frame
39 Engine nacelle

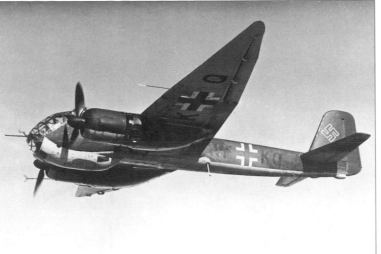

SPECIFICATION

Junkers Ju118

Type

Four-seat medium bomber

Powerplant

Two 1,700-hp (1268-kW) BMW 801D-2 radial piston engines

Performance

Maximum speed 310 mph (500 km/h) at 19,685 ft (6000 m); service ceiling 30,660 ft (9345 m); range 1,209 miles (1945 km)

Weights

Empty equipped 21,737 lb (9860 kg); maximum take-off 31,989 lb (9750 kg)

Dimensions

Wingspan 72 ft 2 in (22.00 m); length 49 ft 1/2 in (14.95 m); height 14 ft 7 in (4.44 m); wing area 602.80 sq ft (56 m2)

Armament

One forward-firing 20-mm MG 151 cannon in nose, a single 0.51-in (13-mm) MG 131 in dorsal turret and at the rear of the cockpit canopy, and one 0.31-in (7.92-mm) MG 18 machine-gun in lower front fuselage firing aft, plus a maximum bombload of 6,614 lb (3000 kg)

The Ju 88 V44 was the second of the Ju 188 development vehicles and introduced the enlarged tail surfaces. As such, it was redesignated as the Ju 188 V1 during mid-1942, and was joined on the flight test programme by another aircraft to hasten development.

92 Tailfin leading edge
93 Tailfin front spar
94 Tailfin structure
95 Rudder post
96 Rudder upper hinge
97 Rudder tabs
98 Tab linkage
99 Rudder frame
100 Tail navigation light
101 Rudder controls
102 Tail bumper
103 Elevator tab
104 Port elevator
105 Elevator balance
106 Tailplane leading edge
107 Tailwheel mudguard
108 Retractable tailwheel
109 Tailwheel doors
110 Oxygen bottles
111 Relay boxes

112 Auto-pilot control
113 Aft fuselage crawlway
114 Wingroot fillet
115 Aft (bomb) bay doors
116 Front spar
117 Front bay doors
118 Oil tank
119 Nacelle aft structure
120 Rear spar
121 Mainwheel well
122 Undercarriage attachment
123 Mainwheel doors
124 Rib station
125 Intermediate ribs
126 Control rods
127 Port flaps
128 Aileron trim tab
129 Aileron servo tab
130 Inner port aileron
131 Outer port aileron
132 Port navigation light
133 Outer rib stations
134 Wing structure
135 Pitot head
136 Landing light
137 Undercarriage retraction strut
138 Mainwheel leg door

139 Strut/leg join
140 Brake drum
141 Port mainwheel
142 Axle
143 Torque links
144 Mainwheel leg
145 Exhaust stubs
146 Undercarriage pivot
147 BMW 801 C radial air-cooled engine
148 Oil cooler circular radiator
149 Cooling fan
150 Three-bladed VDM propeller
151 Spinner
152 Crew ventral entry hatch
153 Wingroot ETC weapon racks for
154 Two bombs, or alternatively
155 Auxiliary fuel tank (Ju 188F) or
156 Aerial torpedo (Ju 188E-2)

40 Armoured radiator ring
41 Cooling fan
42 Spinner
43 Three-bladed VDM propeller
44 Wing leading edge
45 Main rib stations
46 Control rod linkage
47 Tab servo
48 Starboard navigation light
49 Outer aileron
50 Aileron servo tab
51 Inner aileron
52 Starboard flaps
53 Flap mechanism
54 Oil tank access

55 Nacelle reinforced rib
56 Aerial stub
57 Lead-in support
58 Fuselage main frame
59 Front spar/fuselage attachment
60 Forward fuel tank bay
61 Bulkhead
62 Fuel tank support beams
63 Aft spar/fuselage attachment
64 Flaps motor
65 Centre keel
66 Aft fuel tank (or weapons) bay
67 Tail control rod/cable interchange
68 Bulkhead
69 Compass
70 D/F antenna
71 Fuel vent/dump pipe

72 Elevator control cables
73 Water filter
74 Dinghy release cord spool
75 Dinghy stowage
76 Electrics panel
77 First-aid kit
78 Fuselage frames
79 Rudder internal mass balance
80 Oxygen cylinders
81 Rudder control linkage
82 Tailwheel shock-absorber leg
83 Tailwheel retraction strut
84 Elevator torque tube
85 Tailplane spar carry-through
86 Starboard tailplane
87 Elevator tab motor
88 Elevator balance
89 Starboard elevator
90 Tab linkage
91 Elevator tab

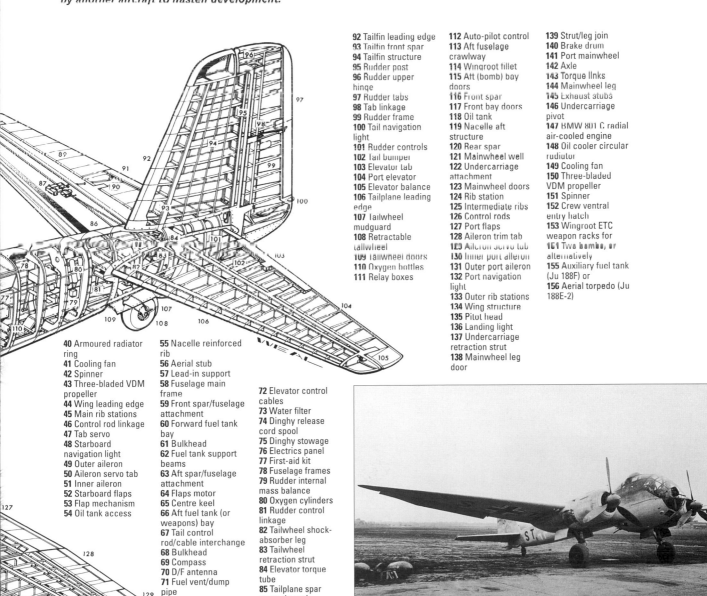

The BMW 801-powered Ju 188E series was delivered ahead of the Jumo 213-powered Ju 188A. This pre-production Ju 188E-0 was modified to act as a fast staff transport for General-Luftzeugmeister Erhard Milch.

Lockheed A-29 Hudson

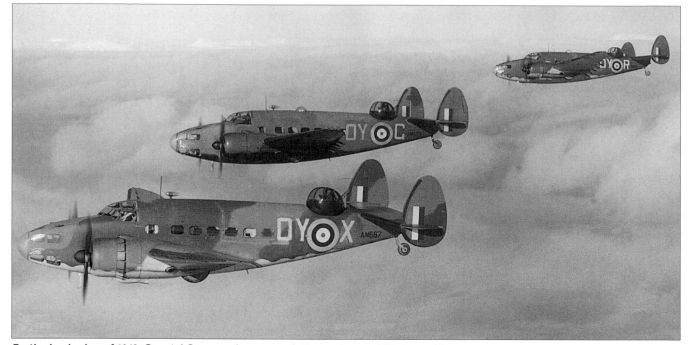

By the beginning of 1942, Coastal Command possessed 12 squadrons of Hudsons (these examples are from No. 48 Sqn), but only five of these were engaged on anti-shipping duties, while the remainder carried out anti-submarine work or air-sea rescue. The Hudsons conducted daylight sorties over the North Sea, along the coasts of Norway and the Netherlands, hunting singly or in small groups.

A-29 Hudson

Cutaway key
1 Starboard navigation/ identification lights
2 Starboard wingtip
3 De-icing slots
4 Internal vanes
5 Aileron internal mass balance
6 Starboard aileron
7 Aileron tab
8 Tab mechanism
9 Control cables
10 Wing main spar structure
11 De-icing tubes
12 Leading-edge de-icing boot
13 Main wing rib stations
14 Wing skinning
15 Flap control cables
16 Flap tracks
17 Flap cables/pulleys
18 Track fairings
19 Port flap (extended)
20 Aerial mast
21 D/F loop fairing
22 Supported structure
23 Aerial lead-in
24 Cockpit cold air
25 Flight deck sun-blind frames
26 Windscreen wiper motor
27 Jettisonable canopy hatch
28 Console light
29 Windscreen wipers
30 Second pilot's jump seat
31 Adjustable quarterlight
32 Windscreen frame support member
33 External gunsight
34 Second-pilot's (back-up) centre column (cantilevered)
35 Central instrument console
36 Starboard nose compartment entry tunnel
37 Bulkhead

38 Starboard engine oil tank
39 Fixed forward firing 0.303-in (7.7-mm) Browning machine-guns (two)
40 Carburettor intake
41 Wright R-1820-GI-02A radial engine
42 Starboard nacelle
43 Cowling nose ring
44 Three-bladed propeller
45 Spinner
46 Nose compartment cold air
47 Machine-gun muzzles
48 Nose structure
49 Roof glazing
50 Window frames
51 Nosecone
52 Navigator's side windows
53 Compass
54 Navigator's table
55 Navigator's (sliding) seat
56 Bomb-aimer's flat panels
57 Bomb-aimer's prone position
58 Bomb selector/switch panel
59 Navigator's instrument panel
60 Forward flare chute

61 Bombsight support
62 Nose frames
63 Nose compartment warm air
64 Windscreen de-icing tank
65 Machine-gun ammunition magazine
66 Rudder pedal assembly
67 Pilot's control column

68 Pilot's seat
69 Pilot's radio control boxes
70 Forward (canted) fuselage frame
71 Frame/wing pick-up
72 Hydraulics reservoir

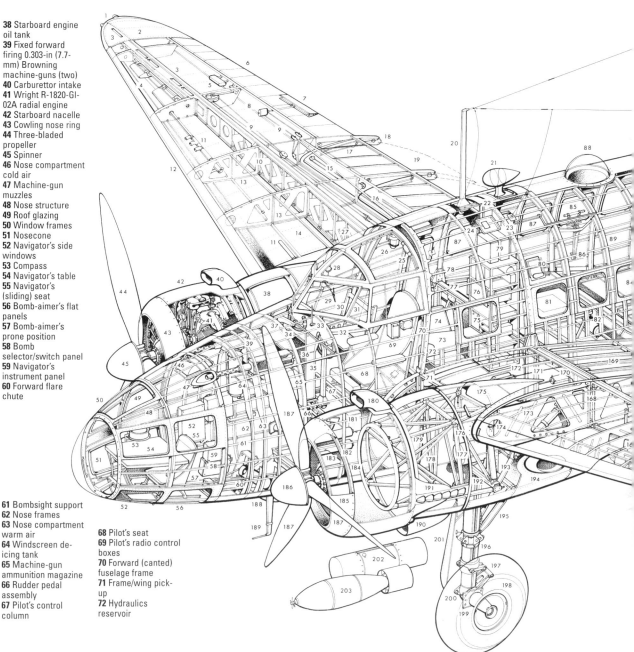

SPECIFICATION

Hudson Mk VI

Dimensions

Length: 44 ft 4 in (13.51 m)
Wingspan: 65 ft 6 in (19.96 m)
Height: 11 ft 11 in (3.63 m)
Wing area: 551 sq ft (51.19 m²)

Powerplant

Two 1,200-hp (895-kW) Pratt & Whitney R-1830-S3C4-G Twin Wasp radial piston engines

Weights

Empty: 12,929 lb (5864 kg)
Loaded: 18,500 lb (8391 kg)
Maximum take-off: 22,360 lb (10,142 kg)

Performance

Maximum speed at 15,000 ft (4572 m): 261 mph (420 km/h)
Cruising speed: 224 mph (360 km/h)
Service ceiling: 27,000 ft (8230 m)
Range: 2,160 miles (3476 km)
Endurance: 6 hours 55 minutes

Armament

Twin 0.303-in (7.7-mm) machine-guns in fixed forward and dorsal turret installations and one 0.303-in (7.7-mm) machine-gun in a ventral position, plus two optional 0.303-in (7.7-mm) machine-guns in beam positions, plus up to 1,000 lb (454 kg) of bombs or depth charges

One Hudson Mk IV was built for, and delivered to, Sperry Gyroscope Co. Registered NX21771, this aircraft was used by Sperry for the testing of aircraft instruments. The aircraft was still being used in 1999 for research and development activities.

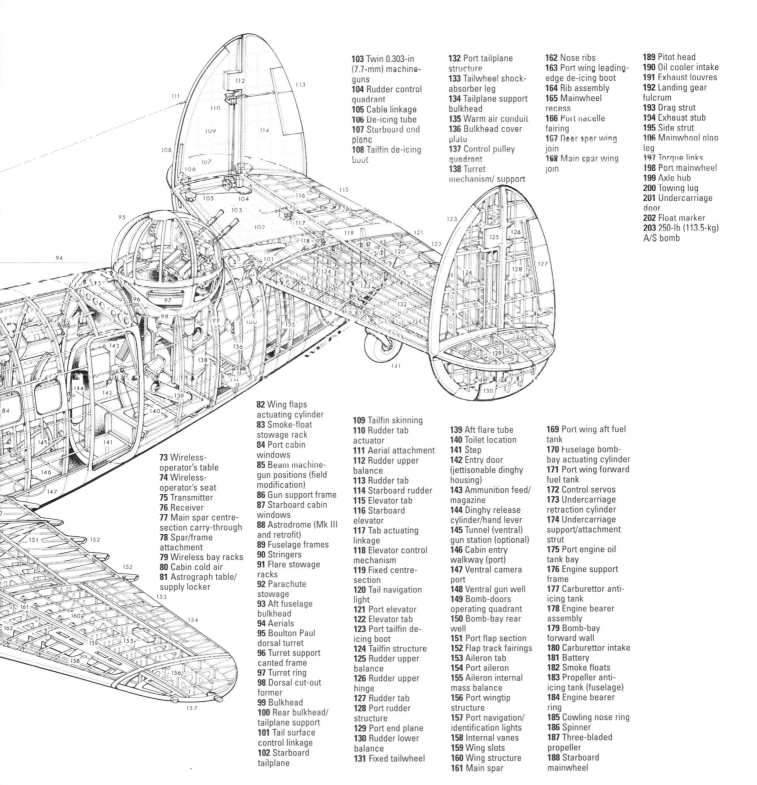

73 Wireless-operator's table
74 Wireless-operator's seat
75 Transmitter
76 Receiver
77 Main spar centre-section carry-through
78 Spar/frame attachment
79 Wireless bay racks
80 Cabin cold air
81 Astrograph table/supply locker
82 Wing flaps actuating cylinder
83 Smoke-float stowage rack
84 Port cabin windows
85 Beam machine-gun positions (field modification)
86 Gun support frame
87 Starboard cabin windows
88 Astrodrome (Mk III and retrofit)
89 Fuselage frames
90 Stringers
91 Flare stowage racks
92 Parachute stowage
93 Aft fuselage bulkhead
94 Aerials
95 Boulton Paul dorsal turret
96 Turret support canted frame
97 Turret ring
98 Dorsal cut-out former
99 Bulkhead
100 Rear bulkhead/tailplane support
101 Tail surface control linkage
102 Starboard tailplane
103 Twin 0.303-in (7.7-mm) machine-guns
104 Rudder control quadrant
105 Cable linkage
106 De-icing tube
107 Starboard end plane
108 Tailfin de-icing boot
109 Tailfin skinning
110 Rudder tab actuator
111 Aerial attachment
112 Rudder upper balance
113 Rudder tab
114 Starboard rudder
115 Elevator tab
116 Starboard elevator
117 Tab actuating linkage
118 Elevator control mechanism
119 Fixed centre-section
120 Tail navigation light
121 Port elevator
122 Elevator tab
123 Port tailfin de-icing boot
124 Tailfin structure
125 Rudder upper balance
126 Rudder upper hinge
127 Rudder tab
128 Port rudder structure
129 Port end plane
130 Rudder lower balance
131 Fixed tailwheel
132 Port tailplane structure
133 Tailwheel shock-absorber leg
134 Tailplane support bulkhead
135 Warm air conduit
136 Bulkhead cover plate
137 Control pulley quadrant
138 Turret mechanism/support
139 Aft flare tube
140 Toilet location
141 Step
142 Entry door (jettisonable dinghy housing)
143 Ammunition feed/magazine
144 Dinghy release cylinder/hand lever
145 Tunnel (ventral) gun station (optional)
146 Cabin entry walkway (port)
147 Ventral camera port
148 Ventral gun well
149 Bomb-doors operating quadrant
150 Bomb-bay rear well
151 Port flap section
152 Flap track fairings
153 Aileron tab
154 Port aileron
155 Aileron internal mass balance
156 Port wingtip structure
157 Port navigation/identification lights
158 Internal vanes
159 Wing slots
160 Wing structure
161 Main spar
162 Nose ribs
163 Port wing leading-edge de-icing boot
164 Rib assembly
165 Mainwheel recess
166 Port nacelle fairing
167 Rear spar wing join
168 Main spar wing join
169 Port wing aft fuel tank
170 Fuselage bomb-bay actuating cylinder
171 Port wing forward fuel tank
172 Control servos
173 Undercarriage retraction cylinder
174 Undercarriage support/attachment strut
175 Port engine oil tank bay
176 Engine support frame
177 Carburettor anti-icing tank
178 Engine bearer assembly
179 Bomb-bay forward wall
180 Carburettor intake
181 Battery
182 Smoke floats
183 Propeller anti-icing tank (fuselage)
184 Engine bearer ring
185 Cowling nose ring
186 Spinner
187 Three-bladed propeller
188 Starboard mainwheel
189 Pitot head
190 Oil cooler intake
191 Exhaust louvres
192 Landing gear fulcrum
193 Drag strut
194 Exhaust stub
195 Side strut
196 Mainwheel oleo leg
197 Torque links
198 Port mainwheel
199 Axle hub
200 Towing lug
201 Undercarriage door
202 Float marker
203 250-lb (113.5-kg) A/S bomb

Hudson Mk VI

No. 48 Sqn was the first RAF unit to receive the Avro Anson, with which it undertook coastal patrols until October 1941. Duties included convoy and anti-submarine flights and Armed Rover reconnaissance patrols. Shortly after receipt of the Hudson, it moved to Gibraltar to cover the Torch landings in North Africa, and remained on the 'Rock' until February 1944, flying patrols over the western Mediterranean and Atlantic, occasionally tangling with Fw 200 Condors. On return to the UK, the squadron was assigned to the transport role with Dakotas, in time for the invasion of France.

Defensive armament

The principal defence for the Hudson lay within a Boulton Paul 'C' Mk II turret mounted on a ring frame. This turret contained a pair of Browning 0.303-in (7.7-mm) machine-guns, fed from magazines beneath the guns. Forward-firing armament was provided by a pair of 0.303-in (7.7-mm) machine-guns in the upper forward fuselage, aimed by the pilot using an external sight and fed from a magazine underneath the weapon. Although not fitted to this aircraft, 0.303-in (7.7-mm) machine-guns could be located on flexible mounts, firing from the beam position. Another option was a single gun, mounted in the lower rear fuselage.

Structure

The single-spar tailplane structure was mounted on top of the rear fuselage, and continued beyond the endplate fins. Large elevators were fitted either side of a small fixed centre-section, each incorporating tabs. Endplate fins were carried by the tailplane, each fitted with de-icing boots on the leading edges. The rudders were large, tabbed and fitted with aerodynamic balances near the top and at the bottom.

Cabin windows

Surprisingly, the Hudson was fitted with airliner-style cabin windows, inherited from the Lockheed Model 14 design from which it was hastily derived. The Mk VI could be reconfigured for passenger and light freight transport if required and many spent the last part of the war in this role.

Camouflage

During the early part of the war, the RAF's Hudson force wore standard Dark Green/Dark Earth camouflage, but later adopted the Coastal Command colour scheme of Dark Green/Ocean Grey upper surfaces and white sides/undersurfaces. Full-colour roundels were carried, but the squadron code letters were not normally worn.

Equipment

A prominent direction-finding loop antenna was fitted to the Hudson (enclosed in a teardrop faring in earlier versions). Behind this was an astrodome for use with a sextant while undertaking celestial navigation. The radio aerials were wires strung between a dorsal mast and the two fintips.

LITTLE NELL

Cockpit

The flight deck had a fixed station for the pilot and a folding jump-seat for the co-pilot, this seat allowing inflight access to the front section. The wireless operator occupied a station immediately behind the pilot on the port side, facing outwards. The glazed nose portion was occupied by the navigator, who was provided with a sliding seat and chart table behind the glazed nosecone. Behind and beneath his seat was a flat pane for bomb-aiming. An important addition to the Coastal Command Hudson fleet from January 1940 was ASV radar, which allowed the detection of surfaced submarines in poor weather or at night. The antennas for the system were positioned under the wings and nose.

Mitsubishi G4M 'Betty'

The 'Flying Cigar' appellation is fully justified in this view of a G4M1. Built in larger numbers than any other Japanese bomber, the type saw considerable success in long-range bombing duties.

G4M 'Betty'

Cutaway key

1 Starboard navigation light
2 Starboard wingtip
3 Wing outboard spars
4 Starboard aileron
5 Aileron hinges
6 Aileron tab linkage
7 Fixed tab
8 Aileron trim tab
9 Wing join station
10 Flap hinge fairings
11 Starboard flap
12 Flap controls
13 Wing spar
14 Starboard wing fuel tanks
15 Starboard outer oil tank
16 Engine nacelle fairing
17 Cooling gills
18 Individual exhaust stubs
19 Engine bearer
20 Intake
21 Cowling ring
22 Four-blade propeller
23 Spinner
24 7.7-mm Type 92 machine-gun
25 Nose turret
26 Nose radar antenna
27 Nose turret drive mechanism
28 Bomb-aimer's flat panel
29 Bomb-aimer's couch
30 Type 90 bombsight
31 Additional cheek gun/drift sight mounting (port and starboard)
32 Bomb panel
33 Ammunition magazine stowage
34 Nose glazing
35 Additional machine-gun (stowed)
36 Rudder pedal assembly
37 Control console
38 Coaming
39 Flat windscreen panels
40 Overhead controls
41 Sun blinds

42 Flight deck emergency escape hatch
43 Pilot's seats
44 Control column
45 Rudder pedal assembly
46 Bomb-aimer's seat
47 Control linkage
48 Flight deck floor level
49 Nose compartment access walkway
50 Fuselage structure
51 Navigation/wireless-operator's station
52 Equipment racks
53 Commander's seat
54 Cockpit roof glazing
55 Front spar carry-through
56 Fuselage centre-section fuel tanks
57 Front spar/fuselage attachment

58 Over-spar centre step section
59 Rear spar carry-through
60 Rear spar/fuselage attachment
61 Gunner's take-off/land jump seats (two)
62 Emergency handhold (down to wing upper surface)
63 Emergency escape hatch
64 Dorsal frames
65 Intake scoop
66 Fuselage window
67 Dorsal gunner's step
68 Dorsal turret mount

69 Ammunition magazine stowage
70 Strengthened longeron section
71 Turret drive mechanism
72 Dorsal turret
73 20-mm Type 99 dorsal cannon
74 Aerial mast
75 Fuselage structure
76 Oxygen cylinders
77 Stepped fuselage floor
78 Gunner's seat
79 Fuselage window
80 Waist gun position
81 Ammunition

82 Gun mounting
83 20-mm Type 99 cannon
84 Fixed upper glazing
85 Sliding (upwards) window section
86 Starboard (asymmetric) waist gun position
87 Fuselage frames

SPECIFICATION

Mitsubishi G4M 'Betty'

Type

Seven-crew long-range bomber

Powerplant

Two 1,825-hp (1361-kW) Mitsubishi MK4T Kasei 25 radial piston engines

Performance

Maximum speed 292 mph (470 km/h) at 16,895 ft (5150 m); service ceiling 30,250 ft (9220 m); maximum range 2,694 miles (4335 km)

Weights

Empty 18,049 lb (8350 kg); maximum take-off 27,558 lb (12500 kg)

Dimensions

Wingspan 82 ft 1/4 in (25.00 m); length 63 ft 113/4 in (19.50 m); height 19 ft 81/4 in (6.00 m); wing area 841.01 sq ft (78.13 m2)

Armament

Four 20-mm cannon and two 7.7-mm (0.303-in) machine-guns, plus one 1,764-lb (800-kg) torpedo or 2,205 lb (1000 kg) of bombs

Unbeknown to the Royal Navy at the time, the G4M made its debut against Allied forces when a number joined G3Ms in attacking and sinking Royal Navy battleships on 10 December 1941. Here IJN personnel load a torpedo aboard a G4M1.

88 Longerons
89 Cannon muzzle trough
90 Crew circular entry hatch
91 Latch
92 Walkway to tail turret
93 Fuselage window

94 Starboard radar aerial internal support
95 Aft fuselage structure
96 Fuselage frame/tailfin support
97 Tailfin join
98 Starboard tailplane skinning

103 Tailfin leading edge
104 Tailfin structure
105 Aerial attachment
106 Rudder balance
107 Rudder frame
108 Rudder post
109 Access panels

116 Open tail turret (glazed side segments)
117 Tail 20-mm Type 99 cannon
118 Elevator tab
119 Port elevator
120 Elevator balance

130 Non-retractable tailwheel
131 Lower longeron
132 Waist station floor level
133 Bulged bomb-bay aft contour
134 Port flap section
135 Wing structure
136 Rear main spar
137 Wing inboard/outboard join
138 Aileron trim tab
139 Fixed tab
140 Port aileron
141 Wing ribs
142 Port wingtip
143 Port navigation light
144 Front main spar
145 Panel joins
146 Nose ribs
147 Port wing fuel tanks (four)
148 Spar join
149 Port wing oil tanks (two)
150 Undercarriage attachment
151 Nacelle fairing
152 Mainwheel leg

159 Individual exhaust stubs
160 Cooling/exhaust stubs
161 Mainwheel bay
162 Mitsubishi Kasei 25 (MK4T) engine
163 Engine upper intake
164 Four-blade Sumitomo VDM propeller
165 Propeller hub
166 Spinner
167 Bulged bomb-bay forward contour
168 Pitot tube (offset/angled to starboard)
169 D/F loop
170 Weapons load, inc:
171 Twelve 110-lb (50-kg) bombs (4 x 3),
172 Four 551-lb (250-kg) bombs (2 x 2),
173 Two 1,102-lb (500-kg) bombs
174 One naval torpedo, or
175 One 1,764-lb (800-kg) bomb

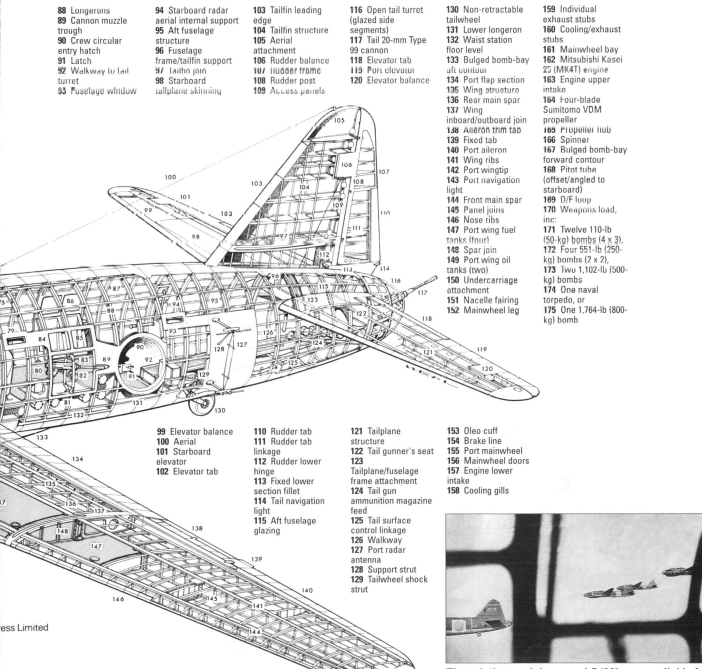

99 Elevator balance
100 Aerial
101 Starboard elevator
102 Elevator tab

110 Rudder tab
111 Rudder tab linkage
112 Rudder lower hinge
113 Fixed lower section fillet
114 Tail navigation light
115 Aft fuselage glazing

121 Tailplane structure
122 Tail gunner's seat
123 Tailplane/fuselage frame attachment
124 Tail gun ammunition magazine feed
125 Tail surface control linkage
126 Walkway
127 Port radar antenna
128 Support strut
129 Tailwheel shock strut

153 Oleo cuff
154 Brake line
155 Port mainwheel
156 Mainwheel doors
157 Engine lower intake
158 Cooling gills

Though the much improved G4M2 was available from 1942, engine shortages kept its predecessor, the G4M1 (pictured), in production until early 1944.

North American B-25 Mitchell

In the Pacific, the B-25 came to be used for missions for which it had never been intended, shining as a low-level strafer and ship-bomber. Illustrated is an attack on Hong Kong harbour.

B-25H Mitchell

Cutaway key
1 Nose machine-gun barrels
2 Hinged nose compartment access door
3 4 x 0.5-in (12.7-mm) machine-guns
4 Ammunition feed chutes
5 Cannon muzzle aperture
6 Nosewheel steering control
7 Aft-retracting nosewheel
8 Torque scissor links
9 Aerial mast
10 Nosewheel leg pivot mounting
11 Cannon barrel
12 Ammunition feed chutes
13 Machine-gun ammunition magazines, 400 rpg
14 Fixed bead sight
15 Armoured bulkhead
16 Windscreen panels
17 Instrument panel shroud
18 Pilot's gunsight
19 Direct vision opening window panel
20 Windscreen de-misting air ducts
21 Instrument panel
22 Control column
23 Rudder pedals
24 Cockpit armoured skin-plating
25 T13E1 75-mm cannon
26 Recoil mechanism
27 Cannon mounting subframe
28 D/F loop aerial
29 HF aerial cable
30 Extending boarding ladder
31 Forward entry hatch
32 Machine-gun blister fairing
33 75-mm cannon loading trough. hand-loaded shells
34 Shell case collector
35 0.5-in (12.7-mm) fixed machine-guns
36 Ammunition magazines
37 Ammunition feed chutes
38 Fire extinguisher bottle
39 Armoured seat backs
40 Pilot's seat
41 Safety harness
42 Sliding side-window panel
43 Navigator/radio operator/cannoneer's seat
44 Armoured headrests
45 Cockpit roof ditching hatch
46 Flight engineer/dorsal gunner's station
47 Cockpit bulkhead
48 Radio equipment racks

B-25H Mitchell

Dimensions

Wingspan: 67 ft 7 in (20.60 m)
Length: 51 ft (15.54 m)
Height: 15 ft 9 in (4.80 m)
Wing area: 610 sq ft (56.67 m²)

Powerplant

Two 1,700-hp (1268-kW) Wright
R-2600-13 14-cylinder air-cooled
radial engines

Weights

Empty: 19,975 lb (9061 kg)
Maximum take-off: 36,047 lb
(16351 kg)

Performance

Maximum speed: 275 mph (443
km/h) at 13,000 ft (3960 m)
Climb to 15,000 ft (4570 m): 19 min
Service ceiling: 23,800 ft (7255 m)
Normal range: 1,350 miles (2173 km)

Armament

One 75-mm T13E1 gun with 21 shells
in nose, four 0.5-in (12.7-mm) machine-
guns in extreme nose, four in 'blisters'
on side of nose, two in dorsal turret,
two in extreme tail and one in each
waist position of rear fuselage, plus up
to eight 5-in (127-mm) rocket
projectiles under the outer wings and
up to 3,000 lb (1361 kg) of bombs
carried internally

During World War II, Britain received B-25s as part of the Lend-Lease agreement. This began in 1942 with the initial allocation of 23 B-25Bs that took the RAF name Mitchell Mk I. However, it was to be the Mitchell Mk II – the equivalent of the USAAC's B-25C and B-25D – that would prove to be the RAF's first operational B-25, and the first of an eventual total of 543 joined the RAF from mid-1942. Deliveries to Britain concluded with 316 Mitchell Mk IIIs (B-25J), although some of these aircraft were diverted to the RCAF.

49 75-mm cannon shell magazines, 21 rounds
50 Turret control foot pedals
51 Cabin heating air duct
52 Fresh air intake
53 Inner wing panel engine pylon mounting front spar
54 Cabin heater unit
55 Hydraulic reservoir
56 Wing panel centre-section carry-through
57 Turret gun ammunition magazines
58 Turret mounting ring
59 Forward/centre fuselage joint frame
60 Twin 0.5-in (12.7-mm) machine-guns
61 Bendix power-operated dorsal gun turret
62 Starboard inner wing pane
63 Nacelle top fairings
64 Cowling air flaps
65 Ejector type exhaust ducts
66 Detachable engine cowlings
67 Starboard Hamilton Standard constant-speed three-bladed propeller
68 Carburettor air intake
69 Outboard auxiliary fuel tank
70 Starboard oil coolers
71 Oil cooler air intake
72 Starboard landing lamp
73 5-in (127-mm) HVAR rockets
74 Pitot head
75 Starboard navigation light
76 Aileron balance weights
77 Starboard fabric-covered aileron
78 Aileron tab
79 Aileron operating linkage
80 Starboard outboard slotted flap
81 Oil cooler air outlets
82 Nacelle tail fairing
83 Starboard inboard slotted flap
84 Gun deflectors (tailplane protection)
85 Bomb bay roof crawlway
86 Bomb-hoisting frame
87 Vertical bomb rack
88 Port bomb stowage, maximum bombload 3,000 lb (1360 kg)
89 Gun turret motor amplidyne
90 Centre/rear fuselage joint frame
91 Rear fuselage heater unit
92 Starboard 0.5-in (12.7-mm) waist machine-gun
93 Dinghy stowage
94 Dinghy hatch
95 Fuselage skin panelling
96 Ammunition feed chutes
97 Starboard waist gun ammunition box
98 Starboard tailgun ammunition box
99 Tailgun feed chute
100 Tailplane centre section
101 Tailplane rib and spar construction
102 Starboard tailfin
103 HF aerial cable
104 Fabric-covered rudder
105 Rudder horn balance
106 Rudder tab
107 Fabric-covered elevator construction
108 Elevator tab
109 Tail gunner's seat
110 Head armour
111 Rearward armoured panel
112 Tail barbette
113 Twin 0.5-in (12.7-mm) machine-guns
114 Elevator tab
115 Port elevator
116 Port rudder rib construction
117 Rudder tab
118 Fin rib construction
119 Fin/tailplane attachment joint
120 Port tailplane
121 Tail gunner's seat
122 Tail compartment access
123 Rear fuselage/tailplane joint frame
124 Tail bumper
125 Fuselage frame construction
126 Port tail gun ammunition box
127 Port waist gun ammunition box
128 Air scoop
129 Fuselage walkway
130 Emergency stores pack
131 Rear entry hatchway
132 Extending boarding ladder
133 Gun pintle mounting
134 Flexible canvas seal
135 Port waist gun cupola
136 Port 0.5-in (12.7-mm) waist machine gun
137 Cartridge case collector
138 Port inboard slotted flap segment
139 Flap rib construction
140 Emergency stores pack
141 Inner wing rear spar
142 Fuselage/wing skin joint strap
143 Rear main fuel tank, 164 US gal (621 litres)
144 Forward main fuel tank, 151 US gal (572 litres)
145 Auxiliary fuel tanks, 152 US gal (575 litres) in three fuel cells per wing
146 Flap actuator links
147 Flap hydraulic jack
148 Port oil coolers
149 Oil cooler exhaust ducts
150 Nacelle tail fairing
151 Port outer-slotted flap segment
152 Outer wing panel rib construction
153 Aileron spar
154 Aileron tab
155 Port aileron rib construction
156 Aileron spar
157 Wingtip rib construction
158 Port navigation light
159 Outerwing panel leading edge ribs
160 Main spar
161 5-in (127-mm) HVAR rockets
162 Port landing lamp
163 Mainwheel doors
164 Main undercarriage wheel bay
165 Outer wing panel joint rib
166 Mainwheel hydraulic retraction jack
167 Nacelle auxiliary fuel tank
168 Mainwheel mounting subframe
169 Oil cooler air intake
170 Mainwheel shock absorber leg strut
171 Mainwheel leg door
172 Port mainwheel
173 Torque scissor links
174 Engine mounting subframe
175 Battery stowage
176 Engine bay firewall
177 Engine bearer struts
178 Accessory equipment bay
179 Cowling air flaps
180 Wright R-2600-13 14-cylinder two-row radial engine
181 Carburettor air intake
182 Detachable cowling panels
183 Propeller reduction gearbox
184 Propeller hub pitch change mechanism
185 Cowling nose ring/ cooling air intake
186 Port three-bladed propeller
187 2,000-lb (907-kg) torpedo

Mike Badrocke

B-25D Mitchell

41-29896 was a B-25D-1-NC Mitchell. The B-25D had the company designation NA-82A, and was essentially similar to the B-25C (NA-82) except that the 2,290 built were constructed at a new North American factory established in Kansas, instead of at the Inglewood, California plant. B-25s saw service in the North African theatre from August 1942, when four bomber groups were brought in to help counter Rommel's *Afrika Korps*. The following year, the Axis forces were on the retreat and some B-25s were modified as strafers, these aircraft going on to participate in every major campaign from Tunisia to the German surrender in northern Italy.

Cockpit
The B-25 was flown by a crew of two, comprising aircraft commander in the left-hand seat and co-pilot/navigator in the right-hand seat. The extensively glazed cockpit gave the crew good visibility. Later versions with fuselage guns had a reflector gunsight added above the dashboard. The B-25C and the B-25D were the first Mitchell models to introduce an autopilot, greatly aiding long-range flying and reducing crew fatigue.

Nose section
The glazed nose section housed the bombardier, equipped with a Norden bombsight. His escape hatch was located at the rear of the compartment on the port side. Two machine-guns were incorporated in the nose section, one fixed to fire forward and the other on a flexible mount, aimed by the bombardier.

Rear fuselage

The empty rear fuselage provided space for the carriage of equipment, as well as the dorsal gunner. Observation panels were incorporated to provide lateral visibility, and in later models were replaced by waist guns. Rear protection was provided by two 0.5-in (12.7-mm) machine-guns located in a Bendix dorsal turret. (The later B-25J had the turret moved forward and a separate tail turret added.) The characteristic twin-fin tail unit was built up around a two-spar central structure, with leading-edge sections and large control surfaces attached.

Payload

The single bomb bay was located between the forward and aft wing carry-through structures. Although short and narrow, it was nearly the height of the fuselage. Bombs were held in side-by-side vertical racks and the maximum payload was 5,200 lb (2359 kg), comprising 3,200 lb (1452 kg) carried internally, plus eight 250-lb (113-kg) bombs on wing racks. B-25Cs and B-25Ds occasionally carried a 2,000-lb (907-kg) torpedo externally for shipping attacks.

Petlyakov Pe-2

The popular 'Peshka' was built in enormous numbers in order to satisfy air force demand: regular series production ended in early 1945, by which date 11,427 examples had been completed. These VVS aircraft are pictured engaging in a high-speed level bomb-run during the war. The foreground Pe-2, an early production example, has been provided with a makeshift upper surface winter camouflage scheme.

Pe-2FT

Cutaway key

1 Glazed nose cone
2 Muzzle of starboard 7.62mm ShKAS machine-gun
3 Muzzle of port 7.62-mm ShKAS machine-gun
4 Nose compartment
5 Lower side glazing
6 Bomb-aimer's optically flat glazing
7 Three-blade VISh-61 constant-speed metal propeller
8 Propeller hub
9 Spinner
10 Starter clog
11 Oil cooler intake
12 Oil cooler installation
13 Adjustable outlet flap
14 Engine bearing lower cross frame
15 Engine bearer assembly
16 Klimov M-105RA 12-cylinder Vee engine
17 Engine cool air
18 Carburettors
19 Ventral D/F loop
20 Rudder pedal assembly
21 Cartridge case collector chute
22 Fixed nose armament (port 7.62-mm ShKAS optional)
23 Ammunition box (500 rpg)
24 Nose panelling
25 Main instrument panel
26 Split windscreen
27 Fixed quarter light
28 Instrument side panel
29 Starter dog
30 Control column
31 Pilot's seat with 9-mm armoured back
32 Control run linkage
33 Navigator's (starboard) seat support frame
34 Three-blade VISh-61 propeller

35 Crew entry hatch
36 Oil cooler intake
37 Propeller hub
38 Pilot's adjustable armoured headrest (9-mm)
39 Cockpit canopy
40 Aerial mast
41 Pitot head
42 Aerials
43 Dorsal flexible 7.62-mm ShKAS machine-gun
44 Canopy hinged aft section
45 Exhaust collector shroud
46 Engine cool air intake
47 Dorsal armament ammunition box (750 rounds)
48 Dorsal gunner's seat 49 Port engine nacelle fasteners
50 Fuselage main fuel tank (114 Imp gal/518 litre capacity)

51 Fuselage port saddle tank (11.65 Imp gal/53 litre capacity)
52 Port engine bearer assembly
53 Cooling pipe
54 Oil cooler
55 Adjustable outlet flap
56 Flap actuating servo motor
57 Carburettor air intake
58 Port undercarriage/wing spar attachment
59 Port engine oil tank
60 End fib profile
61 Port outer radiator intake
62 Radiator ducting

63 Front spar/nacelle fixing
64 Port wing root fuel tank (39.6 Imp gal/80 litre capacity)
65 Undercarriage radius rod/wing spar attachment
66 Part outer radiator assembly

67 Underwing dive-brake (extended)
68 Dive-brake hinge fairings
69 Landing lamp
70 Port outer wing inboard fuel tank (31.5 Imp gal/143 litre capacity)

71 Port outer wing outboard fuel tank (23.5 Imp gal/107 litre capacity)
72 Wing leading-edge strip
73 Wing stiffeners
74 Nose rib stations
75 Wing front spar

76 Wing fibs
77 Wing rear spar
78 Wing skinning
79 Port navigation light
80 Port wingtip
81 Aileron attachment/hinge points

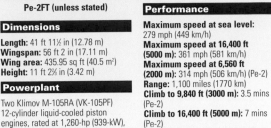

SPECIFICATION

Pe-2FT (unless stated)

Dimensions

Length: 41 ft 11½ in (12.78 m)
Wingspan: 56 ft 2 in (17.11 m)
Wing area: 435.95 sq ft (40.5 m²)
Height: 11 ft 2⅔ in (3.42 m)

Powerplant

Two Klimov M-105RA (VK-105PF) 12-cylinder liquid-cooled piston engines, rated at 1,260-hp (939-kW), with two-speed superchargers

Weights

Empty weight: 13,117 lb (5950 kg)
Loaded weight (normal): 17,130 lb (7770 kg) (Pe-2)
Loaded weight (maximum): 18,783 lb (8520 kg) (Pe-2)
Wing loading: 38.9-43 lb/sq ft (190-210 kg/m²) (Pe-2)

Performance

Maximum speed at sea level: 279 mph (449 km/h)
Maximum speed at 16,400 ft (5000 m): 361 mph (581 km/h)
Maximum speed at 6,560 ft (2000 m): 314 mph (506 km/h) (Pe-2)
Range: 1,100 miles (1770 km)
Climb to 9,840 ft (3000 m): 3.5 mins (Pe-2)
Climb to 16,400 ft (5000 m): 7 mins (Pe-2)
Service ceiling: 29,530 ft (9000 m)

Armament

(Fixed) Typically two 0.3-in (7.62-mm) ShKAS machine-guns firing ahead aimed by pilot, MV-3 dorsal turret with single 0.5-in (12.7-mm) UBT, one ShKAS in rear ventral position, and one ShKAS in left or right rear beam position. (Disposable) See text

The 82-mm calibre RS-82 (Reaktivnyi Snaryad, reaction missile) was the most numerous Soviet air-to-ground rocket of the Great Patriotic War. The weapon, a simple projectile with an ogival nose with a fuze windmill coupled to a drum-shaped central portion and four-fin conical tail, came as a surprise to Nazi and Allied forces alike when first used against German Panzers by Il-2s in June 1941. This Pe-2 is armed with a total of ten RS-82 rockets on underwing rails.

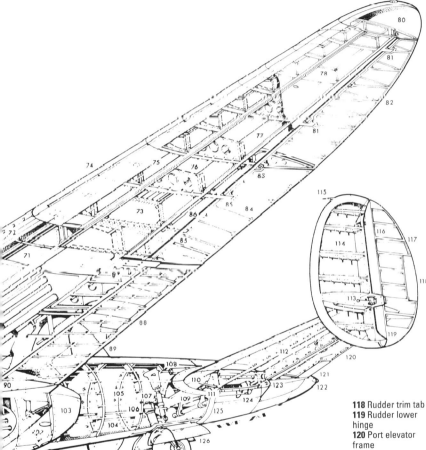

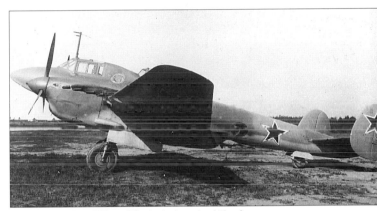

Above: The Pe-2UT multirole trainer had the former No. 1 (fuselage) fuel tank replaced by an extra pilot station at the rear, and was equipped with dual controls.

During TsAGI tests, this Pe-2 had its standard MV-3 rear-facing gun turret replaced by a VUB-1 installation, similarly equipped with a single-blade compensator (weathercock). The 12.7-mm UB gun had the same calibre as the equivalent 0.5-in Browning, but was lighter and faster-firing.

82 Port aileron outer section
83 Aileron actuating control linkage
84 Port aileron inner section
85 Aileron attachment/hinge points
86 Aileron control rod
87 Stiffening plate
88 Port flap outboard section
89 Starboard rudder
90 Flap inboard rib fillet
91 Rear spar/nacelle fixing
92 Fuselage beam window
93 Tail surface control rods
94 Cooling louvres
95 Ventral armament ammunition box 1750 rounds)
96 Ventral machine gun mounting/retraction frame
97 Periscopic sight
98 Control grips
99 Undercarriage radius rods
100 Ventral gunner's (prone) pad
101 Ventral retractable 7.62 mm ShKAS machine-gun
102 Wort nacelle bomb-bay
103 Port nacelle tail cone
104 Tail surface control rods
105 Fuselage structure
106 Tailwheel leg assembly
107 Shock-absorber strut
108 Tailwheel retraction mechanism and cylinder
109 Tailplane centre-section brace
110 Rudder control push-pull rod link
111 Tailplane attachment fillet
112 Tailplane structure
113 Rudder control linkage
114 Tailfin structure
115 Aerial attachment pick-up
116 Rudder upper hinge
117 Rudder frame
118 Rudder trim tab
119 Rudder lower hinge
120 Port elevator frame
121 Port elevator trim tab
122 Tail navigation light
123 Elevator attachment/hinge bracket
124 Elevator actuating rod and internal counterweight
125 Aft fuselage frame/ tailplane front spar join
126 Tailwheel doors
127 Retractable tailwheel
128 Starboard tailfin/rudder
129 Ventral machine gun (deployed)
130 110-lb (50-kg) engine nacelle bay bomb-load
131 Ventral armament wind deflector fairing
132 Port undercarriage doors

133 Undercarriage lower brace strut
134 Retraction jack
135 Door actuating link
136 Mainwheel leg cross-brace
137 Brake lines
138 Mainwheel oleo legs
139 Hub plate
140 Port mainwheel
141 Starboard nacelle bomb bay doors (open)
142 Starboard nacelle bomb bay
143 Fuselage bomb-bay doors
144 Starboard engine nacelle mainwheel well
145 Starboard undercarriage doors
146 Telescopic entry step
147 Crew entry hatch door/integral step
148 Carburettor air intake
149 Mainwheel leg cross-brace
150 Brake lines
151 Undercarriage lower brace strut
152 Mainwheel oleo legs
153 Hub assembly
154 Starboard mainwheel
155 551-lb (250-kg) (optional) underwing bomb load
156 441-lb (200-kg) (4x 110-lb/50-kg) fuselage internal bomb load
157 882-lb (400-kg) (4x 220-lb/100-kg) underwing external bomb load

Pe-2FT

Operated by the 12th Guards Dive-bomber Air Regiment (12 GvBAP) of the Baltic Fleet, Aviatsiya Voenno-Morskovo Flota (AV-MF), flying sorties over the Gulf of Finland in 1944, this Series 205 Pe-2FT (*Frontovii trebovanii*, front-line requirement) wears standard pattern camouflage, consisting of a two-tone green and tan upper surface scheme and pale undersides. The prized '*Guardiya*' badge on the nose signifies that the 12 BAP had been recognised as a Guards unit. Note also the 'Kremlin star' national insignia. The pilot of aircraft '01' was Lt Col Vasili I. Rakov, HSU (Hero of the Soviet Union, awarded 7 February 1940 whilst serving with the 57 BAP), who flew 170 missions, and became commander of the 12 GvBAP after leading a successful attack by 28 Pe-2s on the German anti-aircraft cruiser *Niobe* at the port of Kotka, southern Finland, on 16 July 1944 (an action for which he received a second HSU, on 22 July).

Notable '*Peshka*' operators

As the standard VVS tactical bomber of the Great Patriotic War, the Pe-2 equipped the majority of Soviet bomber regiments by the end of the war. However, among those with particularly distinguished service records were the 5 SBAP (Fast Bomber Aviation Regiment) commanded by Col F. P. Kotlyar (Commander of the 4 GvBAD, Guards Bomber Aviation Division, at the end of the war) and becoming the 8 GvBAP (Guards Bomber Aviation Regiment) in spring 1942, the 6 BAP (Bomber Aviation Regiment) of the 202 BAD (Bomber Aviation Division), the 24th Orlov Red Banner Regiment, the 24 BAP, the 35 GvBAP, the 80 BAP, the 86th Guards Stalingrad Regiment, the 150 BAP commanded by Lt Col I. S. Polbin in early 1942, the 779 BAP and the 82 GvBAP.

Bombload

The Pe-2's offensive stores capability included a standard fuselage bomb bay which could accommodate up to six 100-kg (220-lb) FAB-100 general-purpose HE bombs or four 250-kg (551-lb) FAB-250 bombs, whilst additional 100-kg bombs could be carried singly in the rear of each engine nacelle, with a further two more such weapons carried on racks under each wing centre section. Later in the war, after the power of the Pe-2 had been increased, the four external weapons carried underwing could be increased to 250-kg weapons. Among important roles bestowed upon the Pe-2 was that of dive-bomber. To reduce speed during the dive and stabilise the aircraft, large and powerful slatted 'Venetian-blind' hydraulically-actuated dive-brakes hinged down from under the wing. Carrying a 2,205-lb (1000-kg) bomb load, the Pe-2FT had a range of approximately 817 miles (1315 km).

High-speed capability

In 1941, when Nos. 8 and 134 Sqns, RAF, were sent to Murmansk in order to familiarise Soviet pilots with the Hurricane, the RAF fighters sometimes flew escort to a Pe-2 regiment. Hurricane pilots discovered that 'in an operation that lasted as long as an hour they had to go all-out to keep station', whilst the Pe-2s 'climbed and flew at a rate that that astounded our boys considerably' (Flt Lt H. Griffiths). Maximum permissible speed of the Pe-2 was 450 mph (725 km/h) or 373 mph (600 km/h) with dive-brakes extended. After the introduction of the Bf 109G-2 in late 1942, measures were taken to further improve performance, with the M-105RA engine replaced by the M-105PF/RF rated at 1,260 hp (939-kW) at 2,560 ft (780 m) and 1,180 hp (880-kW) at 8,860 ft (2,700 m), improving take-off performance and increasing maximum speed.

Pe-2FT modifications

Most Pe-2FTs were updated to this standard 'in field' by factory teams who visited operational units. The Pe-2FT offered improved defensive armament in response to requests from crews, who were facing Bf 109Fs by early 1942. The most obvious modification was the replacement of the bomb aimer/navigator's ShKAS with a UBT in the rear turret. A feature of the new lightweight manually operated MV-3 turret was the weathercock. When swung to the side the barrel of the gun caused considerable drag, so the weathercock was fitted in order to offset the large forces required by the bomb aimer/navigator to swing the gun under combat conditions.

Crew positions and duties

The Pe-2 was flown by a crew of three comprising pilot, bomb aimer/navigator and radio operator. The bomb aimer/navigator normally occupied the rear cockpit turret, but just prior to the bombing run would slide forward to the bomb aiming position, lying prone in the nose. The radio operator, who doubled as the ventral gunner, was enclosed in the rear cabin. Although rather spartan by Western standards, Soviet cockpits were provided with all necessary equipment with which the pilot could perform his task. With his head and back protected by 9-mm armour, the pilot also had an adjustable headrest. The distinguishing feature of the Pe-2FT was the bomb aimer/navigator's rear-facing Mozharovsky-Venyevidov MV-3 turret. This mounted a single 0.5-in (12.7-mm) UBT gun, replacing the 0.3-in (7.62 mm) ShKAS weapon of previous variants. The radio operator was responsible for the ventral rear-facing gun aimed from the rear fuselage position. This was aimed using both a periscope and oval side windows. Initially a ShKAS, the weapon was subsequently replaced with a 0.5-in (12.7-mm) calibre UBT machine-gun in some later aircraft, including the example illustrated. However, the one or two beam ShKAS weapons of this Pe-2FT, fired through port and/or starboard hatches, are not visible.

Tupolev Tu-2

Later production Tu-2s (throughout the war the Tu-2S designation was applied to production machines) featured numerous modifications compared to earlier aircraft. Early in production the cowling diameter was reduced (Block 20); small blisters added over the valve gear and a redesigned metal nose. By Block 50, the Tu-2 had been progressively equipped with windows for the ventral gunner, a new VUB-68 gun mount for the radio operator, an additional retractable landing light (all Block 44), improved Lu-68 ventral gun installation (Block 46), extended nose glazing, new straight-top canopy and new VUS-1 navigator's gun mount (Block 48).

Tu-2S

Cutaway key
1 Detachable wingtip
2 Starboard navigation light
3 Corrugated inner skin (upper and lower)
4 Starboard aileron (outer section)
5 Wing construction
6 Skin-strengthening stringers
7 Light bomb or rocket-launching attachments (five per side)
8 Twin landing lights
9 Starboard aileron (inboard section)
10 Rear spar
11 Outboard fuel tank set
12 Inboard fuel tank set
13 Main spar
14 Landing flap assembly
15 Nacelle aft fairing
16 Mainwheel doors
17 Mainwheel well
18 Spar carry-through
19 Mainwheel brake cable
20 Mainwheel oleo
21 Mainwheel retraction scissors
22 Fireproof bulkhead
23 Oil tank
24 Engine bearers
25 Exhaust stub
26 Exhaust collector ring
27 Fire-suppression bottle
28 Radiator outlet shutter
29 Oil radiator
30 Oil cooler intake
31 Detachable cowling panels
32 AV-5-157A three-bladed variable-pitch metal propeller
33 Carburettor air intake
34 Low-drag cowling ring
35 Cooling louvres
36 Propeller boss
37 Hucks-type starter dog
38 Propeller shaft
39 Gear housing

40 Navigator/bomb aimer's 0.5-in (12.7-mm) UBT machine-gun
41 Starboard fixed 20-mm ShVAK cannon
42 Ammunition tank
43 Navigator/bomb aimer's seat
44 Pilot's back armour
45 Pilot's canopy (incorporating downward-hinged side panels and upward-hinged roof

46 Aerial mast
47 Two-piece windscreen
48 Instrument panel and port controls console
49 Control column
50 Rudder pedals
51 Four-panel access hatch

52 Nose side glazing
53 Optically-flat aiming panels
54 Port propeller spinner
55 Shvetsov ASh-82FN (M-82FN) 14-cylinder two-row radial air-cooled engine

SPECIFICATION

Tu-2S (Block 10)

Normal fuel capacity: 615 Imp gal (2800 litre)

Dimensions

Fuselage length: 45 ft 3½ in (13.80 m)
Wing span: 61 ft 10½ in (18.86 m)
Wing area: 525 ft² (48.80 m²)
Height: 14 ¾ ft (4.50 m)

Powerplant:

Two 14-cylinder Shvetsov ASh-82FN (M-82FN) radial piston engines each normally rated at 1,523 hp (1136 kW)

Weights:

Empty weight: 16,477 lb (7474 kg)
Loaded weight: 25,044 lb (11,360 kg)
Maximum take-off weight: 28,219 lb (12,800 kg)

Performance:

Maximum speed: 342 mph (550 km/h) at 17,716 ft (5400 m)
Cruising speed: 275 mph (442 km/h) at 19,030 ft (5800 m)
Service ceiling: 31,170 ft (9500 m)
Maximum range: 1,305 miles (2,100 km)
Range with 3,307 lb (1500 kg) bombs: 1,553 miles (2500 km)
Range with 4,960 lb (2500 kg) bombs: 870 miles (1400 km)
Climb to 16,400 ft (5000 m): 9.5 min
Landing speed: 98 mph (158 km/h))

Andrei Nikolaevich Tupolev (in white hat), pictured visiting a front-line Tu-2 unit, developed the Tu-2, along with his design team, under prison conditions. Tupolev had been imprisoned in a Moscow jail in 1937 but was transferred to Bolshevo, where he worked at the Central Design Bureau N29 of the NKVD (TsKB-29) with other aviation specialists the following year. The full-scale mock-up of Samolyet 103 (the future Tu-2) was constructed from timber in a forest close to the prison.

Right: Initial work on Samolyet 103 (the name derived from that of Tupolev's design team at the TsKB-29: KB-103) began on 1 March 1940, by which time TsKB-29 had been re-located to Tupolev's Moscow offices in Radio Street, which then became a prison. Rolled out on 3 October 1940 after construction of the prototype at factory N156, the first aircraft was then transferred to Chkalovskaya airbase, where it began NII-VVS testing on 1 December. At this stage, Tupolev's continued status as 'enemy of the people' meant that the aircraft had to be known as Samolyet 103, rather than by an ANT-series designation. Series production began and ended in 1941 in favour of fighter production, however, it was restarted in 1943, by which time the aircraft was officially known as the Tu-2.

56 Exhaust pipe cluster
57 Quick-release cowling clips
58 Ejector exhaust pipe
59 Oil cooler intake
60 25-kg (55-lb) OFAB fragmentation bombs
61 Port mainwheel
62 Mainwheel shock-absorber scissors
63 Mainwheel doors
64 Exhaust gill
65 Centre-hinged main bomb bay doors
66 Forward bomb shackle
67 Single FAB-1000 2,205-lb (1000-kg) bomb
68 Access panel
69 Starboard mainwheel
70 Mainwheel fork
71 Aft bomb bay bulkhead
72 Radio operator's position
73 Dorsal glazing
74 Dorsal 0.5-in (12.7-mm) UBT machine-gun
75 Fuselage construction
76 Control cable shroud
77 Stub aerial
78 Ventral gunner's couch
79 Aft crew entry hatch
80 Ventral gunner's aiming periscope
81 Ammunition tank
82 Beam observation window
83 Ventral glazing
84 Ventral 0.5-in (12.7-mm) UBT machine-gun
85 Retractable tailwheel
86 Tailwheel doors
87 Tailwheel retraction mechanisms
88 Aft navigation light
89 Tailplane construction
90 Aerial
91 Starboard tailfin
92 Rudder post
93 Rudder tab
94 Starboard rudder

Above: The five-seat Tu-2DB (ANT-65) long-range bomber introduced a long-span wing, supercharged (exhaust-driven) liquid-cooled engines and a twin-pilot cockpit, whilst retaining the Tu-2's weapons and bombload.

A torpedo-carrying capability had been envisaged during the original Samolyet 103 scheme, and was realised in the Tu-2T (Torpedonosyets), with two prototypes built in 1945-46. Changes included the introduction of a pylon under each wingroot for the carriage of a 45-36-AN aerial torpedo strengthened landing gear, and increased fuel capacity in a sealed bomb bay. The Tu-2T, which had a 2,360 mile (3800 km) range, was built in series for the AV-MF in 1947, it replaced the Il-4T, and served until the mid-1950s with the Baltic, Black Sea and Northern Fleets.

Tu-2S

This Tu-2S (ANT-61) wears a similar camouflage scheme as those aircraft which participated in the Aviation Day parade over Moscow on 18 August 1945. There were several camouflage variations involving two-tone upper surfaces, but many Tu-2s were completed with simple dark green upper surfaces and pale blue undersides. Red star national markings were carried prominently, even during wartime. The first unit to receive the Tu-2 was the 3rd Air Army on the Kalinin Front, which received its first three 103VS aircraft in late April 1942. Following the war, the Tu-2 remained in front-line Soviet air force service until 1950, and was exported to China, North Korea and Warsaw Pact clients, flying Korean War sorties with the Chinese.

Early operational history

The first operational evaluation unit to fly the Tu-2 was Maj. Gen. M. M. Gromov's 3rd Air Army, which received the 103VS (ANT-60) first series production variant in April 1942. From May, the definitive production aircraft (now known as the Tu-2S) was being delivered to the 132 BAP (*Bombardirovochnaya Aviatsionnyi Polk*, Bomber Aviation Regiment), which converted from the SB-2 with assistance of instructors from the Omsk flying school, and a GAZ 166 test pilot. This initial regiment left for the front in September, and a second regiment had become operational by the end of the year.

Design and construction, post-war service

From the outset, Samolyet 103 was envisaged as an all-metal aircraft, utilising smooth duraluminium for the airframe, wings and skin, and steel for the engine mounts and undercarriage. The large bomb compartment beginning just behind the cockpit took up most of the fuselage's volume. Later (post-Block 50) modifications to the construction of the Tu-2S comprised an improved form fixed canopy for the radio operator/gunner and addition of a starboard wingroot walkway and hand-hold (Block 50); metal wingtips (from the 21st aircraft of Block 52) and the introduction of pulsating rubber de-icers for the wing leading edges and tail surfaces, increased-area fins and rudders and new AV-9VF-21K propellers with four square-tipped reduced diameter 'paddle' blades (Block 59). Block 61 saw the enlargement of the engine air inlets in order to incorporate dust filters.

Total Soviet production amounted to 2,257, whilst further aircraft were license-built in China (some of these later being fitted with Chinese HS8 engines and surviving in service until the 1960s). Tu-2s exported to Bulgaria, China, Hungary, North Korea, Poland and Romania tended to be taken from surplus Soviet stocks. The Tu-2 received the ASCC (Allied Standards Co-ordinating Committee) reporting name 'Bat'.

Shvetsov ASh-82FN powerplant
The first powerplant for the Tu-2 family was Mikulin's unreliable 12-cylinder liquid-cooled AM-37, developing 1,400 hp (1044 kW), which was used by the ANT-58, the first prototype Samolyet 103. The ASh-82FN (or M-82FN) was installed on the production Tu 2S (ANT-61), replacing the earlier air-cooled ASh-82 radial piston engine of the Samolyet 103V (ANT-60) production prototype. Both units were developments of the Mikulin M-82, however, the 14-cylinder FN produced between 1,450 hp (1082 kW) at 15,255 ft (4650 m) and 1,850 hp (1380 kW) at 2,500 rpm (for take-off), compared to the 1,330 hp (992 kW) output of the basic ASh-82. Normal rated output for the engine was 1,523-hp (1136-kW). Each powerplant drove a three-bladed 12-ft 6-in (3.8-m) AV-5-157A propeller, with fully feathering constant-speed blades. These metal units replaced the VISh-61T propellers of the Samolyet 103, and the VISh-61E 12-ft 5-in (37.8-m) diameter units of the Samolyet 103U.

Combat record
Despite the fact that the Tu-2 took a long time to appear in numbers within front-line units (due to materials shortages, evacuation of factories, and production schedules favouring the Yak-1 fighter), the Tu-2 was veteran of many battles during the Great Patriotic War. The first major duty was during the Battle of Kursk in June 1944, when 18 aircraft of the 285 BAP bombed enemy forces and attacked positions behind the lines. Over 600 Tu-2s, lead by Col I. Piskok of the 334 BAP took part in the Battle of Vyborg, beginning in 9 June 1944. These aircraft also bombed positions around the pre-Baltic, including the Kiviniemi, Valkiarv and Kivennopa regions. On 7 April 1945, a force of 516 Tu-2s and Pe-8s attacked defences around Koningsberg (Kaliningrad) before the city was captured by the Soviets. During the first day alone of the Battle of Berlin, Tu-2s dropped a total of 97 tonnes of bombs on the German capital.

Gun armament
Forward-firing armament for the Tu-2S consisted of two fixed 20-mm ShVAK cannon, one mounted in each wingroot, and provided with 200 rounds of ammunition per gun. Further defensive armament comprised one manually-operated 0.5-in (12.7-mm) UBT heavy machine-gun (with 250 rounds) behind the pilot, for operation by the navigator/bomb-aimer. Two further manually-operated UBT machine-guns were located in the rear dorsal and ventral positions, operated by the radio operator/gunner and a dedicated gunner, respectively. Sitting on the centreline, the pilot was provided with a PBP-1A reflector sight in order to aim the pair of wingroot ShVAKs. As well as operating the ShKAS mounted on a TSS installation, and firing to the rear of the bulged Plexiglass canopy, the navigator/bomb-aimer could fly the aircraft in an emergency using a folding control wheel.

Tu-2S experimental modifications
Two Tu-2s, unofficially designated Tu-2K (*Katapult*) were utilised for ejection seat tests in 1944-45: two different configurations were trialled, one with the ejection seat in the navigator's position, the other with an open cockpit on the radio operator's station. Another aircraft, the Tu-2N was a series aircraft used to test the Rolls-Royce Nene turbojet in an underslung installation in July 1947. At least two further Tu-2Ls were used as testbeds for other jet engines (at least five types, including the RD-10, RD-20, RD-45, RD-500 and TR-1) at the LII. Other aircraft were used for testing radar systems, bomb sights and guns, whilst the aircraft was also employed as a tanker in early looped-hose refuelling trials with jet aircraft, including the Yak-15. A number of de-militarised Tu-2s were used by Aeroflot as freighters (Tu-2G) with a 4,410-lb (2000-kg) payload; and in 1948-49, a single Block 60 aircraft was modified to carry a GAZ-6TB scout car, which could be air-dropped from a semi-recessed underfuselage position.

Vickers Wellington

Equipped with underwing rockets and a Leigh Light (shown here retracted under the rear fuselage), this Wellington Mk XIV also carries ASV.Mk III radar in a 'chin' radome. These ASW Wellingtons served with 10 RAF Coastal Command squadrons.

Wellington Mk XVI

Cutaway key
1 Nash and Thomson power-operated tail gun turret
2 Four Browning 0.303-in (7.7-mm) machine-guns
3 Cartridge case ejection chute
4 Elevator tab
5 Elevator rib construction
6 Elevator horn balance
7 Tailplane tip construction
8 R.3003 aerial cable
9 Tailplane leading-edge de-icing boot
10 Tailplane geodetic construction
11 Elevator torque shaft
12 Fin/tailplane attachment main frames
13 Gun turret entry doors
14 Rudder tab
15 Tail navigation and formation lights
16 Rudder rib construction
17 Rudder mass-balance weights
18 HF aerial cable
19 Fin tip construction
20 Tailfin geodetic construction
21 leading-edge de-icing boot
22 Starboard fabric-covered elevator
23 Aluminium alloy-skinned tailplane tip segment
24 Port fabric-covered tailplane
25 Tailplane control rods
26 Ammunition feed chutes
27 Tailwheel pivot fixing
28 Castoring tailwheel
29 Ventral aerial mast
30 Tailwheel retraction jack
31 Vacuum flask stowage
32 Tail turret ammunition boxes

33 Boarding ladder stowage
34 Life jacket container
35 Engine turning crank handle
36 Radio altimeter aerial
37 Fuselage fabric covering
38 Lower longeron
39 Footboards
40 Browning 0 303-in (7.7-mm) machine-gun
41 Beam gunner's window, port and starboard
42 Ammunition box
43 Beam gunner's swivelling seat
44 Reconnaissance flares
45 Leigh-Light mounting frames
46 Hydraulic actuator

47 Light extension and retraction mechanism
48 Leigh-Light control panel
49 Fuselage upper longeron
50 Cabin roof geodetic frame construction
51 Beam approach aerial
52 Fabric support stringers
53 Mid-cabin window panels, port and starboard
54 Flare/marker launch tube
55 Rear spar attachment main frame
56 Marine marker stowage
57 Toilet
58 TR.9J transmitter/receiver
59 Dinghy emergency equipment pack

60 ASV radar operator's seat
61 Intercom socket
62 Parachute stowage
63 Astrodome observation hatch
64 ASV Mk III radar receiver
65 Radar equipment rack
66 Wing main spar cut-out
67 Pneumatic system CO_2 bottles
68 Oil filler cap
69 Starboard engine oil tank, 16-Imp gal (73-litre) capacity

70 Nacelle fuel tank, 58-Imp gal (264-litre) capacity
71 Main undercarriage hydraulic retraction jack
72 Dinghy inflation bottle
73 Dinghy stowage
74 Leigh-Light, extended
75 Searchlight cooling air scoop

76 Rear spar
77 Flap shroud ribs
78 Fuel jettison pipe

79 Starboard split trailing-edge flap
80 Aileron trim tab
81 Starboard aileron
82 Aileron rib construction

83 Starboard formation light
84 Wing-tip fairing
85 Starboard navigation light
86 Armoured leading-edge panel
87 Geodetic wing panel construction

© 2001 Mike Badrocke/Aviagraphica

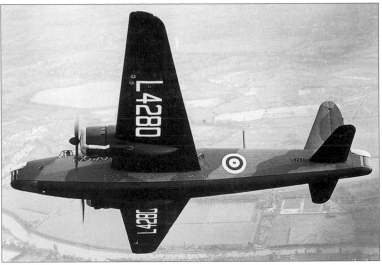

Above: The first production Wellingtons were 180 Mk I aircraft ordered in August 1936, all but the first of which were powered by Bristol Pegasus XVIII radials. The first examples were delivered to No. 99 Sqn in October 1938; L4280 (pictured) went to No. 148 Sqn in March 1939. Also among these first production aircraft were six machines ordered by the RNZAF though, with war looming all remained with the RAF.

SPECIFICATION

Wellington Mk I	Wellington B.Mk X
Dimensions	**Dimensions**
Length: 61 ft 3 in (18.67 m)	**Length:** 64 ft 7 in (19.68 m)
Height: 17 ft 5 in (5.31 m)	**Height:** 17 ft 6 in (5.33 m)
Wingspan: 86 ft (26.2 m)	**Wingspan:** 86 ft 2 in (26.3 m)
Wing area: 840.00 sq ft (78.04 m²)	**Wing area:** 840.00 sq ft (78.04 m²)
Powerplant	**Powerplant**
Two Bristol Pegasus XVIII radial piston engines, each rated at 1,050 hp (783 kW)	Two Bristol Hercules VI/XVI radial piston engines, each rated at 1,675 hp (1249 kW)
Weights	**Weights**
Empty: 18,000 lb (8165 kg)	**Empty:** 22,474 lb (10194 kg)
Gross: 24,850 lb (11272 kg)	**Gross:** 36,500 lb (16556 kg)
Performance	**Performance**
Maximum speed at 15,000 ft (4572 m): 245 mph (394 km/h)	**Maximum speed:** 255 mph (410 km/h)
Initial climb rate: 1,120 ft/min (341 m/min)	**Climb to:** 15,000 ft (4572 m) in 27.7 minutes
Climb to: 15,000 ft (4572 m) in 18 minutes	**Service ceiling:** 22,000 ft (6706 m)
Service ceiling: 21,600 ft (6584 m)	**Range**
Range	1,885 miles (3034 km) at 180 mph (290 km/h) with a 1,500 lb (680 kg) bomb load
3,200 miles (5150 km) at 180 mph (290 km/h)/15,000 ft (4572 m)	**Armament**
Armament	Two 0.303-in (7.7-mm) Browning machine-guns in an FN.5 nose turret, plus four similar weapons in an FN.20A tail turret and a single beam gun either side of the rear fuselage. Offensive load was up to 4,000 lb (1814 kg) of bombs
A single 0.303-in (7.7-mm) Browning machine-gun in a Vickers nose turret, plus a pair of similar weapons in a Vickers tail turret and ventral Fraser Nash FN.9 'dust bin' turret. Offensive load was up to 4,500 lb (2041 kg) of bombs	

88 Outer wing panel spar joint
89 Pitot head
90 60-lb (27-kg) air-to-surface rocket projectile
91 Leading-edge nose ribs
92 Main spar
93 Starboard wing fuel tank bays; total fuel capacity, 750 Imp gal (3410 litres)
94 Front spar
95 Rocket launch rails
96 Mainwheel doors
97 Starboard mainwheel

98 Hydraulic brake pipe
99 Oleo-pneumatic shock absorber leg

100 Main undercarriage pivot fixing
101 Engine bay fireproof bulkhead
102 Engine bearer struts
103 Oil cooler exhaust duct
104 Adjustable engine bay cooling air gills
105 Oil cooler
106 Oil cooler air scoop
107 Three-segment detachable engine cowling panels

108 Flame suppressing exhaust pipe on inboard side
109 Engine mounting ring frame
110 Carburettor air intake duct
111 Reconnaissance flare stowage rack
112 Main spar 'free-floating' centre-section carry-through
113 Beam approach equipment rack
114 Upper identification light

115 Front spar attachment main frame
116 Fire extinguisher bottle
117 Forward cabin window panel
118 Engine cowling nose ring
119 Propeller hub pitch change mechanism
120 Starboard variable pitch propeller
121 Navigator's compartment
122 Chart table
123 Compass mounting
124 Soundproof bulkhead
125 D/F loop aerial
126 Port nacelle fuel tank
127 Nacelle tail fairing
128 Flap hydraulic jack
129 Flap operating links
130 Port split trailing-edge flap
131 Fuel jettison pipe
132 Aileron trim tab
133 Port fabric-covered aileron
134 Aileron hinge control linkage
135 Port formation light
136 Aluminium alloy wing-tip fairing
137 Port navigation light
138 Wing panel fabric skinning
139 Retractable landing lamps
140 Wing aft fuel tank train (60 Imp gal/273 litre inboard, 57 Imp gal/259 litre centre and 50 Imp gal/227 litre outboard)
141 Fuel filler caps
142 Wing forward fuel tank train (52 Imp gal/236 litre inboard, 55 Imp gal/250 litre centre and 43 Imp gal/195 litre outboard)
143 Port rocket launch rails
144 Carburettor filtered air intake
145 Intake trunking
146 Port engine oil tank
147 Engine accessory equipment compartment
148 Aerial mast
149 Armoured bulkhead
150 Radio operator's compartment
151 Electrical distribution panels
152 Main cabin floor level
153 Bomb-bay emergency flotation bags (14)
154 Bomb-bay lateral support beam
155 Flotation bag inflated position
156 Outer bomb doors, open
157 250-lb (113-kg) depth charges; 5,000-lb (2268-kg) maximum internal load
158 Triple cell bomb-bay doors
159 Internal step
160 Cabin heater air duct
161 Hydraulic system hand pump
162 HT battery
163 Cockpit section main frame
164 Second pilot's folding seat
165 Sliding cockpit side window panel
166 Radio equipment racks
167 Pilot's seat
168 Windscreen panels
169 Cockpit roof glazing
170 Bristol Hercules XVII 14-cylinder sleeve-valve two-row radial engine
171 Propeller reduction gearbox
172 Townend ring exhaust collector
173 de Havilland three-bladed variable pitch propeller
174 Spinner
175 Windscreen washer ducts
176 Instrument panel
177 Control column
178 Cockpit floor level
179 Ventral entry hatch
180 Parachute stowage
181 Downward identification lights
182 Reconnaissance camera
183 Hand bearing compass holder
184 Rudder pedals
185 Nose compartment construction
186 Nose gunner's seat
187 Glazed nose compartment
188 Manually-operated 0.303-in (7.7-mm) Browning machine-guns
189 Ammunition box
190 Radar scanner drive mechanism
191 ASV Mk III radar scanner
192 Nose radome
193 Forward navigation light

X3662 was among the aircraft equipping No. 115 Squadron, RAF Bomber Command at RAF Marham, Norfolk between late 1941 and March 1943, when the unit re-equipped with Avro Lancaster B.Mk IIs. A Blackpool-built aircraft, X3662 was one of 500 Mk IC aircraft ordered in 1940, 50 of which were completed as such before the order was amended to one for Mk IIIs. No. 115 Sqn was one of the best-known bomber units in the RAF. Having operated the Handley Page Harrow, it acquired its first Wellingtons (Mk Is) in April 1939. During its time equipped with the 'Wimpy', the squadron became the first RAF unit to bomb a mainland enemy target, attacking the airfield at Stavanger/Sola in April 1940 while 'on loan' to Coastal Command.

Wellington B.Mk III

Crew positions

The Wellington Mk III generally flew with a crew of five, comprising a pilot, bomb-aimer/nose gunner, navigator, radio-operator and rear gunner. The pilot occupied the lefthand seat on the flight deck, a folding seat on the starboard side allowing access to the nose compartment in flight. Just aft of the nose turret was a prone bomb-aiming position. Behind the flight deck were positions for the wireless operator, who faced forward immediately behind the pilot, but seperated from the pilot by a bulkhead, and the navigator, who was further aft facing outwards on the port side. The rear crew positions were defensive in nature, comprising the beam gunner's station in the rear fuselage (manned by the navigator and wireless operator), and the tail turret, which was accessed from under the tail.

Structure and fuel capacity

The Wellington was built on the 'geodetic' principal developed by Dr Barnes Wallis, involving a lattice work of diagonals which provided great strength under both bending and twisting loads. With the various loads borne by this structure, a fabric covering was possible, thus saving weight. Four conventional longerons ran the length of the fuselage to form the basis of the framework. Three bomb bays made up the entire centre fuselage beneath the wing. In the top of the bays were flotation bags which were inflated in the event of ditching to give the crew time to escape. Fuel was carried in the wings and engine nacelles. Tanks in the upper nacelles each had a capacity of 58 Imp gal (284 litres), while those ahead of the main spar held 52 Imp gal (236 litres) inboard, 55 Imp gal (250 litres) in the centre and 43 Imp gal (195 litres) outboard. Another three tanks were fitted aft of the spar, these containing 167 Imp gal (758 litres) in all.

Powerplant

The Wellington Mk I was powered by a pair of Bristol Pegasus XVIII radials, though concerns over supplies of this engine and the continuing need for more power prompted development of the Mk II (with Rolls-Royce Merlin Xs), Mk III and Mk IV (Pratt & Whitney Twin Wasps). The Wellington B.Mk III employed a pair of 14-cylinder, two-row Bristol Hercules XIs, each rated at 1,500 hp (1119 kW) and it was the Hercules that was to be the most widely used of the Wellington's varied powerplants. The most numerous variant, the Mk X (of which 3,803 were completed), employed a pair of 1,675-hp (1249-kW) Hercules XVIs.

Bomb load

Typically the Wellington was able to carry a bomb load of up to 4,500 lb (2041 kg), comprising nine 500-lb (227-kg) bombs. Alternatively, a pair of 2,000 lb (907 kg) bombs could be carried, or (in later machines and earlier aircraft so converted) a single 4,000-lb (1814-kg) 'Cookie' HC device.

Defensive armament

In original Mk I guise the Wellington was lightly armed with Vickers nose and tail turrets, the former with mounting a single Browning 0.303-in (7.7-mm) machine-gun and the latter a pair of similar weapons. A retractable two-gun Fraser Nash FN.9 'dust bin' turret was also fitted. In the Mk IA FN.5 nose and FN.10 tail turrets were fitted in place of the original units, each sporting a pair of 'three-oh-threes'. From the Mk IC the ventral FN.9 turret was deleted and replaced by a single beam gun either side of the rear fuselage. The Merlin-engined Mk II introduced the FN.20A four-gun tail turret; this change was carried forward into the Mk III and Mk X. Concern about the Wellington's defensive capabilities prompted the development of a new ventral turret installation, but this was rejected by Bomber Command on the grounds that its weight would have resulted in a reduced bomb load.

Fighter and Ground Attack Aircraft

Bell P-39 Airacobra

When the fuselage side intakes and turbo supercharger were removed, the XP-39 prototype became the XP-39B. The removal of these features, however, turned the P-39 from a potentially great fighter into something of an 'also ran'.

Airacobra

Cutaway key
1 Aluminium sheet rudder tip
2 Rudder upper hinge
3 Aerial attachment
4 Fin forward spar
5 Tall navigation lights
6 Fin structure
7 Rudder middle hinge
8 Rudder
9 Rudder tab
10 Rudder tab flexible shaft
11 Elevator control quadrant
12 Rudder control quadrant
13 Starboard elevator
14 Starboard tailplane
15 Rudder lower hinge
16 Control cables
17 Fuselage aft frame
18 Diagonal brace
19 Fin root fillet
20 Elevator hinge fairing
21 Elevator tab (port only)
22 Port elevator
23 Aerial
24 Aerial mast
25 Port tailplane
26 Aft fuselage semi-monocoque
27 Radio installation
28 Access panel
29 Radio equipment tray
30 Control quadrant
31 Oil tank armour plate
32 Aft fuselage/central chassis bulkhead
33 Engine oil tank
34 Prestone (cooler) expansion tank
35 Carburettor intake fairing
36 Carburettor intake shutter housing
37 Engine accessories
38 Central chassis web
39 Frame
40 Starboard longitudinal fuselage beam
41 Exhaust stubs
42 Allison V-1710-35 Vee 12-cylinder engine
43 Engine compartment decking
44 Aft-vision glazing
45 Crash turnover bulkhead
46 Turnover bulkhead armour plate
47 Auxiliary air intake
48 Ventral Prestone (coolant) radiator
49 Rear main spar/centre section attachment
50 Cylindrical oil radiator
51 Ventral controllable shutters
52 Auxiliary spar/centre section attachment
53 Hoses
54 Shutter control rod access doors
55 Starboard mainwheel well
56 Mainwheel leg/rear main spar attachment point
57 Wing structure
58 Port flap structure
59 Aileron tab control link fairing
60 Aileron trim tab
61 Aileron servo tab
62 Wing rib
63 Starboard navigation light
64 Ammunition tanks
65 Two 0.3-in (7.62-mm) machine-guns
66 Inboard gun ammunition feed chute
67 Machine-gun barrels
68 Mainwheel door fairing
69 Starboard mainwheel
70 Axle
71 Mainwheel fork
72 Torque links
73 Mainwheel oleo leg
74 Wing fuel cells (6)
75 Fuel filler cap
76 Mainwheel retraction spindle
77 Fuel tank gauge capacity plate
78 Fuel tank access plate
79 Forward main spar
80 Oil cooler intakes
81 Intake duct rib cut-out
82 Wing centre-section
83 Aileron control cables
84 Undercarriage gear motor
85 Aileron control quadrant
86 Undercarriage emergency handcrank
87 Coolant radiator/oil temperature shutter controls
88 Sutton harness
89 Pilot's seat
90 Armoured glass turnover bulkhead frame
91 Cockpit entry doors
92 Internal rear-view mirror
93 Gunsight
94 Armoured glass windscreen
95 Steel plate armour overlap
96 Instrument panel frame
97 Control column
98 Control column yoke/drive shaft
99 Nosewheel retraction chain coupling
100 Rudder pedal assembly
101 Fuselage machine-gun ammunition tank
102 Nosewheel drive motor
103 Nosewheel retraction strut forged 'A'-frame attachments

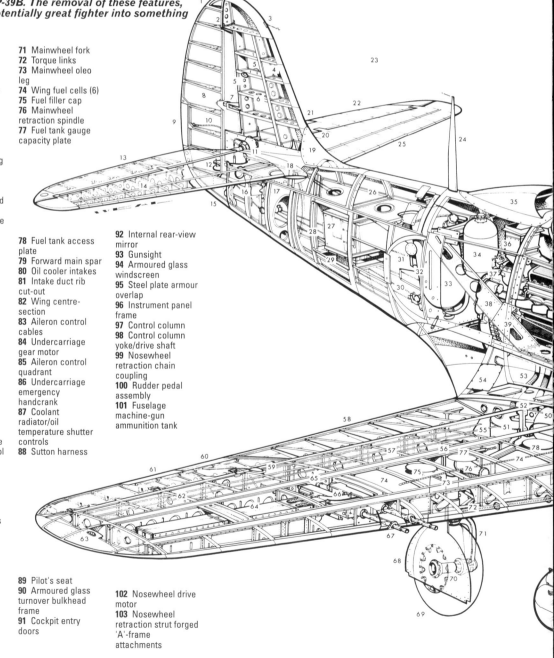

While the P-39 saw only limited in Europe and Africa, it was in the Pacific theatre that the Airacobra, along with the P-40, was the dominant fighter until 1944. These P-39s can be seen escorting a C-47 over New Guinea en route to Wau.

SPECIFICATION

Type
Single-seat fighter and fighter-bomber

Powerplant
One Allison V-1710-85 Vee engine rated at 1,200 hp (895 kW)

Performance
Maximum speed 376 mph (605 km/h) at 15,000 ft (4570 m); cruising speed 200 mph (322 km/h) at optimum altitude; climb to 15,000 ft (4570 m) in 6 minutes 6 seconds; service ceiling 38,270 ft (11665 m); range 975 miles (1569 km)

Weights
Empty 6,400 lb (2903 kg); maximum take-off 8,800 lb (3992 kg)

Dimensions
Wingspan 34 ft (10.36 m); length 30 ft 2 in (9.19 m); height 12 ft 5 in (3.75 m); wing area 213.00 sq ft (19.79 m2)

Armament
One 37-mm T9 fixed forward-firing cannon, two 0.5-in (12.7-mm) fixed forward-firing machine-guns and four 0.3-in (7.62-mm) fixed forward-firing machine-guns, plus one 500-lb (227-kg) bomb carried externally

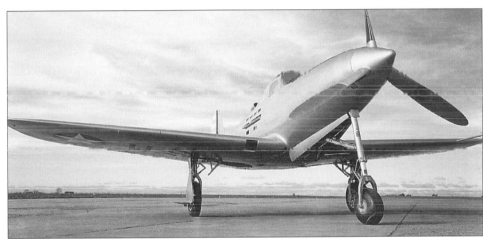

The P-39Q represented the final attempt to mould the Airacobra into a world-class fighter. This is a P-39Q-20, most of which were built for the USSR and delivered without guns, although this example was destined for the USAAF and retained its armament.

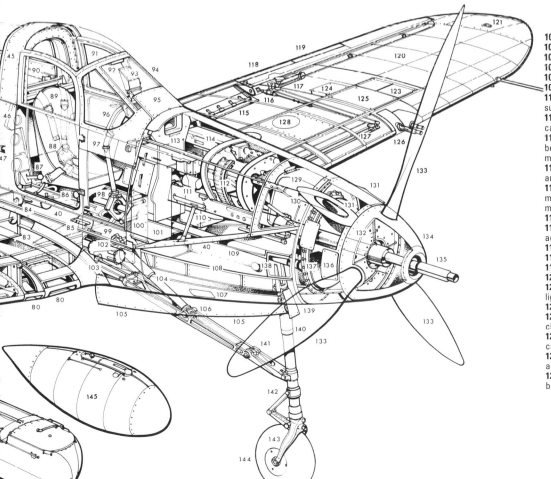

104 Retraction screw
105 Nosewheel doors
106 Link assembly
107 Access plate
108 Nosewheel well
109 Drive shaft
110 Cannon aft support frame
111 37-mm M4 cannon breech
112 Circular endless belt-type cannon magazine (30 rounds)
113 Cockpit forward armoured plate
114 Two 0.5-in (12.7-mm) fuselage machine-guns
115 Flap links
116 Aileron tab actuating link
117 Aileron control
118 Aileron trim tab
119 Aileron servo tab
120 Wing skinning
121 Port navigation light
122 Pitot tube
123 Ammunition feed chute access
124 Gun charge cable access
125 Wing gun service access
126 Machine-gun barrels
127 Aileron and tab control pulleys
128 Fuel tank filler cap
129 Reduction gear oil tank
130 Machine-gun blast tubes
131 Machine-gun ports
132 Reduction gear box frontal armour
133 Three-bladed Curtiss Electric constant speed propeller
134 Spinner
135 Cannon muzzle
136 Blast tube access
137 Reduction gear casing
138 Nosewheel link
139 Nosewheel door forward fairing
140 Nosewheel oleo
141 Link assembly
142 Torque links
143 Axle fork
144 Rearward-retracing nosewheel
145 Ventral stores, options including auxiliary fuel tank, or;
146 Two-man life raft

Bristol Beaufighter

No. 404 Squadron (RCAF) was equipped with Beaufighter TF.Mk Xs. The aircraft, four of which are seen here in June 1944 while based at RAF Davidstow Moor, Cornwall, covered the western Channel during the D-Day invasion of Normandy.

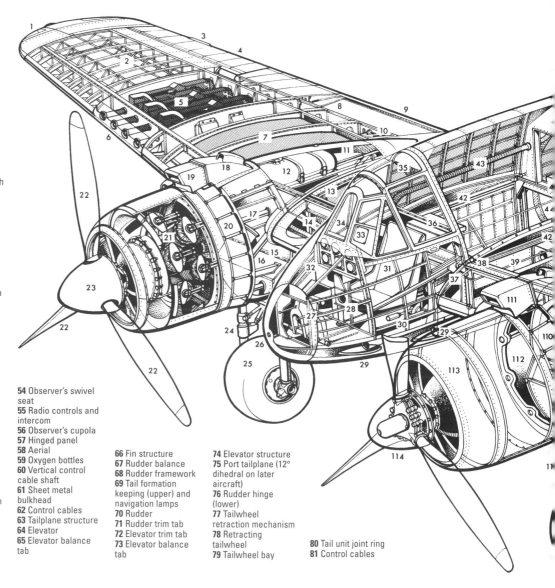

Beaufighter Mk 1

Cutaway key
1 Starboard navigation light (fore) and formation-keeping light (aft)
2 Wing structure
3 Aileron adjustable tab
4 Starboard aileron
5 Four Browning 0.303-in (7.7-mm) machine-guns
6 Machine-gun ports
7 Starboard outer wing fuel tank, capacity 87 Imp gal (395 litres)
8 Split trailing-edge flaps, hydraulically-actuated
9 Starboard flap
10 Flap-operating jack
11 Starboard nacelle tail fairing
12 Oil tank capacity 17 Imp gal (77 litres)
13 Starboard inner wing fuel tank, capacity 188 Imp gal (855 litres)
14 Cabin air duct
15 Hinged leading-edge sections
16 Engine bulkhead
17 Engine bearers
18 Auxiliary intake
19 Supercharger air intake
20 Engine cooling flaps
21 1,560-hp (1164-kW) Bristol Hercules III radial engine
22 de Havilland Hydromatic propeller
23 Propeller spinner
24 Lockheed oleo-pneumatic shock absorber
25 Starboard mainwheel, with Dunlop brakes

26 Forward identification lamp in nose cap
27 Rudder pedals
28 Control column
29 Cannon ports
30 Seat adjusting lever
31 Pilot's seat
32 Instrument panel
33 Clear vision panel
34 Flat bulletproof windscreen
35 Fixed canopy (sideways-hinged on later aircraft)
36 Spar carry-through step
37 Nose centre-section attachment point
38 Fuselage/centre-section attachment point
39 Pilot's entry/emergency escape hatch
40 Underfloor cannon blast tubes
41 Fuselage/centre-section attachment points
42 Centre-section attachment longeron reinforcement
43 Cabin air duct
44 Cannon heating duct
45 Rear spar carry-through
46 Bulkhead cutout (observer access to front hatch)
47 Bulkhead
48 Hydraulic header tank
49 Aerial mast
50 Monocoque fuselage construction
51 Starboard cannon (two 20-mm)
52 Floor level
53 Steps

54 Observer's swivel seat
55 Radio controls and intercom
56 Observer's cupola
57 Hinged panel
58 Aerial
59 Oxygen bottles
60 Vertical control cable shaft
61 Sheet metal bulkhead
62 Control cables
63 Tailplane structure
64 Elevator
65 Elevator balance tab

66 Fin structure
67 Rudder balance
68 Rudder framework
69 Tail formation keeping (upper) and navigation lamps
70 Rudder
71 Rudder trim tab
72 Elevator trim tab
73 Elevator balance tab

74 Elevator structure
75 Port tailplane (12° dihedral on later aircraft)
76 Rudder hinge (lower)
77 Tailwheel retraction mechanism
78 Retracting tailwheel
79 Tailwheel bay
80 Tail unit joint ring
81 Control cables

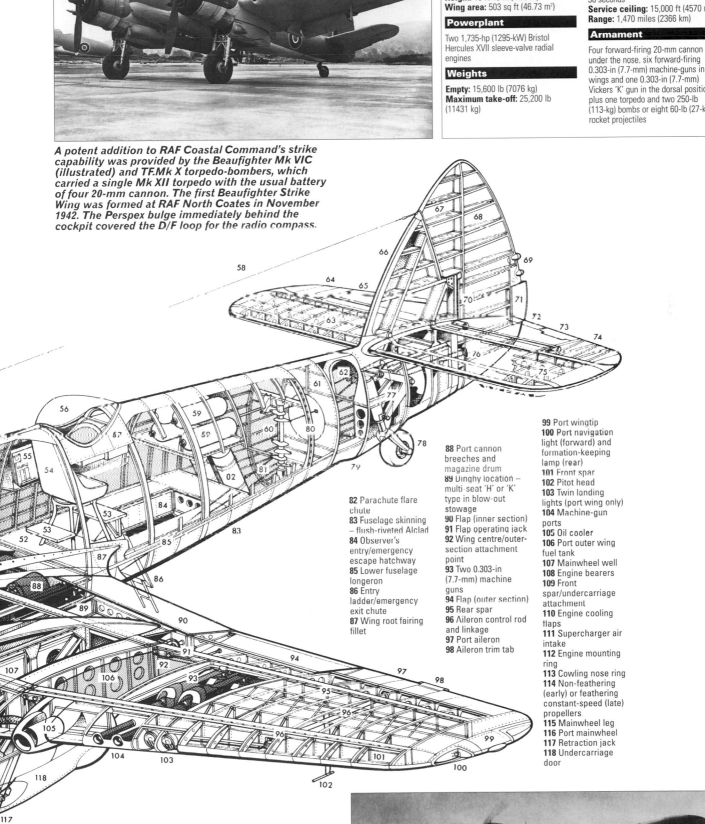

SPECIFICATION

Beaufighter TF.Mk X

Dimensions

Length: 41 ft 8 in (12.70 m)
Wingspan: 57 ft 10 in (17.63 m)
Height: 15 ft 10 in (4.83 m)
Wing area: 503 sq ft (46.73 m²)

Powerplant

Two 1,735-hp (1295-kW) Bristol Hercules XVII sleeve-valve radial engines

Weights

Empty: 15,600 lb (7076 kg)
Maximum take-off: 25,200 lb (11431 kg)

Performance

Maximum speed at 1,300 ft (395 m): 303 mph (488 km/h)
Cruising speed: 249 mph (401 km/h)
Climb to 5,000 ft (1525 m): 3 minutes 30 seconds
Service ceiling: 15,000 ft (4570 m)
Range: 1,470 miles (2366 km)

Armament

Four forward-firing 20-mm cannon under the nose, six forward-firing 0.303-in (7.7-mm) machine-guns in the wings and one 0.303-in (7.7-mm) Vickers 'K' gun in the dorsal position, plus one torpedo and two 250-lb (113-kg) bombs or eight 60-lb (27-kg) rocket projectiles

A potent addition to RAF Coastal Command's strike capability was provided by the Beaufighter Mk VIC (illustrated) and TF.Mk X torpedo-bombers, which carried a single Mk XII torpedo with the usual battery of four 20-mm cannon. The first Beaufighter Strike Wing was formed at RAF North Coates in November 1942. The Perspex bulge immediately behind the cockpit covered the D/F loop for the radio compass.

82 Parachute flare chute
83 Fuselage skinning – flush-riveted Alclad
84 Observer's entry/emergency escape hatchway
85 Lower fuselage longeron
86 Entry ladder/emergency exit chute
87 Wing root fairing fillet

88 Port cannon breeches and magazine drum
89 Dinghy location – multi-seat 'H' or 'K' type in blow-out stowage
90 Flap (inner section)
91 Flap operating jack
92 Wing centre/outer-section attachment point
93 Two 0.303-in (7.7-mm) machine guns
94 Flap (outer section)
95 Rear spar
96 Aileron control rod and linkage
97 Port aileron
98 Aileron trim tab

99 Port wingtip
100 Port navigation light (forward) and formation-keeping lamp (rear)
101 Front spar
102 Pitot head
103 Twin landing lights (port wing only)
104 Machine-gun ports
105 Oil cooler
106 Port outer wing fuel tank
107 Mainwheel well
108 Engine bearers
109 Front spar/undercarriage attachment
110 Engine cooling flaps
111 Supercharger air intake
112 Engine mounting ring
113 Cowling nose ring
114 Non-feathering (early) or feathering constant-speed (late) propellers
115 Mainwheel leg
116 Port mainwheel
117 Retraction jack
118 Undercarriage door

The only variant of the Beaufighter to serve with the USAAF was the Mk VIF. During 1942-43, the USAAF desperately needed a night-fighter aircraft for the Mediterranean theatre, so the RAF provided sufficient aircraft to arm four squadrons of the 12th Air Force. These aircraft saw extensive service during the German withdrawal of North Africa, especially in providing night air cover for the army landings at Anzio and Salerno.

Beaufighter Mk 21

A8-186 was an Australian-built Beaufighter Mk 21 which served with No. 22 Squadron, RAAF during the first half of 1945. The name *'Beau-gunsville'* on the nose of the aircraft refers to the island of Bougainville in the Solomon Islands which saw heavy fighting by Australian forces in late 1944 and early 1945. No. 22 Sqn was part of the RAAF's No. 77 (Attack) Wing which flew strike missions against the Celebes and surrounding Japanese-held islands from its base on the island of Morotai. In the last months of the war, the unit moved to newly-captured islands and was mainly involved in harrying the retreating Japanese forces. This particular aircraft is one of the few Australian Beaufighters to survive intact and is currently on display at the Camden Museum of Aviation, New South Wales.

Cockpits

The single-place cockpit was dominated by the large reflector sight mounted above the dashboard. Flight controls were effected by a yoke-style control column which incorporated the firing button. Engine controls were located to the port side, while the starboard had navigation and general function controls. A distinguishing feature of the Beaufighter Mk 21 was the bulge ahead of the cockpit, intended to cover a Sperry autopilot although this was not, in the end, fitted on operational aircraft. The rear cockpit enclosed a rearward-facing observer/radio operator beneath a 'bubble' canopy. In some variants a machine-gun was provided giving a measure of self defence from the rear. The second crew member was also tasked, when necessary, with reloading the four 20-mm cannon located in the rear of the front fuselage.

Powerplant

The Australian-built Beaufighter Mk 21 was powered by a pair of Bristol Hercules Mk XVIII radial engines. Each had 14 cylinders in two rows with sleeve valves, and developed 1,735 hp (1295 kW). Large air inlets on the upper surface of each engine nacelle provided air for the engine's supercharger. Further forward, a ring of cooling flaps around the rear of the cowling admitted cooling air during taxiing and low-speed flight. They were closed shut at high speeds when ram air on the front of the engine provided adequate cooling.
A 17-Imp gal (77-litre) oil tank was mounted in the top of each nacelle, aft of the engine.

Gun armament

The Beaufighter Mk 21's main gun armament was four 20-mm cannon mounted in the lower fuselage, firing from beneath the cockpit. The ammunition drum and firing mechanisms for these reached back to a point level with the trailing edge of the wing. Unlike British Beaufighters, which were mostly equipped with six 0.303-in (7.7-mm) machine-guns in the wings (two in the port and four in the starboard), the Australian Mk 21 introduced four 0.5-in (12.7-mm) machine-guns (two in each wing). The barrels of the guns projected forward of the leading edge of the wing.

Australian markings

Royal Australian Air Force aircraft adopted RAF-style squadron codes during World War II. 'DU' was the code for No. 22 Squadron. The standard RAAF serial consisted of a type designator (in this case A8) followed by a serial number. British-built examples of the Beaufighter serving with the RAAF were given the prefix 'A19'. This aircraft was the 186th from the Fisherman's Bend factory in Australia. The roundels of all RAF and RAAF aircraft serving in the Far East theatre had the red centre omitted to avoid confusion with Japanese aircraft. The fin flash also only featured blue and white segments.

Fuselage

The exceptional strength of the Beaufighter was based on an enormously strong centre-section, which also included the engine bearers. To this all-metal structure was added the forward and rear fuselage, engines and outer wing panels. The rear fuselage behind the observer accommodated oxygen bottles in the upper section. Parachute flares could be carried in the lower section for illuminating targets at night. The lower fuselage of the rear centre section housed a dinghy to be deployed in the event of a ditching. A rotating shaft aft of the rear cockpit transferred the flight control run from the lower to the upper fuselage.

Wing structure

The two-spar wing was built in four major sections: the centre-section, two outer sections (one containing the wing guns) and a detachable tip. Fuel was contained in large tanks between the engines and the guns, and between the engines and the fuselage. The pitot sensor for the air speed indicator was held on a long mast beneath the port wing, which ensured that it was situated in undisturbed airflow. On the same wing, large twin landing lights were fitted behind a flush transparent cover. Australian Mk 21s also had provision for underwing armament which normally consisted of up to two 250-lb (113-kg) bombs and eight rocket projectiles.

Curtiss P-40 Warhawk

Encouraged by the performance being demonstrated by European interceptors powered by liquid-cooled inline engines, Curtiss decided, in 1938, to install a 1,160-hp (865-kW) supercharged Allison V-1710-19 in its radial-powered P-36A. Designated XP-40, the aircraft was the first American fighter to enter mass production. This early P-40C wears pre-war markings possibly belonging to the 20th Pursuit Group, stationed at Hamilton Field, California.

P-40E Warhawk

Cutaway key
1 Rudder aerodynamic balance
2 Rudder upper hinge (port external)
3 Radio aerial bracket/ insulator
4 Rear navigation light (port and starboard)
5 Tailfin structure
6 Rudder post/support tube
7 Rudder structure
8 Rudder trim tab
9 Rudder trim tab push-rod (starboard external)
10 Elevator tab
11 Elevator structure
12 Elevator aerodynamic balance
13 Tailplane structure
14 Rudder lower hinge
15 Rudder control horn
16 Tab actuator flexible drive shafts
17 Tailplane attachment lugs
18 Elevator control horn
19 Tab control rear sprocket housing/chain drive
20 Tailwheel retraction mechanism
21 Access panel
22 Tailwheel door
23 Retractable tailwheel
24 Tailwheel leg
25 Lifting point
26 Tailwheel lower attachment
27 Trim control cable turnbuckles
28 Elevator control cables
29 Tailwheel upper attachment
30 Access panel
31 Port tailplane
32 Port elevator
33 Radio aerials
34 Monocoque fuselage structure
35 Hydraulic reserve tank
36 Automatic recognition device
37 Aerial lead-in
38 Radio aerial mast
39 Hand starter crank stowage
40 Radio bay access door (port)
41 Radio receiver/ transmitter
42 Support frame
43 Battery stowage
44 Ventral aerial (optional)
45 Hydraulic system vent and drain
46 Rudder control cable turnbuckle
47 Oxygen bottles
48 Radio equipment installation (optional)
49 Hydraulic tank
50 Hydraulic pump
51 Wingroot fillet
52 Streamline ventral cowl
53 Wing centreline splice
54 Fuselage fuel tank, capacity 51.5 Imp gal (234 litres)
55 Canopy track
56 Fuel lines
57 Rear-vision panels
58 Pilot's headrest
59 Rearward-sliding cockpit canopy
60 Rear view mirror (external)
61 Bulletproof windshield
62 Instrument panel coaming
63 Electric gunsight
64 Throttle control quadrant
65 Trim tab control wheels
66 Flap control lever
67 Pilot's seat
68 Elevator control cable horn
69 Seat support (wing upper surface)
70 Hydraulic pump handle
71 Control column
72 Rudder pedal/brake cylinder assembly
73 Bulkhead
74 Oil tank, capacity 108 Imp gal (491 litres)
75 Ring sight
76 Flap control push rod rollers
77 Aileron control cables
78 Aileron cable drum
79 Aileron trim tab drive motor
80 Aileron trim tab
81 Port aileron
82 Port navigation light

83 Pitot head
84 Wing skinning
85 Ammunition loading panels
86 Bead sight
87 Coolant expansion tank, capacity 29 Imp gal (132 litres)
88 Carburettor intake
89 Engine bearer support attachment
90 Air vapour eliminator
91 Hydraulic emergency reserve tank
92 Junction box
93 Engine support tubes
94 Engine mounting vibration absorbers
95 Exhaust stacks
96 Cowling panel lines
97 Allison V-1710-39 engine
98 Carburettor Intake fairing
99 Propeller reduction gear casing
100 Coolant thermometer
101 Propeller hub shaft
102 Spinner
103 Curtiss Electric propeller
104 Radiator (divided) intakes

105 Intake trunking
106 Oil cooler radiator (centreline)
107 Glycol radiators (port and starboard)
108 Radiator mounting brackets
109 Glycol radiator intake pipe
110 Port mainwheel
111 Controllable cooling gills
112 Access panel (oil drain)
113 Engine bearer support truss
114 Fresh air intake
115 Wingroot fairing
116 Fuselage frame/wing attachment
117 Walkway
118 Wing/fuselage splice plate
119 Split flap structure
120 Aileron fixed tab
121 Starboard aileron
122 Starboard wingtip construction
123 Starboard navigation light
124 Wing rib

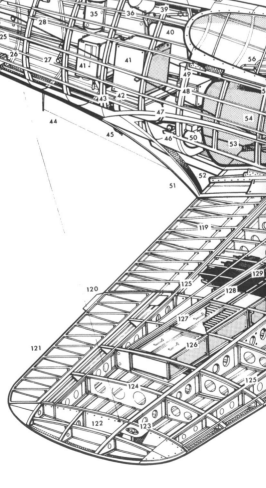

A Randolph Field-based *P-40E* illustrates the type's standard olive Drab paint scheme. The first of Warhawk variant to serve with the *USAAF* in Europe in 1942, the *P-40E* flew with a number of American squadrons in the Mediterranean theatre, but proved generally inferior to most other Allied fighters.

SPECIFICATION	
P-40E (Model H87-B2) Warhawk	**P-40N (Model H87-V) Warhawk**
Dimensions	**Dimensions**
Length: 31 ft 2 in (9.49 m) **Height:** 10 ft 7 in (3.22 m) **Wingspan:** 37 ft 3½ in (11.35 m) **Wing area:** 236 sq ft (21.92 m²)	**Length:** 33 ft 4 in (10.16 m) **Height:** 12 ft 4 in (3.75 m) **Wingspan:** 37 ft 3½ in (11.35 m) **Wing area:** 236 sq ft (21.92 m²)
Powerplant	**Powerplant**
One 1,150-hp (857-kW) Allison V-1710 inline piston engine	One 1,360-hp (1014-kW) supercharged Allison V-1710 inline piston engine
Weights	**Weights**
Empty: 6,350 lb (2880 kg) **Gross:** 8,280 lb (3756 kg) **Maximum take-off:** 9,200 lb (4173 kg)	**Empty:** 6,000 lb (2722 kg) **Gross:** 4,400 lb (2903 kg) **Maximum take-off:** 8,850 lb (4014 kg)
Fuel	**Fuel**
Normal: 147 Imp gal (558 litre) **Maximum:** 200 Imp gal (756 litre)	**Normal:** 122 Imp gal (462 litre) **Maximum:** 292 Imp gal (1105 litre)
Performance	**Performance**
Maximum speed (clean) at 15,000 ft (4572 m): 366 mph (589 km/h) **Climb to 15,000 ft (4572 m):** 7 min 36 seconds **Climb in one minute:** 2,050 ft (625 m) **Cruising speed:** 308 mph (496 km/h) **Speed for maximum range:** 190 mph (306 km/h) **Landing speed:** 82 mph (132 km/h) **Service ceiling:** 29,000 ft (8830 m) **Range:** 350 miles (563 km) **Maximum range:** 950 miles (1529 km)	**Maximum speed (clean) at 15,000 ft (4572 m):** 343 mph (552 km/h) **Climb to 15,000 ft (4572 m):** 6 min 42 seconds **Climb in one minute:** 2,120 ft (646 m) **Cruising speed:** 263 mph (423 km/h) **Speed for maximum range:** 198 mph (319 km/h) **Landing speed:** 85 mph (137 km/h) **Service ceiling:** 31,000 ft (9449 m) **Range:** 750 miles (1207 km) **Maximum range:** 1,400 miles (2253 km)
Armament	**Armament**
Six 0.5-in (12.7-mm) machine-guns in the wings; plus provision for six 20-lb (9 kg) bombs or one 500-lb (227 kg) bomb mounted under the fuselage	Six 0.5-in (12.7-mm) machine-guns in the wings; plus up to 700-lb (318-kg) of bombs

125 Multi (7)-spar wing structure
126 Inboard gun ammunition box (235 rounds)
127 Centre gun ammunition box (235 rounds)
128 Outboard gun ammunition box (235 rounds)
129 Three 0.50-in (12.7-mm) M-2 Browning machine-guns
130 Ammunition feed chute
131 Starboard wheel well
132 Wing centre section main fuel tank, capacity 42.1 Imp gal (191 litres)
133 Undercarriage attachment
134 Wing centre section reserve fuel tank, capacity 29.2 Imp gal (133 litres)
135 Retraction cylinder
136 Retraction arm/links
137 Machine-gun barrel forward support collars
138 Blast tubes
139 Bevel gear
140 Undercarriage side support strut
141 Gun warm air
142 500-lb (227-kg) bomb (ventral stores)
143 Undercarriage oleo leg fairing
144 Undercarriage fairing door
145 Machine/gun ports
146 Hydraulic brake line
147 One (or two) underwing 40-lb (18-kg) bomb(s)
148 Oleo leg

149 Torque links
150 Axle
151 30-in (782-mm) diameter smooth contour mainwheel tyre
152 Tow ring/jack point
153 Ventral auxiliary tank, capacity 43.3 Imp gal (195 litres)
154 Vent line
155 Sway brace pads
156 External fuel line
157 Shackle assembly
158 Filler neck
159 Alternative ventral 250 lb (114 kg) bomb with:
160 Extended percussion fuse

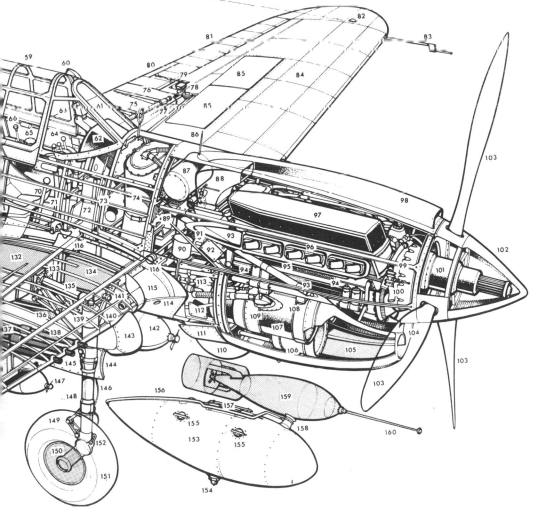

A quartet of *P-40F Warhawks* performs a classic fighter peel-off. The 'F' was identified by the lack of an intake above the engine, denoting the fitment of a Packard-built V-1650 Merlin engine. In total, 1,311 of this model were completed, many with a lengthened rear fuselage.

P-40E Warhawk

In 1941 Madam Chiang Kai-shek, the National Secretary of Aviation (regarded by many as the real power in Nationalist China) gave Brig. Gen. Claire L. Chennault – founder of the American Volunteer Group in China (AVG) – nearly $9 million via the China Defence Supplies Corporation to obtain the fighters he wanted. At the time, the standard fighter used by the AVG (later called the 'Flying Tigers') in China was the Curtiss P-36 Hawk. A batch of 100 P-40Cs had originally been intended for supply to Great Britain under Lend-Lease, but as they were not of a sufficiently high performance to take on German fighters over Western Europe, they were transferred to the Chinese air force, which in turn forwarded them to the AVG in the southern China/Burma area. The P-40s went into action for the first time during December 1941. Among these aircraft was this example flown by Lt Dallas Clinger. Flying with the 76th Fighter Squadron, 23rd Fighter Group, he achieved 'ace' status in the Chinese theatre, scoring five kills over Japanese aircraft.

Powerplant

The P-40E was powered by an Allison V-1710-39 12-cylinder inline engine, with an output of 1,150 hp (857 kW). Most P-40s were Allison-powered, although the P-40F (1,311 built) featured the Packard V-1650 licence-built Merlin. A long inlet duct which admitted air for the carburettor positioned at the rear of the engine was mounted prominently above the cowling. Just forward of the cockpit and the engine bulkhead was an oil tank, containing 10.8 Imp gal (49 litres). Immediately forward of this was an expansion tank for the coolant system, containing 2.9 Imp gal (13 litres). Cooling air for the three radiators mounted underneath the engine was admitted by a characteristic chin intake. The central unit cooled the oil, while the two outer radiators cooled glycol for the main cooling system.

Fuel and radio equipment

Fuel was held in three main internal tanks. The fuselage tank was located behind the cockpit in the lower fuselage, holding 51.5 Imp gal (234 litres). Two tanks were located in the centre section, the main one holding 42.1 Imp gal (191 litres), and a reserve holding 29.2 Imp gal (133 litres). From a point on the fin ran a cable antenna for the radio set, extending to the rear fuselage, wingtips and the prominent mast behind the cockpit. Equipment for the radio set was carried in the rear fuselage.

Cockpit

Despite the glazed rear-vision panels incorporated into the decking behind the pilot's headrest, the P-40 did not have good vision in the all-important rear quadrant. A mirror mounted on the canopy rail, offset to port, allowed the pilot to check his 'six'. The P-40E was provided with an electric reflector gunsight on top of the dashboard, providing range and offset information. If this unit failed, a back-up ring and bead sight was fitted to the upper fuselage decking for emergency use.

Tail surfaces and insignia

The large rudder and elevators were both balanced aerodynamically by horns. Trimming was by tabs, that on the rudder actuated by an external rod on the starboard side. 'Hold'n My Own' was a typically derisory tail marking which left no doubt as to the pilot's intentions. In reality, the P-40 was barely adequate in combat against Japanese fighters such as the Nakajima Ki-43 'Oscar' and Mitsubishi A6M 'Zeke', both of which possessed a much higher degree of manoeuvrability. However, a high level of training and superior tactics enabled AVG air crew to gain limited air superiority.

Wing surfaces

The wing was built up around three spars. A main spar was located at about quarter-chord, with two others mounted forward and aft of this. Leading-edge sections and trailing-edge control surfaces were attached to these spars. The wingtips were separate structures. Roll control was provided by simple tabbed ailerons, connected by cables to the control column, while the trailing-edge flaps were simple split units.

Undercarriage and wing guns

Fairings under the wing held the main undercarriage struts. The main wheels were held flat within the wing section, deploying forwards. The wheel had to rotate through 90° during the deployment process to be correctly aligned for landing. The P-40E introduced a six 0.50-in (12.7-mm) calibre machine-gun armament. Each gun had 235 rounds available, all armament held in quick-change boxes outboard of the guns. Many P-40s carried a centrally-mounted drop tank, holding 43.3 Imp gal (197 litres), to augment their internal fuel load. The normal range of the aircraft was in the region of 350 miles (563 km).

Dewoitine D.520

After a heroic, yet ultimately futile, effort against the superior Messerschmitt Bf 109 during the Battle of France, the D.520 found itself fighting alongside its former enemy against Allied Forces in North Africa.

Dewoitine D.520

Cutaway key
1 Cannon port
2 Spinner
3 Three-blade Ratier Electric propeller
4 Cannon barrel blast tube
5 Coolant water tank
6 Safety vent
7 Cowling forward frame
8 Auxiliary intake
9 Chin intake
10 Coolant piping
11 Oil cooler intake
12 Intake duct
13 Oil radiator
14 Engine bearer frames
15 Engine accessories
16 Exhaust stubs
17 Hispano-Suiza 12Y45 engine
18 Cowling rear frame
19 Cannon ammunition drum (60 rounds)
20 Oil tank
21 Starboard wing fuel tank
22 Wing skinning
23 Starboard navigation light
24 Starboard aileron
25 Aileron hinge
26 Emergency ring and bead gunsight
27 Fuselage main fuel tank
28 Fuselage main frame upper member
29 Engine bearer upper attachment
30 Bulkhead
31 20-mm HS 404 cannon breech
32 Compressor outlet

33 Extinguisher
34 Szydlowski compressor
35 Engine bearer support frame
36 Wing root fairing
37 Starboard mainwheel
38 Port mainwheel well
39 Ventral radiator bath intake

40 Undercarriage retraction mechanism
41 Mainwheel leg pivot
42 Wing machine-gun blast tubes
43 Machine-gun ports
44 Mainwheel leg
45 Port mainwheel
46 Mainwheel cover

47 Mainwheel leg door
48 Port wing fuel tank
49 Wing nose ribs
50 Pitot head
51 Port navigation light
52 Wingtip
53 Port aileron frame
54 Aileron hinge
55 Wing rear false spar
56 Wing skinning

57 Wing ribs
58 Two 7.5-mm MAC 1934 machine-guns
59 Ammunition feed
60 Wing main spar
61 Ammunition boxes (675 rpg)
62 Gun hot air
63 Radiator bath
64 Wing flap inboard profile

65 Radiator outlet flap
66 Port wing flap
67 Retractable radio aerial
68 Wing root fairing
69 Fuselage main frame lower member
70 Wing flap control linkage
71 Rudder pedal bar
72 Instrument panel
73 Command radio receiver

74 Control column grip
75 HF receiver
76 Windscreen
77 OPL RX 39 gunsight
78 Canopy track
79 Pilot's seat
80 Seat adjustment lever
81 Seat mounting frame

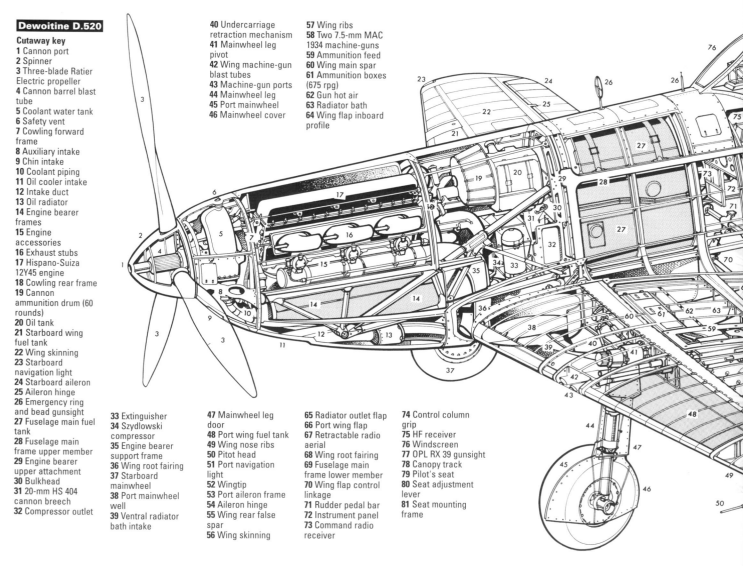

SPECIFICATION	
Dewoitine D.520	

Type

Single-seat fighter

Powerplant

One Hispano-Suiza 12Y-45 Vee piston engine rated at 935 hp (967 kW)

Performance

Maximum speed 332 mph (534 km/h) at 18,045 ft (5500 m); cruising speed 230 mph (370 km/h) at optimum altitude; climb to 13,125 ft (4000 m) in 5 minutes 48 seconds; service ceiling 34,450 ft (10500 m); range 950 miles (1530 km)

Weights

Empty 4,449 lb (2036 kg); maximum take off 5,902 lb (2677 kg)
Dimensions
wingspan 33 ft 5 1/2 in (10.20 m); length 28 ft 2 1/2 in (8.60 m); height 8 ft 5 1/4 in (2.57 m); wing area 171.91 sq ft (15.97 m2)

Armament

One 20-mm Hispano-Suiza HS-404 fixed forward-firing cannon between the engine's cylinder banks, and four 0.295-in (7.5-mm) MAC 34 M39 fixed forward-firing machine-guns in the leading edges of the wing

The extensive use of the D.520 by Luftwaffe fighter schools was an expression of the desperation faced by that service late in the war. Accident rates among the young students were high.

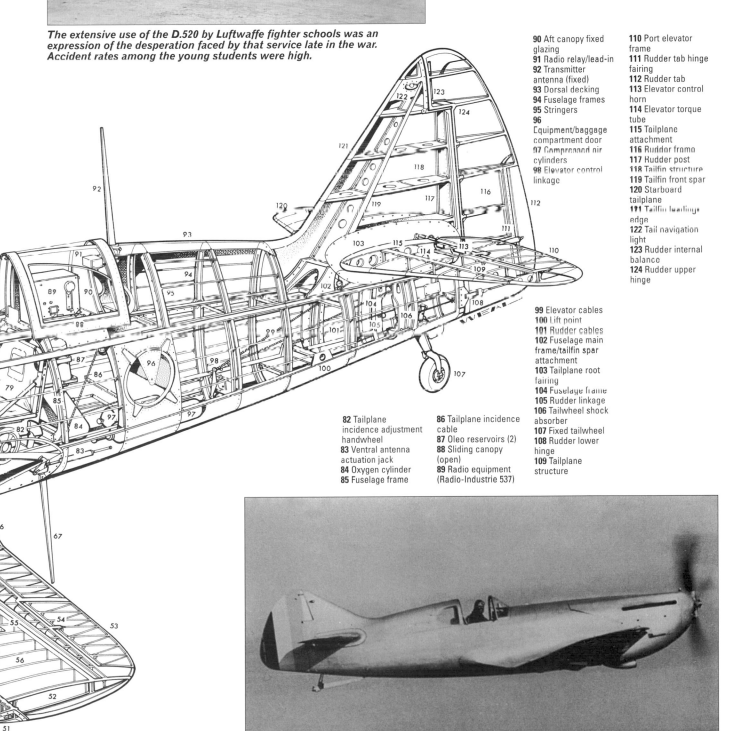

90 Aft canopy fixed glazing
91 Radio relay/lead-in
92 Transmitter antenna (fixed)
93 Dorsal decking
94 Fuselage frames
95 Stringers
96 Equipment/baggage compartment door
97 Compressed air cylinders
98 Elevator control linkage

110 Port elevator frame
111 Rudder tab hinge fairing
112 Rudder tab
113 Elevator control horn
114 Elevator torque tube
115 Tailplane attachment
116 Rudder frame
117 Rudder post
118 Tailfin structure
119 Tailfin front spar
120 Starboard tailplane
121 Tailfin leading edge
122 Tail navigation light
123 Rudder internal balance
124 Rudder upper hinge

99 Elevator cables
100 Lift point
101 Rudder cables
102 Fuselage main frame/tailfin spar attachment
103 Tailplane root fairing
104 Fuselage frame
105 Rudder linkage
106 Tailwheel shock absorber
107 Fixed tailwheel
108 Rudder lower hinge
109 Tailplane structure

82 Tailplane incidence adjustment handwheel
83 Ventral antenna actuation jack
84 Oxygen cylinder
85 Fuselage frame

86 Tailplane incidence cable
87 Oleo reservoirs (2)
88 Sliding canopy (open)
89 Radio equipment (Radio-Industrie 537)

Marcel Doret is seen at the controls of the first D.520 on its second flight on 8 October 1938. The short fin gave the type the appearance of a racer rather than a fighting machine.

Dornier Do335

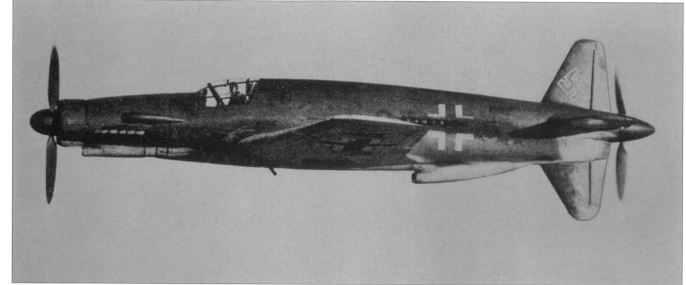

During initial tests at Oberpfaffenhofen and Rechlin, the Do 335 V1 demonstrated superb acceleration and generally good handling.

Dornier Do335

Cutaway key

1 Upper rudder trim tab
2 Upper rudder
3 Upper tailfin (jettisonable by means of explosive bolts)
4 VDM airscrew of 3.30 m (10.83 ft) diameter
5 Airscrew spinner
6 Airscrew pitch mechanism
7 Starboard elevator
8 Elevator tab
9 Metal stressed-skin tailplane
10 Ventral rudder
11 Tail bumper
12 Tail bumper oleo shock-absorber
13 Ventral tailfin (jettisonable for belly landing)
14 Coolant outlet
15 Rear navigation light
16 Explosive bolt seatings
17 Rudder and elevator tab controls
18 Hollow airscrew extension shaft
19 Rear airscrew lubricant feeds
20 Aft bulkhead
21 Coolant trunking
22 Oil cooler radiator
23 Coolant radiator
24 Fire extinguisher
25 Ventral air intake
26 FuG 25a IFF
27 FuG 125a blind landing receiver
28 Rear engine access cover latches
29 Exhaust stubs
30 Supercharger intake
31 Coolant tank
32 Engine bearer
33 Aft Daimler-Benz DB 603E-1 12-cylinder inverted-Vee liquid-cooled engine rated at 1340 kW (1,800 hp) for take-off and 1415 kW (1,900 hp) at 1800 m (5,905 ft)
34 Supercharger
35 Aft firewall
36 FuG 25a ring antenna
37 Fuel filler cap

38 Main fuel tank (1230-litre/270 Imp gal capacity)
39 Secondary ventral fuel tank
40 Two (45-litre/9.9-Imp gal capacity) lubricant tanks (port for forward engine and starboard for rear engine)
41 Pilot's back armour
42 Rearview mirror in glazed teardrop
43 Headrest
44 Pilot's armoured ejection seat
45 Clear-vision panel
46 Jettisonable canopy (hinged to starboard)
47 Protected hydraulic fluid tank (45-litre/9.9-Imp gal capacity)
48 Undercarriage hydraulics cylinder
49 Oxygen bottles
50 Port flaps
51 Aileron tab
52 Port wing fuel tank
53 Port aileron
54 Master compass
55 Pitot head
56 Twin landing lights
57 Cannon muzzle of 30-mm Rheinmetall Borsig MK 103
58 Cannon fairing

59 Ammunition tray
60 Windscreen
61 Port control console (trim settings)
62 Control column
63 Twin 20-mm Mauser MG 151/20 cannon
64 Ammunition box

65 Forward firewall
66 Breech of nose-mounted MK 103 cannon
67 Engine bearer
68 Forward DB 603E-1 engine
69 MG 151 cannon blast tubes
70 Gun trough
71 Hydraulically-operated cooling gills
72 Coolant radiator (upper segment)
73 Oil cooler radiator (lower segment)

74 VDM airscrew of 11,48 ft (3.50 m) diameter
75 Airscrew spinner
76 MK 103 cannon port
77 Armoured radiator ring

Ten pre-production Do 335A-0 fighter-bombers were completed, the second (illustrated) being evaluated in the US post-war.

SPECIFICATION

Dornier Do335

Type

Single-seat fighter-bomber

Powerplant

Two Daimler-Benz DB 603A-2 inverted Vee piston engines each rated at 1,750 hp (1305 kW)

Performance

Maximum speed 478 mph (770 km/h) at 21,000 ft (6400 m); cruising speed 426 mph (685 km/h) at 23,295 ft (7100 m); climb to 26,245 ft (8000 m) in 14 minutes 30 seconds; service ceiling 37,400 ft (11400 m); range 857 miles (1380 km)

Weights

Empty 16,314 lb (7400 kg); maximum take-off 21,164 lb (9600 kg)

Dimensions

Wingspan 45 ft 3¼ in (13.80 m); length 45 ft 5¼ in (13.85 m); height 16 ft 4¾ in (5.00 m); wing area 414.42 sq ft (38.50 m2)

Armament

One 30-mm MK 103 fixed forward-firing cannon between the cylinder banks of the forward engine and two 15-mm MG 151/15 fixed forward-firing cannon in the upper part of the forward fuselage, plus one 500-kg (1,102-lb) SC500 or two 250-kg (551-lb) SC250 bombs carried in a lower-fuselage weapons bay and two 250-kg (551-lb) SC250 bombs carried under the wing

78 Coolant tank (15-litre/3.3-Imp gal capacity)
79 Exhaust stubs
80 Nosewheel oleo leg
81 Nosewheel scissors
82 Damper
83 Nosewheel
84 Mudguard
85 Retraction strut
86 Nosewheel door
87 MK 103 cannon ammunition tray
88 Collector tray

89 Accumulator
90 Electric systems panel
91 Ejector seat compressed air bottles
92 Rudder pedals
93 Ammunition tray
94 Armour
95 Cannon fairing
96 MK 103 barrel
97 Muzzle brake
98 Ammunition feed chute

99 Starboard MK 103 wing cannon
100 Mainwheel retraction strut
101 Oleo leg
102 Starboard mainwheel
103 Mainwheel door
104 Forward face of box spar
105 Stressed wing skinning
106 Starboard navigation light

107 Wingtip structure
108 Starboard aileron
109 Aileron trim tab
110 Starboard wing fuel tank
111 Aileron control rod
112 Trim tab linkage
113 Oxygen bottles
114 Starboard flaps
115 Starter fuel tank
116 Flap hydraulic motor
117 Starboard mainwheel well

118 Boxspar
119 Compressed air bottles (emergency undercarriage actuation)
120 Mainspar/fuselage attachment points

Focke Wulf Fw 190

Restored in the markings of JG 3 'Udet', this Fw 190D-9 belongs to the US National Air and Space Museum. The 'Dora-9' was in most respects an excellent fighter at low level (acquiring the nickname 'Downstairs Maid') but by the time it appeared the Luftwaffe's fortunes were in a spiral descent from which there could be no recovery.

Fw 190A-8

Cutaway key
1 Pitot head
2 Starboard navigation light
3 Detachable wingtip
4 Pitot tube heater line
5 Wing lower shell floating rib
6 Aileron hinge points
7 Wing lower shell stringers
8 Leading-edge ribs
9 Front spar
10 Outermost solid rib
11 Wing upper shell stringers
12 Aileron trim tab
13 Aileron structure
14 Aileron activation/control linkage
15 Ammunition box (125 rpg)
16 Starboard 20-mm MG 151/20E wing cannon (sideways mounted)
17 Ammunition box rear suspension arm
18 Flap structure
19 Wing flap under skinning
20 Flap setting indicator peephole
21 Rear spar
22 Inboard wing construction
23 Undercarriage indicator
24 Wing rib strengthening
25 Ammunition feed chute
26 Static and dynamic air pressure lines
27 Cannon barrel
28 Launch tube bracing struts
29 Launch tube carrier strut
30 Mortar launch tube (auxiliary underwing armament)
31 Launch tube internal guide rails
32 21-cm (WfrGr 21) spin-stabilised Type 42 mortar shell

33 VDM three-bladed adjustable-pitch constant-speed propeller
34 Propeller boss
35 Propeller hub
36 Starboard undercarriage fairing
37 Starboard mainwheel
38 Oil warming chamber
39 Thermostat
40 Cooler armoured ring (0.25-in/6.5-mm)
41 Oil tank drain valve
42 Annular oil tank (12.1 Imp gal/55 litres)
43 Oil cooler
44 12-bladed engine cooling fan
45 Hydraulic-electric pitch control unit
46 Primer fuel line
47 Bosch magneto
48 Oil tank armour (0.22-in/5.5-mm)
49 Supercharger air pressure pipes
50 BMW 801D-2 14-cylinder radial engine
51 Cowling support ring
52 Cowling quick-release fasteners
53 Oil pump
54 Fuel pump (engine rear face)
55 Oil filter (starboard)
56 Wingroot cannon synchronisation gear
57 Gun troughs/cowling upper panel attachment
58 Engine mounting ring
59 Cockpit heating pipe
60 Exhaust pipes (cylinders 11-14)
61 MG 131 link and casing discard chute
62 Engine bearer assembly
63 MG 131 ammunition boxes (400 rpg)
64 Fuel filter recess housing

65 MG 131 ammunition cooling pipes
66 MG 131 synchronisation gear
67 Ammunition feed chute
68 Twin fuselage 13-mm MG 131 machine-guns
69 Windscreen mounting frame
70 Emergency power fuse and distributor box
71 Rear hinged gun access panel
72 Engine bearer/bulkhead attachment
73 Control column
74 Transformer
75 Aileron control torsion bar
76 Rudder pedals (EC pedal unit with hydraulic wheelbrake operation)
77 Fuselage/wing spar attachment
78 Adjustable rudder push rod
79 Fuel filler head
80 Cockpit floor support frame
81 Throttle lever
82 Pilot's seat back plate armour (0.31-in/8-mm)
83 Seat guide rails
84 Side-section back armour (0.19-in/5-mm)
85 Shoulder armour (0.19-in/5-mm)
86 Oxygen supply valve
87 Steel frame turnover pylon
88 Windscreen spray pipes
89 Instrument panel shroud
90 1.18-in/30-mm armoured glass quarterlights
91 1.96-in/50-mm armoured glass windscreen
92 Revi 16B reflector gunsight
93 Canopy
94 Aerial attachment
95 Headrest

96 Head armour (0.47-in/12 mm)
97 Head armour support strut
98 Explosive charge canopy emergency jettison unit
99 Canopy channel side
100 Auxiliary tank: fuel (25.2 Imp gal/115 litres) or GM-1 (18.7 Imp gal/85 litres)
101 FuG 16ZY transmitter-receiver unit
102 Handhold cover
103 Primer fuel filler cap
104 Autopilot steering unit (PKS 12)
105 FuG 16ZY power transformer
106 Entry step cover plate
107 Two tri-spherical oxygen bottles (starboard fuselage wall)
108 Auxiliary fuel tank filler point
109 FuG 25a transponder unit
110 Autopilot position integration unit
111 FuG 16ZY homer bearing converter
112 Elevator control cables
113 Rudder control DUZ flexible rods
114 Fabric panel (bulkhead 12)
115 Rudder differential unit
116 Aerial lead-in
117 Rear fuselage lift tube
118 Triangular stress frame
119 Tailplane trim unit
120 Tailplane attachment fitting
121 Tailwheel retraction guide tube

122 Retraction cable lower pulley
123 Starboard tailplane
124 Aerial
125 Starboard elevator
126 Elevator trim tab
127 Tailwheel shock strut guide
128 Fin construction
129 Retraction cable under pulley
130 Aerial attachment strut
131 Rudder upper hinge
132 Rudder structure

The first operational Fw 190s were sent to France to equip JG 2 and JG 26, which faced the RAF across the English Channel. These Fw 190As are from 7. Staffel/Jagdgeschwader 2 'Richthofen'. A feature of many Fw 190s was a painted design aft of the engine cowling to mask the prolific exhaust stains.

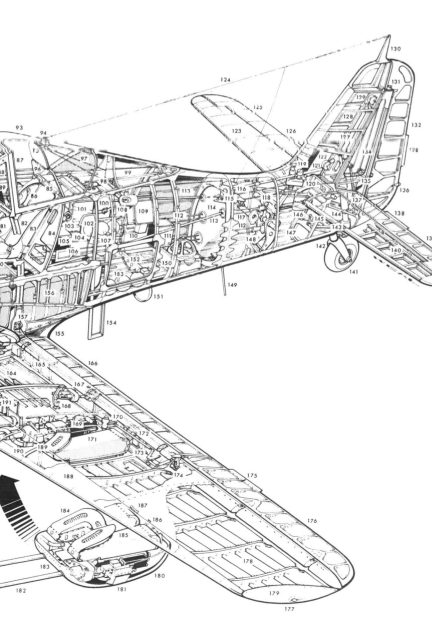

133 Rudder trim tab
134 Tailwheel retraction mechanism access panel
135 Rudder attachment/actuation fittings
136 Rear navigation light
137 Extension spring
138 Elevator trim tab
139 Port elevator structure
140 Tailplane construction
141 Semi-retracting tailwheel
142 Forked wheel housing
143 Drag yoke
144 Tailwheel shock strut
145 Tailwheel locking linkage
146 Elevator actuation lever linkage
147 Angled frame spar
148 Elevator differential bellcrank
149 FuG 25a ventral antenna
150 Master compass sensing unit
151 FuG 16ZY fixed loop homing antenna
152 Radio compartment access hatch
153 Single tri-spherical oxygen bottle (port fuselage wall)
154 Retractable entry step
155 Wingroot fairing
156 Fuselage rear fuel tank (64.5 Imp gal/293 litres)
157 Fuselage/rear spar attachment
158 Fuselage forward fuel tank (51 Imp gal/232 litres)
159 Port wingroot cannon ammunition box (250 rpg)

160 Ammunition feed chute
161 Port wingroot MG 151/20E cannon
162 Link and casing discard chute
163 Cannon rear mount support bracket
164 Upper and lower wing shell stringers
165 Rear spar
166 Spar construction
167 Flap position indicator scale and peephole
168 Flap actuating electric motor
169 Port 20-mm MG 151/20E wing cannon (sideways mounted)
170 Aileron transverse linkage
171 Ammunition box (125 rpg)
172 Ammunition box rear suspension arm
173 Aileron control linkage
174 Aileron control unit
175 Aileron trim tab
176 Port aileron structure
177 Port navigation light
178 Outboard wing stringers
179 Detachable wingtip
180 A-8/R1 variant underwing gun pack (in place of outboard cannon)
181 Link and casing discard chute
182 Twin unsynchronised 20-mm MG 151/20E cannon
183 Light metal fairing (gondola)
184 Ammunition feed chutes
185 Ammunition boxes (125 rpg)
186 Carrier frame restraining cord

187 Ammunition box rear suspension arms
188 Leading-edge skinning
189 Ammunition feed chute
190 Ammunition warming pipe
191 Aileron bellcrank
192 Mainwheel strut mounting assembly
193 EC-oleo shock strut
194 Mainwheel leg fairing
195 Scissors unit
196 Mainwheel fairing
197 Axle housing
198 Port mainwheel
199 Brake lines
200 Cannon barrel
201 FuG 16ZY Morane antenna
202 Radius rods
203 Rotating drive unit
204 Mainwheel retraction electric motor housing
205 Undercarriage indicator
206 Sealed air jack
207 BSK 16 gun camera
208 Retraction locking hooks
209 Undercarriage locking unit
210 Armament collimation tube
211 Camera wiring conduits
212 Wheel well
213 Cannon barrel blast tube
214 Wheel cover actuation strut
215 Ammunition hot air
216 Port inboard wheel cover
217 Wingroot cannon barrel
218 ETC 501 carrier unit
219 ETC 501 bomb rack
220 SC 500 bomb (500 kg/1,102 lb)

Fw 190F-2

First appearing in combat in the skies over France in September 1941, the Focke-Wulf Fw 190A was an unpleasant shock to the RAF, for this pugnacious-looking radial-engined fighter was clearly superior to the RAF's Spitfire Mk Vs. Enjoying a considerable period of dominance in the Western Front fighter v. fighter war, the type also came to be increasingly used as a fighter-bomber. This role was developed further with the Fw 190F series, which became dedicated close support aircraft and served with distinction on the Russian Front, where the type rapidly superseded the Junkers Ju 87 as the main Luftwaffe ground attack aircraft. Around 550 Fw 190F-1s, F-2s and F-3s were built between late 1942 and mid-1943. They were so successful that the F model was reinstated in production as the Fw 190F-8 in spring 1944, this version being based on the Fw 190A-8 and upgunned with 13-mm MG 131s in the upper fuselage. This aircraft is an Fw 190F-2 of 5. Staffel, II. Gruppe of Schlachtgeschwader 1, and is shown as it would have appeared in 1943 on the Russian Front.

Powerplant
The Fw 190 smashed the theory that only sleek inline-engined fighters could achieve good performance. The Fw 190F-2 was based on the Fw 190A-5 airframe, and featured the BMW 801D-2 powerplant. This engine developed 1,700 hp (1268 kW) for take-off and 1,440 hp (1074 kW) at 18,700 ft (5700 m). MW-50 water-methanol boosting was fitted as standard. Around the front of the engine was an annular oil cooler, and a 12-bladed cooling fan which built up pressure in the engine compartment. Cooling air was ejected at the rear of the cowling, downstream of the flush exhaust outlets.

Armament
Gun armament consisted of a pair of o.31-in (7.9-mm) MG 17 machine-guns in the upper fuselage decking, featuring a characteristic bulge over the breech block and each armed with 1,000 rounds. In each wingroot was a 20-mm MG 151/20 cannon with 200 rounds. A centreline ETC 250 bomb rack was used for a single 250-kg (551-lb) weapon or four 50-kg (110-lb) bombs on an ER 4 adaptor. Two ETC 50 racks (for 50-kg/110-lb) bombs could be fitted under each wing. In addition to standard SC 250 and SC 50 bombs, the Fw 190F regularly carried the AB 250 *splitterbombe* (cluster bomb) which could dispense a variety of sub-munitions. These included 224 SD 1, 144 SD 2, 30 SD 4 or 17 SD 10 anti-personnel/armour minelets, 184 B 1 incendiaries or 116 B 2 steel-nosed incendiaries. The widely-used SD 2 was the feared 'butterfly' bomb, which deployed small wings to slow its descent to earth.

Radio

The Fw 190F-2 used the FuG 16Z radio equipment, which had first been introduced to the family by the Fw 190A-4. The wire aerial stretched from a short mast on top of the fin to a spool mounted on the canopy. This was spring-loaded to take up the wire antenna when the canopy was slid backwards and to maintain tension in flight.

Cockpit

Well laid out and effectively armoured, the cockpit provided the pilot with good visibility in flight, but the broad nose and tail-down stance made ground visibility poor. Introduced on late Fw 190Fs was a bulged canopy which dramatically improved the pilot's view of the world.

Undercarriage

The stalky mainwheel units retracted inward to lie in the wingroots. In turn this gave the Fw 190 a very wide track, which made the aircraft very stable when operating from the primitive airstrips prevalent on the Russian Front. During the spring and autumn months, when the airstrips could turn into bogs, the lower undercarriage doors were often removed to prevent the wheels clogging with mud.

Markings

This Fw 190F-2 is finished in typical camouflage with a light grey base, two-tone splinter top surfaces and mottling along the fuselage. The Russian Front theatre markings consisted of a yellow fuselage band and yellow panels under the wingtips and cowling. The Schlachtgeschwadern originally used symbols as unit identifications, Schlachtgeschwader 1 employing a black triangle. The red colour of the individual aircraft code signified 5. Staffel, as did the red background to the unit badge and similarly-coloured spinner. The gun-toting Mickey Mouse badge was applied by all II./SchG 1 staffeln, and had been inherited from one of the Gruppe's predecessors – IV.(Schlacht)/Lehrgeschwader 2.

Fuel

Fuel was accommodated in two self-sealing tanks located beneath the pilot's seat. They were separated by the rear spar tie-through member (the Fw 190 was built using a very strong through-spar construction). The forward tank held 51 Imp gal (232 litres) while the rear tank held 64.5 Imp gal (293 litres).

Gloster Meteor

As the operational life of the Meteor began to draw to a close, a large number of Meteor F.Mk 8s was modified to become target-towing tugs and advanced trainers. The target tugs were unofficially designated 'F(TT).Mk 8' and the trainers 'T.Mk 8'. Both types received high-visibility markings and a 'T.Mk 8' of No. 85 Sqn, with bright orange Dayglo markings, is seen here accompanying a Lightning of No. 5 Sqn.

Meteor F.Mk III

Cutaway key
1 Starboard detachable wingtip
2 Starboard navigation light
3 Starboard recognition light
4 Starboard aileron
5 Aileron balance tab
6 Aileron mass balance weights
7 Aileron control coupling
8 Aileron torque shaft
9 Chain sprocket
10 Cross-over control runs
11 Front spar
12 Rear spar
13 Aileron (inboard) mass balance
14 Nacelle detachable tail section
15 Jet pipe exhaust
16 Internal stabilising struts
17 Rear spar 'spectacle' frame
18 Fire extinguisher spray ring
19 Main engine mounting frame
20 Engine access panel(s)
21 Nacelle nose structure
22 Intake internal leading-edge shroud
23 Starboard engine intake
24 Windscreen de-icing spray tube
25 Reflector gunsight
26 Cellular glass bulletproof windscreen
27 Aft-sliding cockpit canopy
28 Demolition incendiary (cockpit starboard wall)

29 RPM indicators (left and right of gunsight)
30 Pilot's seat
31 Forward fuselage top deflector skin
32 Gun wobble button
33 Control column grip

34 Main instrument panel
35 Nosewheel armoured bulkhead
36 Nose release catches (10)
37 Nosewheel jack bulkhead
38 Nose ballast weight location
39 Nosewheel mounting frames
40 Radius rod (link and jack omitted)
41 Nosewheel pivot bearings
42 Shimmy-damper/self-centring strut
43 Gun camera
44 Camera access
45 Aperture
46 Nose cone
47 Cabin cold-air intake
48 Nosewheel leg door
49 Picketing rings
50 Tension shock absorber
51 Pivot bracket
52 Mudguard
53 Torque strut
54 Doorhoop
55 Wheel fork
56 Retractable nosewheel
57 Nosewheel doors

58 Port cannon trough fairings
59 Nosewheel cover
60 Intermediate diaphragm
61 Blast tubes
62 Gun front mount rails
63 Pilot's seat pan

64 Emergency crowbar
65 Canopy de-misting silica gel cylinder
66 Bulletproof glass rear view cut-outs
67 Canopy track
68 Sea bulkhead
69 Entry step
70 Link ejection chutes

71 Case ejection chutes
72 20-mm Hispano Mk III cannon
73 Belt feed mechanism
74 Ammunition feed necks
75 Ammunition tanks
76 Aft glazing (magazine bay top door)

77 Leading ramp
78 Front spar bulkhead
79 Oxygen bottles (2)
80 Front spar carry-through
81 Tank bearer frames
82 Rear spar carry-through
83 Self-sealing (twin compartment) main fuel tank, capacity 165 Imp gal (750 litres) in each half

84 Fuel connector pipe
85 Return pipe
86 Drain pipes
87 Fuel filler caps
88 Tank doors (2)
89 T.R.1143 aerial mast
90 Rear spar bulkhead (plywood face)
91 Aerial support frame

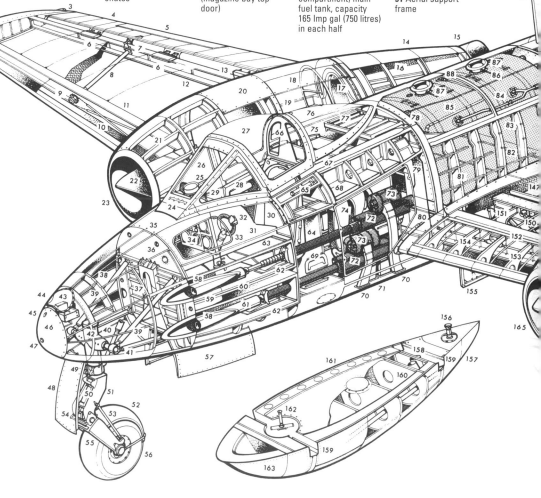

EE389 was the first Meteor involved in inflight-refuelling trials, in April 1949. Here it is seen, with its airbrakes deployed and probe clearly evident, about to refuel from a Lancaster Mk III tanker. The neat probe installation in the nose of the aircraft served as the basis of a similar fitting applied to a number of Mk 4s and Mk 8s.

SPECIFICATION

Meteor F.Mk 8

Dimensions

Length: 44 ft 7 in (13.59 m)
Wingspan: 37 ft 2 in (11.33 m)
Height: 13 ft (3.96 m)
Wing area: 350 sq ft (32.515 m²)
Aspect ratio: 3.9
Root chord: 11 ft 9 in (3.6 m)

Powerplant

Two 3,500-lb (15.5-kN) thrust Rolls-Royce Derwent 8 turbojets

Weights

Empty: 10,684 lb (4846 kg)
Maximum overload: 15,700 lb (7122 kg)

Performance

Maximum speed at sea level: 592 mph (953 km/h)
Maximum speed at 30,000 ft (9144 m): 550 mph (885 km/h)
Climb to 30,000 ft (9144 m): 6 minutes 30 seconds
Service ceiling: 44,000 ft (13410 m)
Range without wing drop tanks: 690 miles (1111 km)
Endurance at 40,000 ft (12192 m) with 420 Imp gal (1909 litres) of fuel: 592 mph (953 km/h)

Armament

Four fixed 20-mm British Hispano cannon in the nose with 195 rounds per gun

92 R.3121 (or B.C.966M IFF installation
93 Tab control cables
94 Amplifier
95 Fire extinguisher bottles (2)
96 Elevator torque shaft
97 T.R.1143 transmitter/ receiver radio installation
98 Pneumatic system filler
99 Pneumatic system (compressed) air cylinders
100 Tab cable fairlead
101 Elevator control cable
102 Top longeron
103 Fuselage frame
104 IFF aerial
105 DR compass master unit
106 Rudder cables
107 Starboard lower longeron

108 Cable access panels (port and starboard)
109 Tail section joint
110 Rudder linkage
111 Tail ballast weight location
112 Fin spar/fuselage frame
113 Rudder tab control
114 Fin structure
115 Torpedo fairing
116 Tailplane spar/upper fin attachment plates
117 Upper fin section
118 Starboard tailplane
119 Elevator horn and mass balance
120 Starboard elevator
121 Rudder horn and mass balance
122 Rudder upper hinge
123 Rudder frame

124 Fixed tab
125 Rear fairing
126 Tail navigation light
127 Elevator torque shaft
128 Elevator trim tab
129 Elevator frame
130 Elevator horn and mass balance
131 Tailplane structure
132 Rudder combined balance trim tab
133 Rudder lower section
134 Elevator push rod linkage
135 Rudder internal/ lower mass balance weight
136 Emergency landing tailskid
137 Tail section riveted joint
138 Port lower longeron
139 Fuselage stressed skin
140 Wingroot fairing
141 Inboard split flap
142 Airbrake (upper and lower surfaces)
143 Flap indicator transmitter
144 Rear spar
145 Inter-coupler cables (airbrake/airbrake and flap/flap)
146 Port mainwheel well
147 Roof rib station
148 Front diaphragm
149 Undercarriage beam
150 Undercarriage retraction jack
151 Undercarriage sidestay/downlock
152 Front spar
153 Nose ribs
154 Aileron control runs
155 Mainwheel door inner section
156 Ventral tank transfer pipe
157 Tank rear fairing
158 Filler stack pipes
159 Ventral tank attachment strap access doors
160 Anti-surge baffles
161 Fixed ventral fuel tank, capacity 105 Imp gal (477 litres)
162 Air pressure inlet
163 Tank front fairing

164 Port mainwheel
165 Starboard engine intake
166 Intake internal leading edge shroud
167 Auxiliary gearbox drives (vacuum pump/generator)
168 Nacelle nose structure
169 Starter motor
170 Oil tank
171 Rolls-Royce W.2B/23C Derwent I
172 Main engine mounting frame
173 Combustion chambers
174 Rear spar spectacle frame
175 Jet pipe thermo-coupling
176 Nacelle aft frames
177 Nacelle detachable tail section
178 Jet pipe suspension link
179 Jet pipe exhaust
180 Gap fairing tail section
181 Rear-spar outer wing fixing
182 Outer wing rib No. 1
183 Engine end rib
184 Engine mounting/ removal trunnion
185 Gap fairing nose section
186 Front-spar outer wing fixing
187 Nose ribs
188 Intermediate riblets
189 Wing ribs
190 Aileron drive chain sprocket
191 Aileron torque shaft
192 Retractable landing lamp
193 Port aileron
194 Aileron balance tab
195 Rear spar
196 Front spar
197 Pitot head
198 Port navigation light
199 Outer wing rib No. 10/wingtip attachment
200 Port recognition light

Meteor NF.Mk 12

RAF Fighter Command aircraft adopted colourful squadron markings during the 1950s, these replacing the two-letter codes which dated from the war years. A stylised adaptation of the traditional squadron badge was usually worn on the fin, with colourful bars flanking the roundel. No. 153 Squadron, of No. 11 Group based at RAF West Malling, Kent, used black-edged white bars, with inward-pointing red chevrons, and carried a version of the squadron's official bat and six pointed star on the fin. The flight markings of No. 153 Squadron came in the shape of coloured intake leading edges and fin bullet fairings. 'A' Flight used red as its identifying colour.

Cockpit

Like the NF.Mk 11, the Meteor NF.Mk 12 retained the same heavily framed, sideways-opening cockpit as the T.Mk 7 trainer. The port windscreen side panel was split diagonally and one portion could be opened to act as a direct vision panel if the canopy iced up. Although a handful of Meteor single-seaters was fitted with ejection seats, the two-seaters (including the night-fighters) were never thus equipped. Abandoning the aircraft was fraught with difficulties, and was impossible at low level.

Radome

With the arrival of the NF.Mk 12 the Meteor night-fighter lost its distinctive undernose bulge. This had housed the scanner mounting-bracket, which was redesigned on the APS.21. The Mk 12 used this American-built radar rather than the British AI Mk 10 used in the NF.Mk 11. This necessitated a slight increase in fuselage length (17 in/43 cm), and to balance this, an increase in fin area. This increase was obtained by adding fillets to the fin leading edge which faired towards into the leading-edge tailplane bullet fairing.

Armament

The Meteor night-fighters retained the same four British Hispano Mk V 20-mm cannon armament as the day-fighter and fighter-reconnaissance Meteors, but these were relocated to the wings, outboard of the engine nacelles. This was a major modification, as the cannon access doors had to be part of the stressed structure of the wings, which had to be strengthened to withstand this variant's higher IAS (Indicated Air Speed) limits. One hundred and sixty rounds of ammunition were carried for each gun in ammunition tanks further outboard.

Powerplant

The Meteor NF.Mk 12 was powered by a pair of 3,800-lb (16.9-kN) thrust Rolls-Royce Derwent 9s. These replaced the 3,600-lb (16-kN) Derwent 8s of the slightly lighter NF.Mk 11, and raised the limiting Mach number from 0.79 to 0.81, necessitating some airframe strengthening. The turbojets were fed by simple, round, pitot intakes, inside which the front spar continued unbroken, immediately ahead of the engine, enclosed in a fairing approximating in shape to the wing leading edge outboard of the engine nacelle. The NF.Mk 12 had the enlarged, so-called 'deep breather' intakes fitted to late F.Mk 8s.

Tail

Although they used the round-tipped wings of the early Meteors, the Meteor night-fighters had the square-cropped horizontal tailplanes of the F.Mk 8. These were fixed, with conventional trailing-edge elevators, and trim tabs inboard. The two-piece rudder, above and below the tailplane, was joined together by a torque tube, and acted as a single control surface. The lower section incorporated a manually adjustable trim tab.

Outer wing panels

Day-fighter Meteors after the F.Mk III had their outer wings redesigned with square-cropped wingtips and reduced span to improve roll-rate. The original outer wing was re-introduced on the photo-reconnaissance PR.Mk 10 and retained on the night fighters. The night fighters were originally to have had swept outer-wing panels, but this idea was soon abandoned.

Drop tanks

The Meteor could carry a single 100-Imp gal (455-litre) external fuel tank under each wing. These augmented the main tanks in the fuselage, immediately aft of the cockpit, which contained 325 Imp gal (1477 litres). A further 175 Imp gal (796 litres) could be carried in a bulged belly tank

Grumman F4F Wildcat

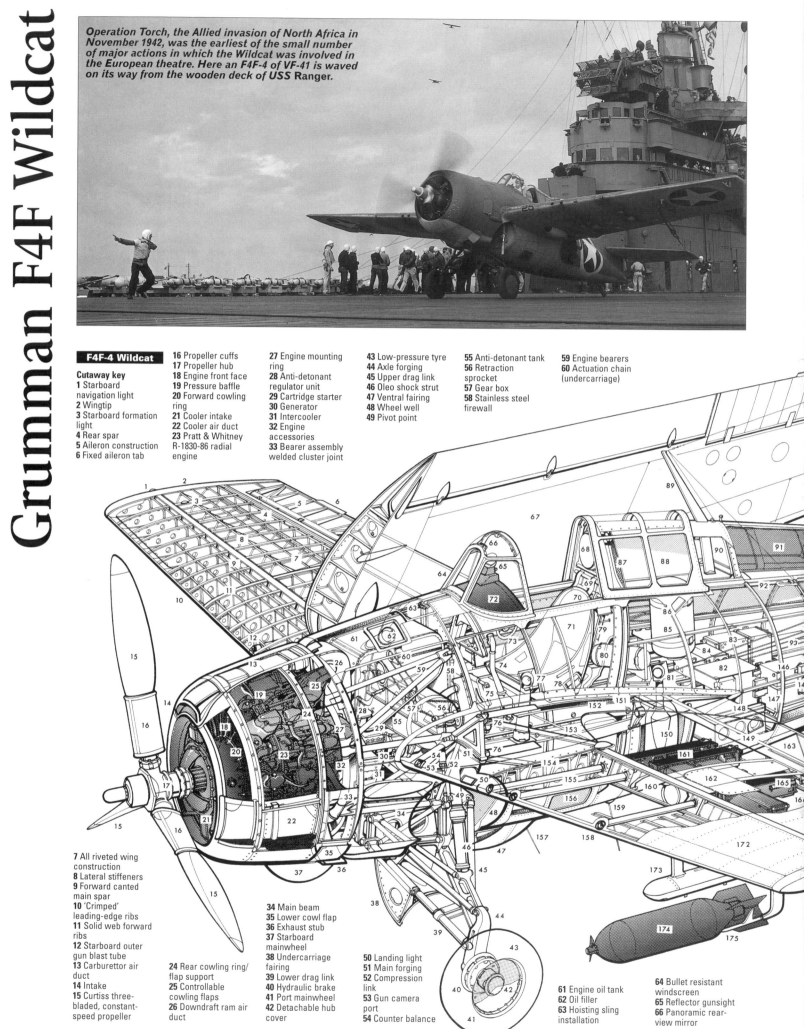

Operation Torch, the Allied invasion of North Africa in November 1942, was the earliest of the small number of major actions in which the Wildcat was involved in the European theatre. Here an F4F-4 of VF-41 is waved on its way from the wooden deck of USS Ranger.

F4F-4 Wildcat

Cutaway key
1 Starboard navigation light
2 Wingtip
3 Starboard formation light
4 Rear spar
5 Aileron construction
6 Fixed aileron tab
7 All riveted wing construction
8 Lateral stiffeners
9 Forward canted main spar
10 'Crimped' leading-edge ribs
11 Solid web forward ribs
12 Starboard outer gun blast tube
13 Carburettor air duct
14 Intake
15 Curtiss three-bladed, constant-speed propeller

16 Propeller cuffs
17 Propeller hub
18 Engine front face
19 Pressure baffle
20 Forward cowling ring
21 Cooler intake
22 Cooler air duct
23 Pratt & Whitney R-1830-86 radial engine
24 Rear cowling ring/flap support
25 Controllable cowling flaps
26 Downdraft ram air duct

27 Engine mounting ring
28 Anti-detonant regulator unit
29 Cartridge starter
30 Generator
31 Intercooler
32 Engine accessories
33 Bearer assembly welded cluster joint
34 Main beam
35 Lower cowl flap
36 Exhaust stub
37 Starboard mainwheel
38 Undercarriage fairing
39 Lower drag link
40 Hydraulic brake
41 Port mainwheel
42 Detachable hub cover

43 Low-pressure tyre
44 Axle forging
45 Upper drag link
46 Oleo shock strut
47 Ventral fairing
48 Wheel well
49 Pivot point
50 Landing light
51 Main forging
52 Compression link
53 Gun camera port
54 Counter balance

55 Anti-detonant tank
56 Retraction sprocket
57 Gear box
58 Stainless steel firewall
59 Engine bearers
60 Actuation chain (undercarriage)
61 Engine oil tank
62 Oil filler
63 Hoisting sling installation
64 Bullet resistant windscreen
65 Reflector gunsight
66 Panoramic rear-view mirror

122

The F4F-3S Wildcatfish was an attempt to produce a floatplane fighter in the same mould as the Japanese A6M2 'Rufe'. One hundred were ordered, but the aircraft's poor performance (including a top speed of 266 mph/428 km/h) led to their completion as conventional F4F-3 training aircraft.

SPECIFICATION

FM-2 Wildcat

Dimensions

Length: 28 ft 11 in (8.81 m)
Height: 9 ft 11 in (3.02 m)
Wingspan: 38 ft 0 in (11.58 m)
Wing area: 260 sq ft (24.15 m²)

Powerplant

One Wright R-1820-56/-56A or -56W/-56WA (with water injection) Cyclone 9 radial piston engine rated at 1,350 hp (1007 kW)

Weights

Empty: 5,448 lb (2471 kg)
Loaded: 7,487 lb (3396 kg)
Maximum take-off: 8,271 lb (3752 kg)

Fuel

Internal fuel: 117 US gal (443 litres)

Maximum external load: two 58-US gal (220-litre) drop tanks

Performance

Maximum speed at 28,800 ft (8780 m): 332 mph (534 km/h)
Cruising speed: 164 mph (264 km/h)
Climb rate: 3,650 ft (1113 m) per minute
Service ceiling: 34,700 ft (10577 m)

Range

Normal: 900 miles (1448 km)
Maximum: 1,310 miles (2108 km) with external fuel

Armament

Four wing-mounted 0.5-in (12.7-mm) Browning M2 machine-guns each with 430 rounds of ammunition, plus six underwing rocket projectiles or up to 500 lb (227 kg) of bombs

The Fleet Air Arm trialled the installation of rocket projectiles on a number of its fighter types, including the Wildcat. Experiments conducted at A&AEE Boscombe Down involved several machines, including this Wildcat Mk IV, with three 25-lb (11-kg) rockets beneath each wing. British Mk I rails (seen here) and American Mk V zero-length launchers were tested, with some success, between 1942 and 1944, but the weapon was never used operationally from FAA Wildcats.

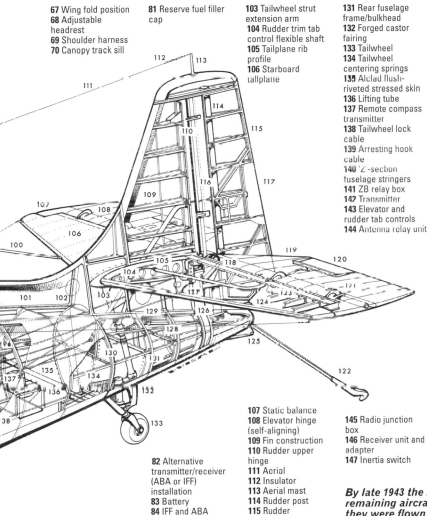

67 Wing fold position
68 Adjustable headrest
69 Shoulder harness
70 Canopy track sill

81 Reserve fuel filler cap

103 Tailwheel strut extension arm
104 Rudder trim tab control flexible shaft
105 Tailplane rib profile
106 Starboard tailplane

131 Rear fuselage frame/bulkhead
132 Forged castor fairing
133 Tailwheel
134 Tailwheel centering springs
135 Alclad flush-riveted stressed skin
136 Lifting tube
137 Remote compass transmitter
138 Tailwheel lock cable
139 Arresting hook cable
140 'Z'-section fuselage stringers
141 ZB relay box
142 Transmitter
143 Elevator and rudder tab controls
144 Antenna relay unit

82 Alternative transmitter/receiver (ABA or IFF) installation
83 Battery
84 IFF and ABA dynamotor units
85 Wing flap vacuum tank
86 Handhold
87 Turnover bar
88 Rearward-sliding Plexiglas canopy
89 Streamlined aerial mast
90 Mast support
91 One-man Mk IA life-raft stowage
92 Upper longeron
93 Toolkit
94 Aerial lead-in
95 Elevator and rudder control runs
96 'L'-section fuselage frames
97 IFF aerial
98 Dorsal lights
99 Whip aerial
100 Wing-fold jury strut
101 Fin fairing
102 Access panel

107 Static balance
108 Elevator hinge (self-aligning)
109 Fin construction
110 Rudder upper hinge
111 Aerial
112 Insulator
113 Aerial mast
114 Rudder post
115 Rudder construction
116 Aluminium alloy leading-edge
117 Rudder trim tab
118 Elevator torque tube
119 Port elevator
120 Elevator trim tab
121 Elevator hinge (self-aligning)
122 Arresting hook (extended)
123 Tailplane spar
124 Rear navigation light
125 Towing lug
126 Rudder torque tube support
127 Elevator control linkage
128 Rudder control cable
129 Arresting hook spring
130 Tailwheel shock strut

145 Radio junction box
146 Receiver unit and adapter
147 Inertia switch

148 Radio equipment support rack
149 Entry foothold
150 Reserve fuel tank, capacity 27 US gal (102 litres)
151 Fuselage/rear spar attachment
152 Wing hinge line
153 Main (underfloor) fuel tank, capacity 117 US gal (443 litres)
154 Stub wing end rib and fairing
155 Inboard gun blast tubes

156 Plexiglas observation panel
157 Ventral antenna
158 Outboard gun port
159 ZB antenna
160 Fixed D/F loop
161 Two 0.50-in (12.7-mm) Browning M2 machine-guns
162 Outboard gun access/loading panels
163 ABA antenna
164 Flap profile
165 Outboard 0.50-in (12.7-mm) Browning M2 machine-gun

166 Aileron control linkage
167 Aileron trim tab
168 Port aileron
169 Aileron hinges (self-aligning)
170 Port formation light
171 Port navigation light
172 Wing skinning
173 Bomb rack (optional)
174 Fragmentation bomb
175 Pitot head

71 Pilot's adjustable seat
72 Instrument panel shroud
73 Undercarriage manual crank
74 Control column
75 Rudder pedals
76 Fuselage/front spar attachment
77 Main fuel filler cap
78 Seat harness attachment
79 Back armour
80 Oxygen cylinder

By late 1943 the F4F-4 had disappeared from front-line service, the few remaining aircraft having been issued to training units in the US where they were flown by the next generation of Wildcat pilots, destined to fly the FM-2 in combat. Large fuselage codes identify these aircraft as training machines; the red 'star and bar' surrounds date the picture at between July and October 1943.

F4F-3 Wildcat

This F4F-3 carries the markings of Marine Corps Fighting Squadron 121 (VMF-121) and was flown by Bruce Porter during his time with the unit between September 1941 and February 1942, based at Tafuna, Samoa. Porter also flew Wildcats with VMF-441 and VMF-111 before returning to VMF-121 at Guadalcanal in March 1943. By then the squadron was equipped with F4U-1s and it was in a Corsair that he scored his first three Zero kills, plus a pair of 'probables'. Towards the end of the war in the Pacific, Porter achieved ace status with two bomber kills gained while flying F6F-5N Hellcat night-fighters with VMF(N)-542 from Okinawa. VMF-121 was the top-scoring Wildcat unit of the war, claiming 160 kills in all.

Powerplant

The XF4F-2 Wildcat prototype was first flown in 1937 powered by a 1,050-hp (783-kW) Pratt & Whitney R-1830-66 Twin Wasp (with single-stage, single-speed supercharging), but this engine suffered major teething problems (including crankshaft failures) and was replaced during the 1938 redesign of the aircraft with a 1,200-hp (895-kW) R-1830-76, with two-stage, two-speed supercharging. This more reliable powerplant was subsequently fitted to the first 100 F4F-3s, later aircraft being powered by the similarly-rated R-1830-86, with twin magnetos. Concerns that supplies of this engine could not be maintained led to a batch of 95 F4F-3As employing an R-1830-90 derivative, with a single-stage supercharger, but in the F4F-4 the R-1830-86 was reinstated.

Fuel stowage

Most Wildcat variants carried fuel in a 117-US gal (443-litre) main tank situated beneath the cockpit and in a 27-US gal (102-litre) emergency tank in the rear fuselage. The F4F-3 was able to carry a non-jettisonable 42-US gal (159-litre) external tank, flush-mounted under each wing, though this installation appears not to have been used in service. For ferrying purposes a number of USMC aircraft were modified in Hawaii, during 1942, to carry a single, jettisonable version of this tank under the centreline. A proper drop tank installation was designed for the F4F-4; a 58-US gal (220-litre) teardrop-shaped tank could be carried by this and subsequent variants. The F4F-7 long-range reconnaissance variant (of which just 21 were completed) had a rigid wing containing additional fuel tanks. With a total capacity of no less than 555 US gal (2101 litres), the F4F-7 had an endurance of 25 hours. As a safety measure, a special fuel dump system was also installed.

Wing folding

F4F-3s and G-36As for the Aéronavale did not have a folding mainplane. Known by Grumman as the 'sto-wing' this was introduced in the F4F-4 and was an important innovation, especially where the Wildcat was operated from small escort aircraft-carriers with limited (or even non-existent) below-deck space. In the XF4F-4 prototype wing folding was accomplished hydraulically, though this equipment was omitted in production aircraft, presumably to save weight. Aircraft-carrier capacity was improved by 150 per cent when aircraft with folding wings were embarked, the Wildcat's span being just 14 ft 4 in (4.37 m) in its folded state.

Offensive armament

In its original guise the XF4F-2 carried a pair of 0.5-in (12.7-mm) machine-guns in the upper engine cowling and had the option of another pair mounted in the wings. The first production F4F-3s had 0.3-in (7.62-mm) cowl-mounted guns and a pair of '50-calibers' in the wings, but most of these machines (including the aircraft depicted here) dispensed with the cowl guns and were fitted with four wing-mounted '50s' instead. In the F4F-4 armament was improved, each wing carrying three 0.5-in (12.7-mm) machine-guns, a pair near the wing fold and another further outboard. The General Motors-built FM-1 derivative had four guns (with more rounds per weapon) and this configuration was continued in the XF4F-8 (FM-2) as a weight-saving measure. The F4F-7 reconnaissance variant was unarmed.

Undercarriage

The Wildcat's undercarriage was very similar in configuration to that of Grumman's earlier amphibian and FF/SF, F2F and F3F fighter designs, and retracted into the sides of the lower forward fuselage. Gear retraction was a manual operation, requiring 30 full turns of a hand crank in the cockpit. This operation required the F4F's pilot to change hands on the stick during take-off, often resulting in 'porpoising' as the pilot attempted to maintain control.

Grumman F6F Hellcat

The Hellcat remained in USN service following the conclusion of the Pacific war, in particular with units from the Naval Air Reserve. Additional war-surplus airframes were converted to unmanned F6F-5K status, with wingtip camera pods for the tracking of air-to-air missiles (AAMs) and surface-to-air missiles (SAMs).

F6F-5 Hellcat

Cutaway key

1 Radio mast
2 Rudder balance
3 Rudder upper hinge
4 Aluminium alloy fin ribs
5 Rudder post
6 Rudder structure
7 Rudder trim tab
8 Rudder middle hinge
9 Diagonal stiffeners
10 Aluminium alloy elevator trim tab
11 Fabric-covered (and taped) elevator surfaces
12 Elevator balance
13 Flush-riveted leading-edge strip
14 Arrester hook (extended)
15 Tailplane ribs
16 Tail navigation (running) light
17 Rudder lower hinge
18 Arrester hook (stowed)
19 Fin main spar lower cut-out
20 Tailplane end rib
21 Fin forward spar
22 Fuselage/finroot fairing
23 Port elevator
24 Aluminium alloy-skinned tailplane
25 Section light
26 Fuselage aft frame
27 Control access
28 Bulkhead
29 Tailwheel hydraulic shock-absorber
30 Tailwheel centring mechanism
31 Tailwheel steel mounting arm
32 Rearward-retracting tailwheel (hard rubber tyre)
33 Fairing
34 Steel plate door fairing
35 Tricing sling support tube
36 Hydraulic actuating cylinder
37 Flanged ring fuselage frames
38 Control cable runs

39 Fuselage longerons
40 Relay box
41 Dorsal rod antenna
42 Dorsal recognition light
43 Radio aerial
44 Radio mast
45 Aerial lead-in
46 Dorsal frame stiffeners
47 Junction box
48 Radio equipment (upper rack)
49 Radio shelf
50 Control cable runs

51 Transverse brace
52 Remote radio compass
53 Ventral recognition lights (three)
54 Ventral rod antenna
55 Destructor device
56 Accumulator
57 Radio equipment (lower rack)
58 Entry hand/footholds
59 Engine water injection tank
60 Canopy track
61 Water filler neck
62 Rear-view window
63 Rearward-sliding cockpit canopy (open)
64 Headrest
65 Pilot's head/shoulder armour
66 Canopy sill (reinforced)
67 Fire extinguisher
68 Oxygen bottle (port fuselage wall)
69 Water tank mounting
70 Underfloor self-sealing fuel tank (60 US gal/227 litres)
71 Armoured bulkhead
72 Starboard console
73 Pilot's seat
74 Hydraulic handpump

75 Fuel filler cap and neck
76 Rudder pedals
77 Central console
78 Control column
79 Chart board (horizontal stowage)
80 Instrument panel
81 Panel coaming
82 Reflector gunsight
83 Rear-view mirror

84 Armoured glass windshield
85 Deflection plate (pilot forward protection)
86 Main bulkhead (armour-plated upper section with hoisting sling attachments port and starboard)
87 Aluminium alloy aileron trim tab
88 Fabric-covered (and taped) aileron surfaces
89 Flush-riveted outer wing skin
90 Aluminium alloy sheet wingtip (riveted to wing outer rib)
91 Port navigation (running) light
92 Formed leading-edge (approach/landing light and camera gun inboard)
93 Fixed cowling panel
94 Armour plate (oil tank forward protection)
95 Oil tank (19 US gal/72 litres)
96 Welded engine mount fittings

97 Fuselage forward bulkhead
98 Aileron control linkage
99 Engine accessories bay
100 Engine mounting frame (hydraulic fluid reservoir attached to port frames)
101 Controllable cooling gills

102 Cowling ring (removable servicing/access panels)
103 Pratt & Whitney R-2800-10W twin-row radial air-cooled engine
104 Nose ring profile
105 Reduction gear housing

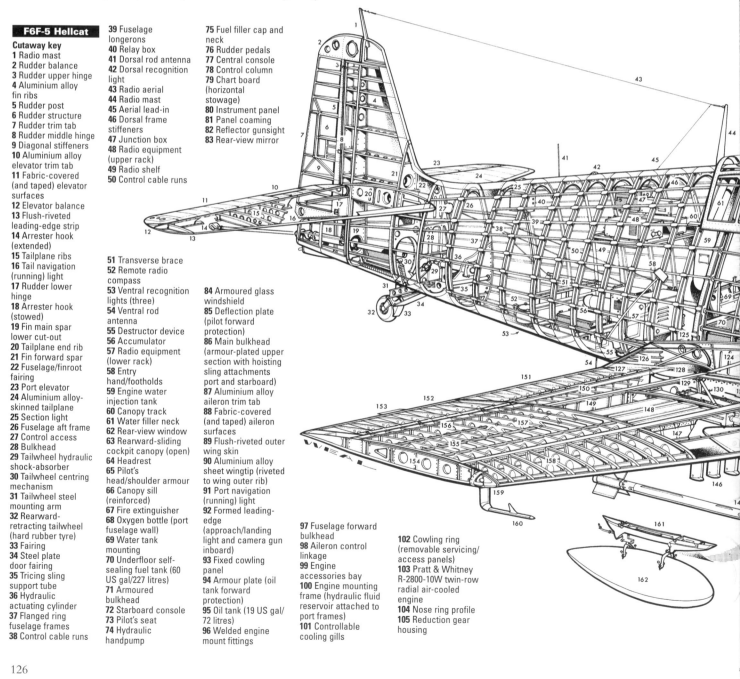

F6F-5 Hellcat

Dimensions

Span: 42 ft 10 in (13.08 m)
Span (wings folded): 16 ft 2 in (4.93 m)
Length: 33 ft 7 in (10.23 m)
Height: 13 ft 1 in (3.99 m)
Wing area: 334 sq ft (31.03 m²)
Wing loading: 38.17lb/sq ft (410.87 kg/m²)

Powerplant

One 2,200-hp (1641-kW) Pratt & Whitney R-2800-10W Double Wasp 18-cylinder radial piston engine

Weights

Empty: 9,153 to 9,239 lb (4152 to 4191 kg)
Normal take-off: 12,500 lb (5670 kg)
Maximum take-off: 15,413 lb (6991 kg)

Fuel

Internal fuel: 250 US gal (66 litres)
External fuel: 150 US gal (39 litres)

Performance

Maximum speed at medium altitude: 386 mph (621 km/h)
Initial climb rate (clean): 3,410 ft (1039 m) per minute
Service ceiling: 37,300 ft (11369 m)
Cruising speed: 168 mph (270 km/h)
Time to altitude: 7 min 30 secs to 20,000 ft (6096 m)

Range

Range on internal fuel: 1,040 miles (1674 km)

Armament

Six 0.5-in (12.7-mm) Browning machine-guns each with 400 rounds, plus provision for two or three bombs up to a maximum total of 2,000 lb (907 kg), plus up to six 5-in (127-mm) High Velocity Aircraft Rockets (HVAR)

Five VF-6 F6F-3 Hellcats are seen on the flight deck of the USS Intrepid (CV-11). Pictured during February 1944, off the Marshall Islands, the unit claimed a total of 14.66 kills during that year alone. VF-6 Hellcat aces included F. J. Blair with five kills before being killed in action; C. J. Chambers with 5.3; T. T. Coleman Jr with 10 kills (he also saw service with VF-83); H. G. Odenbrett with seven victories; J. D. Robbins with five victories and the legendary Alex Vraciu with 19 aerial victories.

106 Three-bladed Hamilton Standard Hydromatic controllable-pitch propeller
107 Propeller hub
108 Engine oil cooler (centre) and supercharger intercooler
109 Oil cooler deflection plate under-protection
110 Oil cooler duct
111 Intercooler intake duct
112 Mainwheel fairing
113 Port mainwheel
114 Auxiliary tank support/attachment arms
115 Cooler outlet and fairing
116 Exhaust cluster
117 Supercharger housing
118 Exhaust outlet scoop
119 Wing front spar web
120 Wing front spar/fuselage attachment bolts
121 Undercarriage mounting/pivot point on front spar
122 Inter-spar self-sealing fuel tanks (port and starboard: 87.5 US gal (133 litres) each)
123 Wing rear spar/fuselage attachment bolts

124 Structural end rib
125 Slotted wing flap profile
126 Wing flap centre-section
127 Wing fold line
128 Starboard wheel well (doubler-plate reinforced edges)
129 Gun bay
130 Removable diagonal brace strut
131 Three 0.5-in (12.7-mm) Colt Browning machine-guns
132 Auxiliary tank aft support
133 Blast tubes
134 Folding wing joint (upper surface)
135 Machine-gun barrels
136 Fairing
137 Undercarriage actuating strut
138 Mainwheel leg oleo hydraulic shock strut
139 Auxiliary tank sling/brace
140 Long-range auxiliary fuel tank (jettisonable)
141 Mainwheel aluminium alloy fairing
142 Forged steel torque link
143 Low pressure balloon tyre
144 Cast magnesium wheel
145 Underwing 5-in (12.7-cm) air-to-ground RPS
146 Mark V zero length rocket launcher installation
147 Canted wing front spar
148 Inter-spar ammunition box bay (lower surface access)
149 Wing rear spar (normal to plane of wing)
150 Rear sub spar
151 Wing flap outer-section
152 Frise type aileron
153 Aileron balance tab
154 Wing outer rib
155 Wing lateral stiffeners
156 Aileron spar
157 Wing outer-section ribs
158 Leading-edge rib cut-outs
159 Starboard navigation (running) light
160 Pitot head
161 Underwing stores pylon (mounted on fixed centre-section inboard of mainwheel leg)
162 Auxiliary fuel tank

VF-16 Hellcats are pictured aboard USS Randolph (CV-15) in March 1945. Later that year the unit would prove to be the second most successful F6F squadron operator, with 18 kills between July and August 1945, putting it just one behind the leading VF-31, aboard the Belleau Wood.

F6F-5P Hellcat

Incorporating a rear fuselage camera installation, the Grumman F6F-5P was unique among Hellcat variants in possessing a limited tactical reconnaissance capability. This example served with Fighter Squadron VF-84, aboard the carrier USS *Bunker Hill*, during February 1945. The aircraft is depicted as it appeared during raids on Tokyo, when the Hellcats involved wore a distinctive yellow cowling, repainted in midnight blue following the campaign. A pre-dawn launch on 16 February began the series of strikes on Tokyo, led by 16 aircraft-carriers, whose often inexperienced Hellcat pilots met the opposition in great numbers. USS *Bunker Hill* operated a mixture of VF-84's Hellcats, as well as two Marine F4U Corsair units, making its major combat debut over Tokyo. The Hellcat unit that saw most action over the Japanese capital during the first days of the operation was the 'Vipers' of VF-80, who claimed 24 aircraft on the morning of the 16th, when one of the unit's pilots, Lt A. L. Anderson, destroyed four different aircraft types – two 'Oscars', one 'Tojo', one 'Tony' and a Zero.

Wing and tail structure

The Hellcat's robust wing was comprised of two strong central spars, the outer panels of which folded backwards, skewing through 90° in order to lie flat against the rear fuselage. Outboard of the wing-fold mechanism for carrier stowage, the Hellcat wing featured a slight dihedral. The fin and tailplane were both built around a single central spar for structural strength, the part of the spar that comprised the fin running from the fintip to the bottom of the fuselage. The rudder carried a small balance near the top, and a central tab. The fixed section of the fin carried a radio mast. Full-span elevators on the tailplane had tabs, and were slotted to allow the uninterrupted movement of the rudder.

Wing-mounted weapons

Typical fixed armament for the Hellcat comprised six 0.5-in (12.7-mm) Browning machine-guns. Mounted in a staggered formation, each weapon was armed with 400 rounds of ammunition. Later production F6F-5s often replaced two of the machine-guns with two 20-mm cannon. In addition to the six Brownings, this Hellcat carries a load of six 5-in (127-mm) rocket projectiles, mounted on Mk V zero-length launch rails. A favourite ground-attack weapon of the Hellcat units during the latter stages of the Pacific war, the unguided rockets were heavily utilised during the assaults on Iwo Jima and Okinawa.

Reconnaissance equipment and undercarriage

Ahead of the 'sting'-type arrester hook that projected from the extreme rear of the fuselage was the camera installation, unique to the F6F-5P. This sloped downwards on the port side of the rear fuselage underside. Around 200 of the 8,100 F6F-5 airframes built were equipped with this reconnaissance package. Other equipment situated in the rear fuselage included radio and navigation systems aft of the cockpit, and a radio compass further back on the floor of the rear fuselage. The Hellcat's undercarriage was developed to withstand the punishment imposed by carrier operations, and comprised a single main oleo that rotated through 90° to lie flat within the wing structure. The tailwheel unit was also fully retractable.

Cockpit and systems

The Hellcat pilot was seated high in the fuselage under a sliding canopy. Well protected by armour plating, particularly at his rear, the pilot did, however, suffer from poor rear quadrant visibility. A reflector gunsight ahead of him enabled the pilot to aim his weapons. Distinctive external systems included the starboard wingtip air speed indicator pitot head, mounted in the undisturbed airflow beneath the wingtip, just by the starboard wingtip navigation light. The radio aerial, stretched between the fintip mast and dorsal mast, led to the rear fuselage equipment bay. The F6F-5 introduced an upright dorsal mast, as opposed to the forward-sloping mast of the F6F-3.

Powerplant and fuel

The F6F-5 Hellcat was powered by a single Pratt & Whitney R-2800-10W Double Wasp radial engine, with two rows of nine cylinders each. Developing 2,200 hp (1641 kW), the unit was angled down by three degrees to allow the fitment of a zero-incidence wing. The engine drove a three-bladed Hamilton Standard Hydromatic controllable-pitch propeller, ahead of a reduction gear housing. Internal self-sealing fuel tanks under the cockpit and in the inner wing structure carried a total of 235 US gal (889 litres). Tanks were filled through fuselage side and wingroot caps.

Colour scheme

The standard Pacific colour scheme of Non-Specular Sea Blue over Intermediate Blue had given way later in the war to just Specular Blue, which has been weathered here by hectic periods of maritime combat. White fin markings reveal the individual unit of the aircraft, in this case VF-84.

External loads

The later F6F variants were capable of carrying up to 2,000 lb (907 kg) of external stores, although all models were equipped to carry a single 150-US gal (500-litre) auxiliary fuel tank, slung under the fuselage centreline. Another later variant, the F6F-5N, was equipped with night-interception radar, carried in a starboard wing-mounted pod. The faired-in housing contained the AN/APS-6 centrimetric radar, the scope of which was mounted on the centre of the pilot's instrument panel. Pilot radar controls allowed alteration of the radome calibration, signal level adjustment, and the changing of the focus and intensity of the received image.

Intakes and exhaust

Three auxiliary intakes situated beneath the main cowling fed cool air to the engine oil supply (centre section), and the supercharger (two side sections). The main aperture cooled the engine, aided by a series of cooling gills on the rear of the cowling, which promoted a greater flow of air through the engine at low speeds, particularly for the rear row of cylinders. Cylinder exhaust gases were collected in ducts prior to passage through a cluster of exhausts on either side of the engine. These ejected the exhaust fumes from under the rear of the engine cowling and into shallow troughs.

Hawker Hurricane

Having served their time with operational squadrons, early-production Hurricane Mk Is often found their way into training units, in this case the Empire Central Flying School, Hullavington. This unarmed Hurricane Mk IA (seen with a pair of Spitfire Mk IIAs) was on charge with the ECFS in 1942.

Hurricane Mk I

Cutaway key
1 Starboard navigation light
2 Wingtip fairing
3 Fabric-covered aileron
4 Aluminium alloy wing skin panelling
5 Aileron hinge control
6 Starboard outer wing panel
7 Inboard torsion box heavy-gauge skin panel
8 Starboard landing lamp
9 Rotol three-bladed propeller
10 Spinner
11 Propeller hub pitch change mechanism
12 Spinner back plate
13 Propeller reduction gearbox
14 Cowling fairing
15 Starboard machine-gun muzzles
16 Upper engine cowling
17 Coolant pipes
18 Rolls-Royce Merlin III 12-cylinder liquid-cooled Vee engine
19 Exhaust stubs
20 Engine-driven generator
21 Forward engine mounting
22 Ignition control unit
23 Engine bearer struts
24 Lower engine cowlings
25 Starboard mainwheel
26 Manual-type inertia starter
27 Hydraulic pumps
28 Carburettor air intake
29 Cooling air scoop
30 Rear engine mounting
31 Single-stage supercharger
32 Port magneto

33 Coolant system header tank
34 External bead sight
35 Coolant filler cap
36 Starboard wing gun bay
37 Ammunition magazines
38 Starboard Browning 0.303-in (7.7-mm) machine-guns (4)
39 Fuel filler cap
40 Engine bay canted bulkhead
41 Rear engine mounting struts
42 Pneumatic system air bottle (gun firing)
43 Wing spar centre-section carry-through
44 Lower longeron/wing spar joint
45 Rudder pedals
46 Pilot's foot boards
47 Control column linkage
48 Fuselage (reserve) fuel tank, capacity 28 Imp gal (127 litre)
49 Fuel tank bulkhead
50 Control column hand grip
51 Instrument panel
52 Reflector gunsight
53 Starboard split trailing-edge flap
54 Bulletproof windscreen panel
55 Canopy internal handle
56 Rear view mirror
57 Sliding cockpit canopy cover
58 Plexiglass canopy panels
59 Canopy framework
60 Canopy external handle
61 Starboard side 'break-out' emergency exit panel
62 Safety harness
63 Seat height adjustment lever
64 Oxygen supply cock

65 Engine throttle lever
66 Elevator trim tab control handwheel
67 Oil pipes to radiator
68 Radiator flap control lever
69 Cockpit section tubular fuselage framework
70 Coolant system piping
71 Pilot's oxygen cylinder
72 Boarding step
73 Seat back armour
74 Pilot's seat
75 Armoured headrest
76 Turn-over crash pylon struts
77 Canopy rear fairing construction
78 Sliding canopy rail
79 Battery
80 TR 9D radio transmitter/receiver
81 Radio shelf
82 Downward identification light
83 Flare launch tube
84 Handgrip
85 Plywood skin panel
86 Dorsal fairing stringers
87 Upper identification light
88 Aerial mast
89 Aerial lead-in
90 Wooden dorsal section formers
91 Fuselage upper longeron
92 Rear fuselage fabric covering

93 Aluminium alloy tailplane leading edge
94 Starboard fabric-covered tailplane
95 Fabric-covered elevator
96 Aluminium alloy fin leading edge
97 Forward fin mounting post
98 Tailplane spar attachment joint
99 Elevator hinge control
100 Fin rib construction
101 Tailfin fabric covering
102 Diagonal bracing strut

103 Stern post
104 Rudder mass balance weight
105 Aileron cable
106 Rear aerial mast
107 Fabric-covered rudder
108 Aluminium alloy rudder framework
109 Tail navigation light
110 Rudder tab
111 Elevator trim tab
112 Port elevator rib construction
113 Elevator horn balance
114 Port tailplane rib construction
115 Diagonal spar bracing struts
116 Rudder control horn
117 Tail control access panel
118 Ventral tailwheel fairing
119 Fixed, castoring tailwheel
120 Dowty shock absorber tailwheel strut

121 Ventral fin framework
122 Lifting bar socket
123 Aluminium alloy lateral formers
124 Tail control cables
125 Rear fuselage tubular framework
126 Diagonal wire bracing
127 Lateral stringers
128 Fuselage lower longeron
129 Pull-out boarding step
130 Wing root trailing-edge fillet
131 Ventral access hatch
132 Walkway
133 Flap hydraulic jack
134 Inner wing panel rear spar
135 Outer wing panel spar attachment joint
136 Gun heater air duct
137 Wing panel joint cover strip

138 Flap shroud ribs
139 Port split trailing-edge flap
140 Aluminium alloy aileron rib construction
141 Port fabric-covered aileron
142 Aileron hinges
143 Wingtip fairing construction
144 Port navigation light
145 Leading-edge nose ribs
146 Front spar
147 Intermediate spars
148 Ventral pitot head
149 Rear spar
150 Aluminium alloy wing rib construction
151 Wing stringers
152 Port landing lamp

153 Inboard double-web strengthened spar section
154 Outboard ammunition magazines, 338 rounds each

155 Port Browning 0.303-in (7.7-mm) machine-guns (4)
156 Inboard ammunition magazines, 324 and 338 rounds

Twelve-gun Hurricane Mk IIBs of No. 601 (County of London) Squadron are seen over the English countryside, some time in 1941. This Royal Auxiliary Air Force unit operated Mk IIBs for most of 1941, on sweeps over the English Channel and escort sorties. Towards the end of the year, it began its short stint as the only operational RAF Bell P-39 Airacobra unit. Later, the unit was equipped with Spitfires and served with distinction in the Mediterranean.

157 Diagonal gun bay ribs
158 Gun barrel blast tubes
159 Machine-gun muzzles
160 Main undercarriage leg strut
161 Oleo pneumatic shock absorber strut
162 Port mainwheel
163 Mainwheel leg fairing
164 Side-locking strut
165 Main undercarriage leg pivot fixing
166 Outer wing panel front spar bolted joint
167 Fuel filler cap

168 Port wing main fuel tank, capacity 34.5 Imp gal (157 litre)
169 Centre-section strut framework
170 Ventral oil and coolant radiator
171 Main undercarriage wheel bay
172 Oil tank attachments
173 Mainwheel hydraulic retraction jack
174 Oil filler cap
175 Leading-edge oil tank, capacity 9 Imp gal (41 litre), port side only

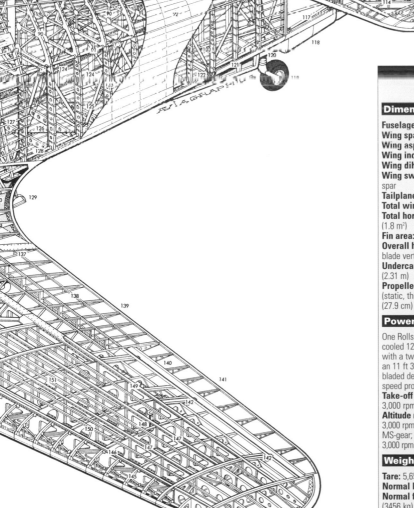

SPECIFICATION

Hurricane Mk IIC

Dimensions

Fuselage length: 32 ft 2¼ in (9.81 m)
Wing span: 40 ft (12.19 m)
Wing aspect ratio: 6.2
Wing incidence: 2
Wing dihedral angle: 3.5˚
Wing sweepback angle: 3˚ on front spar
Tailplane span: 11 ft (3.35 m)
Total wing area: 258 sq ft (23.97 m²)
Total horizontal tail area: 19.6 sq ft (1.8 m²)
Fin area: 8.82 sq ft (0.82 m²)
Overall height: (Rotol propeller, top blade vertical) 12 ft 11½ in (3.95 m)
Undercarriage track: 7 ft 7 in (2.31 m)
Propeller ground clearance: (static, thrust line horizontal) 11 in (27.9 cm)

Powerplant

One Rolls-Royce Merlin XX liquid-cooled 12-cylinder Vee piston engine with a two-speed supercharger, driving an 11 ft 3-in (3.43-m) diameter three-bladed de Havilland or Rotol constant-speed propeller
Take-off rating: 1,300 hp (969 kW) at 3,000 rpm
Altitude ratings: 1,260 hp (940 kW) at 3,000 rpm at 11,750 ft (3581 m) in MS-gear; 1,160 hp (865 kW) at 3,000 rpm at 20,750 ft (6325 m) in S-gear

Weights

Tare: 5,658 lb (2566 kg)
Normal loaded: 7,544 lb (3422 kg)
Normal ferry weight: 7,619 lb (3456 kg) with two 44-Imp gal (200-litre) drop tanks
Overload combat: 8,044 lb (3648 kg)

Fuel and load

Total internal fuel: 97 Imp gal (441 litre), comprising two wing fuel tanks each of 34.5-Imp gal (157-litre) capacity, plus one reserve tank in rear fuselage of 28-Imp gal (127-litre) capacity
External fuel: provision for two 44-Imp gal (200-litre) drop tanks or two 88-Imp gal (400-litre) ferry tanks
Maximum external load: 1,000 lb (454 kg)

Performance

Maximum level speeds: (clean) 260 mph (418 km/h) at sea level; 329 mph (529 km/h) at 17,800 ft (5425 m)
Rate of climb: 2,760 ft (841 m) per minute at sea level; 1,670 ft (509 m) per minute at 15,000 ft (4572 m)
Service ceiling: 32,400 ft (9875 m)
Absolute ceiling: 35,600 ft (10850 m)
Time to climb: 15,000 ft (4572 m) in 5.7 minutes; 20,000 ft (6096 m) in 7.7 minutes

Range

460 miles (740 km) clean at optimum range speed (178 mph; 286 km/h); 920 miles (1481 km) with two 44-Imp gal (200-litre) drop tanks at optimum range speed

Armament

Fixed: four wing-mounted 20-mm Hispano cannon, with a total of 364 rounds (91 per gun)
External stores: provision for two underwing racks, each able to carry a 250-lb (113-kg) or 500-lb (227-kg) bomb

Hurricane Mk IID

HV663/'U' was a Hurricane Mk IID completed by Hawker Aircraft Ltd towards the end of 1943 and shipped to North Africa. Initially allocated to No. 71 Operational Training Unit at Carthago, Sudan in February 1943, the aircraft would have been utilised in the training of fighter pilots in desert conditions. Later in 1943, it was transferred to No. 6 Squadron, RAF which had operated this Hurricane variant since June 1942, in an anti-tank role against Rommel's Afrika Korps. After a period based in Egypt on shipping protection duties, No. 6 Squadron returned to the desert the following February, again in the anti-tank role, eventually moving westwards into Tunisia. The Mk IID's effectiveness as a 'tank buster' earned the unit the nickname 'The Flying Can-Openers' – a motif (a can-opener with a set of wings) to be found on the squadron's aircraft to this day. In common with a number of RAF units in the Western Desert, No. 6's aircraft dispensed with unit codes (though they carried 'JV' for a time), but retained an individual aircraft letter.

Powerplant and propeller

Early-production Hurricane Mk Is were fitted with a Rolls-Royce Merlin II rated at 1,030 hp (768 kW) at 16,250 ft (4953 m) and driving a Watts two-bladed, fixed-pitch wooden propeller with a diameter of 11 ft 6 in (3.5 m). Later-production aircraft benefited from a de Havilland three-bladed, constant-speed propeller which much improved take-off performance, climb rate and maximum speed at altitude. This and a similar Rotol design appeared from late 1938 and necessitated modifications to the aircraft's engine, which became the Merlin III. The Hurricane Mk II introduced the Merlin XX engine with two-stage supercharging and a rating of 1,260 hp (940 kW) at 11,750 ft (3580 m). Early Mk IIs were equipped with an enlarged coolant header tank which lengthened the nose of these aircraft by some 6.5 in (16.5 cm). However, as this change presented handling problems, it was abandoned after a handful of aircraft were completed. The illusion that most other Hurricane Mk IIs had longer noses than Mk Is was a result of the longer Rotol propeller spinner fitted to these machines. Hurricane Mk IVs benefited from a Merlin 27, modified to produce peak power (1,620 hp; 1208 kW) on take-off and operate more efficiently at high temperatures. Canadian-built Hurricane Mk Xs were fitted with Packard-built Merlin 28s (equivalent to the Merlin XX), while Mk XIIs had an improved Packard Merlin 29, rated at 1,300 hp (970 kW). Vokes tropical filters were fitted to aircraft intended for operation in the Mediterranean and Far East, including most Mk IIDs and Mk IVs.

Gun armament

Eight Browning 0.303-in (7.7-mm) machine-guns equipped Hurricane Mk IAs and Mk IIAs. The Mk IIB introduced an additional pair of Brownings in each wing, making this variant popular with pilots. However, with the recognition that rifle-calibre guns had their limitations against the armour and self-sealing fuel tanks installed in Luftwaffe aircraft, cannon were soon introduced. After trials with Oerlikon and Hispano 20-mm designs, the latter was chosen, four being fitted to the Hurricane Mk IIC (two of which were sometimes removed in service, especially in the Middle East, to save weight). Mk IIDs featured two Vickers 40-mm 'S' guns but retained a pair of Browning guns for sighting purposes, firing tracer ammunition. The 'E' wing, as fitted to the Mk IV (originally known as the Mk IIE), was a 'universal' design intended to be reconfigured according to the role of the squadron to which the aircraft was issued. Four Hispano cannon could be installed, but the most common armament fits were external – rockets (four per wing), a pair of 'S' guns or two 250-lb (113-kg) or 500-lb (227-kg) bombs.

Armour

Successive Hurricane variants were fitted with increased amounts of armour, largely for protection from ground fire. Later-production Mk IIDs were fitted with an additional 368 lb (167 kg) of armour plate over early-build examples and Mk IICs. The Mk IV had still more armour fitted, mainly around the nose and radiator intake under the fuselage. This variant had a considerably reduced top speed and an all-up weight of 8,462 lb (3838 kg), compared to the 6,218 lb (2820 kg) of the earliest Mk I aircraft.

Structure and markings

Among the changes made to the Hurricane's airframe during early production, in light of service experience, were the introduction of locally strengthened, metal-skinned wings, a slightly enlarged rudder and a ventral underfin on later-build Hurricane Mk Is. The rear fuselage remained fabric-covered throughout the life of the design, this ironically contributing to the machine's ability to sustain battle damage without loss of the aircraft (and its pilot). Repairs were also more straightforward and thus often easier to accomplish at squadron level, compared to the all-metal monocoque airframe of the Spitfire. This Mk IID is finished in the standard RAF Dark Earth/Middle Stone/Azure Blue applied to aircraft in the Mediterranean theatre.

Hawker Tempest

Seen fresh from the Hawker factory at Langley, this Tempest Mk II was fitted with bomb racks and was delivered to the A&AEE at Boscombe Down in September 1945 for weapons trials with 1,000-lb (454-kg) bombs.

Hawker Sea Fury

Cutaway key

1 Spinner
2 Rotol five-bladed constant-speed propeller of 12 ft 9 in (3.89 m) diameter
3 Propeller hub pitch change mechanism
4 Spinner backplate
5 Engine cowling ring
6 Cooling air intake
7 Propeller reduction gear casing
8 Detachable engine cowlings
9 Bristol Centaurus Mk 18 18-cylinder two-row radial sleeve valve engine
10 Exhaust stubs
11 Carburettor intake ducting
12 Starboard British Hispano Mk 5 20-mm cannon
13 Recoil springs
14 Cannon muzzles
15 60-lb (27.22 kg) ground attack rocket projectiles
16 Zero-length rocket launcher rails
17 Wing folding jack
18 Wing fold latching mechanism
19 Starboard outer wing panel
20 Starboard navigation light
21 Wing tip fairing
22 Starboard aileron
23 Aileron hinge control
24 Push-button control rod
25 Aileron spring tab
26 Retractable landing/taxiing lamp
27 Ammunition box (290 rounds port and starboard)
28 Starboard wing folded position
29 Outer split trailing edge flap
30 Ammunition feed drum blister fairings
31 Cannon breeches
32 Oil tank (14 Imp

gal/63.65 litre capacity)
33 Engine cartridge starter
34 Engine bearer struts
35 Hydraulic reservoir
36 Accessory drive gearbox
37 Engine cooling air outlet
38 Wing front spar attachment joint
39 Fireproof engine compartment bulkhead
40 Fuselage double frame
41 Main fuel tank (97 Imp gal/441 litre)
42 Fuel tank vent
43 Filler cap
44 Fuselage top longeron
45 Rudder pedals
46 Auxiliary fuselage fuel tank (30 Imp gal/136 litre)
47 Fuselage bottom longeron
48 Rear wing spar attachment joint
49 Oxygen bottle
50 Control column
51 Instrument panel
52 Bullet proof windscreen
53 Mk 4B reflector sight
54 Windscreen framing
55 Pilot's starboard side console
56 Pilot's seat
57 Engine throttle and propeller controls
58 Radio equipment
59 Port side console
60 Seat back armour plate
61 Safety harness
62 Headrest
63 Armoured headrest support
64 Sliding cockpit canopy cover
65 Canopy rails
66 Tailplane control rod
67 Rear fuselage joint frame
68 Whip aerial

69 Fuselage skin plating
70 Elevator push-pull control rod
71 Tailplane attachment joint frame
72 Fin root fillet
73 Starboard tailplane
74 Starboard elevator
75 Tailfin construction
76 Curved fin leading edge
77 Sternpost
78 Rudder construction
79 Mass balance weight
80 Rudder tab
81 Deck arrester hook
82 Elevator trim tab
83 Port elevator
84 Tailplane construction
85 Tailplane spar joints
86 Rudder hinge control
87 Tail navigation light
88 Arresting hook attachment link
89 Tailwheel hydraulic retraction jack
90 Tailwheel
91 Tailwheel doors
92 Rear fuselage double bulkhead
93 Tailwheel bay
94 Tailwheel bay bulkhead
95 Fuselage frame and stringer construction
96 Rudder push-pull control rod
97 Remote compass transmitter
98 Ventral aerial
99 Handgrip
100 Radio transmitter/receiver
101 Trailing edge wing root fillet
102 Retractable 'stirrup-type' step
103 Inboard split trailing edge flap
104 Flap shroud structure
105 Gun heater duct
106 Inboard ammunition box

107 Ammunition guide track
108 Port British Hispano Mk 5 20-mm cannon
109 Ammunition feed drums
110 Outer ammunition box (145 rounds)
111 Outer split trailing edge flap
112 Port retractable landing/taxiing lamp
113 Aileron spring tab
114 Aileron construction
115 Wing tip fairing
116 Port navigation light
117 Pitot tube
118 Rear spar
119 Wing rib construction
120 Main spar
121 Leading edge nose ribs
122 1,000-lb (453.6-kg) HE bomb
123 60-lb (27.22-kg) ground attack rockets
124 Port drop tank (45 or 90 Imp gal/204.5 or 409 litres)
125 Tank pylon
126 Wing fold hydraulic jack
127 Wing fold hinge joints
128 Cannon barrel mountings

129 Port interspar fuel tank (28 Imp gal/127 litres)
130 Main undercarriage wheel bay
131 Mainwheel door
132 Hydraulic retraction jack
133 Port carburettor air intake
134 Oil cooler ram air intake
135 Oil radiator (starboard leading edge has 17 Imp gal/77 litre fuel tank)
136 Port cannon muzzles
137 Pivoted main undercarriage shock absorber leg strut

138 Undercarriage leg fairing door
139 Port mainwheel

© Pilot Press Limited

SPECIFICATION

Hawker Tempest Mk V Series 2

Type

single-seat fighter and fighter-bomber

Powerplant

one Napier Sabre IIA H-type piston engine rated at 2,180 hp (1626 kW)

Performance

maximum speed 426 mph (686 km/h) at 18,500 ft (5640 m); cruising speed 391 mph (629 km/h) at 18,800 ft (5730 m); initial climb rate 4,700 ft (1433 m) per minute; climb to 20,000 ft (6095 m) in 6 minutes 6 seconds; service ceiling 36,000 ft (10975 m); range 1,300 miles (2092 km) with drop tanks or 820 miles (1320 km) with standard fuel

Weights

Empty 9,000 lb (4082 kg); maximum take-off 13,540 lb (6142 kg)

Dimensions

Wingspan 41 ft (12.50 m); length 33 ft 8 in (10.26 m); height 16 ft 1 in (4.90 m); wing area 302.00 sq ft (28.06 m2)

Armament

Four 20-mm Hispano Mk V fixed forward-firing cannon in the leading edges of the wing, plus up to 2,000 lb (907 kg) of disposable stores carried on two underwing hardpoints, and generally comprising two 1,000- or 500-lb (454- or 227-kg) bombs or eight 60-lb (27-kg) air-to-surface unguided rockets.

British piston-engined fighter design reached a pinnacle in the Hawker Fury and Sea Fury, which had its origins in a lightweight derivative of the Tempest. In this view of the second prototype, the Fury's raised cockpit and reduced wingspan are evident. Though it failed to see RAF service during World War II, a naval version – the Sea Fury – served the post-war Fleet Air Arm well.

Seen at Newchurch in the spring of 1944, No. 486 Squadron, RNZAF was to become, along with No. 3 Squadron, one of the RAF's most successful units against the V-1 flying-bombs.

Hawker Tempest Mk II

The Tempest Mk II was powered by the Bristol Centaurus V 18-cylinder two row radial engine. The origins of the Tempest II can be traced to a proposal by Hawker Aircraft for a Typhoon Mk II with a radial engine. The prototype of the Centaurs-Typhoon Mk II was abandoned without being flown because sufficient experience had already been amassed with the Centaurus-powered Tornado, another Hawker design. However, delays in the engine's development meant that the Mk II entered service after the Mk V, which had a Napier Sabre engine.

Construction
The Tempest pilot enjoyed an excellent all-round view, which was a considerable improvement over that of its predecessor, the Hawker Typhoon. Production of the Tempest F. Mk.II was originally to be undertaken jointly by Hawker and Gloster Aircraft, but by the time the second prototype flew on 18 September, 1943, the number of aircraft on order had increased to 600 and some of the production work was switched to the Bristol Aeroplane Company because of Gloster's other commitment, the Meteor jet fighter

Markings
This aircraft has the markings of No 16 Squadron RAF, based in northern Germany in 1946-47 as part of the 2nd Tactical Air Force. The squadron only flew Tempests for about two years before converting to the de Havilland Vampire Mk 5 jet fighter-bomber. The squadron originally formed part of the Fassberg Wing, the other two squadrons being Nos 33 and 26. In November 1947 the Wing moved to Gütersloh, where it spent the remainder of its Tempest days. The first Tempest II squadron, No 33, later redeployed to Malaya.

Cockpit

A reflector gun sight was mounted on a bar above the instrument panel. A dimmer switch was also mounted on the instrument panel and had three positions, marked 'off', 'night' and 'day'. A supply of warm air to the cockpit was controlled by a lever on the starboard cockpit wall, the lever being moved downwards from 'off' to 'on'. Two ventilators were provided, one on each side of the instrument panel. The radio installation, fitted behind the pilot, comprised a TR1143 transceiver and A1271 beam approach equipment. Provision was also made for IFF (Identification Friend or Foe) equipment.

Armament

The Tempest two carried a fixed armament of four 0.79in (20mm) Hispano V cannon, specially designed to fit inside the aircraft's very thin wing section, and 800 rounds of ammunition. The type could also carry up 907kg (2000lb) of underwing stores, including eight rocket projectiles, as seen here. The Tempest Mk II gave excellent postwar service in the fighter-bomber role with the RAF in the Far East, carrying out many attacks on communist terrorist hideouts during the early stages of Operation Firedog, the counter-insurgency operations in Malaya.

Fuel capacity

The Tempest had less internal fuel tankage than the Typhoon, as its new, thin wing prevented the installation of wing fuel tanks. To compensate for this a new tank was installed behind the engine. Although the Tempest had a shorter endurance than the Typhoon, its higher speed meant that it had a similar range. Hawker designed a 45 gal streamlined long-range fuel tank for the Tempest, replacing the cylindrical tank that had been used on the Hurricane and Typhoon. Napalm tanks were also developed, but were detrimental to handling.

Hawker Typhoon/Tempest

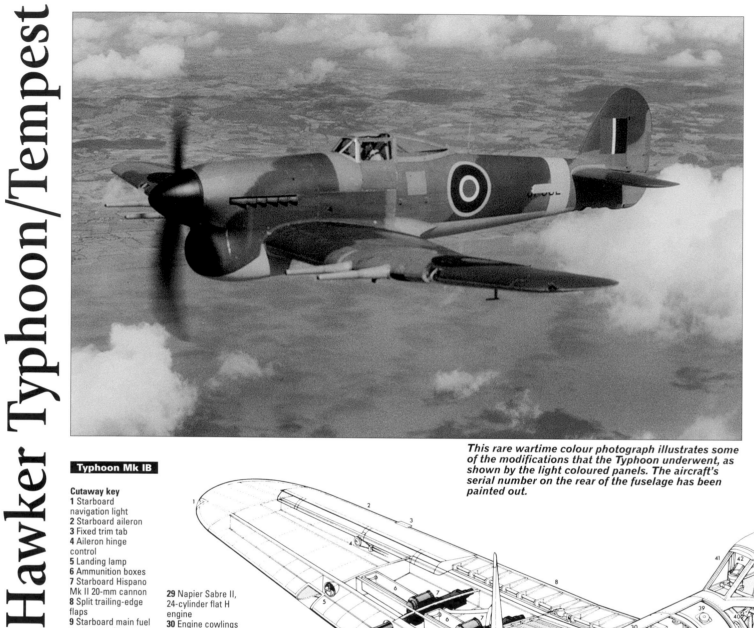

This rare wartime colour photograph illustrates some of the modifications that the Typhoon underwent, as shown by the light coloured panels. The aircraft's serial number on the rear of the fuselage has been painted out.

Typhoon Mk IB

Cutaway key
1 Starboard navigation light
2 Starboard aileron
3 Fixed trim tab
4 Aileron hinge control
5 Landing lamp
6 Ammunition boxes
7 Starboard Hispano Mk II 20-mm cannon
8 Split trailing-edge flaps
9 Starboard main fuel tank, capacity 40 Imp gal (182 litres)
10 Self-sealing leading-edge fuel tank, capacity 35 Imp gal (159 litres)
11 Cannon barrel fairings
12 Rocket launcher rails
13 60-lb (27-kg) ground attack rockets
14 Main undercarriage leg fairing
15 Starboard mainwheel
16 de Havilland four-bladed propeller
17 Air intake
18 Propeller pitch change mechanism
19 Spinner
20 Armoured spinner backplate
21 Coolant tank, capacity 7¼ Imp gal (33 litres)
22 Supercharger ram air intake
23 Oil radiator
24 Coolant radiator
25 Radiator shutter
26 Engine mounting block
27 Tubular steel engine support framework
28 Exhaust stubs

29 Napier Sabre II, 24-cylinder flat H engine
30 Engine cowlings
31 Cartridge starter
32 Engine compartment fireproof bulkhead
33 Oxygen bottle
34 Gun heating air duct
35 Hydraulic reservoir
36 Footboards
37 Rudder pedals
38 Oil tank, capacity 18 Imp gal (46.6 litres)
39 Oil tank filler cap
40 Instrument panel
41 Bullet-proof windscreen
42 Reflector sight
43 Control column handgrip
44 Engine throttle controls
45 Trim handwheels
46 Emergency hydraulic hand pump
47 Forward fuselage steel tube construction
48 Pilot's seat
49 Safety harness
50 Back and head armour plate
51 Pneumatic system air bottle
52 Rearward-sliding canopy cover
53 Aft fuselage joint
54 Canopy rails
55 Radio transmitter/receiver

56 Fuselage double frame
57 Whip aerial
58 Fuselage skinning
59 Starboard tailplane
60 Starboard elevator
61 Elevator trim tab
62 Fin leading edge
63 Fin construction
64 Rudder sternpost
65 Fabric-covered rudder construction
66 Rudder trim tab
67 Tail navigation light
68 Elevator trim tab
69 Port tailplane construction
70 Tailplane spar attachments
71 Tailwheel hydraulic jack

72 Forward-retracting tailwheel
73 Dowty oleo-pneumatic tailwheel strut
74 Tailplane spar fixing double bulkhead
75 Tailplane attachment joint strap
76 External strengthening fishplates
77 Elevator mass balance

A fine 1945 photograph of an echelon of Tempests from the CFE, the busy RAF Central Fighter Establishment at West Raynham, where most of the RAF's trials and evaluations on fighter-type aircraft were conducted. All are Mk V Series 2: SN328, SN108 and EJ884. SN328 has eight of the lengthened rocket rails fitted.

SPECIFICATION

Typhoon Mk IB (early production)

Dimensions

Length: 31 ft 11 in (9.73 m)
Height: 14 ft 10 in (4.52 m)
Wing span: 41 ft 7 in (12.67 m)
Wing area: 279 sq ft (25.90 m²)

Powerplant

One 2,180-hp (1626-kW) Napier Sabre IIA inline piston engine

Weights

Empty: 8,800 lb (3992 kg)
Maximum take-off: 13,250 lb (6010 kg)

Performance

Maximum speed (clean) at 18,000 ft (5486 m): 405 mph (652 km/h)
Climb to 15,000 ft (4572 m) from sea level: 5 minutes 55 seconds
Service ceiling: 34,000 ft (10670 m)
Range: (clean) 610 miles (982 km), and with 2,000-lb (910-kg) bombload 510 miles (021 km)

Armament

four 20-mm Hispano cannon each with 140 rounds, plus two bombs of up to 1,000-lb (454-kg) each, or eight 60-lb (27-kg) rockets or other stores such as 45-Imp gal (205-litre) drop tanks.

Tempest Mk V

Dimensions

Length: 33 ft 8 in (10.26 m)
Height: 16 ft 1 in (4.90 m)
Wing span: 41 ft (12.50 m)
Wing area: 302 sq ft (28.06 m²)

Powerplant

One 2,180-hp (1626-kW) Napier Sabre IIA inline piston engine

Weights

Empty: 9,000 lb (4082 kg)
Maximum take-off: 13,540 lb (6142 kg)

Performance

Maximum speed (clean) at 18,500 ft (5639 m): 426 mph (686 km/h)
Service ceiling: 36,500 ft (11125 m)
Maximum Range: 1,530 miles (2462 km)

Armament

four 20-mm Hispano cannon, plus two bombs of up to 1,000-lb (454-kg) each, or rocket projectiles

99 Wingtip construction
100 Port navigation light
101 Wing rib construction
102 Wing stringers
103 Front spar
104 Leading-edge nose ribs
105 Gun camera
106 Camera port
107 Landing lamp
108 1,000-lb (454-kg) bomb
109 Long-range tank, capacity 90 Imp gal (409 litres)
110 Underwing stores pylon
111 Cannon barrel fairings
112 Recoil spring
113 Leading-edge construction
114 Main undercarriage leg
115 Undercarriage leg fairing door
116 Oleo-pneumatic shock absorber strut
117 Port mainwheel
118 Undercarriage locking mechanism
119 Mainwheel hydraulic jack
120 Wing spar inboard girder construction
121 Port leading-edge fuel tank, capacity 35 Imp gal (159 litres)

78 Elevator cross shaft
79 Cable guides
80 Tailplane control cables
81 Rear fuselage frame and stringer construction
82 Wing root fillet
83 Spar root pin joints
84 Undercarriage door hydraulic jack
85 Mainwheel door
86 Main undercarriage bay
87 Rear spar
88 Port main fuel tank, capacity 40 Imp gal (182 litres)
89 Flap shroud construction
90 Port split trailing-edge flaps
91 Flap hydraulic jack
92 Port gun bays
93 Port Hispano Mk II 20-mm cannon
94 Ammunition feed drum
95 Ammunition boxes, 140 rounds per gun
96 Gun heater air ducts
97 Port aileron
98 Fixed aileron tab

Hawker could not handle the mass-production of the Typhoon on top of its continuing commitment to making the Hurricane, so the Typhoon was assigned to Gloster, a sister-firm in the Hawker-Siddeley group. Clearly visible in this view are the armoured backplates to the spinner. The delivery of Typhoons to the RAF was hindered by strikes when the Gloster workers tried to obtain a pay rise because of the complex construction methods used in making the new aircraft.

Typhoon Mk IB

Pictured unleashing a pair of rockets against a ground target in the Normandy area during August 1944, this Typhoon operated with No. 175 Squadron as part of the 2nd Tactical Air Force. Known as 'The Seven-Ton Brute', the Typhoon excelled in the ground-attack role, not only striking enemy airfields, but also lines of communication, river and canal barges and trains and locomotives. Often operating in pairs on missions known as 'Rhubarbs', Typhoon pilots were simply given the order to attack targets of opportunity, if not required by ground forces to provide specific close-air support missions. During these sorties pilots often showed great initiative in the bid to inflict maximum damage on the Third Reich. Perhaps one of the most sensational attacks was by No. 609 and 198 Squadrons on Rommel's headquarters in a château on the Cherbourg peninsula on the eve of D-Day. Rommel was in charge of the German defences against the coming invasion, but had left the château shortly before the Typhoons swept in. Had he been in residence at the time, his chances of survival would have been slight. However, a few weeks later in July Allied aircraft, believed to be Typhoons of No. 193 Squadron, attacked Rommel's staff car, wounding him and ending his military career.

Powerplant
Bias against radial engines ensured that the best engine for the Typhoon, the Bristol Centaurus, was not selected. Instead prototypes were ordered with the Rolls-Royce Vulture (to be known as the Hawker Tornado) and the Napier Sabre (to be known as the Hawker Typhoon). The Vulture engine proved unreliable beyond redemption and was cancelled, and the Sabre-engined Typhoon entered service almost by default. The Napier Sabre IIA was a 24-cylinder, inline water/glycol cooled monster, with sleeve valves. Power output was 2,180 hp (1624 kW) at sea level and 1,830 hp (1363 kW) at 11,500 ft (3500 m). Power from the Sabre was transmitted by a three-bladed de Havilland Hydromatic constant-speed propeller, although later a four-bladed unit was occasionally fitted. Both units had a diameter of 14 ft (4.27 m).

Canopy, oil tank and aerial

Early Typhoons featured a heavily-framed canopy with a car-type outward-hinging door manufactured by Rover. Complaints from pilots about the lack of visibility particularly to the rear, led to the development of a one-piece teardrop sliding canopy, with much improved vision. In addition the solid radio mast of early versions was replaced by a whip aerial further back on the spine. By the end of 1943 most Typhoons had this important modification, as did all the Tempests. Housed in the upper fuselage slightly ahead of the cockpit was the oil tank for the Sabre engine. Since it had a capacity of 18 Imp gal (46.6 litres) many pilots were initially wary that ground-fire would set the tank alight. However, additional armour plating fitted around this area relieved any fears pilots held.

Tail plane and armoured fuselage

The tailplane featured a two-spar box structure, but the fin was built around a multi-spar, multi-rib construction. Both rudder and elevators incorporated sizeable trim tabs. During the development of the Typhoon tailplane problems resulted in several fatal crashes. Diagnosis of the fault took some time, the delay claiming many lives before the simple expedient of attaching fishplate strengtheners to the rear fuselage joint cured the weakness. Because it operated at low altitude and would face heavy enemy ground fire the Typhoon was well provided with armour plating to protect the pilot and vital systems. A thick back and head plate was mounted behind the pilot, and a bullet-proof windscreen was fitted. The backplate of the propeller spinner was armoured to protect the front of the engine.

Identification markings

To avoid confusion with the Focke-Wulf Fw 190 a yellow band was initially applied overwing, and on the outboard leading edge. After a few months only the leading edge strip was retained. Black and white stripes were applied underwing and on the rear of the fuselage during the D-Day landings to help 'trigger-happy' Allied infantry units to identify friendly aircraft.

Underwing pylons

For bombing missions, the Typhoon could lift a pair of 1,000-lb (454-kg) bombs on underwing racks. Alternatively, the racks could carry 45- or 90-Imp gal (205- or 410-litre) drop tanks for extended range, although from June 1944 onwards most missions were short-range attacks close in front of friendly lines. For these sorts of missions rockets were used. Depicted here is a Typhoon from No. 175 Squadron, which worked up with rockets during the spring of 1944 and proved its expertise with this devastating weapon throughout the final year of the war. Eight Rocket Projectiles (RPs) could be carried by the Typhoon, each a 3-in (76-mm) rocket with a 60-lb (27-kg) warhead. These proved more than enough to penetrate the armour of German battle tanks.

Heinkel He 162 Salamander

This He 162A-2 was allocated to 3. Staffel/JG 1 at its Leck base in May 1945. By this time, the 50 aircraft had been reorganised into one single Gruppe, Einsatz-Gruppe I./JG 1; many pilots from other fragmented units at Leck were absorbed by this new Gruppe.

He 162

Cutaway key
1 Pitot tube
2 Moulded plywood nose cap
3 Nosewheel retraction mechanism
4 Spring-loaded nosewheel extension assembly
5 Shock absorber scissor
6 Nosewheel
7 Nosewheel fork
8 Nosewheel leg
9 Nosewheel door
10 Gun trough
11 Nosewheel well
12 Rudder pedal
13 Window panel (visual nosewheel retraction check)
14 Wooden instrument panel
15 One-piece moulded windscreen
16 Revi 16G gunsight (interchangeable with the Revi 16B)
17 Jettisonable hinged clear-vision canopy
18 Ventilation disc
19 Heinkel cartridge-operated ejection seat
20 Ejection seat handle grip
21 Throttle control quadrant

22 Retractable entry step
23 Gun barrel shroud in cockpit wall
24 Port 20-mm MG 151 cannon
25 Ammunition chute
26 Main oxygen supply bottle (3.5-pint/2-litre capacity)
27 Explosive charge ejector rail
28 Pilot's headrest
29 Canopy hinge
30 Ammunition box behind cockpit (120 rounds per gun)
31 Flexible main tank (153-Imp gal/695 litre capacity)
32 Fuel lines
33 FuG 25a IFF radio compartment
34 Beech plywood wing skinning
35 Jet intake
36 Riedel two-stroke starter motor bullet
37 Oil tank
38 BMW 003E-1 Sturm axial-flow turbojet
39 Auxiliary intake
40 Seven-stage axial compressor casing
41 FuG 24 R/T homing loop
42 Annular combustion chamber
43 Exhaust centre body
44 Exhaust outlet
45 Jet efflux fairing

46 Heat-resistant aft dorsal decking
47 Light metal tailplane
48 Starboard fin housing R/T receiver aerial
49 Starboard rudder
50 Rudder tab
51 Elevator
52 Elevator tab
53 Tailcone (movable through +3° to −2°)
54 Port tailfin structure
55 Rudder structure
56 Tailplane/tailfin

attachment
57 Port tailfin upper and lower plates (housing R/T transmitter and IFF aerials)
58 Tailskid
59 Dural fuselage skinning
60 Monocoque fuselage construction
61 Control cables
62 Downswept wingroot fillet
63 Hydraulically-operated flaps
64 Port aileron

SPECIFICATION

Heinkel He 162A-2 Salamander

Type

Single-seat fighter

Powerplant

One BMW 003A-1 turbojet engine
rated at 1,764 lb st (7.85 kN)

Performance

Maximum speed 522 mph (840
km/h) at 19,685 ft (6000 m); initial
climb rate 3,780 ft (1152 m) per
minute; service ceiling 39,370 ft
(12000 m); endurance 57 minutes at
35,990 ft (10970 m)

Weights

Empty 4,520 lb (2050 kg); maximum
take-off 5,941 lb (2695 kg)

Dimensions

Wingspan 23 ft 7½ in (7.20 m);
length 29 ft 8⅓ in (9.05 m); height
8 ft 6⅓ in (2.60 m); wing area
120.56 sq ft (11.20 m2)
Armament: two 20-mm MG 151/20
fixed forward-firing cannon in the
underside of the nose

*Considerable numbers of Heinkel He 162s
were captured by the Allies in varying
degrees of repair and some still exist in
museums. This aircraft was flown on 26
flights by the British RAE at Farnborough.
It was restored for display at RAF St Athan.*

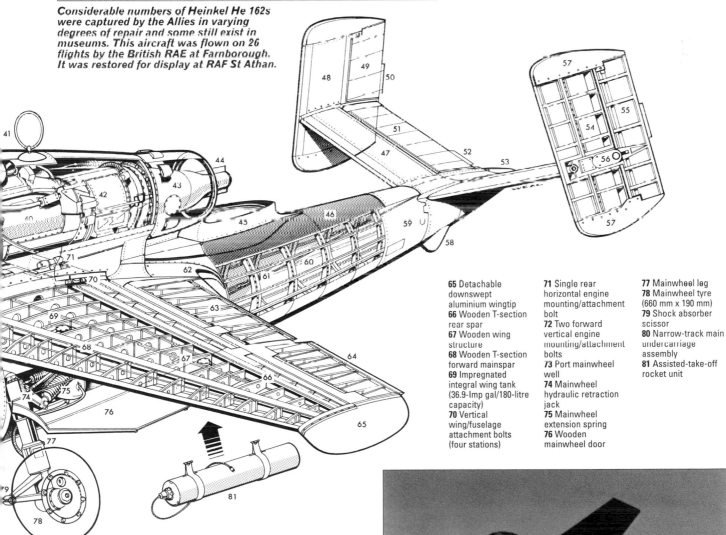

65 Detachable
downswept
aluminium wingtip
66 Wooden T-section
rear spar
67 Wooden wing
structure
68 Wooden T-section
forward mainspar
69 Impregnated
integral wing tank
(36.9-Imp gal/180-litre
capacity)
70 Vertical
wing/fuselage
attachment bolts
(four stations)

71 Single rear
horizontal engine
mounting/attachment
bolt
72 Two forward
vertical engine
mounting/attachment
bolts
73 Port mainwheel
well
74 Mainwheel
hydraulic retraction
jack
75 Mainwheel
extension spring
76 Wooden
mainwheel door

77 Mainwheel leg
78 Mainwheel tyre
(660 mm x 190 mm)
79 Shock absorber
scissor
80 Narrow-track main
undercarriage
assembly
81 Assisted-take-off
rocket unit

*An He 162A-1 shows the turned-down
wingtips first introduced on the V3 to
overcome excessive dihedral problems.
The A-1s were manufactured in parallel
with the prototypes, the latter being
regarded as A-0 pre-production airframes.*

Ilyushin Il-2/10 'Bark'/'Beast'

As an attack aircraft more 'feared even than the German Stuka or the British Typhoon, the Il-2 was one of the world's all-time great military aircraft. In terms of numbers built, it is unsurpassed. An Il-2M3 is illustrated.

Il-2M3

Cutaway key
1 Rear navigation light
2 Elevator tab
3 Elevator tab hinge
4 Starboard elevator frame
5 Non-retractable tailwheel
6 Wooden tailplane structure
7 Tailwheel leg assembly
8 Elevator torque tube
9 Tailwheel shock-absorber
10 Tail cone fairing
11 Rudder tab
12 Rudder tab actuating rod
13 Rudder frame
14 Rudder hinge
15 Rudder post
16 Rudder upper hinge
17 Rudder mass balance
18 Aerial attachment
19 Wooden tail fin structure
20 Tail fin spars
21 Rudder control cables
22 Fuselage aft frames
23 Elevator internal mass balance
24 Tailplane spar/fuselage attachment
25 Fuselage intermediate frame
26 Strengthened wooden frame
27 Plywood skinning
28 Elevator control rods
29 Rudder control cable pulleys
30 Aerial lead-in
31 Aerial
32 Fuselage frame
33 Provision for camera (portside window) or DAG-10 grenade launcher
34 Wingroot fairing
35 Armour protection (13-mm) for rear gunner
36 Ammunition tank (150 rounds)
37 Ammunition feed
38 Gun mounting post

39 0.5-in (12.7-mm) Berezin UBT machine-gun
40 K-8T sight
41 Canopy aft frame
42 Starboard-folding canopy section

43 Gunner's station
44 Gunner's canvas seat cradle
45 Cockpit area side armour (6-mm)
46 CO_2 fire extinguisher
47 Fuselage main fuel tank (63 Imp gal/286 litre capacity)
48 Fixed canopy centre section
49 RSI aerial mast
50 Pilot's armoured (13-mm) headrest and turnover pylon
51 8-mm armour glass side panels
52 Aft-sliding canopy section
53 Canopy track
54 Pilot's seat (vertically adjustable)
55 ESBR ZP selection panel for rockets (forward) and bombs (aft)
56 Control column (incorporating brake lever, bomb and rocket release buttons, cannon and machine gun firing buttons)
57 Rudder pedal assembly
58 Instrument panel
59 Forward fuel tank (38.50 Imp gal/175 litre capacity)
60 55-mm armour glass windscreen (embodying VV-1 sight)
61 Aileron control linkage
62 Port aileron outer hinge
63 Port aileron
64 Port wingtip
65 Port navigation light
66 Wooden outer panel wing structure
67 Leading edge
68 Rocket launching rails
69 RS-82 rocket projectiles (RS-132 optional)
70 Landing lamp
71 VV-1 external front sight
72 Fuel filler access
73 Foam suppressant tank
74 Intake duct

75 Engine bearer attachment
76 Cowling panel
77 Engine accessories
78 Cooling louvres
79 Starboard oil tank (total capacity 17.80 Imp gal/81 litres)
80 Ejector exhausts
81 Mikulin AM-38F engine
82 Radiator intake
83 Intake cowling trough
84 Armoured (6-mm) engine cowling
85 Cowling forward frame
86 Expansion tank
87 Auxiliary side intakes
88 Spinner armoured (6-mm) backplate
89 Propeller hub assembly
90 Spinner
91 Hucks-type starter dog
92 AV-57-158 three-bladed constant-speed propeller
93 Auxiliary intake

94 Underside armour (9-mm) protection
95 Engine support bearer
96 Bearer attachment
97 Port mainwheel
98 Filter intake
99 Intake duct
100 Radiator assembly
101 Radiator ventral intake
102 Exhaust trunking
103 Fuselage under floor fuel tank (59 Imp gal/269 litre capacity)
104 Wing inboard bomb bay (for two 220-lb/100-kg bombs or canisters of PTAB 3½- to 5½-lb/1.5- to 2.5-kg hollow-charge bomblets)
105 Mainspar
106 Aileron control cable transition
107 Flap actuating cylinder

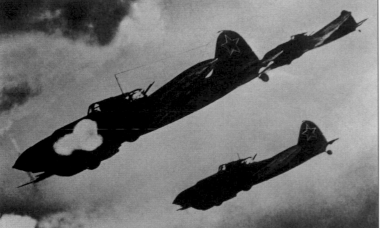

SPECIFICATION

Il-2M3

Dimensions

Length: 38 ft 2½ in (11.65 m)
Height: 13 ft 8 in (4.17 m)
Wingspan: 47 ft 10¾ in (14.60 m)
Wing area: 414.42 sq ft (38.50 m²)

Powerplant

One 1,720-hp (1282-kW) Mikulin AM-38F piston engine

Weights

Empty: 9,976 lb (4525 kg)
Empty (with NS-37 cannon): 10,196 lb (4625 kg)
Loaded: 14,021 lb (6360 kg)
Loaded (with NS-37 cannon): 13,580 lb (6160 kg)

Fuel

Internal: 1,179 lb (535 kg)

Range

Normal: 475 miles (765 km)

Performance

Maximum speed at sea level: 242 mph (390 km/h)
Maximum speed at 4,920 ft (1500 m): 255 mph (410 km/h)
Climb to 3,280 ft (1000 m): 2 minutes 12 seconds
Climb to 9,843 ft (3000 m): 6 minutes 54 seconds
Service ceiling: 19,685 ft (6000 m)
Take-off run: 1,296 ft (395 m)
Landing run at 90 mph (145 km/h): 1,755 ft (535 m)

Armament

Two 23-mm VYa cannon and two 0.3-in (7.62-mm) ShKAS machine-guns (all wing-mounted) and one 0.5-in (12.7-mm) UBT machine-gun for the gunner, plus 220-lb (100-kg) bombs (four carried internally and two under the fuselage), or two 551-lb (250-kg) bombs (under the fuselage), eight RS-82 rockets or four RS-132 rockets under the outer wing panels

This trio of Shturmoviks was photographed on the Voronezh Front during the Kursk campaign in July 1943. During this campaign, as with all the others in which the type was engaged, the Il-2 proved devastating against German armour. Note the 37-mm cannon being fired in this view of an attack.

108 Starboard flap inboard section
109 Flap outboard section profile
110 Aileron tab
111 Tab hinge
112 Starboard aileron control
113 Aileron profile
114 Starboard wingtip assembly
115 Starboard navigation light
116 Wing outer rib
117 Aileron outer hinge

118 Wooden wing structure
119 Flap control linkage
120 Wing ribs
121 Aileron tab control
122 Flap rods
123 Wing centre/outer section joint/capping strake
124 Wing attachment points
125 Undercarriage retraction cylinder

126 Forward extremity of weapons bay
127 ShKAS 0.3-in (7.62-mm) machine gun
128 Machine-gun barrel support
129 Cannon barrel fairing
130 Volkov Yartsev VYa 23 23-mm cannon
131 Ammunition access panel
132 Magazine for starboard VYa-23 cannon (150 rounds)

These aircraft represent the Il-2M3 in its ultimate form. All have 37-mm cannon, and the second aircraft at least, has yet to fire its underwing RS-82 rockets. All four of these machines have similar canopy shapes, but at least five main variations on canopy design have been noted, along with a range of minor changes. Such differences resulted from variations during manufacture and from local field modifications.

133 Forward spar
134 Leading edge panels
135 Alternative pitot head positions
136 Undercarriage retraction linkage
137 Mainwheel leg cross-brace
138 Undercarriage fairing doors
139 Starboard mainwheel
140 Axle
141 Undercarriage oleo legs
142 Barrel of VYa-23 cannon

143 Undercarriage pivot point
144 Fairing nose section
145 Starboard bomb load comprising three (two internal and one external) 220-lb (100-kg) bombs which could be released singly or in salvo
146 Alternative main armament (Il-2 Type M3) of 37-mm Nudelman-Suranov NS-11-37 (NSK-OKB-16) cannon

Il-2M3

This aircraft flew with the 566th Shturmovik Aviation Squadron of the 277th Shturmovik Aviation Division, Frontal Aviation, Soviet Air Forces. It is illustrated as it appeared while in action on the Leningrad Front in the Summer of 1944, while being flown by the squadron commander Lt V. I. Mykhlik. The slogan to the rear of the fuselage star read 'Revenge for Khristenko', while that in front stated 'For Leningrad'. Khristenko had been a pilot on the squadron, but was killed earlier in 1944, while Mykhlik was awarded two Hero of the Soviet Union awards and survived to finish the war as a Captain.

Rear fuselage structure

From 1944, the Il-2M3 was produced with an all-Dural fuselage structure. Prior to this however, the rear fuselage of earlier models, including the Il-2 and Il-2M, had been a wooden monocoque structure. This created many problems early in the type's service career, with glue often failing where sections were jointed and, indeed, the whole rear fuselage being prone to failure. These problems were cured by A. K. Belyenkov, a repair engineer who devised a fix employing four steel strengthening pieces and which later became standard in the composite-structure production aircraft. The rear fuselage contained a battery, the flap actuation equipment, oxygen bottles, a pneumatic bottle and the radio system.

Flying surfaces

On the earliest production Il-2s, the fin was of wooden construction, while the tailplanes, wings and all control surfaces were generally of all-metal construction. There were exceptions however, with a number of basic Il-2 aircraft having wooden outer wing and tailplane structures. The leading edges of the outer wing panels of the Il-2 and Il-2M were swept at 5° in order to improve longitudinal stability. In the Il-2/AM-38F (which preceded the ultimate late-production Il-2m3), this sweep angle was increased to 15° with a view to decreasing drag, and aircraft with this revised wing were first in action over Stalingrad in January 1943. The wing centre section had two spars, with a box in between used to accommodate bombs. Two bomb cells were created in each wing, each covered by a pair of doors that were opened manually by the pilot for bomb release, and typically carrying a 100-kg (220-lb) FAB-100 high-explosive general purpose bomb.

Armour protection

Armour plate of 4-, 5-, 6-, 8- and 12-mm thickness was used to protect the Il-2's crew and vital systems. The engine was protected by 4-mm thick armour at the front and 5-mm material covered the lower and under sides. Other armour included a 7-mm thick section protecting the bulkhead behind the rear crew member. In order to minimise the weight penalties inherent in adding armour to an aircraft, Ilyushin, along with Mikoyan-Gurevich and Sukhoi, was working on methods of making the armour part of the load-bearing structure of the airframe. In the case of the Il-2, this was only possible around the engine and all three manufacturers suffered grievous problems in making accurate sections of armour. Bolt and rivet holes frequently failed to match up on armour sections that were supposed to be joined together and this problem persisted until an armour-welding process was perfected for use on the Il-2M and subsequent models.

Passengers

It was not uncommon for the Il-2 to carry passengers. These were normally carried only in times of urgent need, where a normal transport might be too vulnerable, and were normally accommodated lying on the floor of the gunners cockpit. Many downed crews were rescued from crash sites by their fellow Il-2 flyers, sometimes by using the lying in the cockpit method, but also by securing themselves to the main undercarriage units, which were then kept extended for the return to base.

Weapons

The rockets leaving the underwing racks of this machine are twin-finned, 51-lb (23.10-kg) RS-132 weapons. These rockets were 36⅞ in (93.50-cm) long and were common Il-2 rockets along with the four-finned RS-82, although RS-132 compatibility was not introduced until mid-1941. Early Il-2s could only carry six such rockets, while this was later upgraded to eight. The Il-2/AM-38 introduced a new two-tier launch rack for the RS-82, which allowed up to 32 RS-82s to be carried. These weapons were normally aimed using either the PBP-1 optical sight or the less-complicated VV-1 sight, although crews also made markings on the windscreen and canopy to provide references for gun and rocket firing and for bombing. As well as conventional high-explosive bombs, the Il-2 frequently employed cluster weapons, in the form of canisters containing 200 3⅓- to 5½-lb (1.5- to 2.5-kg) hollow-charge PTAB bomblets for use against armour. Other options included the unusual DAG-10 grenade launcher, which released infantry grenades on small parachutes, hopefully into the path of any pursuing fighters. Fixed armament originally consisted of four forward-firing machine-guns in the form of two ShVAK and two ShKAS weapons in the wings. From mid-1941, the 20-mm ShVAK weapons were replaced by a pair of 23-mm calibre VYa-23 guns and with the introduction of the second crew member in the Il-2M, a 0.5-in (12.7-mm) UBT machine-gun was added on a flexible mount in the rear cockpit. The ultimate Il-2 gun configuration was displayed by a number of Il-2M3s, which featured two ShVAKs, the UBT and a pair of 37-mm NS-OKB-16 cannon. Being of such a large calibre, the NS-OKB-16s were restricted to just 50 rounds each, but these were capable of penetrating the armour of the formidable PzKW VI Tiger tank.

Tactics

The basic Il-2 operating group consisted of 4-12 aircraft and an attack might involve several groups. Standard echelon, line abreast, line astern and vic formations were employed, although the favourite attack formation was the 'circle of death'. Approached in echelon right, the 'circle of death' was flown with the aircraft in line astern and spaced at 1,970-ft (600-m) intervals. The circle was off-set to one side of the target, the aircraft attacking from behind and making attack runs in turn until all ammunition had been expended. This tactic frequently kept the enemy under constant attack by at least one aircraft for up to 30 minutes. Bombs were often delivered in steep diving attacks, while for attacks against emplacements, infantry and vehicles in the open, Il-2s would often run in to the target at an altitude between 15 and 30 ft (4.57 and 9.00 m), firing their fixed armament and rockets horizontally.

Kawasaki Ki-61 Hien

This Ki-61-I of the 37th Sentai was among those that fought in the last stages of the defence of the Philippines, before being forced to redeploy to Formosa and Okinawa in the last year of the war.

Kawasaki Ki-61

Cutaway key
1 Starboard navigation light
2 Wing rib bracing
3 Wing spar
4 Starboard aileron
5 Aileron tab
6 Starboard flap
7 Wing gun access panel
8 Gun port
9 Three-blade constant-speed propeller
10 Auxiliary drop-tank (43.9 Imp gal/200 litres)
11 Propeller boss
12 Propeller reduction gear housing
13 Air intake duct
14 Starboard mainwheel
15 Lower cowling quick-release catches
16 Exhaust stubs
17 Anti-vibration mounting pad
18 Engine bearer
19 Upper cowling quick-release catches
20 Kawasaki Ha-40 (Army Type 2) engine
21 Engine accessories
22 Gun port
23 Cannon barrels
24 Firewall
25 Cowling panel line
26 Supercharger
27 Supercharger intake
28 Ammunition tanks
29 Ammunition feed chute
30 Two 20-mm Ho-5 cannon
31 Sloping windscreen
32 Gunsight
33 Control column

34 Pilot's seat (armoured)
35 Fuselage frame
36 Rearward-sliding cockpit
37 Pilot's headrest
38 Rear-vision cut-out
39 Aft glazing
40 Canopy track
41 Spring-loaded handhold
42 Fuselage fuel tank (36.2 Imp gal/165 litres)
43 Fuselage equipment access door (upward hinged)
44 Radio pack (Type 99-111)
45 Aerial mast
46 Aerial lead-in
47 Aerial
48 Elevator control cables
49 Upper longeron
50 Rudder cable
51 Fuselage join
52 Starboard tailplane
53 Starboard elevator
54 Tailfin root fairing
55 Tailfin structure
56 Rear navigation light (port and starboard)
57 Aerial stub mast
58 Rudder balance
59 Rudder fixed trim tab
60 Rudder post
61 Rudder framework
62 Elevator tab
63 Elevator fixed trim tab
64 Port elevator
65 Elevator control cable
66 Rudder hinge
67 Rear fuselage frame/tailplane attachment
68 Tailwheel retraction jack
69 Tailwheel doors

70 Retractable tailwheel
71 Tailwheel shock absorber oleo
72 Lower longeron
73 Radiation bath air outlet
74 Adjustable gill
75 Radiator
76 Radiator intake ducting
77 Intake
78 Main spar/fuselage attachment point
79 Inboard mainwheel doors
80 Mainwheel well
81 Landing light
82 Mainwheel pivot point
83 Mainwheel leg
84 Oleo shock-absorber section (leather-sleeved)
85 Mainwheel single fork
86 Port mainwheel
87 Mainwheel door
88 Separate mainwheel leg fairing
89 Gun port
90 Machine gun barrel
91 Wing-mounted 12.7-mm Ho-103 machine-gun
92 Gun access panel
93 Bomb/tank shackle
94 Port flap
95 Main spar
96 Wing ribs
97 Auxiliary drop-tank (43.9 Imp gal/200 litres)
98 Pitot head
99 Metal wing skin
100 Aileron tab
101 Port aileron
102 Wingtip structure
103 Port navigation light

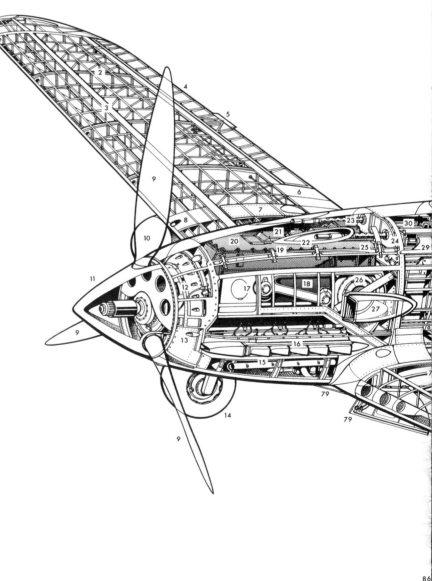

Kawasaki Ki-61-Ic

Type

Single-seat fighter

Powerplant

One 1,175-hp (876-kW) Kawasaki Ha-40 V-12 piston engine

Performance:

Maximum speed 348 mph (560 km/h); service ceiling 32,810 ft (10000 m); maximum range 1,181 miles (1900 km)

Weights

Empty 5,798 lb (2630 kg); maximum take-off 7,650 lb (3470 kg)

Dimensions

Wingspan 39 ft 4½ in (12.00 m); length 29 ft 4¼ in (8.95 m); height 12 ft 11 in (3.70 m); wing area 215.29 sq ft (20.00 m2)

Armament

As detailed under variants, plus provision for two drop tanks or two 551-lb (250-kg) bombs

By Western standards the Japanese 53-US gal (200-litre) drop tank carried by all operational versions of the Ki-61 was a crude store, which reduced its maximum speed by around 50 mph (80 km/h) but increased the range of the Ki-61-II KAIa from 684 miles (1100 km) to 995 miles (1600 km).

Ki-61-KAIs of the Akeno Flying Training School, the main home-based Hien training unit, are run up before another training sortie. KAI variants had strengthened wings and cannon armament.

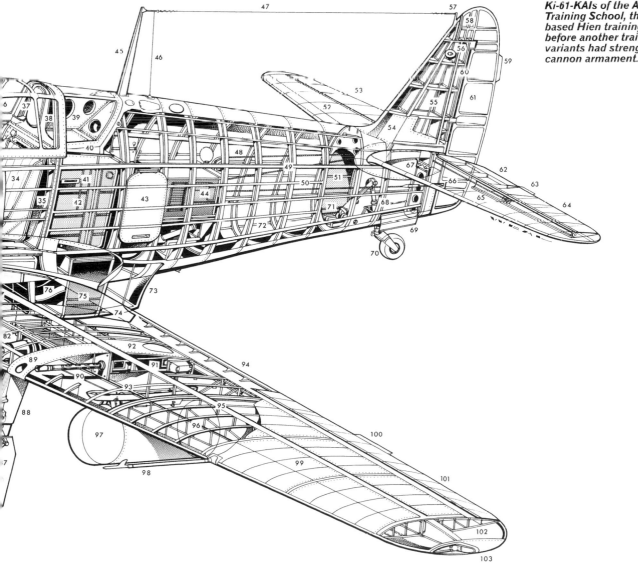

149

Lavochkin La-5/7

With the La-5 and La-7, Lavochkin created one of the most capable fighter families of World War II. Operating from a typically rough airstrip, this La-5 was engaged in combat against the Luftwaffe's Luftflotte 4 during the Battle of Kursk in the summer of 1943.

La-5FN

Cutaway key

1 Hucks-type starter dog
2 Spinner
3 Propeller balance
4 Controllable frontal intake louvres
5 VISh-105V metal propeller
6 Nose ring profile
7 Intake centrebody
8 ShVAK cannon port
9 Supercharger air intake
10 Supercharger intake trunk fairing
11 Blast tube
12 Shvetsov ASh-82FN 14-cylinder two-row radial
13 Cowling ring
14 Cowling panel hinge line
15 Exhaust pipes
16 Exhaust outlet cluster (seven per side)
17 Outlet cover panel
18 Engine accessories
19 Mainspar/fuselage attachment
20 Ammunition tanks (200 rpg)
21 Link and cartridge ejection chutes
22 Engine bearer upper support bracket
23 Cannon breech fairing
24 Paired 20-mm ShVAK cannon
25 Supercharger intake trunking
26 Stressed Bakelite-ply skinning
27 Automatic leading-edge slat (obliquely-operated)
28 Pitot head

29 Starboard navigation light
30 Wingtip
31 Dural-framed fabric-covered aileron
32 Aileron trim tab
33 Armoured glass windscreen (2$\frac{1}{10}$ in/55 mm thick)
34 PBP-1A reflector gunsight
35 Cockpit air intake
36 Control column
37 Outlet louvres
38 Rudder pedal assembly
39 Underfloor control linkage
40 Rear spar/fuselage attachment
41 Rudder and elevator trim hand wheels
42 Seat height adjustment
43 Boost controls
44 Seat harness
45 Pilot's seat
46 Throttle quadrant
47 Hydraulics main valve
48 Aft-sliding cockpit canopy
49 Fixed aft transparent cockpit fairing
50 Armoured glass screen (2$\frac{3}{5}$ in/66 mm thick)
51 Canopy track
52 RSI-4KhF HF R/T installation
53 Radio equipment shelf
54 Dural fuselage side panels
55 Control cables
56 Plywood-sheathed birch frames with triangular-section wooden stringers
57 Stressed Bakelite-ply skinning

58 Accumulator
59 Accumulator access panel
60 Tailfin front spar attachment
61 Aerial mast
62 Radio aerials
63 Starboard tailplane
64 Elevator hinge
65 Dural-framed fabric-covered elevator
66 Tailfin leading edge
67 Tailfin wooden structure (plywood skinning)
68 Aerial stub
69 Rudder balance
70 Rudder upper hinge
71 Dural-framed fabric-covered rudder
72 Rudder trim tab
73 Rear navigation light
74 Rudder centre hinge
75 Elevator control lever
76 Tailplane/fuselage attachment
77 Rudder control lever
78 Elevator trim tab
79 Dural-framed fabric-covered elevator
80 Wooden two-spar tailplane structure (plywood skinning)
81 Tailwheel doors
82 Aft-retracting tailwheel (sometimes locked in extended position)
83 Tailwheel leg
84 Tailwheel shock strut
85 Retraction mechanism
86 Stressed Bakelite-ply skinning

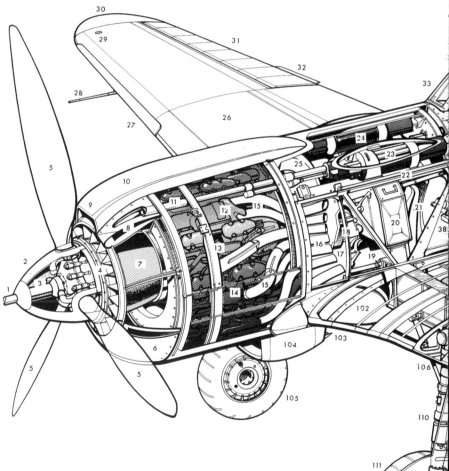

SPECIFICATION

La-5FN

Dimensions

Length: 28 ft 5½ in (8.67 m)
Height: 8 ft 4 in (2.54 m)
Wingspan: 32 ft 1¾ in (9.80 m)
Wing area: 189 sq ft (17.59 m²)

Powerplant

One Shvetsov ASh-82FN 14-cylinder, twin-row, air-cooled, direct fuel injection radial piston engine rated at 1,850 hp (1380 kW) or 1,470 hp (1096 kW) at altitude

Weights

Empty: 5,743 lb (2605 kg)
Gross: 7,323 lb (3322 kg)

Fuel and load

Internal fuel: 102 Imp gal (464 litres)
Maximum external load: 880 lb (400 kg)

Performance

Maximum speed at 21,325 ft (6500 m): 403 mph (648 km/h)
Maximum speed at sea level: 356 mph (573 km/h)
Climb to 16,400 ft (5000 m): 5 minutes
Service ceiling: 36,090 ft (11000 m)
Take-off run: 951 ft (290 m)
Landing run: 1,673 ft (510 m)
Time for a 360° turn: 18 seconds

Range

Operational: 360 miles (580 km)

Armament

Two ShVAK 20-mm cannon with 200 rounds per gun, plus provision for two 50-kg (110-lb) AO-25M, FAB-50 or FAB-50M bombs on two underwing D3-40 racks or up to six RS-82 82-mm (3½-in) unguided rockets

Semyon Lavochkin (second from the right) posed for this photograph with Soviet naval pilots, beside an La-7. The Naval Air Forces also contributed to the Soviet victory, acting as four distinct air forces – the Red Banner Baltic Fleet, the Northern Fleet, the Black Sea Fleet and the Pacific Fleet. None of the constituent units appears to have operated the La-7 during the war, although both the 3rd GvIAP-KBF and the 4th GvIAP-KBF flew La-5 variants.

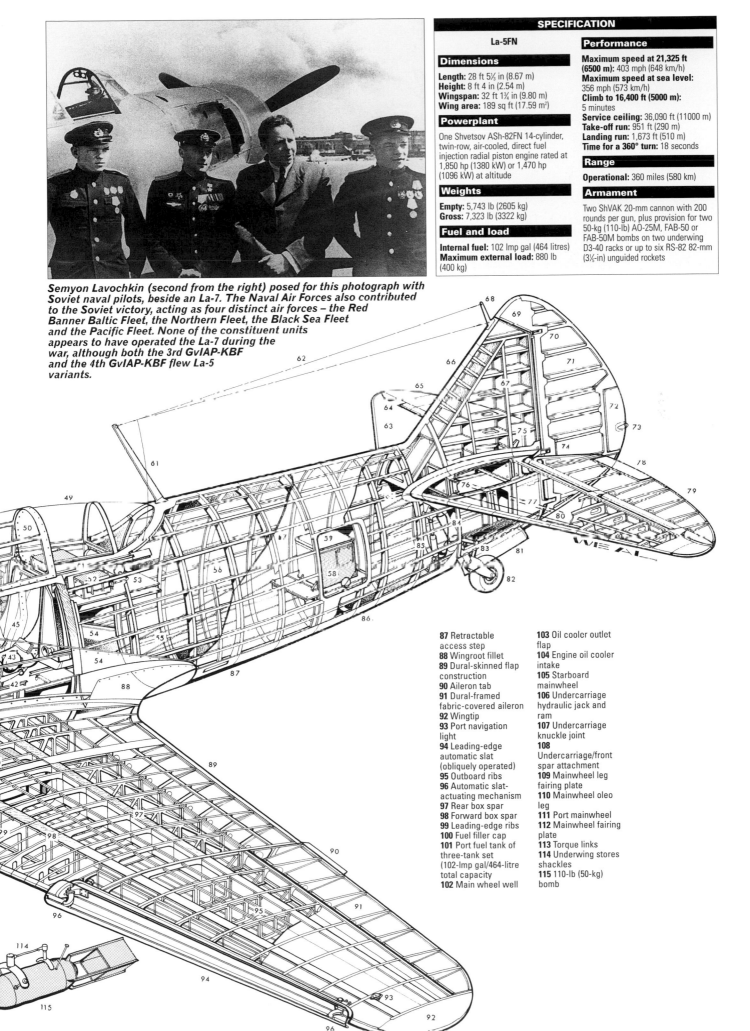

87 Retractable access step
88 Wingroot fillet
89 Dural-skinned flap construction
90 Aileron tab
91 Dural-framed fabric-covered aileron
92 Wingtip
93 Port navigation light
94 Leading-edge automatic slat (obliquely operated)
95 Outboard ribs
96 Automatic slat-actuating mechanism
97 Rear box spar
98 Forward box spar
99 Leading-edge ribs
100 Fuel filler cap
101 Port fuel tank of three-tank set (102-Imp gal/464-litre total capacity
102 Main wheel well

103 Oil cooler outlet flap
104 Engine oil cooler intake
105 Starboard mainwheel
106 Undercarriage hydraulic jack and ram
107 Undercarriage knuckle joint
108 Undercarriage/front spar attachment
109 Mainwheel leg fairing plate
110 Mainwheel oleo leg
111 Port mainwheel
112 Mainwheel fairing plate
113 Torque links
114 Underwing stores shackles
115 110-lb (50-kg) bomb

La-5FN

Kapitan Petr Yakovlevich Likholetov served with the 159th IAP for the entirety of his operational career. From 1941 to summer 1942, the unit was equipped with Yak-7 fighters, Likholetov probably gaining his first 12 victories on this type. From summer 1942 onwards, the 159th flew the P-40, La-5 and La-5FN in succession. Some confusion surrounds the allocation of Likholetov's final score, although he notched up at least 30 individual/group kills, of which certainly one was scored by ramming a Bf 109 with his Yak-7. He finished his flying career on the La-5FN, since at the end of 1944 he was seriously injured in a car accident and died of his injuries on 13 July 1945.

M-82 engine

Shvetsov's M-82 (later ASh-82) was a 14-cylinder, twin-row radial piston engine displacing 41.20 litres. In its ASh-82FN form for the La-5FN, the engine carried the *forsirovanny neprosredstvenno*, or directly boosted, designation, the letters 'FN' stencilled on the cowling of this aircraft in Cyrillic referring to this. In fact, the engine used a direct fuel injection system, which finally solved the inverted flight/engine cut-out problem that had previously dogged the La-5. A change associated with the introduction of the -82FN engine, and a key La-5FN recognition feature, was the addition of a new supercharger air intake stretching across the entire chord of the upper cowling. The intake beneath the centre forward fuselage in line with the wing leading edge served the oil cooler. The location of this item was moved to be in line with the wing trailing edge on the La-7. A flap at the rear of the intake controlled the through-flow of air.

Canopy design and gunsight

Early production La-5s, in common with the prototype, used the canopy and curved windscreen design of the earlier LaGG-3. Later aircraft used a redesigned windscreen with a flat forward panel which enabled the use of a PBP-1A gunsight. This modified arrangement also allowed the installation of a 2¹⁄₁₀-in (55-mm) thick armoured glass panel behind the windscreen, while a 2⅜-in (66-mm) thick armoured glass panel was fitted behind the pilot's head. The La-5F featured entirely revised rear glazing, which was combined with a cut-down rear fuselage to improve visibility to the rear. The La-5FN featured at least three distinctly different canopy arrangements. The first FNs shared the canopy design of the La-5F, while later aircraft added a small external grab handle to the port-side lower canopy frame and a vertical frame was added up the centre of the canopy at a later date. The aircraft illustrated demonstrates only the former canopy modification. Early La-7s employed a similar canopy/windscreen arrangement to the early La-5FN. The La-7 also introduced the much improved PBP-1B(V) reflector gunsight. This device overcame the limitations of the simple PBP-1A gunsight, whose inherent lack of accuracy led to pilots using three bursts of fire for each target – one before, one during and one after the target had passed through the sight.

Cannon armament

All the La-5 variants were armed with a pair of 20-mm ShVAK (*Shpital'nyi/Vladimirov Aviatsionnyi Krupnokaliber*, or Shpital'nyi/Vladimirov large-calibre cannon) weapons mounted in the upper part of the engine cowling to either side of the fuselage centreline. Boris G. Shpital'nyi and S. V. Vladimirov developed the weapon from the earlier ShKAS 0.3-in (7.62-mm) machine-gun. Each cannon weighed 92½ lb (45 kg), with a barrel 49 in (1.25 m) long and an overall length of 69⅛ in (1.76 m). Some 200 rounds per gun were carried in ammunition tanks between the cockpit and the engine, while the cannon were cable of firing at between 750 and 800 rounds per minute. The majority of La-7s was delivered with a three-gun ShVAK installation, although aircraft delivered from 1945 introduced the 20-mm calibre Berezin B-20 cannon. As with the ShVAKs, these weapons were installed in the form of two to the left of the centreline, with the third to the right, but in the same general position as those of the La-5. However, supplies of this weapon could not keep up with demand – it was also used in the PV-20 gun-turret system for Soviet bombers such as the Tu-4 'Bull' – and many La-7s flew with just two B-20s installed.

Disposable stores

All La-5/7-family aircraft were equipped to mount a single D3-40 bomb rack beneath each wing for bombs of up to 110 lb (50 kg) in weight. Though rarely used, these could include the FAB-50 GP bomb or AO-25M or FAB-50M fragmentation bombs. With the La-5FN already established in service, the capability to carry two or three RS-82 rockets under each wing was introduced. At least 2.5 million of these rockets were built, each 34 in (86.40 cm) long and weighing 15 lb (6.82 kg). The La-5's rocket capability was also little used.

Structure

Aft of the engine mounting bulkhead, the La-5 airframe was more or less identical to the desperately inadequate LaGG-3. As such, the fuselage was a semi-monocoque wooden structure utilising plywood-sheathed birch frames and wooden stringers as its basis with Bakelite-ply skinning. The wooden components were made of a specially developed material known as DSP-10 delta wood in the initial production La-5s. This material used between five and eight birch strips glued together across their grain and impregnated with a substance known as VIAM-B3. The latter consisted of boric acid, borax and phenol-formaldehyde resin. Predictably, supplies of the German-supplied resin soon dried up and the majority of production machines used pine rather than delta wood components. Bakelite ply was made by gluing layers of birch strip together and then combining them with Bakelite film at a temperature of 302°F (150°C). As La-5 development continued, metal was increasingly introduced in to the structure, starting with the wing spars in later La-5FNs.

Antennas and radios

Many changes of aerial mast and wire antenna arrangement occurred throughout the service life of the La-5/7 series, this aircraft exhibiting the standard La-5FN installation. RSI-4 radio was standard in early-build FNs, but later machines featured the RSI-4KhF unit. The main controls for the radio, including the knobs used to change frequencies, were mounted beneath the instrument panel. Changing frequencies could be a little awkward, but pilots praised the simple transmit switch on the throttle. This was pressed when the pilot wished to talk, and released at all other times.

Pressurised fuel tanks

In an effort to prevent fuel tank fires, especially in combat, the La-5/7 series featured a gas pressurisation system for the fuel tanks. Gas from the left-side exhaust manifold was piped to a filter in the rear fuselage. It was then cooled and filtered before passing to the fuel tanks in the wing/fuselage centre section. The system was operated by a cock in the cockpit, the pilot having to remember to switch the system on when entering combat and to deactivate it afterwards. If the system was used for too long, the fuel tanks were prone to deformation due to the excess pressure.

Camouflage and markings

It was commonplace for Soviet fighters to carry slogans on their fuselage sides, proclaiming or urging victory over Germany or loyalty to the Soviet Motherland. The inscription on Likholetov's aircraft translates as 'For Vasek and Zhora' and while it appears here in white, it may have been applied in yellow. A variety of camouflage colours and schemes was used, this aircraft being illustrated in what appears to have become a standard La-5FN pattern of two shades of blue grey over light grey.

Lockheed P-38 Lightning

An F-4 Lightning of the 3rd Photographic Reconnaissance Group banks towards the photographer, displaying the type's unique lines. The 3rd Group arrived at La Senia, Algeria, in mid-December 1942 and flew countless photographic missions in support of the Allied armies.

P-38 Lightning

Cutaway key
1 Starboard navigation light
2 Wingtip trailing edge strake
3 Landing light (underwing)
4 Starboard aileron
5 Aileron control rod/quadrant
6 Wing outer spar
7 Aileron tab drum
8 Aileron tab control pulleys
9 Aileron tab control rod
10 Aileron trim tab
11 Fixed tab
12 Tab cable access
13 Flap extension/retraction cables
14 Control pulleys
15 Flap outer carriage
16 Fowler-type flap (extended)
17 Control access panel
18 Wing spar transition
19 Outer section leading-edge fuel tanks (P-38J-5 and subsequent) capacity 46 Imp gal (208 litres) each
20 Engine bearer/bulkhead upper attachment
21 Firewall
22 Triangulated tubular engine bearer supports
23 Polished mirror surface panel (undercarriage visual check)
24 Cantilever engine bearer
25 Intake fairing
26 Accessories cooling intake
27 Oil radiator (outer sections) and intercooler (centre section) tripleintake
28 Spinner
29 Curtiss-Electric three blade (left) handed propeller
30 Four machine gun barrels
31 Cannon barrel

32 Camera-gun aperture
33 Nose panel
34 Bulkhead
35 Machine gun blast tubes
36 Four 0.5-in (12.7-mm) machine guns
37 Cannon flexible hose hydraulic charger
38 Chatellerault-feed cannon magazine (150 rounds)
39 Machine gun firing solenoid
40 Cannon ammunition feed chute
41 Nose armament cowling clips
42 Case ejection chute (port lower machine gun)
43 Ammunition box and feed chute (port lower machine gun)
44 Case ejection chute (port upper machine gun)
45 Ammunition box and feed chute (port upper machine gun)
46 Radio antenna
47 Ejection chute exit (shrouded when item 52 attached)
48 Nosewheel door
49 Nosewheel shimmy damper assembly and reservoir
50 Torque links
51 Towing eye
52 Type M10 triple-tube 4.5-in (11.4-cm) rocket-launcher
53 Rearward-retracting nosewheel
54 Alloy spokes cover plate
55 Fork
56 Rocket-launcher forward attachment (to 63)
57 Nosewheel lower drag struts
58 Nosewheel oleo leg
59 Nosewheel pin access
60 Side struts and fulcrum
61 Actuating cylinder
62 Upper drag strut

63 Rocket-launcher forward attachment bracket
64 Rudder pedal assembly
65 Engine controls quadrant
66 Instrument panel
67 Spectacle grip cantilevered control wheel
68 Non-reflective shroud
69 Lynn-3 reflector sight mounting
70 Optically-flat bullet-proof windscreen

71 External rear-view mirror
72 Armoured headrest
73 Rearward-hinged canopy
74 Pilot's armoured seat back
75 Canopy bracing
76 Downward-winding side windows
77 Wing root fillets
78 Nosewheel well
79 Port reserve fuel tank, capacity 50 Imp gal (227 litres)
80 Fuel filler cap

81 Main (double I-beam) spar
82 Fuel filler cap
83 Flap inner carriage
84 Port main fuel tank, capacity 75 Imp gal (341 litres)
85 Flap control access
86 Flap structure

87 Entry ladder release
88 Flap drive motor
89 Fuel surge tank and main hydraulic reservoir in aft nacelle
90 Radio equipment compartment
91 Turnover support pylon

154

P-38Hs were the first to have the bar added to the national insignia (illustrated). This factory-fresh example is seen on a test flight from Lockheed's Burbank facility in California, prior to delivery to the USAAF.

SPECIFICATION

Lockheed P-38L Lightning

Type

Single-seat fighter

Powerplant

Two 1,475-hp (1100-kW) Allison V-1710-111/-113 V-12 piston engines

Performance

Maximum speed 414 mph (666 km/h) at 25,000 ft (7620 m); service ceiling 44,000 ft (13410 m); normal range 450 miles (724 km)

Weights

Empty 12,800 lb (5806 kg); maximum take-off 21,600 lb (9798 kg)

Dimensions

Wingspan 52 ft (15.85 m); length 37 ft 10 in (11.53 m); height 12 ft 10 in (3.91 m); wing area 328 sq ft (30.47 m2)

Armament

Four 0.5-in (12.7-mm) machine-guns and one 20-mm cannon, plus up to 3,200 lb (1451 kg) of bombs

92 Flap control access
93 Aerial attachment
94 Starboard inner flap
95 Flap push-pull rod
96 Starboard main fuel tank, capacity as 84
97 Main spar
98 Engine control runs
99 Starboard reserve fuel tank, capacity as 79
100 Starboard oil tank
101 Cooling louvres
102 Cabin heater intake
103 Turbo-supercharger cooling intakes
104 Turbine cooling duct
105 Exhaust turbine
106 Supercharger housing
107 Wingroot/boom fillet
108 Coolant/radiator return pipe (left and right)
109 Exhaust waste gate outlet
110 Access panel
111 Boom Joint (Station 265)
112 Radiator/coolant supply pipe
113 Mainwheel well
114 Mainwheel doors
115 Radiator intake
116 Starboard outer radiator fairing
117 Radiator grille
118 Engine coolant radiator assembly
119 Exit flap
120 Tool and baggage compartment
121 Boom structure
122 D/R master compass housing
123 Boom/tail attachment joint (Station 393)
124 Starboard lower fin
125 Tail bumper skid shoe
126 Elevator control pulley
127 Rudder stop
128 Elevator control horn
129 Fixed tip
130 Radio aerials
131 Tail surface control pulleys
132 Aerodynamic mass balance
133 Aerial attachments
134 Starboard rudder
135 Tab control rod and drum
136 Rudder trim tab
137 Elevator abbreviated torque tube
138 Tailplane stressed skin
139 Elevator pin hinges (eight off)
140 Elevator
141 Upper and lower mass balances
142 Elevator trim tab
143 Tailplane structure
144 Stiffeners
145 Port fin structure
146 Elevator pulley access
147 Rudder tab drum access
148 Tail running light (port)
149 Aerodynamic mass balance
150 Rudder framework
151 Rudder trim tab
152 Fixed tip structure
153 Tail surfaces/boom (quatrefoil bulkhead) attachment flanges
154 Rudder lower section
155 Tail bumper skid shoe
156 Elevator pulley access
157 Port lower fin
158 Elevator, rudder, and table cables
159 Battery compartment
160 Radiator exit flap
161 Engine coolant radiator assembly
162 Radiator housing
163 Radiator/coolant supply pipe
164 Radiator intake
165 Coolant/radiator return pipe
166 Oxygen cylinder
167 Port inner radiator fairing
168 Flare tube (port and starboard booms)
169 Mainwheel doors
170 Mainwheel well
171 Exhaust waste gate outlet
172 Turbine cooling duct
173 Exhaust turbine
174 Supercharger assembly
175 Supercharger/intercooler duct
176 Carburettor intake duct
177 Carburettor air intake
178 Abbreviated rear spar
179 Flap outer section
180 Tab cable access
181 Fixed tab
182 Aileron trim tab
183 Aileron full-span piano-wire hinge
184 Underwing pitot attachment
185 Raked web stiffener (outboard of rear spar)
186 Aileron structure
187 Outer wing pressed sheet ribs
188 Aileron counterweight
189 Junction box
190 Port navigation lights
191 Port wingtip structure
192 Leading-edge ribs
193 Pitot head
194 Wing leading-edge skin join (fabric-covered piano-wire hinge)
195 Wing outer section I-beam box spar
196 Leading-edge stringers (no fuel tanks in early P-38 Js)
197 Wing inner surface corrugation
198 Spar single/double I-beam box spar transition
199 Mainwheel leg doors
200 Rearward-retracting mainwheel
201 Mainwheel oleo leg
202 Alloy spoked hub
203 Cantilever axle
204 Torque links
205 Hydraulic brake cable
206 Drag strut
207 Side strut
208 Drag links
209 Fulcrum
210 Actuating cylinder
211 Multi-bolt outer wing fixings
212 Turbo-supercharger cooling intakes
213 Cabin heater intake
214 Cooling louvres
215 Carburettor duct
216 Outer section wing fillet
217 Insulated exhaust shroud duct
218 Intercooler/carburettor duct
219 Supercharger/intercooler duct
220 Outlet
221 Oil radiator shutter
222 Intercooler
223 Exhausts
224 Allison V 1710 89/91 twelve-cylinder Vee engine
225 Magnetos/distributors
226 Intake fairing
227 Header feed pipes
228 Port outer oil radiator
229 Spark-plug and magneto cooling intake
230 Coolant header tank
231 Propeller hub
232 Oil radiator (outer sections) and intercooler (centre section tripleintake
233 Curtiss-Electric three-blade (right) handed propeller
234 Inner section underwing stores including
235 Jettisonable auxiliary fuel tank, or
236 Smoke generator, or
237 1,000-lb (454-kg) bomb

Macchi MC.200/202/205

*The **Cucaracham** (cockroach) device on the rear fuselage of these early MC.200s identifies the aircraft as belonging to 22° Gruppo, 52° Stormo, based at Ciampino for the defence of Rome in 1940. In fact, these machines are from 371ª Squadriglia.*

MC.200 Saetta (Serie XIX)

Cutaway key
1 Propeller hub
2 Variable-pitch propeller
3 Hub plate
4 Casing
5 Pitch control mechanism
6 Oil radiator
7 Cowling ring
8 Fiat A.74 RC.38 14-cylinder radial air-cooled engine
9 Cowling rocker arm fairings
10 Carburettor intake
11 Intake housing
12 Starboard mainwheel
13 Intake filter
14 Exhaust outlet
15 Engine mounting ring
16 Exhaust collector ring
17 Adjustable cowling gills
18 Zenith compressor
19 Engine ring bearer frames
20 Oil filler access
21 Undercarriage retraction jack attachment
22 Firewall bulkhead
23 Cooling louvres
24 Oil tank (9-Imp gal/42-litre capacity)
25 Machine-gun muzzle ports
26 F.M.62 gun camera (mounted mid-chord starboard wing join)
27 Starboard mainplane 28
Starboard pitot tube (heated)
29 Starboard navigation light
30 Aerial attachment
31 Starboard aileron
32 Cowling access panels
33 Fuel filler cap
34 Allocchio Bacchini B.30 R/T set
35 Battery

36 Twin 0.5-in (12.7-mm) Breda-SAFAT guns
37 Gun synchronisation mechanism
38 Link and case ejector chute
39 Gun mounting arm
40 Ammunition feed chute

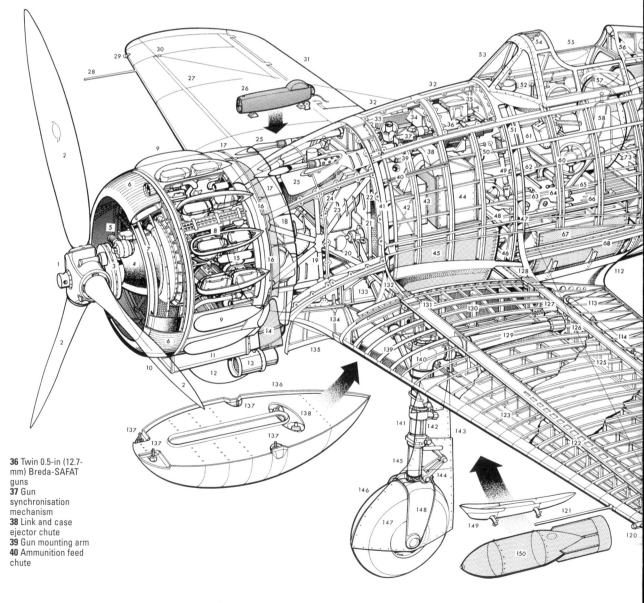

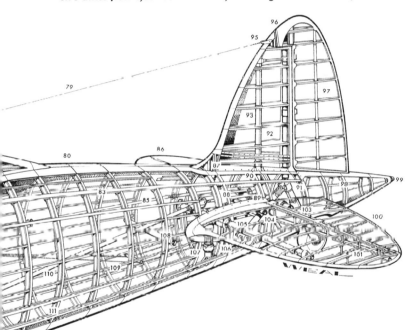

Late-production MC.200s such as these of 81ª Squadriglia, 6º Gruppo, 1º Stormo (based at Catania, Sicily late in 1940), took part in many sorties over Malta during this period. Deployed to North Africa in April 1941, the Saetta soon proved no match for the RAF's Hurricane Mk II and P-40 in air combat. So it was that, the following year, the MC.200 was used for the first time as a fighter-bomber, usually escorted by more modern fighters. By the time of the Allied invasion of Sicily the type was wholly outdated, though 42 remained in the front-line order of battle, of which 23 were still in use in September 1943. The Saetta also saw some use on the Eastern Front, 22º and, later, 21º Gruppi deploying to Russia in April 1941. These two units flew 6,361 sorties in all, claiming 85 Soviet kills for 15 losses.

SPECIFICATION

	MC.200 Saetta	MC.205V Veltro
Dimensions		

MC.200 Saetta — Dimensions
Length: 26 ft 10¼ in (8.19 m)
Height: 11 ft 5¾ (3.50 m)
Wingspan: 34 ft 8½ in (10.58 m)
Wing area: 180.84 sq ft (16.80 m²)

MC.205V Veltro — Dimensions
Length: 29 ft 0½ in (8.58 m)
Height: 9 ft 11½ in (3.04 m)
Wingspan: 34 ft 8½ in (10.58 m)
Wing area: 180.84 sq ft (16.80 m²)

MC.200 Saetta — Powerplant
One Fiat A.74 RC.38 14-cylinder air-cooled radial piston engine delivering 870 hp (649 kW)

MC.205V Veltro — Powerplant
One Fiat RA.1050 RC.58 Tifone 12-cylinder inverted Vee piston engine delivering 1,475 hp (1100 kW)

MC.200 Saetta — Weights and loads
Empty: 4,178 lb (1895 kg)
Maximum take-off: 5,710 lb (2590 kg)

MC.205V Veltro — Weights and loads
Empty: 5,691 lb (2581 kg)
Maximum take-off: 7,514 lb (3408 kg)

MC.200 Saetta — Performance
Maximum speed at 14,765 ft (4500 m): 312 mph (502 km/h)
Cruising speed: 283 mph (455 km/h)
Service ceiling: 29,200 ft (8900 m)
Range with auxiliary fuel: 540 miles (870 km)

MC.205V Veltro — Performance
Maximum speed at 23,620 ft (7200 m): 399 mph (642 km/h)
Cruising speed: 310 mph (500 km/h)
Service ceiling: 37,090 ft (16370 m)
Range: 646 miles (1040 km)

MC.200 Saetta — Armament
Two 0.5 in (12.7 mm) Breda SAFAT machine-guns in upper cowling; later aircraft had two additional 0.303-in (7.7-mm) guns mounted in the wings. Late-production aircraft were also able to carry up 882 lb (400 kg) of bombs on underwing pylons

MC.205V Veltro — Armament
Two 0.5-in (12.7-mm) Breda-SAFAT machine guns in upper cowling, plus two wing-mounted 0.303-in (7.7-mm) machine-guns; late series aircraft had the wing-mounted guns replaced by two 20-mm cannon

MC.201 – a one-off prototype

Answering the Regia Aeronautica's call in 1938 for an 'economical interceptor' to follow on from the Fiat G.50 and Macchi MC.200, a number of proposals were received. Macchi's was the MC.201, effectively a Saetta fitted with the new 1,000-hp (746-kW) Fiat A.76 RC.40 radial. A single prototype (MM436) was constructed, but development of the A.76 was abandoned so this first flew with the Saetta's A.74 engine installed. By early 1940 interest in the 'economical interceptor' had waned and a second MC.201 was completed with a DB 601 engine, as a forerunner to the MC.202.

41 Fuselage forward frame (Frame 0)
42 Supplementary magazine
43 Ammunition magazine
44 Link/spent case collector
45 Main fuel tank (52.3-Imp gal/238-litre capacity)
46 Centre-section rear spar carry-through
47 Fuselage frame (Frame 4)
48 Rudder pedal/heel rest assembly
49 Control column
50 Aerial attachment
51 Instrument panel
52 San Giorgio reflector gunsight
53 Windscreen
54 Canopy side-panel lock/release
55 Cutaway canopy side-panels
56 Cutaway canopy side-panels
57 Turnover pylon structure
58 SILMA CO₂ fire extinguisher bottle (fuselage starboard wall)
59 Pilot's seat
60 Adjustable tailplane trim wheel
61 Throttle quadrant
62 Pilot's oxygen cylinder (to right of seat)
63 Control linkage
64 Seat adjustment handle
65 Seat main frame
66 Cockpit floor
67 Underfloor fuel tank (16.5-Imp gal/75-litre capacity)
68 Lower longeron
69 Entry foothold
70 Cylinder support frame
71 Compressed air cylinder (2.2-Imp gal/10-litre capacity)
72 Hydraulic reservoir (flap actuation)
73 Garelli compressor (fuselage starboard wall)
74 Hydraulic reservoir (undercarriage actuation)
75 Auxiliary fuel tank (18-Imp gal/83-litre capacity)
76 Fuel filler access cut-out
77 Fairing formers
78 Stub aerial mast
79 Aerial
80 Fuselage skin
81 Fuselage structure
82 Frame
83 Upper longeron
84 Stringer
85 Rudder control rod
86 Starboard horizontal tail surfaces
87 Tailfin front attachment
88 Fuselage frame (Frame 16)
89 Elevator control horns
90 Tailplane attachment (Frame 17)
91 Fuselage aft frame (Frame 18)
92 Tailfin structure
93 Support tube
94 Rudder post
95 Aerial attachment
96 Rudder balance
97 Rudder frame
98 Tail cone
99 Tail navigation light
100 Port elevator
101 Port tailplane structure
102 Non-retractable tailwheel
103 Tailwheel shock strut
104 Tailplane incidence torque tube (+ 1° 45' to -5° 30')
105 Tailplane support tube
106 Tailwheel strut attachment
107 Tailplane incidence screw
108 Lifting tube
109 Tailplane incidence control cables
110 Elevator control rod
111 Lower longeron
112 Wingroot fillet
113 Flap profile
114 Flap-operating rod
115 Flap structure
116 Wing rear spar
117 Port aileron structure
118 Wing outer section ribs
119 Port wingtip structure
120 Port navigation light
121 Port pitot tube (unheated)
122 Wing front spar
123 Leading-edge rib sections
124 Wing skin
125 Aerial
126 Undercarriage/rear spar attachment
127 Wing outer/inner section front spar join
128 Wing root fairing former
129 Undercarriage rotation spindle
130 Centre-section outer rib
131 Wing outer/inner section front spar join
132 Frame 0 carry-through
133 Undercarriage retraction strut
134 Port mainwheel well
135 Mainwheel door inner section
136 Auxiliary jettisonable fuel tank (33-Imp gal/ 150-litre capacity)
137 Attachment lugs
138 Fuel connections
139 Mainwheel leg well
140 Undercarriage pivot
141 Mainwheel leg
142 Retraction strut attachment
143 Leg doors (hinged)
144 Torque links
145 Shock strut
146 Port mainwheel
147 Mainwheel door outer section
148 Axle fork
149 Underwing stores pylon
150 Bomb

MC.202 Folgore

MM9066 is an MC.202 Serie VII of 151ª Squadriglia, 20° Gruppo, 51° Stormo of the Regia Aeronautica, based in Sicily towards the end of 1942. Named *Dai Banana!* (Go, banana!) the aircraft was flown by Italian ace Sergeant Ennio Tarantola, who had been a banana importer before the war. Seven of his eventual eight kills are marked on the Folgore's tail. As well as Macchi, both Breda and SAI-Ambrosini were given contracts to build Folgores, the seventh production batch (Serie VII) of 100 aircraft being completed by Macchi. In all, 1,300 aircraft in 15 batches were authorised, though only about 1,150 were completed before the Italian surrender.

National insignia

In addition to the white cross on the tail, Regia Aeronautica aircraft carried the *fasces* national insignia of the Italian Fascist party on the fuselage. The symbol was of Roman origin, consisting of a bundle of rods with an axe-head protruding, and symbolised the power of the magistrates. Wing roundels comprised three black *fasces* devices in a black circle.

Control surfaces

The statically- and aerodynamically-balanced ailerons were of high aspect ratio and reached right to the wingtip. The MC.202 was considered to be one of the most manouevrable and, above all, one of the most beautifully harmonised fighters of the war.

Wing and tail structure

The wing was built around a two-spar structure, which carried through the lower fuselage. Apart from the wing root fuel tank and the gun/ammunition installation, there was nothing contained within the structure itself. The tail surfaces exhibited classical curves, the moveable surfaces being metal-framed but fabric-skinned. The large rudder had an auxiliary spar and featured an aerodynamic horn balance at the tip.

Armament

Though comparatively fast and agile the Folgore was inadequately armed. Aircraft in the first six production batches carried a pair of 0.5-in (12.7-mm) Breda-SAFAT machine-guns mounted in the upper fuselage decking ahead of the cockpit. These were armed with 400 rounds each. From Serie VII the MC.202 featured a gun in each wing in an attempt to redress this problem. These were 0.303-in (7.7-mm) Breda-SAFAT guns, each with 500 rounds. This armament arrangement was repeated in early-production MC.205Vs, though a pair of 20-mm MG 151 cannon replaced the wing machine-guns in later aircraft.

Powerplant

Alfa Romeo acquired a licence for the Daimler-Benz DB 601A inverted vee-12 engine, which was built for the MC.202 as the RA.1000 RC.41 Monsoni. The engine developed 1,075 hp (802 kW) for take-off at 2,500 rpm and had a normal maximum rating of 1,040 hp (776 kW) at 2,400 rpm. The first production MC.202s were fitted with German-built engines, 400 of which were supplied. Alfa Romeo began DB 601 production at its Pomigliano d'Arco plant, initially using components supplied from Germany. The first wholly Italian-made engines came off the line in the summer of 1941. Eventually 2,000 were completed. The Monsoni engine drove a Piaggio P.1001 three-bladed, constant-speed propeller of 10 ft (3.05 m) diameter.

Cockpit

In the Folgore's cockpit the pilot was provided with a San Giorgio reflector sight, offset to starboard, and secondary ring-and-bead sight, offset to port. The framed canopy hinged to starboard for access. The characteristic fairing behind the cockpit improved aerodynamics and incorporated a cut-out on either side so that rearward visibility was impaired as little as possible. An armoured seat was provided and, from Serie VII onward, an armoured glass windscreen was fitted.

Camouflage and markings

Depending on the theatre, MC.202s were mostly finished in greens and browns. This aircraft has the classic 'sand-and-spinach' finish, the basic desert scheme being overpainted with green patterns for a disruptive effect. The prominent marking applied over the white fuselage band is that of 51° Stormo, depicting 'Sorci Verdi' (Green Mice, representing bomber aircraft) being chased by a black cat (a 51° Stormo fighter). This insignia was retained by the Gruppo post-war and is displayed on its AMX aircraft in 2000. The small 'AS' marking under the aircraft's serial number stands for Africa Settentrionale (North Africa) and indicated that the aircraft had been tropicalised for service in the Mediterranean threatre.

Fuel

The Folgore's main fuel tank was located in the fuselage between the cockpit and engine, this holding 60 Imp gal (270 litres). Either side of this was a pair of wing root tanks, each holding 9 Imp gal (40 litres), while an overload fuel tank was available in the rear fuselage behind the pilot's seat for a further 18 Imp gal (80 litres). The Serie XI aircraft introduced plumbing for drop tanks.

Messerschmitt Bf 109E

A Bf 109E-7/Trop of JG 5 over the northern sector of the Eastern Front in 1942. This example was fitted with dust and sand filters and a survival kit. This was standard for tropical versions of the Bf 109.

Bf 109E-4

Cutaway key
1 Hollow propeller hub
2 Spinner
3 Three-bladed VDM variable-pitch propeller
4 Propeller pitch-change mechanism
5 Spinner back plate
6 Glycol coolant header tank
7 Glycol filler cap
8 Cowling fastener
9 Chin intake
10 Coolant pipe fairing
11 Exhaust forward fairing
12 Additional (long-range) oil tank
13 Daimler-Benz DB 601A engine
14 Supplementary intakes
15 Fuselage machine-gun troughs
16 Anti-vibration engine mounting pads
17 Exhaust ejector stubs
18 Coolant pipes (to underwing radiators)
19 Oil cooler intake
20 Coolant radiator
21 Radiator outlet flap
22 Cowling frame
23 Engine mounting support strut
24 Spent cartridge collector compartment
25 Ammunition boxes (starboard loading)
26 Engine supercharger
27 Supercharger air intake fairing
28 Forged magnesium alloy cantilever engine mounting
29 Engine mounting/forward bulkhead attachment
30 Ammunition feed chutes

31 Engine accessories
32 Two fuselage-mounted MG17 machine-guns
33 Blast tube muzzles
34 Wing skinning
35 Starboard cannon access
36 20-mm MG FF wing cannon
37 Leading-edge automatic slot
38 Slot tracks
39 Slot actuating linkage
40 Wing main spar
41 Intermediate rib station
42 Wing end rib
43 Starboard navigation light
44 Aileron outer hinge
45 Aileron metal trim tab
46 Starboard aileron
47 Aileron/flap link connection
48 Combined control linkage
49 Starboard flap frame
50 Cannon ammunition drum access
51 Fuselage machine-gun cooling slots
52 Gun mounting frame
53 Firewall/bulkhead
54 Instrument panel near face (fabric covered)
55 Oil dipstick cover
56 Control column
57 Oil filler cap (tank omitted for clarity)
58 Rudder pedal assembly
59 Aircraft identity data plate (external)
60 Mainspar centre-section carry-through
61 Underfloor control linkage

This Bf 109E-1 of I/JG 20 is seen in August/September 1939, i.e. upon the outbreak of World War II. This Gruppe did not participate in the Polish campaign, remaining in eastern Germany on metropolitan defence duties around Dresden. In July 1940 I./JG 20 became III./JG 51 and the 'black cat' emblem was used by 8/JG 51.

SPECIFICATION

Bf 109 E-4

Dimensions

Length overall: 28 ft 6 in (8.7 m)
Wing span: 32 ft 6 in (9.9 m)
Wing area: 176 sq ft (16.4m²)

Powerplant

One Daimler Benz DB 601Aa 12 cylinder inverted-Vee liquid cooled engine with direct fuel injection. Rated at 1,020 hp (761 kW) at 14,7675 ft (4500 m).

Weights

Empty: 4,440 lb (2018 kg)
Maximum take-off: 5,520 lb (2509 kg)

Performance

Maximum speed: 357 mph (575 km/h) at 19,700 ft (3200 m)
Service ceiling: 36,000 ft (10972 m)

Range

434 miles (700 km) on internal fuel

Armament

Two 20-mm (Oerlikon) MG FF cannon with 60 r.p.g in wings and two fuselage-mounted 0.312-in (7.9-mm) Rheinmetall Borsig MG 17 machine guns with 500 r.p.g. E-4/B fighter-bombers were capable of carrying either four 110-lb (50-kg) bombs or one 551-lb (250-kg) bomb.

Bf 109 T-2

generally similar to Bf 109 E-4 except

Dimensions

Length overall: 28 ft 9 in (8.76 m)
Wing span: 36 ft 4¼ in (11.08 m)
Wing area: 188,368 sq ft (17.5m²)

Powerplant

One Daimler Benz DB 601N cylinder inverted-Vee liquid cooled engine with direct fuel injection. Rated at 1,270 hp (947 kW) at 16,400 ft (5000 m).

Weights

Empty: 4,409 lb (2000 kg)
Maximum take-off: 6,786 lb (3078 kg)

Performance

Service ceiling: 34,450 ft (10500 m)

Range

568 miles (914 km) (with 66-lmp gal/300-litre drop tank)

62 Oxygen regulator
63 Harness adjustment lever
64 Engine priming pump
65 Circuit breaker panel
66 Hood catch
67 Starboard-hinged cockpit canopy
68 Revi gunsight (offset to starboard)
69 Windscreen panel frame
70 Canopy section frame
71 Pilot's head armour
72 Pilot's back armour
73 Seat harness
74 Pilot's seat
75 Seat adjustment lever
76 Tailplane incidence handwheel
77 Cockpit floor diaphragm
78 Landing flaps control hand wheel
79 Seat support frame
80 Contoured ('L' shape) fuel tank
81 Tailplane incidence cables
82 Fuselage frame
83 Rudder cable
84 Oxygen cylinders
85 Fuel filler/overspill pipes
86 Baggage compartment
87 Entry handhold (spring-loaded)
88 Canopy fixed aft section
89 Aerial mast
90 Aerial
91 Fuel filler cap
92 Fuel vent line
93 Radio pack support brackets
94 Anti-vibration bungee supports
95 FuG VII transmitter/receiver radio pack
96 Aerial lead-in
97 Tailplane incidence cable pulley
98 Rudder control cable
99 Monocoque fuselage structure
100 Radio access/first-aid kit panel
101 Elevator control cables
102 Fuselage frame
103 Lifting tube
104 Tailfin root fillet
105 Tailplane incidence gauge (external)
106 Tailplane support strut
107 Starboard tailplane
108 Elevator outer hinge
109 Elevator balance
110 Starboard elevator
111 Tailfin structure
112 Aerial stub
113 Rudder balance
114 Rudder upper hinge
115 Rudder frame
116 Rudder trim tab
117 Tail navigation light
118 Port elevator frame
119 Elevator balance
120 Rudder control quadrant
121 Tailplane structure
122 Elevator torque tube sleeve
123 Tailplane end rib attachment
124 Fuselage end post
125 Elevator control rod
126 Port tailplane support strut
127 Non-retractable tailwheel
128 Tailwheel leg
129 Elevator control cable rod link
130 Tail wheel leg shock-absorber
131 Rudder control cable
132 Fuselage stringer
133 Accumulator
134 Fuselage half ventral join
135 Electrical leads
136 Fuselage panel
137 Radio pack lower support frames
138 Entry foothold (spring loaded)
139 Wingroot fillet
140 Flap profile
141 Port flap frame
142 Port aileron frame
143 Aileron trim tab
144 Rear spar
145 Port wingtip
146 Port navigation light
147 Wing main spar outer section
148 Solid ribs
149 Leading-edge automatic slot
150 Rib cut-outs
151 Control link access plate
152 Wing rib stations
153 Port wing 20 mm MG FF cannon installation
154 Ammunition drum access panel
155 Inboard rib cut-outs
156 Flap visual position indicator
157 Control access panel
158 Main spar/fuselage attachment fairing
159 Wing control surface cable pulleys
160 Port mainwheel well
161 Wheel well (zipped) fabric shield
162 20 mm MG FF wing cannon
163 Wing front spar
164 Undercarriage leg tunnel rib cut-outs
165 Undercarriage lock mechanism
166 Wing/fuselage end rib
167 Undercarriage actuating cylinder
168 Mainwheel leg/fuselage attachment bracket
169 Leg pivot point
170 Mainwheel oleo leg
171 Mainwheel leg door
172 Brake lines
173 Torque links
174 Mainwheel hub
175 Axle
176 Port main wheel
177 Mainwheel half-door
178 Ventral ETC centre-line stores pylon, possible loads include:
179 Early-type (wooden) drop tank
180 66-lmp gal (300-litre) [Junkers] metal drop tank
181 551-lb (250-kg) HE bomb, or
182 551-lb (250-kg) SAP bomb

Bf 109E-4

This Messerschmitt Bf 109E-4 is part of I. Gruppe, Jagdgeschwader 3 and was based at Grandvillier, France in August 1940. Gruppenkommandeur Hans von Hahn's aircraft, it displays the *Tatzelwurm* (a dragon resembling a crested or spiked worm) on the nose, a symbol carried by all the aircraft in I. Gruppe of JG 3. The emblem was applied in green to Stab (staff) aircraft, in white to aircraft of 1. Staffel, in red to aircraft of 2. Staffel, and in yellow to aircraft of 3. Staffel. The foremost part of the spinner was painted in the same colour.

Up-engined 'Emils'

The Bf 109E-4/N was powered by a DB 601N engine, whose flattened (instead of concave) piston heads gave a higher compression ratio, and which used higher octane fuel. The Bf 109E-7 was similarly powered, and the Bf 109E-7/Z introduced a nitrous oxide (GM1) supercharger injection system, which boosted altitude performance and was known as the 'Ha-Ha' system. A similar performance increase was provided both in the Bf 109E-8 and the recce-roled Bf 109E-9 by the new DB 601E engine, with increased maximum rpm, improved supercharging, and a take-off power of 1,350 hp (1006 kW). The downside was that the new engine was considerably less economical and, even with a 22-Imp gal (100-litre) increase in fuel capacity (to 88 Imp gal/400 litres), the Bf 109E's already inadequate reach was not greatly improved.

Armament

Throughout its career, the Bf 109 was given progressively heavier armament. The prototype was originally specified with two cowling-mounted 0.312-in (7.92-mm) MG 17 machine-guns (each with 500 rounds of ammunition), with a third later added between the banks of cylinders to fire through the propeller hub, subsequently replaced by a 20-mm MG FF/M cannon. However, this 'through the hub' system proved unsuccessful and so later models received two more 0.312-in (7.92-mm) machine-guns in the wings. On the Bf 109E-3/4, the wing armament was the hard-hitting MG FF 20-mm cannon. The Bf 109E-4 was the first 109 variant to see service in the fighter-bomber (Jabo) role. A rudimentary ETC 500 bomb rack sat between the main wheels and was capable of carrying four 110-lb (50-kg) bombs or a single 551-lb (250-kg) bomb. After successful trials, each Bf 109 Gruppe was ordered to convert some of its Staffeln to the Jabo role. These aircraft received the designation BF 109E-4/B to illustrate their new role.

Aircraft markings

In the confused cut-and-thrust of fighter-versus-fighter combat, a means of easy recognition was regarded as essential and, from mid-August, the Bf 109Es had wing and tail tips painted in white or yellow, together with a patch at the top of the rudder. Whole rudders were soon painted in yellow, and the tips of noses (and sometimes whole cowlings) followed. Some aircraft had tail units that were painted yellow in their entirety, but this was unusual.

Camouflage

The Luftwaffe's Messerschmitt Bf 109s originally wore dark-green upper surfaces, with light blue-grey (Hellblau) undersides, but these colours were replaced by a disruptive two-tone green camouflage on the top surfaces. The two shades of green were so similar that they looked almost like a single colour, and weathering further reduced the differentiation between the shades. In the winter of 1939, the top surface colours were limited to the upper surfaces of the wings and tailplanes, plus the top decking of the fuselage. The fuselage sides and fin were painted Hellblau. On most aircraft, the top surface camouflage was repainted, with RLM 71 Dunkelgrün (the lighter of the two tones used previously) and RLM 02 Grau (a pale grey-green). These had a greater tonal variation than the previous colours. The basic new camouflage scheme was then modified at unit level during the Battle of Britain. Some aircraft had a neutral grey area painted along the wing leading-edge to soften the demarcation between the dark topsides and light undersurfaces. Fuselage sides were often overpainted with a mottled RLM 02 Grau, as seen on this aircraft.

Personal markings

The aircraft belonging to the Gruppenkommandeur of JG 3's I. Gruppe, Hans 'Vadder' ('Daddy') von Hahn, carried his own distinctive version of the standard double chevron (Winkel) or 'triangle and chevron' Gruppenkommandeur's marking. Under the cockpit was a cockerel's head, a play on his name (Hahn meaning cockerel in German), an insignia also used by his better-known namesake, Hans 'Assi' Hahn. Von Hahn began the war as the adjutant of JG 53, later becoming the Staffelkapitän of 8./JG 53 under Werner Mölders during the Battle of France. At the height of the Battle of Britain, when Herman Göring replaced his older fighter leaders (many of whom, like Theo Osterkamp and Dr Mix, had fought and even become aces in World War I), von Hahn was promoted to become the Gruppenkommandeur of I./JG 3, replacing Gunther Lützow who was, in turn, promoted to become Geschwaderkommodore. Von Hahn took the *Tatzelwurm* Gruppe to Russia in June 1941 and returned with the Gruppe in January 1942, having added 17 kills to his tally, thus bringing his total to 34 in 300 missions. The Gruppe was redesignated II./JG 1 and started converting to the Fw 190, and von Hahn began the first of a succession of staff and training appointments, ending the war as Jafü (fighter leader) Oberitalien (Upper Italy). He died in Frankfurt in 1957, aged 53.

Anatomy

The Bf 109 was built as a semi-monocoque fuselage, constructed in two halves and joined at the centreline. The undercarriage was attached directly to the fuselage, allowing the wing to be easily removed without the need for assembling jacks. The wing itself was a single-spar construction, the cannon-armed variants having a strengthened cut-out in the spar to accommodate the weapon. Similarly, the tail and tailplanes were simple single-spar structures, the tailplanes being externally braced by a single strut. The incidence of the tailplane could be altered via a torque tube in landing configuration to offset the effects of deploying both the flaps and the drooping ailerons. The wing slots, flaps and ailerons were actuated by rods, but the tail surfaces had cable runs through the rear fuselage, the rudder having a simple left/right pivoting arm. A tube was located transversely across the fuselage just forward of the tail unit, through which a rod could be inserted for lifting the aircraft's tail. The rear fuselage was largely empty but did provide housing for the two oxygen bottles and the FuG 7 radio equipment, which was supported on brackets attached to both the upper and lower fuselage frames. In the forward fuselage, the engine was cantilevered on A-frame engine bearers, above which were mounted the guns. The ammunition tanks were located below and behind the engine, feeding upwards into the weapons. The glycol coolant was held in a header tank just aft of the propeller.

Messerschimitt Bf 109G/K

It was not until the development of the G model that the Messerschmitt Bf 109 went into mass-scale production and with this new variant came the hitherto unseen practice of producing a myriad of versions. By the middle of the war, the Bf 109 had lost its supremacy, yet continued to remain the backbone of the Luftwaffe until the end of the war. Even during the final days of the Reich, the late-model Bf 109Gs and Ks managed to put up fierce resistance to the invading Allies.

Bf 109G-14

Cutaway key

1 Starboard navigation light
2 Starboard wingtip
3 Fixed trim tab
4 Starboard Frise-type aileron
5 Flush-rivetted stressed wing skinning
6 Handley Page automatic leading-edge slot
7 Slot control linkage
8 Slot equaliser rod
9 Aileron control linkage
10 Fabric-covered flap section
11 Wheel fairing
12 Port fuselage machine-gun ammunition feed fairing
13 Port 13-mm Rheinmetall-Borsig MG 131 machine-gun
14 Engine accessories
15 Starboard machine-gun trough
16 Daimler-Benz DB 605AM 12-cylinder inverted-Vee liquid-cooled engine
17 Detachable cowling panel
18 Oil filter access
19 Oil tank
20 Propeller pitch-change mechanism
21 VDM electrically-operated constant-speed propeller
22 Spinner
23 Engine-mounted cannon muzzle
24 Blast tube
25 Propeller hub
26 Spinner back plate
27 Auxiliary cooling intakes
28 Coolant header tank
29 Anti-vibration rubber engine mounting pads
30 Elektron forged engine bearer
31 Engine bearer support strut attachment
32 Plug leads

33 Exhaust manifold fairing strip
34 Ejector exhausts
35 Cowling fasteners
36 Oil cooler
37 Oil cooler intake
38 Starboard mainwheel
39 Oil cooler outlet flap
40 Wingroot fillet
41 Wing/fuselage fairing
42 Firewall/bulkhead
43 Supercharger air intake
44 Supercharger assembly
45 20-mm cannon magazine drum
46 13-mm machine-gun ammunition feed
47 Engine bearer upper attachment
48 Ammunition feed fairing
49 13-mm Rheinmetall-Borsig MG 131 machine-gun breeches
50 Instrument panel
51 20-mm Mauser MG 151/20 cannon breech
52 Heelrests
53 Rudder pedals
54 Undercarriage emergency retraction cables
55 Fuselage frame
56 Wing/fuselage fairing
57 Undercarriage emergency retraction handwheel (outboard)
58 Tail trim handwheel (inboard)
59 Seat harness
60 Throttle lever
61 Control column
62 Cockpit ventilation inlet
63 Revi 16B reflector gunsight (folding)
64 Armoured windshield frame
65 Anti-glare gunsight screen
66 3½-in (90-mm) armoured glass windscreen
67 Erla-Haube clear-vision hinged canopy

68 Galland-Panzer framed armourglass head/back panel
69 Canopy contoured frame
70 Canopy hinges (starboard)
71 Canopy release catch

72 Pilot's bucket-type seat (0.3-in/8-mm back armour)
73 Underfloor contoured fuel tank (88 Imp gal/ 400 litres of 87 octane B4)
74 Fuselage frame
75 Circular access panel
76 Tail trimming cable conduit
77 Wireless leads
78 MW-50 (methanol/water) tank (25-Imp gal/114-litre capacity)
79 Handhold

80 Fuselage decking
81 Aerial mast
82 D/F loop
83 Oxygen cylinders (three)
84 Filler pipe
85 Wireless equipment packs (FuG 16ZY communications and FuG 25 IFF)

86 Main fuel filler cap
87 Aerial
88 Fuselage top keel (connector stringer)
89 Aerial lead-in
90 Fuselage skin-plating sections
91 'U' stringers

As the tide of war turned in favour of the Allies, the retreating Germans left a number of aircraft in their wake. This Bf 109G-2/Trop was captured at Gambut in Libya and made airworthy by an RAAF crew. It was initially transported around the Middle East for testing and eventually made it to England, where it was used in comparative trials against Allied fighters. It survived the war and remained in storage for many years until it was restored to an airworthy condition. The aircraft's first post-rebuild flight took place on 17 March 1991 and the '109 received its old identification of 'Black 6'. However, in 1998 the aircraft made a forced landing and was damaged to such an extent that it will spend the rest of its days in the static line at Duxford Air Museum.

SPECIFICATION

Bf 109G-6

Dimensions

Length: 29 ft 7 in (9.02 m)
Wingspan: 32 ft 6½ in (9.92 m)
Height: 8 ft 2½ in (2.50 m)
Wing area: 172.75 sq ft (16.05 m²)

Powerplant

One Daimler Benz DB 605AM 12-cylinder inverted-Vee liquid-cooled engine rated at 1,475 hp (1100 kW) for take-off and 1,355 hp (1010 kW) at 18,700 ft (5700 m)

Weights

Empty: 5,953 lb (2700 kg)
Loaded: 6,495 lb (3150 kg)

Performance

Maximum speed at 22,967 ft (7000 m): 387 mph (623 km/h)
Maximum speed at sea level: 338 mph (544 km/h)
Climb to 19,868 ft (6000 m): 6 minutes
Service ceiling: 38,551 ft (11750 m)
Absolute ceiling: 39,700 ft (12100 m)

Range

Normal: 450 miles (725 km)
Maximum: 615 miles (990 km)

Armament

One 30-mm Rheinmetall Borsig MK 108 engine-mounted cannon with 60 rounds or two 20-mm Mauser MG 151/20 cannon with 150 rounds, and two 13-mm Rheinmetall-Borsig MG 131 fuselage-mounted machine-guns with 300 rounds per gun

Bf 109K-4

Same as Bf 109G except for:

Powerplant

One Daimler Benz DB 605DCM 12-cylinder inverted-Vee liquid-cooled engine rated at 2,000 hp (1492 kW) for take-off and 1,800 hp (1343 kW) at 16,400 ft (5000 m)

Weights

Loaded: 7,438 lb (3370 kg)

Performance

Maximum speed at 24,610 ft (7500 m): 387 mph (623 km/h)
Maximum speed at sea level: 378 mph (608 km/h)

92 Fuselage frames (monocoque construction)
93 Tail trimming cables
94 Tailfin root fairing
95 Starboard fixed tailplane
96 Elevator balance
97 Starboard elevator
98 Geared elevator tab
99 All-wooden tailfin construction
100 Aerial attachment
101 Rudder upper hinge bracket
102 Rudder post
103 Fabric-covered wooden rudder structure
104 Geared rudder tab
105 Rear navigation light
106 Port elevator
107 Elevator geared tab
108 Tailplane structure
109 Rudder actuating linkage
110 Elevator control horn
111 Elevator connecting rod
112 Elevator control quadrant
113 Tailwheel leg cuff
114 Castoring non-retractable tailwheel
115 Lengthened tailwheel leg
116 Access panel
117 Tailwheel shock strut
118 Lifting point
119 Rudder cable
120 Elevator cables
121 First-aid pack
122 Air bottles
123 Fuselage access panel
124 Bottom keel (connector stringer)
125 Ventral IFF aerial
126 Master compass
127 Elevator control linkage
128 Wingroot fillet
129 Camber changing flap
130 Ducted coolant radiator
131 Wing stringers
132 Wing rear pick-up point
133 Spar/fuselage upper pin joint (horizontal)
134 Spar/fuselage lower pin joint (vertical)
135 Flap equaliser rod
136 Rüstsatz-3 auxiliary fuel tank ventral rack
137 Undercarriage electrical interlock
138 Wing horizontal pin forward pick-up
139 Undercarriage retraction jack mechanism
140 Undercarriage pivot bevel
141 Auxiliary fuel tank (Rüstsatz-3) of 66-Imp gal/300-litre capacity
142 Mainwheel leg fairing
143 Mainwheel oleo leg
144 Brake lines
145 Mainwheel fairing
146 Port mainwheel
147 Leading-edge skin
148 Port mainwheel well
149 Wing spar
150 Flap actuating linkage
151 Fabric-covered control surfaces
152 Slotted flap structure
153 Leading-edge slot-actuating mechanism
154 Slot equaliser rod
155 Handley Page automatic leading-edge slot
156 Wing stringers
157 Spar flange decrease
158 Wing ribs
159 Flush-rivetted stressed wing skinning
160 Metal framed Frise-type aileron
161 Fixed trim tab
162 Wingtip construction
163 Port navigation light
164 Angled pitot head
165 Rüstsatz-6 optional underwing cannon gondola
166 14-point plug connection
167 Electrical junction box
168 Cannon rear mounting bracket
169 20-mm Mauser MG 151/20 cannon
170 Cannon front mounting bracket
171 Ammunition feed chute
172 Ammunition magazine drum
173 Underwing panel
174 Gondola fairing
175 Cannon barrel

This mixed bag of 'Gustavs' consists of a Bf 109G-3 (nearest the camera) fitted with the large, fixed tailwheel, a G-6 (centre), and an early machine (background) with retractable tailwheel, probably a G-2.

Bf 109K-4

III./JG 77 and III./JG 27 were the first units to re-equip with the Bf 109K-4, the first of which came off the production line in August 1944. The first recorded combat engagement involving K-4s came on 2 November, when JG 27 engaged Allied fighters escorting a large bomber force near Leipzig. In the ensuing fight, JG 27 suffered its worst one-day losses of the war to date – 27 pilots were killed and 11 wounded. Seven Allied 'kills' were claimed by the unit – all Mustangs. Later in the month other units received K-4s, including III./JG 3, III./JG 4, III./JG 26 and I./JG 27, and by 1 January 1945, the day of the Luftwaffe's ill-fated Operation Bodenplatte against Allied airfields, the following Gruppen had also received the variant: II./JG 2, I./JG 4, IV./JG 4 and II./JG 11. It is believed that no unit was exclusively equipped with the Bf 109K; a mix of Gs and Ks was the norm. During January 1945, a number of units equipped with K-4s transferred to the Eastern Front, including III./JG 27, and during late January and February a number of eastern Gruppen was issued with the type.

Engine and propeller

Bf 109K-0 pre-production aircraft and the first K-4s were powered by the DB 605DB variant of Daimler-Benz's inverted-Vee, 12-cylinder, liquid-cooled DB 605. (The DB 605D series was derived from the 605A, featuring a larger supercharger derived from that designed for the DB 603 engine.) Later machines utilised the DB 605DC, differing from the 605DB in having a higher maximum supercharger boost pressure and being strengthened accordingly. The higher boost pressure allowed maximum power output to be attained while using lower-octane fuel, a valuable feature as shortages of first-rate fuel worsened as the war continued. Like its predecessors, the Bf 109K-4 also used MW-50 (methanol-water) injection to boost power, but only when the engine was running on lower-octane fuel. The DB 605 drove a wide-bladed VDM9-12159A propeller with a 10-ft (3-m) diameter, and used fuel that was held in an 88-Imp gal (400-litre) tank located behind the pilot. A Rüstsatz kit (R3) was applied to some aircraft to improve range, with a 66-Imp gal (300-litre) drop tank suspended under the fuselage.

Reconnaissance variants

Among the Rüstzustände kits planned for the K-4 were three which gave the type a reconnaissance capability: the R2, R5 and R6. The R2 was to carry an Rb 50/30 or Rb 70/30 vertical camera behind the cockpit, the R5 an Rb 32/7x9 or Rb 12/7x9 and the R6 a BSK 16 gun camera in the port wing leading edge for bomber and fighter-bomber units.

Identifying features

Several features of the Bf 109K-4's airframe had been carried over from late-production 'Gustavs'. These included rectangular upper wing surface bulges to accommodate wider, low-pressure main gear tyres (fitted to improve ground-handling), a bulged DB 605D series sump cover (below the leading exhaust nozzle) and the FuG 16ZY radio aerial under the port wing. The rudder usually had a Flettner tab and two fixed trim tabs (to obviate the need for rudder applications when diving and climbing), although some aircraft did not have the fixed tabs. Unique to the K-4 were a relocated DF loop, a refined lower engine cowling design, a relocated fuselage access hatch, a taller, retractable tailwheel and additional main gear wheel well doors (often removed in the field). Fixed aileron trim tabs were also a feature of the K-4; a few aircraft were additionally equipped with hinged Flettner aileron tabs.

Armament

Bf 109K-4s carried the standard Bf 109G-6 armament of a single, engine-mounted, Rheinmetall-Borsig 30-mm MK 108 cannon and a pair of Rheinmetall-Borsig MG 131 13-mm machine-guns above the engine, each with 300 rounds. The MK 108 was a highly effective weapon, but was prone to jamming during hard manoeuvring, leaving the aircraft with just two machine-guns. As an alternative to the MK 108, the earlier Mauser MG 151/20 20-mm cannon, as fitted to early Bf 109Gs, could be installed, but this seems not to have been deemed necessary in production K-4s. The wing of the Bf 109K was built to accommodate not only Mauser MG 151/20 cannon but, alternatively, two MK 108s using an internal mount. An anti-bomber variant, the K-6, was to be equipped to the same standard as the late K-4, but with the addition of an MK 108 cannon in each wing. The weight penalty was considerable and handling suffered accordingly. Although prototype service trials, probably with III./JG 3, were carried out from February 1945, the K-6 is thought not to have entered production. Various Rüstsätze kits of the type developed for the Bf 109G could be applied to the K-4. The R1 was a fighter-bomber modification allowing the carriage of a 551-lb (250-kg) or 1,102-lb (500-kg) bomb under the fuselage, while the R4 allowed the installation of an additional MG 151/20 under each wing.

Messerschmitt Me 110

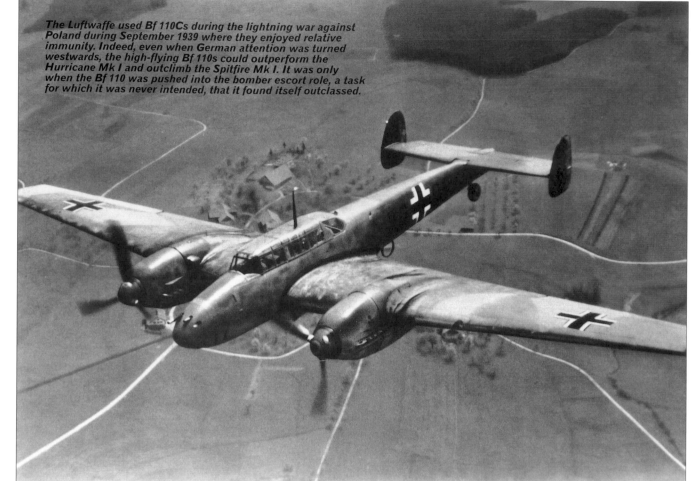

The Luftwaffe used Bf 110Cs during the lightning war against Poland during September 1939 where they enjoyed relative immunity. Indeed, even when German attention was turned westwards, the high-flying Bf 110s could outperform the Hurricane Mk I and outclimb the Spitfire Mk I. It was only when the Bf 110 was pushed into the bomber escort role, a task for which it was never intended, that it found itself outclassed.

Bf110G-4b/R3

Cutaway key
1 *Hirschgeweih* (stag's antlers) array for the FuG 220b Lichtenstein SN-2 radar
2 Quad di-pole type antenna for the FuG 212 Lichtenstein C-1 radar
3 Camera gun
4 Cannon muzzles
5 Cannon ports
6 Blast tubes
7 Starboard mainwheel
8 Armour plate (0.4 in; 10 mm)
9 Twin 30-mm Rheinmetall Borsig Mk 103 (Rüstsatz/ Field Conversion Set 3) with 135 rpg
10 Armoured bulkhead
11 Supercharger intake
12 Position of nacelle-mounted instruments on day-fighter model
13 Exhaust flame damper
14 Auxiliary tank
15 Three-bladed VDM airscrew
16 Leading-edge automatic slat
17 Pitot tube
18 FuG 227/1 Flensburg homing aerial fitted to some aircraft by forward maintenance units (to home onto Monica tailwarning radar emissions)

19 Stressed wing skinning
20 Starboard aileron
21 Trim tab
22 Slotted flap
23 Hinged canopy roof
24 Armoured glass windscreen (2.4 in; 60 mm)
25 Instrument panel
26 Cockpit floor armour (0.16 in; 4 mm)
27 Twin 20-mm Mauser MG 151 cannon with 300 rounds (port) and 350 rounds (starboard)
28 Pilot's seat
29 Control column
30 Pilot's back and head armour (0.315 in; 8 mm)
31 Cannon magazine
32 Centre section carrythrough
33 Radar operator's swivel seat
34 D/F loop
35 Aerial mast
36 Upward-firing cannon muzzles
37 Two 30-mm MK 108 cannon in *schräge Musik* (oblique music) installation firing obliquely upward (optional installation supplied as an Umrust-Bausatz/Factory Conversion Set)
38 Ammunition drums
39 Aft cockpit bulkhead
40 FuG 10P HF R/T set
41 FuB 12F airfield blind-approach receiver

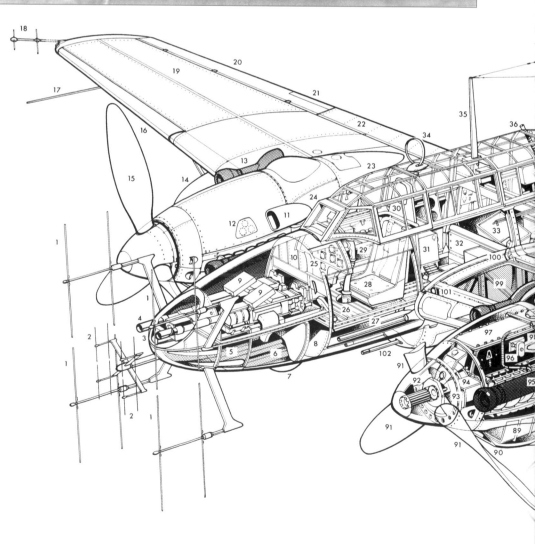

SPECIFICATION

Bf 110C-4

Dimensions
Length: 41 ft 6 in (12.65 m)
Height: 11 ft 6 in (3.50 m)
Wingspan: 53 ft 3 in (16.27 m)
Wing area: 413.3 sq ft (38.40 m²)

Powerplant
Two 1,100-hp (821-kW) Daimler Benz DB 601A inverted-Vee 12-cylinder piston engines

Weights
Empty: 11,454 lb (5200 kg)
Maximum take-off: 14,881 lb (6750 kg)

Performance
Maximum speed at 22,965 ft (7000 m): 349 mph (560 km/h)
Initial climb rate: 2165 ft (660 m) per minute
Cruising speed 22,965 ft (7000 m): 301 mph (480 km/h)
Service ceiling: 32,810 ft (10000 m)
Normal range: 482 miles (775 km)
Maximum range: 565 miles (910 km)

Armament
Two 20-mm MG 151 cannon and four 0.311-in (7.92-mm) MG 17 guns in the nose firing forward, and one 0.311-in (7.92-mm) MG 15 gun in the rear cockpit firing aft. Provision was also made for the carriage of two 551-lb (250-kg) bombs for the *Jabo* role

*Sharkmouths adorned numerous wartime aircraft, few as strikingly as the gaping **Haifisch** jaws on the **Bf 110s** of II./ZG 76, the source of many of the crews and aircraft that would go on to equip **NJG 1**. The sharkmouth markings were retained on individual ZG 76 aircraft transferred to the night-fighter arm, though in some cases the white teeth were oversprayed in black, this being the standard colour for night-fighters before serious investigation into night camouflage began. Aircraft adorned like this were often photographed, more frequently than their plain counterparts, so as so to generate morale for the Luftwaffe's new night-fighting unit. Below the cockpit, the first of eight flags (representing the nations against which ZG 76 fought) can just be seen.*

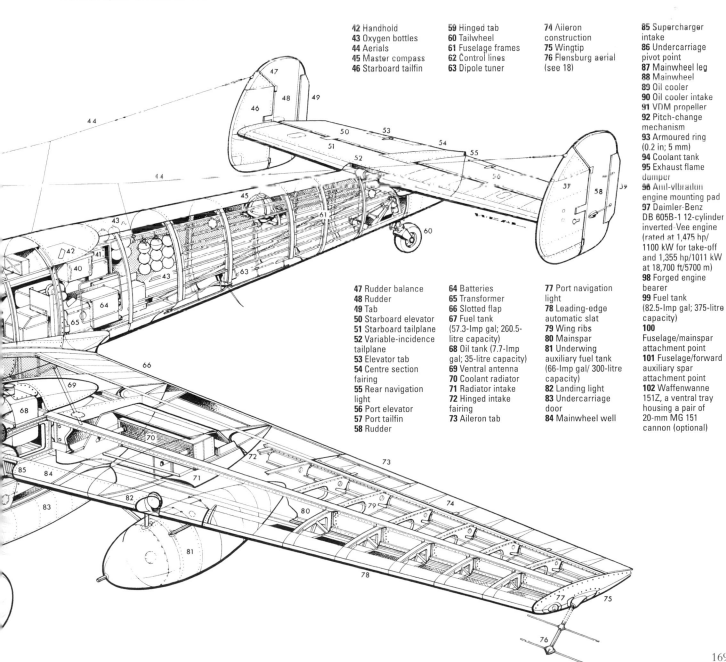

42 Handhold
43 Oxygen bottles
44 Aerials
45 Master compass
46 Starboard tailfin

47 Rudder balance
48 Rudder
49 Tab
50 Starboard elevator
51 Starboard tailplane
52 Variable-incidence tailplane
53 Elevator tab
54 Centre section fairing
55 Rear navigation light
56 Port elevator
57 Port tailfin
58 Rudder

59 Hinged tab
60 Tailwheel
61 Fuselage frames
62 Control lines
63 Dipole tuner

64 Batteries
65 Transformer
66 Slotted flap
67 Fuel tank (57.3-Imp gal; 260.5-litre capacity)
68 Oil tank (7.7-Imp gal; 35-litre capacity)
69 Ventral antenna
70 Coolant radiator
71 Radiator intake
72 Hinged intake fairing
73 Aileron tab

74 Aileron construction
75 Wingtip
76 Flensburg aerial (see 18)

77 Port navigation light
78 Leading-edge automatic slat
79 Wing ribs
80 Mainspar
81 Underwing auxiliary fuel tank (66-Imp gal/ 300-litre capacity)
82 Landing light
83 Undercarriage door
84 Mainwheel well

85 Supercharger intake
86 Undercarriage pivot point
87 Mainwheel leg
88 Mainwheel
89 Oil cooler
90 Oil cooler intake
91 VDM propeller
92 Pitch-change mechanism
93 Armoured ring (0.2 in; 5 mm)
94 Coolant tank
95 Exhaust flame dumper
96 Anti-vibration engine mounting pad
97 Daimler-Benz DB 605B-1 12-cylinder inverted-Vee engine (rated at 1,475 hp/ 1100 kW for take-off and 1,355 hp/1011 kW at 18,700 ft/5700 m)
98 Forged engine bearer
99 Fuel tank (82.5-Imp gal; 375-litre capacity)
100 Fuselage/mainspar attachment point
101 Fuselage/forward auxiliary spar attachment point
102 Waffenwanne 151Z, a ventral tray housing a pair of 20-mm MG 151 cannon (optional)

Bf 110C-4/B

Bf 110s sported many camouflage schemes depending on season and theatre. This aircraft bears what was to become the standard scheme – light-grey fuselage and undersurfaces with darker mottling on the fuselage sides, and disruptive camouflage on the upper surfaces. The most famous marking applied to a Bf 110 was the *Wespen* (wasp) of Zerstörergeschwader 1. The nucleus of II./SKG (schnelles Kampfgeschwader) 210 was provided by 1. Staffel of ZG 1, so the wasp markings stayed with the unit. In 1942 II./SKG 210 returned to ZG 1 control, reuniting the markings with their original operator. The Erprobungsgruppe 210 was established with ZG 1 personnel as an experimental unit for the evaluation of *Jabo* (fighter-bomber) tactics, and it was assigned the first Bf 110C-4/Bs. It commenced cross-Channel raids in July 1940, and became effective at surprise low-level attacks. After being renamed as a Schnellkampfgeschwader (fast bomber wing), the unit dispatched its II. Gruppe to the Eastern Front. The unit fought through the southern sector to Stalingrad, by which time it had been redesignated II./ZG 1 and had been all but decimated.

Cockpit
The Bf 110's cockpit was designed for a crew of three comprising, from front to rear, a pilot, radio operator and gunner. This three-man configuration, which was to prove so unwieldy as the war progressed, had also been adopted by British and French aircraft of the time. In operational conditions, however, the roles of rear gunner and radio operator were usually combined. The view forward and above was extremely good for both crew members, whereas little could be seen downward with this overall layout. The Bf 110C-4 was the first model to introduce some armour protection for the crew.

Powerplant
In deference to its newly-found Jabo role, the Bf 110C-4/B featured the uprated Daimler Benz DB 601N engines (as opposed to the DB 601A of the regular Bf 110C-4). Although standard power outputs were similar, the DB 601N offered 1,200 hp (895 kW) with full boost for one minute at take-off, and an emergency power rating of 1,270 hp (947 kW) for a similar period at 16,400 ft (5000 m). The extra power was achieved by the use of 96 octane C3 fuel, increased compression ratio and redesigned piston heads. Early models of the Bf 110 featured a deep radiator bath under each engine, but the Bf 110C introduced shallow glycol radiators under the wings, outboard of each engine. The radiator intake led back up into the wing, air flow being controlled by electrically-operated exit flaps. The oil cooler for each engine was mounted underneath, fed with air by a small chin inlet. The oil tank was situated behind the engine block and had a capacity of 9 Imp gal (43 litres).

Armament

The nose of the Bf 110C-4B carried four 0.311-in (7.9-mm) MG 17 machine-guns, staggered so that they fitted into the slim fuselage. Each weapon was provided with 1,000 rounds, held in magazines beneath the guns. Two MG FF 20-mm cannon were mounted in the lower fuselage beneath the pilot's seat, but firing through blast troughs underneath the nose. Each had 180 rounds, manually loaded from tanks in the gunner's compartment. To protect the Bf 110 from rear attack, the gunner/radio operator was provided with a single 0.311-in (7.9-mm) MG 15 machine-gun with 750 rounds on a flexible Arado mount. His station was provided with an upward-hinging hood which provided a better field of fire and some protection from the airflow when firing. The Bf 110C-4/B was the first version to be dedicated to the *Jabo* role, for which it was provided with a pair of ETC 250 bomb racks, nestling under the fuselage centre-section. These each carried a 551-lb (250 kg) bomb.

Tail/wing units

The Bf 110's tail was mounted simply on the top of the rear fuselage. The tailplane was small, as the long rear fuselage provided a large moment. Two elevators were fitted, each tabbed and balanced with a notch to allow full rudder deflection. The endplate fins had aerodynamically-balanced rudders. As with that of the Bf 109, the Bf 110's wing featured a single spar, joined to a carry-through member in the fuselage, running behind the pilot's seat. The trailing edge of the wing had large single-slotted flaps inboard, unbroken even behind the engine nacelle. Outboard were slotted ailerons with external mass balances. On the outer section of the leading edge were automatic Handley Page slots.

Fuel

Fuel was provided in four tanks, located in the inner wings either side of the main spar. The forward tanks each held 82 Imp gal (373 litres), while the rear tanks each held 58 Imp gal (264 litres). Later versions could carry drop tanks to increase range.

Undercarriage

The main undercarriage was a sturdy and simple single-strut, single-wheel construction, retracting to the rear into bays in the rear of the engine nacelles, where it was fully enclosed by two doors. The tailwheel was not retractable. The extended tailcone shown here housed a dinghy and survival equipment.

Armament

The nose of the Bf 110C-4B carried four 0.311-in (7.9-mm) MG 17 machine-guns, staggered so that they fitted into the slim fuselage. Each weapon was provided with 1,000 rounds, held in magazines beneath the guns. Two MG FF 20-mm cannon were mounted in the lower fuselage beneath the pilot's seat, but firing through blast troughs underneath the nose. Each had 180 rounds, manually loaded from tanks in the gunner's compartment. To protect the Bf 110 from rear attack, the gunner/radio operator was provided with a single 0.311-in (7.9-mm) MG 15 machine-gun with 750 rounds on a flexible Arado mount. His station was provided with an upward-hinging hood which provided a better field of fire and some protection from the airflow when firing. The Bf 110C-4/B was the first version to be dedicated to the *Jabo* role, for which it was provided with a pair of ETC 250 bomb racks, nestling under the fuselage centre-section. These each carried a 551-lb (250 kg) bomb.

Messerschmitt Me 163

Above: An Me 163B-1a launching at Bad Zwischenahn, home of the trials unit Erprobungskommando 16, which accepted its first Me 163B during May 1944.

Me 163B Komet

Cutaway key

1 Generator drive propeller
2 Generator
3 Compressed air bottle
4 Battery and electronics packs
5 Cockpit ventilation intake
6 Solid armour (⅖-in; 15-mm) nosecone
7 Accumulator pressuriser
8 Direct cockpit air intake
9 FuG 25a radio pack
10 Rudder control assembly
11 Hydraulic and compressed air points
12 Elevon control rocker-bar
13 Control relay
14 Flying controls assembly box
15 Plastic rudder pedals
16 Radio tuning controls
17 Torque shaft
18 Port T-Stoff cockpit tank (13 Imp gal/60 litre capacity)
19 Control column
20 Hinged instrument panel
21 Armourglass windscreen brace
22 Revi 16B gunsight
23 Armourglass internal windscreen (3½-in; 90-mm)
24 Armament and radio switches (starboard console)
25 Pilot's seat
26 Back armour (½-in; 8-mm)
27 Head and shoulder armour ½-in/13-mm)
28 Radio frequency selector pack
29 Headrest
30 Mechanically jettisonable hinged canopy
31 Ventilation panel
32 Fixed leading-edge wing slot

33 Trim tab
34 Fabric-covered starboard elevon
35 Position of underwing landing flap
36 Inboard trim flap
37 FuG 16yz radio receiving aerial
38 T-Stoff filler cap
39 Main unprotected T-Stoff fuselage tank (229 Imp gal/1040 litre capacity)
40 Aft cockpit glazing
41 Port cannon ammunition box (60 rounds)
42 Starboard cannon ammunition box (60 rounds
43 Ammunition feed chute
44 T-Stoff starter tank
45 Rudder control upper bell crank
46 C-Stoff filler cap
47 HWK 509A-1 motor turbine housing
48 Main rocket motor mounting frame
49 Rudder control rod
50 Disconnect point
51 Aerial matching unit
52 Fin front spar/ fusetage attachment point
53 Tailfin construction
54 Rudder horn balance
55 Rudder upper hinge
56 Rudder frame
57 Rudder trim tab
58 Rudder control rocker-bar
59 Linkage fairing
60 Fin rear spar/ fuselage attachment point
61 Rocket motor combustion chamber
62 Tailpipe
63 Rudder root fairing
64 Rocket thrust orifice
65 Vent pipe outlet
66 Hydraulic cylinder
67 Lifting point
68 Tailwheel fairing
69 Steerable tailwheel

70 Tailwheel axle fork
71 Tailwheel oleo
72 Tailwheel steering linkage
73 Coupling piece/ vertical lever
74 Wing root fillet

75 Combustion chamber support brace
76 Gun-cocking mechanism
77 Trim flap control angle gear (bulkhead mounted)
78 Worm gear
79 Trim flap mounting
80 Port inboard trim flap
81 Elevon mounting
82 Rocker-bar
83 Elevon actuation push rod
84 Port elevon
85 Wing rear spar
86 Trim tab
87 Elevon outboard hinge
88 Wingtip bumper
89 Wing construction
90 Fixed leading-edge wing slot
91 Elevon control bell crank
92 Position of port underwing landing flap
93 Push-rod in front spar
94 Front spar
95 FuG 25a aerial
96 Pitot head
97 Wing tank connecting pipe fairing

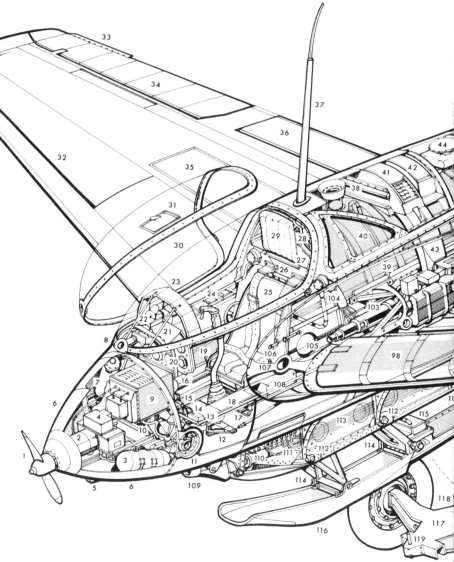

SPECIFICATION

Me 163B-1a Komet

Dimensions

Length: 19 ft 2 in (5.85 m)
Height on take-off dolly: 9 ft (2.76 m)
Wingspan: 30 ft 7 in (9.40 m)
Wing area: 199.10 sq ft (18.50 m²)

Powerplant

One Walter HWK 509A-1 or A-2 rocket motor pump-fed with hypergolic (spontaneously reacting) T-stoff and C-stoff, with high-altitude thrust of 3,748 lb (16.67 kN)

Weights

Empty: 4,190 lb (1900 kg)
Maximum take-off: 9,502 lb (4310 kg)

Performance

Maximum speed at low level: about 510-520 mph (830 km/h)
Maximum speed above 9,845 ft (3000 m): 597 mph (960 km/h)
Initial climb rate: 16,080 ft (4900 m) per minute
Practical range (not allowing for combat): 80 miles (130 km)
Maximum rocket endurance (allowing for periods at reduced thrust): 7 minutes 30 seconds
Service ceiling: 39,370 ft (12000 m)

Armament

Two 30-mm Rheinmetall MK 108 cannon each with 60 rounds

Above: Two of the Me 163B prototypes, V6 and V18, were modified with prototypes of the HWK 509C-1 motor with main and cruising thrust chambers, to give much better flight endurance. Here the V6 blows steam through its propellant lines in the summer of 1944. Note the repositioned retractable tailwheel.

First unit

In early 1943 a special Me 163B test squadron was formed at Karlshagen under Hauptmann Wolfgang Späte, but while this was still in its early stages Peenemünde was raided by the RAF and the unit, Erprobungskommando 16, was moved to Bad Zwischenahn. This was the centre for most Komet flying for the next year, and the aircraft became known to the Allies from high-flying reconnaissance photographs taken here in December 1943. By this time the programme had been further delayed by a raid of the very kind the Komet had been invented to prevent. The Messerschmitt factory at Regensburg was heavily hit by Boeing B-17s on 17 August 1943, many of the pre-production batch being destroyed. The main production, however, was to be dispersed throughout Germany under the control of Klemm Technik, with final assembly at a secret Schwarzwald (Black Forest) centre and then guarded rail shipment to the flight test base at Lechfeld.

This giant production plan suffered many further problems, and the flow did not begin to arrive at Lechfeld until February 1944. The production interceptor was designated Me 163B-1a, and although in many ways seemingly crude it was actually a very refined aircraft as a result of the prolonged experience with earlier variants. The first operational flight of the new machine came on 14 May 1944, when Späte, now a Major, took the red-painted V41 into action.

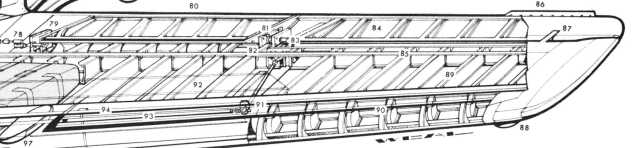

This Me 163B-1a was flown to the UK in 1945 in an Arado Ar 232B-0. It was test flown as a glider in Britain, being towed to altitude by a Spitfire Mk IX, but crashed on 15 November. Parts of the aircraft were incorporated into the Me 163 subsequently exhibited at the Imperial War Museum.

98 C-Stoff leading-edge tank (16 Imp gal/73 litre capacity)
99 Gun-cocking compressed air bottle
100 Main C-Stoff wing tank (38 Imp gal/173 litre capacity)
101 Port 30-mm MK 108 short-barrel cannon
102 Expanding shell and link chute
103 Gun forward mounting frame
104 Pressure-tight guncontrol passage
105 Blast tube
106 Gun alignment mechanism
107 Cannon port
108 FuG 23a FF pack
109 Tow-bar attachment point
110 Compressed-air ram for landing skid
111 Hydraulics and compressed-air pipes
112 Landing skid pivots
113 Landing skid keel mounting
114 Landing skid mounting brackets
115 Trolley jettison mechanism
116 Landing skid
117 Take-off trolley frame
118 Take-off trolley retaining lugs
119 Take-off trolley alignment pins
120 Low-pressure tyre

Me 163B Komet

This aircraft carried the Baron von Munchhausen badge of JG 400's I. Gruppe when flying from Brandis, near Leipzig, in late 1944. JG 400 was activated at Bad Zwischenahn in February 1944 and was soon transferred to Wittmundhaven, where a second staffel was formed. The unit then moved on to Venlo, Holland in June, before moving on to Brandis in August. It conducted operations against USAAF heavy bombers from the latter base and a second Gruppe was formed for a similar role in November 1944. I. Gruppe was subsequently dissolved in April 1945, but II. Gruppe continued to the end, retreating eventually to Nordholz. I. Gruppe claimed nine bombers destroyed for 14 Me 163s shot down and many more lost in accidents, while II. Gruppe made no claims.

Cockpit

The cockpit was comfortable, although there was no system available for pressurisation other than a plain ram inlet at the front. The canopy was a flimsy Plexiglas moulding, hinged on the right side and with little ability to resist hail or birds at the speeds the Komet could attain. There was a hinged ventilation window on the left side of the hood, and another air inlet on the underside of the nose. Nose and back armour was provided, but the seat was not of the new ejection type and it was impossible to get out at high airspeeds.

Powerplant

The Me 163B was powered by a single Hellmuth Walter Werke R II-211 rocket motor, with fuel for six minutes at full throttle. Derived from Von Braun's 650-lb st (2.89-kN) A 1 rocket engine of 1935, the engine was closely based on Walter's TP-1 and TP-2 'Cold' rockets using hydrogen peroxide (T-stoff) with an aqueous solution of sodium or calcium permanganate (Z-stoff) as a catalyst. Essentially the engine consisted of a steam generator into which the two fuels were sprayed using compressed air. This drove a turbine, which powered the pump that delivered T-stoff to the combustion chamber. The TP-2 was redesignated as the HWK (Hellmuth Walter Kiel) R I-203, and was developed progressively into the R II-203, redesignated HWK 509A in production form, which powered early Me 163 prototypes. Substitution of a solution of 30 per cent hydrazine hydrate, 57 per cent methyl alcohol, 13 per cent water and 17 per cent cupracyanide (C-stoff) for the Z-stoff resulted in a hot rocket engine with more thrust and greater reliability, which did not generate a white vapour trail. Before each flight the entire system had to be drained and flushed through with scrupulous care, using vast amounts of water. The motor was started with T-stoff fed from a separate starter tank in the top of the rear fuselage, while an electric motor cranked up the turbopumps. The tanks were pressurised, and once the feed reached the turbopumps the liquids were supplied under high pressure at the rate of 17.64 lb (8 kg) per second, combusting spontaneously on contact in the chamber. Sea-level thrust was about 3,307 lb (14.71 kN), rising with reducing atmospheric pressure to 3,748 lb (16.61 kN) at high altitude. The Type 509A could be throttled back to 220 lb st (0.98 kN) idling rating, but it was inefficient at this level and could often stop entirely. The entire rear fuselage and motor could readily be detached. Although crude compared with later units, the Type 509A was a remarkable achievement and, although over 7 ft (2.13 m) long, weighed little over 220 lb (100 kg).

Wing

The Me 163's wing was smaller and simpler than those of the precursor aircraft, and although it appeared swept it was mainly its taper that gave a quarter-chord sweep angle of 23° 20'. The wooden structure was simple, with two widely spaced spars and a skin of fabric-covered ply usually 0.31 in (8 mm) thick. Outboard on the trailing edge were the only control surfaces, other than the rudder: large manual fabric-covered elevons used for both pitch and roll. The trim tabs were plain metal bent on the ground with pliers to give the required behaviour. Inboard were large, plain, hinged flaps which were lowered hydraulically by screwjacks before landing, in unison with main landing flaps ahead of them on the underside of the wing. The landing flaps caused strong nose-up trim, and the trailing-edge flaps cancelled this out with equal nose-down trim. Trials with the Me 163 V1 and V4 during October 1941 saw the aircraft reaching speeds of up to 550 mph (885 km/h), with maximum speed limited by fuel capacity. To get around this, Heini Dittmar had the Me 163 V4 fully tanked and then towed into the air behind a Bf 110C tug. Lighting the rocket, Dittmar accelerated to 623.85 mph (1003.96 km/h - equivalent to Mach 0.84) when compressibility effects forced the aircraft into a steep dive, from which Dittmar recovered by cutting the engine. The sudden change in pitch stability was due to the fact that the Me 163 V4 had essentially retained the wing of the DFS 194, with considerable washout which caused wingtip compressibility stalls. On the Me 163B the wing was considerably redesigned, with reduced sweep on the trailing edge, constant sweep on the leading edge and with low drag fixed slots on the outer 40 per cent of the wing leading edge. These removed the danger of tip stalling, and also made the Me 163 unspinnable. Even with fully crossed controls, the aircraft would only sideslip.

Fuselage and armament

The small fuselage was of light alloy, covered mainly with detachable panels to gain access to the densely packed interior. The largest item was the T-stoff tank of 229-Imp gal (1040-litre) capacity, which filled the space between the cockpit and the motor. Smaller T-stoff tanks filled each side of the cockpit. The C-stoff was housed in two 38-Imp gal (173-litre) tanks between the wing spars and two 16-Imp gal (73-litre) tanks in the leading edges. The Z-stoff originally used as a catalyst in the Me 163A was prone to clogging feed pipes, but the T-stoff fuel had even worse characteristics. Highly unstable and prone to spontaneous combustion when exposed to organic material (such as human flesh), T-stoff was also highly corrosive. The Me 163 pilot was surrounded by T-stoff tanks in flight, and had to wear a non-organic flying suit made of asbestos-Mipolamfibre. The C-stoff catalyst used in the Me 163 was also highly reactive, and had to be stored in glass or enamelled containers. The Me 163B was initially armed with a pair of Mauser 20-mm MG 151 cannon, but from the 47th pre-production aircraft these were replaced by 30-mm Rheinmetall-Borsig MK 108 cannon, each with 60 rounds of ammunition.

Keith Fretwell

Messerschmitt Me 262 Schwalbe

The Me 262 was among the fastest aircraft operating in any theatre during World War II, capable of overhauling the Mosquito and the Mustang, but its lack of manoeuvrability made it vulnerable, and like all aircraft, it was a sitting duck when in the circuit to land, a fact used to full advantage by the Allies. This machine, III./EJG 2's 'White 10', is seen flown by Leutnant Kurt Bell during the making of a Luftwaffe training film.

Me 262A-1a/b

Cutaway key
1 Flettner-type geared trim tab
2 Mass-balanced rudder
3 Rudder post
4 Tail fin structure
5 Tailplane structure
6 Rudder tab mechanism
7 Flettner-type servo tab
8 Starboard elevator
9 Rear navigation light
10 Rudder linkage
11 Elevator linkage
12 Tailplane adjustment mechanism
13 Fuselage break point
14 Fuselage construction
15 Control runs
16 FuG 25a loop antenna (IFF)

17 Automatic compass
18 Aft auxiliary self-sealing fuel tank (132 Imp gal/600 litre capacity)
19 FuG 16zy R/T
20 Fuel filler cap
21 Aft cockpit glazing
22 Armoured aft main fuel tank (198 Imp gal/900 litre capacity)
23 Inner cockpit shell
24 Pilot's seat
25 Canopy jettison lever
26 Armoured 0.59-in (15-mm) head rest
27 Canopy (hinged to starboard)
28 Canopy lock
29 Bar-mounted Revi 16B sight (for both cannon and R4M missiles)
30 Armourglass windscreen 3.54-in (90-mm)

31 Instrument panel
32 Rudder pedal
33 Armoured forward main fuel tank (198 Imp gal/900 litre capacity)
34 Fuel filler cap
35 Underwing wooden rack for 12 R4M 2.17-in (55-mm) rockets (Me 262A-1b)
36 Port outer flap section

37 Frise-type aileron
38 Aileron control linkage
39 Port navigation light
40 Pitot head
41 Automatic leading-edge slats
42 Port engine cowling
43 Electrical firing mechanism
44 Firewall

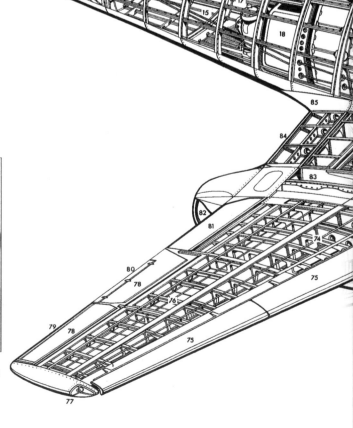

So vulnerable was the Me 262 during the take-off and landing phases that two Staffeln of Fw 190D-9s were assigned for the protection of Kommando Nowotny based at Achmer and Hesepe after this unit's early losses. Although the pictured aircraft wears superficially similar markings to that flown for the camera by Kurt Bell, this 'White 10' is an Me 262A-1a/Jabo of EKdo 262, identified by the presence of forward fuselage bomb pylons.

Kommando Nowotny line-up, probably at Achmer in late September 1944. Whilst 'White 19' and 'White 4' are serviced, in the foreground 'Green 3' is towed out towards the runway by a Kettenkrad motorcycle half-track. Austrian-born Major Walter Nowotny, already a Russian front expert, was chosen by Adolf Galland to head the new Kommando, of which he assumed control on 20 September 1944. Kommando Nowotny's first combat sorties were undertaken on 7 October, when the two-Staffel strong jet unit flew against bombers returning from raids on oil targets within Germany. Flying from Achmer, two of the unit's pilots, Franz Schall and his wingman Helmut Lennartz, each claimed a B-24D Liberator destroyed.

SPECIFICATION

bMe 262A-1a/b

Dimensions:

Length: 34 ft 9 in (10.58 m)
Height: 12 ft 7 in (3.83 m)
Span: 40 ft 11 in (12.5 m)
Wing area: 234 sq ft (21.73 m²)
Wing leading edge sweepback: 18° 32'

Powerplant:

Two Junkers Jumo 004B-1, -2 or -3 axial-flow turbojets each rated at 1,984 lb st (8.83 kN)

Weights:

Empty: 3,778 lb (3795 kg)
Empty equipped: 9,742 lb (4413 kg)
Maximum take-off: 14,080 lb (6387 kg)

Performance:

Maximum speed at sea level: 514 mph (827 km/h)

Maximum speed at 9,845 ft (3000 m): 530 mph (852 km/h)
Maximum speed at 19,685 ft (6000 m): 540 mph (869 km/h)
Maximum speed at 26,245 ft (8000 m): 532 mph (856 km/h)
Initial climb rate: 3,937 ft (1200 m) per minute
Service ceiling: over 40,000 ft (12190 m)
Range: 652 miles (1050 km) at 29,530 ft (9000 m)
Landing speed: 109 mph (175 km/h)

Armament:

Four 30-mm Rheinmetall-Borsig Mk 108A-3 cannon with 100 rounds per gun for the upper pair and 80 rounds per gun for the lower pair, and aimed with a Revi 16.B gunsight or EZ.42 gyro-stabilised sight. Provision for 12 R4M air-to-air rockets under each wing (Me 262A-1b)

*'White 4' wears a typical **Kommando Nowotny** camouflage scheme, comprising a principally solid fuselage colour applied together with distinctive mottled vertical tail surfaces. Following the death of Nowotny on 8 November 1944, control of the unit was passed to Oberleutnant Georg-Peter Eder, however, the unit flew its final mission from Achmer on 17 November. Former pilots went on to form the nucleus of JG 7, the first and only Luftwaffe jet fighter Geschwader.*

45 Spent cartridge ejector chutes
46 Four 30-mm Rheinmetall Borsig Mk 108 cannon (100 rpg belt-fed ammunition for upper pair and 80 rpg for lower pair)
47 Cannon muzzles
48 Combat camera
49 Camera aperture
50 Nosewheel fairing
51 Nosewheel leg
52 Nosewheel
53 Torque scissors
54 Retraction jack
55 Hydraulic lines
56 Main nosewheel door (starboard)
57 Compressed air bottles
58 Forward auxiliary fuel tank (37 Imp gal/ 170 litre capacity)
59 Mainwheel well
60 Torque box
61 Main spar
62 Mainwheel leg pivot point
63 Mainwheel door
64 Mainwheel retraction rod
65 Engine support arch
66 Leading-edge slat structure
67 Auxiliaries gearbox
68 Annular oil tank
69 Riedel starter motor housing
70 Engine air intake
71 Hinged cowling section
72 Junkers Jumo 004B-2 axial-flow turbojet
73 Starboard mainwheel
74 Wing structure
75 Automatic leading-edge slats
76 Mainspar
77 Starboard navigation light
78 Frise-type ailerons
79 Trim-tab
80 Flettner-type geared tab
81 Starboard outer flap section
82 Engine exhaust orifice
83 Engine support bearer
84 Starboard inner flap structure
85 Faired wing root

Me 262A-1a Schwalbe

This Me 262A-1a operated from Parchim in north east Germany with
9 Staffel, Jagdgeschwader III, during the early months of 1945. JG III was
part of III Gruppe, and was responsible to 1 Jagddivision of I Jagdkorps.
Blue and red 'Defence of the Reich' bands were worn on the rear fuselage,
and the Gruppe's leaping greyhound emblem was painted on the fuselage
forward of the cockpit. This aircraft was captured at Lechfeld, shipped to
the United States from France, and evaluated by the USAF at Freeman Field
in Indiana before being passed on to the National Air and Space Museum
in Washington DC where it still resides.

Wings
The Me 262 was equipped with leading edge slots which opened
automatically in a turn or in a climb if the airspeed fell below 280
mph (451 km/h), or to below 185 mph (298 km/h) in a gliding
attitude. Fighter versions of the type were able to carry up to 12
R4M unguided 2.16-in (55-mm) rocket projectiles under each wing,
fired from a wooden rack. The trajectory of the rockets was similar
to that of the cannon, so the same sight could be used. The
rockets scattered to fill the same space as that occupied by a four-
engined bomber at a range of 600 yards. Each rocket had a 16-oz
(4.54-kg) warhead, with a considerable blast effect.

Powerplants
The Me 262 was powered by a pair of Junkers Jumo 004B-1 axial
flow turbojets, each rated at about 1,984 lb (8.82 kN) static thrust.
This gave a maximum speed of approximately 540 mph (869 km/h)
at 20,000 ft (6096 m). The aircraft could exceed this speed in a
dive, soon reaching its limiting Mach number. The Germans
experienced extreme difficulties in maintaining engine production,
the factories producing the jet engines being primary targets for
Allied bombers. This led to poor reliability of the powerplants, and
shortages of chrome and nickel prevented the turbine blades from
being manufactured with sufficient strength to withstand the
extreme temperatures encountered, thus making the life of the
engine very short.

Elevators and ailerons

Pre-production Me 262s were fitted with fabric-covered elevators, but these proved highly susceptible to ballooning in high-speed dives, and on several occasions the fabric actually tore. Thereafter all production aircraft were fitted with metal-skinned elevators. The Me 262 had good aileron control at all altitudes, and the aircraft showed very little tendency to spin following a stall. Directional stability, however, was not so good, although the powerful rudder enabled the pilot to keep the aircraft under control.

Armament

Fighter Me 262s were armed with four 30-mm Rheinmetall Borsig Mk 108A-3 cannon, with 100 rounds for each of the upper guns and 80 for the lower guns. The guns were clustered closely together on the centreline, packing a substantial punch without tricky harmonisation problems. The fighter-bomber version of the Me 262 was dubbed *Sturmvogel* (Stormbird) to distinguish it from the standard fighter. It differed from the latter only in having bomb fusing equipment and provision for two undernose pylons, which could accomodate a pair of 551-lb (250-kg) bombs, or a single 1,102-lb (500-kg) bomb. These aircraft were referred to as 'Super Speed Bombers', because Hitler hated the use of the term 'fighter', even in the phrase 'fighter-bomber'.

Messerschmitt Me 410 Hornisse

With its neatly cowled engines and purposeful nose contours, the Me 210 looked the part, but it was plagued with vicious and unpredictable handling qualities. This aircraft is one of those fitted with a longer rear fuselage, which largely cured the design's major faults.

Me 410 Hornisse

Cutaway key

1 Starboard navigation light
2 Starboard detachable wingtip
3 Main spar
4 Wing leading-edge slat
5 Aileron control rods
6 External balance (underwing)
7 Starboard aileron
8 Tab (ground-adjustable only)
9 Aileron trim tab
10 Trim tab control
11 Slatted airbrakes (above and below wing)
12 Wing centre/outer section join
13 Starboard underwing radiator
14 Boundary layer bleed
15 Radiator flap section
16 Radiator flap motor (in flap section)
17 Starboard oil filter
18 Cowling panelling
19 Starboard engine supercharger intake
20 Starboard nacelle
21 Exhaust stub cover
22 Oil cooler intake (adjustable flap)
23 Auxiliary intake
24 Coolant filter access
25 Spinner
26 Three-bladed constant-speed VDM propeller
27 Starboard mainwheel
28 Bomb-bay doors (open)
29 Two 7.9-mm MG 17 machine-gun ports
30 Two 20-mm MG 151 cannon ports
31 Cabin air intake
32 Cabin air heater
33 Nose glazing
34 Rudder pedals
35 Instrument panel side sections

36 Instrument panel lower section
37 Control column
38 Pilot's heelboards
39 MG 151 cannon blast tube
40 Bomb bay
41 Bomb winch cable hoist
42 Port instrument console
43 Throttle quadrant
44 Pilot's seat
45 Starboard instrument console (weapons/oxygen)
46 Revi C/12D weapons sight
47 Armoured windscreen
48 Hinged cockpit canopy
49 Pilot's armoured head/backrest
50 Canopy internal bracing
51 Ammunition magazines (1,000 rounds 7.9-mm/350 rounds 20-mm)
52 Pilot's entry handhold
53 Ammunition feed chutes
54 Port weapons breeches
55 Mainspar centre-section carry-through
56 Observer's seat
57 Electrical main distribution panel
58 Beam armament master switch and ammunition counter
59 Sighting head for FDSL beam barbettes
60 Hinged cockpit canopy section
61 Aerial mast (angled to starboard)
62 D/F loop aerial housing
63 Optically flat side windows
64 Barbette elevation input shaft
65 Barbette traverse input shaft
66 Observer's entry handhold

67 EZ2 D/F receiver remote control unit
68 FuG 10 radio receiver
69 EZ2 D/F receiver
70 FuG 10 radio transmitter
71 Rear spar centre-section carry-through
72 Wingroot fairing
73 Barbette electrics junction box
74 Access panel/handhold
75 Barbette torque amplifier
76 Barbette ring gears
77 Barbette centre rotating drum
78 Ammunition around drum (500 rpg)
79 Port beam gun fairing
80 10-mm MG 131 beam gun
81 Aerial unit

82 Rear fuselage access panel
83 FuG 25 IFF transformer
84 FuG 25 transponder
85 Aerial lead-in
86 Master compass
87 Fuselage frames
88 Course control drive
89 Skin panelling dorsal join
90 Rear fuselage structure
91 Control rods
92 Tailwheel support frame

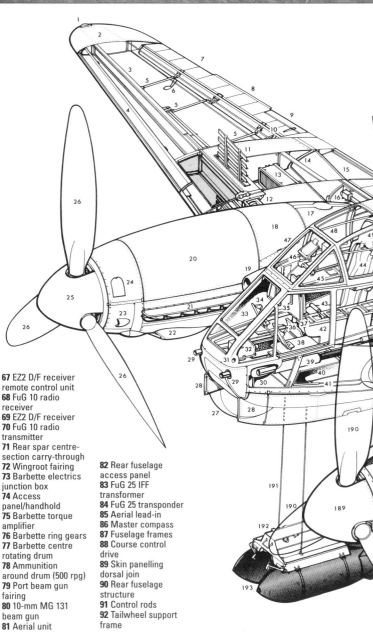

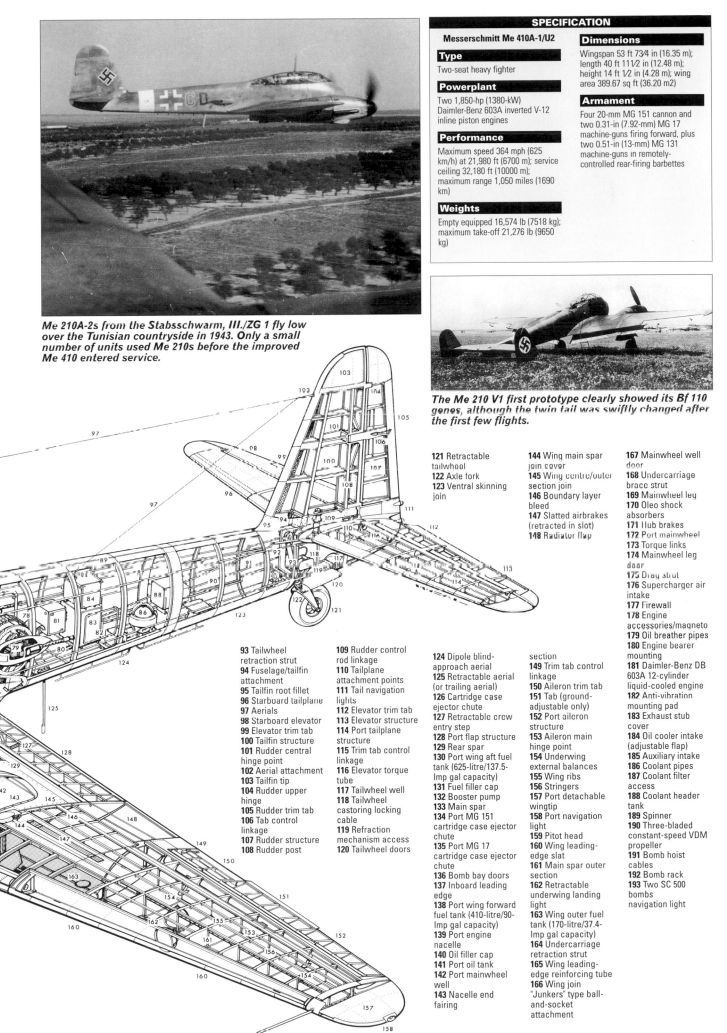

Me 210A-2s from the Stabsschwarm, III./ZG 1 fly low over the Tunisian countryside in 1943. Only a small number of units used Me 210s before the improved Me 410 entered service.

The Me 210 V1 first prototype clearly showed its Bf 110 genes, although the twin tail was swiftly changed after the first few flights.

SPECIFICATION

Messerschmitt Me 410A-1/U2

Type
Two-seat heavy fighter

Powerplant
Two 1,850-hp (1380-kW) Daimler-Benz 603A inverted V-12 inline piston engines

Performance
Maximum speed 364 mph (625 km/h) at 21,980 ft (6700 m); service ceiling 32,180 ft (10000 m); maximum range 1,050 miles (1690 km)

Weights
Empty equipped 16,574 lb (7518 kg); maximum take-off 21,276 lb (9650 kg)

Dimensions
Wingspan 53 ft 7¾ in (16.35 m); length 40 ft 11½ in (12.48 m); height 14 ft 1½ in (4.28 m); wing area 389.67 sq ft (36.20 m2)

Armament
Four 20-mm MG 151 cannon and two 0.31-in (7.92-mm) MG 17 machine-guns firing forward, plus two 0.51-in (13-mm) MG 131 machine-guns in remotely-controlled rear-firing barbettes

93 Tailwheel retraction strut
94 Fuselage/tailfin attachment
95 Tailfin root fillet
96 Starboard tailplane
97 Aerials
98 Starboard elevator
99 Elevator trim tab
100 Tailfin structure
101 Rudder central hinge point
102 Aerial attachment
103 Tailfin tip
104 Rudder upper hinge
105 Rudder trim tab
106 Tab control linkage
107 Rudder structure
108 Rudder post
109 Rudder control rod linkage
110 Tailplane attachment points
111 Tail navigation lights
112 Elevator trim tab
113 Elevator structure
114 Port tailplane structure
115 Trim tab control linkage
116 Elevator torque tube
117 Tailwheel well
118 Tailwheel castoring locking cable
119 Refraction mechanism access
120 Tailwheel doors
121 Retractable tailwheel
122 Axle fork
123 Ventral skinning join
124 Dipole blind-approach aerial
125 Retractable aerial (or trailing aerial)
126 Cartridge case ejector chute
127 Retractable crew entry step
128 Port flap structure
129 Rear spar
130 Port wing aft fuel tank (625-litre/137.5-Imp gal capacity)
131 Fuel filler cap
132 Booster pump
133 Main spar
134 Port MG 151 cartridge case ejector chute
135 Port MG 17 cartridge case ejector chute
136 Bomb bay doors
137 Inboard leading edge
138 Port wing forward fuel tank (410-litre/90-Imp gal capacity)
139 Port engine nacelle
140 Oil filler cap
141 Port oil tank
142 Port mainwheel well
143 Nacelle end fairing
144 Wing main spar join cover
145 Wing centre/outer section join
146 Boundary layer bleed
147 Slatted airbrakes (retracted in slot)
148 Radiator flap
149 Trim tab control linkage
150 Aileron trim tab
151 Tab (ground-adjustable only)
152 Port aileron structure
153 Aileron main hinge point
154 Underwing external balances
155 Wing ribs
156 Stringers
157 Port detachable wingtip
158 Port navigation light
159 Pitot head
160 Wing leading-edge slat
161 Main spar outer section
162 Retractable underwing landing light
163 Wing outer fuel tank (170-litre/37.4-Imp gal capacity)
164 Undercarriage retraction strut
165 Wing leading-edge reinforcing tube
166 Wing join "Junkers" type ball-and-socket attachment
167 Mainwheel well door
168 Undercarriage brace strut
169 Mainwheel leg
170 Oleo shock absorbers
171 Hub brakes
172 Port mainwheel
173 Torque links
174 Mainwheel leg door
175 Drag strut
176 Supercharger air intake
177 Firewall
178 Engine accessories/magneto
179 Oil breather pipes
180 Engine bearer mounting
181 Daimler-Benz DB 603A 12-cylinder liquid-cooled engine
182 Anti-vibration mounting pad
183 Exhaust stub cover
184 Oil cooler intake (adjustable flap)
185 Auxiliary intake
186 Coolant pipes
187 Coolant filter access
188 Coolant header tank
189 Spinner
190 Three-bladed constant-speed VDM propeller
191 Bomb hoist cables
192 Bomb rack
193 Two SC 500 bombs
navigation light

Mitsubishi A6M Reisen 'Zeke'

Many Zeros were captured by the Allies and used for test and evaluation purposes. The first was captured in 1942, following an inconclusive Japanese attack on Dutch Harbor in the Aleutians. An A6M2 flown by Petty Officer Koga was forced to make an emergency landing at Akutan Island and, upon touching down, the aircraft flipped over and the pilot was killed. The machine was transported to San Diego, repaired, and flown for evaluation against Allied aircraft.

A6M2 Reisen

Cutaway key

1 Tail navigation light
2 Tail cone
3 Tailfin fixed section
4 Rudder lower brace
5 Rudder tab (ground adjustable)
6 Fabric-covered rudder
7 Rudder hinge
8 Rudder post
9 Rudder upper hinge
10 Rudder control horn (welded to torque tube)
11 Aerial attachment
12 Tailfin leading edge
13 Forward spar
14 Tailfin structure
15 Tailfin nose ribs
16 Port elevator
17 Port tailplane
18 Piano-hinge join
19 Fuselage dorsal skinning
20 Control turnbuckles
21 Arrester hook release/retract steel cable runs
22 Fuselage frame/tailplane centre brace
23 Tailplane attachments
24 Elevator cables
25 Elevator control horns/torque tube
26 Rudder control horns
27 Tailwheel combined retraction/shock strut
28 Elevator trim tab
29 Tailwheel leg fairing
30 Castored tailwheel
31 Elevator frame (fabric-covered)
32 Elevator outer hinge
33 Tailplane structure
34 Forward spar
35 Elevator trim tab control rod (chain-driven)
36 Fuselage flotation bag rear wall
37 Arrester hook (extended)
38 Arrester hook pivot mounting
39 Elevator trim tab cable guide
40 Fuselage skinning

41 Fuselage frame stations
42 Arrester hook position indicator cable (duralumin tube)
43 Elevator cables
44 Rudder cables
45 Trim tab cable runs
46 Arrester hook pulley guide
47 Fuselage stringers
48 Fuselage flotation bag front
49 Fuselage construction join
50 Wingroot fillet formers
51 Compressed air cylinder (wing gun charging)
52 Transformer
53 'Ku' type radio receiver
54 Oxygen cylinder (starboard) carbon dioxide fire extinguisher cylinder (port)
55 Battery
56 Radio tray support
57 Radio transmitter
58 Canopy/fuselage fairing
59 Aerial mast support/lead-in
60 Aerial
61 Aerial mast (forward raked)
62 Canopy aft fixed section
63 Aluminium and plywood canopy frame
64 Crash bulkhead/headrest support
65 'Ku' type D/F frame antenna mounting (late models)
66 Canopy track
67 Turnover truss
68 Pilot's seat support frame
69 Starboard elevator control bell crank
70 Aileron control push-pull rod
71 Wing rear spar/fuselage attachment
72 Fuselage aft main double frame
73 Aileron linkage
74 Landing-gear selector lever
75 Flap selector lever

76 Seat adjustment lever
77 Pilot's seat
78 Cockpit canopy rail
79 Seat support rail
80 Elevator tab trim handwheel
81 Fuel gauge controls
82 Throttle quadrant
83 Reflector gunsight mounting (offset to starboard)
84 Sliding canopy
85 Plexiglas panels
86 Canopy lock/release
87 Windscreen
88 Fuselage starboard 0.303-in (7.7-mm) machine-gun
89 Control column
90 Radio control box
91 Radio tuner
92 Elevator control linkage
93 Rudder pedal bar assembly
94 Cockpit underfloor fuel
95 Wing front spar/fuselage attachment
96 Fuselage forward main double frame
97 Ammunition magazine

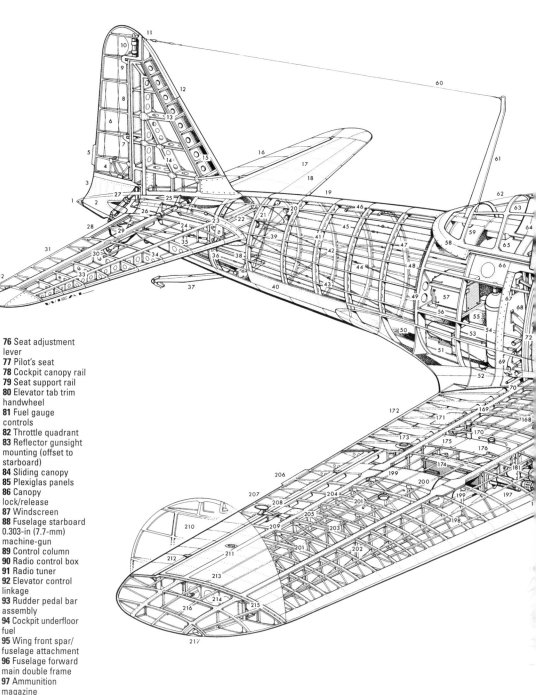

As the A6M2 began to reach service units, it gradually replaced the IJN's previous single-seat fighter, the ultra-manoeuvrable Mitsubishi A5M. The latter served on into the early war years as is proved by this collection of A6M2s and A5Ms lined up on an airfield at the beginning of the war in the Pacific. The US Navy received its first taste of Japanese airpower during the attack on Pearl Harbor, which was planned in great secrecy and took months of preparation. The 'Zekes' which escorted the attacking bombers destroyed four US aircraft in the air without a single loss. Subsequent operations in the Java Sea, against Wake Island and against Darwin proved equally successful.

SPECIFICATION

Mitsubishi Zero A6M2 Model 21

(unless otherwise noted)

Dimensions

Wingspan: 39 ft 4⁷⁄₁₆ in (12 m)
A6M3, 5, 8: 36 ft 1¹⁄₁₆ in (11 m)
Length (including A6M3): 29ft 8¹⁄₁₆ in (12 m)
A6M5: 29 ft 11²³⁄₃₂ in (9.12 m)
A6M8: 30 ft 3²¹⁄₃₂ in (9.24 m)
Height: 10 ft ¹⁄₁₆ in (3.05 m)
A6M3, 5: 11 ft 6⁹⁄₃₂ in (3.51 m)
Wing area: 241.541 sq ft (22.44 m²)
A6M3: 231.746 sq ft (21.53 m²)
A6M5, 8: 229.27 sq ft (21.30 m²)

Powerplant

One Nakajima NK1C Sakae 12 14-cylinder air cooled radial engine, rated at 940 hp (700 kW) at take-off and 950 hp (708 kW) at 13,780 ft (4200 m), driving a three-bladed metal propeller.
A6M3, 5a, b, c: One Nakajima NK1F Sakae 21 14-cylinder air cooled radial engine, rated at 1,130 hp (843 kW) at take-off and 1,100 hp (820 kW) at 9,350 ft (2050 m) and 900 hp (731 kW) at 19,685 ft (6000 m), driving a three-bladed metal propeller.
A6M8: One Mitsubishi MK8P Kinsei 62 14-cylinder radial, rated at 1,560 hp (1163 kW) at take-off, 1,340 hp (999 kW) at 2,100 ft (6890 m) and 1,180 hp (880 kW) at 5,800 ft (19030 m) driving a three-bladed metal propeller.

Weights

Empty: 3,704 lb (1680 kg)
A6M3: 3,984 lb (1807 kg)
A6M5: 4,136 lb (1876 kg)
A6M8: 4,740 lb (2150 kg)
Loaded: 5,313 lb (2410 kg)
A6M3: 5,609 lb (2544 kg)
A6M5: 6,025 lb (2733 kg)
A6M8: 6,945 lb (3150 kg)
Maximum: 6,104 lb (2790 kg)
Wing loading: 22 lb/sq ft (107.4 kg/m²)
A6M3: 24.2 lb/sq ft (118.1 kg/m²)
A6M5: 26.6 lb/sq ft (120.0 kg/m²)
A6M8: 30.3 lb/sq ft (147.9 kg/m²)

Fuel and load

Normal fuel: 130 Imp gal (590.98 litres)
A6M3: 134 Imp gal (609.16 litres)
Maximum fuel: 202 Imp gal (918.29 litres)
External fuel: 72.6 Imp gal (330 litres)
Maximum weapon load: 1,790 lb (811.92 kg)

Performance

Maximum speed: 288 kt (332 mph; 534 km/h) at 14,930 ft (4550 m)
A6M3: 294 kt (338 mph; 545 km/h) at 19,685 ft (6000 m)
A6M5: 305 kt (351 mph; 565 km/h) at 19,685 ft (6000 m)
A6M8: 309 kt (365 mph; 573 km/h) at 19,685 ft (6000 m)
Cruising speed: 180 kt (207 mph; 334 km/h)
A6M3, 5: 200 kt (230 mph; 370 km/h)
Service ceiling: 32,810 ft (10000 m)
A6M3: 36,250 ft (11050 m)
A6M5: 38,520 ft (11740 m)
A6M8: 37,075 ft (11200 m)

Range

Normal range: 1,010 nm (1,162 miles; 1870 km)
Maximum range: 1,675 nm (1930 miles; 1162 km)

Armament

Fixed: Two 0.303-in (7.7-mm) Type 97 machine-guns in the upper fuselage decking and two wing-mounted 20-mm Type 99 cannon. The A6M8 carried two wing mounted 0.6-in (15.2-mm) Type 3 machine-guns and two wing-mounted 20-mm Type 99 cannon.
External: Normal load was two 132-lb (60-kg) bombs. For suicide missions, one 551-lb (250-kg) bomb was carried. Maximum external load for A6M7 and A6M8 was 1,102 lb (500 kg). Eight 22-lb (10-kg) or two 132-lb (60-kg) air-to-air rockets could be carried by the A6M6c and A6M8. There were also hardpoints for drop tanks; usually a 72.6-Imp gal (330-litre) tank was carried, but the A6M7 and A6M8 carried a 77-Imp gal (350-litre) tank.

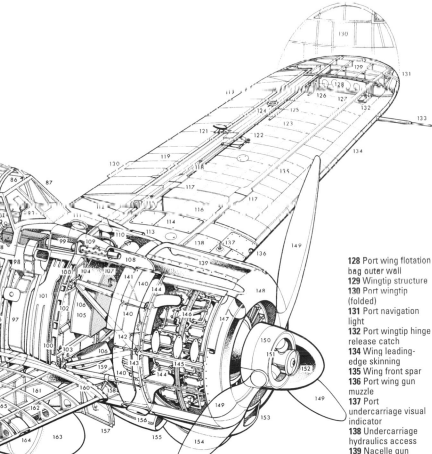

98 Ammunition feed
99 Blast tube
100 Cooling louvres
101 Fuselage fuel tank capacity 34 Imp gal (155 litres)
102 Firewall bulkhead
103 Engine bearer lower attachment
104 Engine bearer upper attachment
105 Oil tank capacity 12.7 Imp gal (58 litres)
106 Bearer support struts
107 Cooling gill adjustment control
108 Machine-gun muzzle trough
109 Barrel fairing
110 Oil filler cap
111 Fuselage fuel tank filler cap
112 Port flap profile
113 Port fuselage machine-gun
114 Port wing gun access panels
115 Port inner wing identification light
116 Port wing flotation bag inner wall
117 Wing spar joins
118 Aileron control rods
119 Port aileron (fabric covered)
120 Aileron tab (ground adjustable)
121 Aileron external counter-balance
122 Control linkage
123 Wing skinning
124 Port inner wing identification light
125 Port navigation light lead conduit
126 Wingtip hinge
127 Wing end rib
128 Port wing flotation bag outer wall
129 Wingtip structure
130 Port wingtip (folded)
131 Port navigation light
132 Port wingtip hinge release catch
134 Wing leading-edge skinning
135 Wing front spar
136 Port wing gun muzzle
137 Port undercarriage visual indicator
138 Undercarriage hydraulics access
139 Nacelle gun troughs
140 Cooling gills
141 Fuselage gun synchronisation cable
142 Bearer support strut assembly
143 Carburettor
144 Exhaust manifold
145 Cowling panel fastener clips
146 950 hp Nakajima Sakae 12 radial engine
147 Cowling inner ring profile
148 Cowling nose ring
149 Three-bladed propeller
150 Spinner
151 Propeller gears
152 Hub
153 Carburettor intake
154 Port main wheel
155 Oil cooler intake
156 Exhaust outlet
157 Starboard mainwheel inner door fairing
158 Engine bearer support brace
159 Oil cooler
160 Wingroot fasteners
161 Starboard mainwheel well
162 Front auxiliary spar cutouts
163 Auxiliary fuel tank
165 Intake trunking
166 Front main spar
167 Starboard wing fuel tank capacity 43 Imp gal (195 litres)
168 Fuel filler cap
169 Rear main spar
170 Flap actuating cylinder
171 Access cover
172 Starboard flap structure
173 Starboard inner wing identification light
174 Starboard wing 20-mm cannon
175 Access panels
176 Ammunition magazine (underwing loading)
177 Landing gear hydraulic retraction jack
178 Hydraulic lines
179 Starboard undercarriage visual indicator
180 Landing gear pivot axis
181 Undercarriage/spar mounting
182 Starboard wing gun muzzle
183 Starboard undercarriage leg
184 Oleo travel
185 Welded steel wheel fork
186 Wheel uplock latch
187 Starboard mainwheel
188 Wheel door fairing ball and swivel closure
189 Mainwheel door fairing
190 Axle hub
191 Access plate
192 Hinge
193 Left fairing attachments
194 Brake line
195 Leg fairing
196 Leg fairing upperflap
197 Wing gun barrel support collar
198 Wing nose ribs
199 Cartridge ejection chute
200 Wing spar joins
201 Wing outer structure
202 Front spar outer section
203 Inter-spar ribs
204 Rear spar outer section
205 Aileron control access
206 Aileron (ground adjustable)
207 Starboard aileron frame
208 Aileron external counter balance
209 Control linkage
210 Starboard wingtip (folded)
211 Starboard outerwing identification light
212 Aileron outer hinge
213 Starboard wing flotation bag outer wall
214 Wing end rib
215 Starboard wingtip hinge release catch
216 Wingtip structure
217 Starboard navigation light

A6M2 Reisen 'Zeke'

This A6M2 Reisen belonged to the 2nd Sentai, 1st Koku Kentai (air fleet) flying from the carrier *Hiryu* during the Battle of Midway in June 1942. Wearing typical markings for the period, the aircraft is painted overall light grey and features a black cowling and a borderless Hinomaru (national insignia). The Imperial Japanese Navy concentrated its Reisens in large formations for maximum effect although, with four Japanese carriers being sunk at Midway by the US Navy Pacific Fleet, the Imperial Fleet was unable to mount further mass air attacks.

Sturdy undercarriage

For sustained operations at sea, the Zero featured a strong undercarriage which was necessary to withstand the heavy pounding of repeated deck landings. The main undercarriage legs were tall but sturdy, retracting inwards to lie flat in their wells. The tailwheel was also retractable. The wide undercarriage track resulted in an aircraft which was easy to manoeuvre on the ground and able to use the rudimentary airstrips which were common in the South Pacific with few problems.

Armour

An endurance of up to eight hours had been one of the original requirements specified by the IJN. In order to achieve this, the Zero was of very light construction, while relying on an engine of marginal power. Its greatest weakness lay in its lack of adequate armour or self-sealing fuel tanks. The airframe was, in fact, so fragile, that several aircraft are said to have broken up while attempting high-speed dives. The interim A6M5 variant introduced a strengthened airframe and an armoured glass screen behind the pilot, but was heavier and less agile than the A6M2, as evidenced by the 'Great Marianas turkey shoot', when a force of A6M5s was annihilated by Grumman F6F Hellcats.

Handling characteristics

All control surfaces were fabric covered. Although highly agile, the A6M2 was sluggish to roll and took time to build up speed once in a dive. Allied pilots used this to their advantage, often scoring a kill while the Zero attempted to dive away. Early Reisens suffered from aileron flutter and, on at least one occasion, this prevented the pilot from pulling out of a dive, his aircraft crashing into the sea. The ailerons on subsequent aircraft were modified as a result.

Fuselage and canopy

With the exception of the control surfaces, the Zero was of all-metal construction. There was no armour for the pilot, no bulletproof windshield and no jettisonable hood. The cockpit arrangement was typical for fighters of the era except for its size. While big enough for a Japanese pilot, a typical Western pilot in full flying gear would find the cockpit cramped. The canopy used ordinary glass, which was all flat plate except for the segments in the curved top.

Engine

The standard engine of the A6M2 variant was a 14-cylinder Nakajima NK1C Sakae 12 radial piston engine. Fitted with a single-stage supercharger and driving a three-bladed airscrew, it produced 950 hp (708 kW). Even by 1940 standards, this was not a particularly powerful engine, and the excellent agility and performance of the Zero could only be maintained in later, heavier models by the substitution of a more powerful engine. The A6M3 introduced an improved Sakae 21 with a two-stage supercharger, boosting power output to 1,130 hp (843 kW). Throughout the war, the chief engineer on the Zero, Jiro Horikoshi, had favoured the 1,560-hp (1163-kW) Mitsubishi Kinsei 62 radial as the original powerplant and was finally granted his wish with the construction of the A6M8. Approximately 6,300 of this variant were ordered but Allied bombing hindered its development and only two prototypes were built.

Fuel

A6M2s had three fuel tanks, one in each wingroot and a fuselage tank directly in front of the pilot. During operations in the Pacific, most Reisens also carried a single drop tank under the fuselage, extending maximum range out to 1,864 miles (3000 km) and endurance to eight hours on intermediate engine power.

Propeller

The A6M1 prototype was completed in March 1939 and first flew in April. One of the key changes during the flight test programme was the change from a two-bladed variable-pitch propeller to a Sumitomo-Hamilton three-bladed constant-speed unit. The three-bladed metal propeller became standard on all subsequent variants.

Armament

Although the Zero's designers sacrificed protection to save weight, they decided from the very beginning to equip their nimble fighter with heavy 20-mm cannon. Although slow-firing, these hard-hitting weapons gave the Zero a decided advantage over US fighters armed only with machine-guns. Later versions of the Zero carried a number of different weapon configurations, one of the most radical being that of the night-fighter version of the A6M5. It had two 0.303-in (7.7-mm) Type 97 machine-guns in the upper fuselage decking, two wing-mounted 20-mm Type 99 cannon and one fuselage-mounted oblique-firing Type 99 cannon for engaging bombers from relative safety.

Mitsubishi Ki-46 'Dinah'

This 16 Dokuritsu Hiko-tai Ki-46-III has the upward/oblique-firing 1.45-in (37-mm) cannon that was typical of the variant.

Ki-46 'Dinah'

Cutaway key
1 Starboard navigation light
2 Starboard wingtip
3 Wing front spar
4 Main spar
5 Auxiliary rear spar
6 Starboard aileron
7 Aileron hinges
8 Aileron actuating hinge fairing
9 Aileron fixed tab
10 Access plates
11 Control rods
12 Leading-edge fuel tank
13 Filler/access points
14 Rib station
15 Centre spar
16 Centre fuel tank
17 Aft fuel tank
18 Flap profile
19 Starboard flap outer section
20 Starboard nacelle aft fairing
21 Wing inner aft fuel tank
22 Wing inner centre fuel tank
23 Nacelle panels
24 Access
25 Engine bearer ring support
26 Cooling gills
27 Exhaust slots
28 Cowling inner ring
29 Inner trunking
30 Intake slot
31 Spinner
32 Three-blade propeller
33 Starter dog
34 Propeller hub
35 Reduction gear housing
36 Cowling nose ring
37 Mitsubishi Ha-112 Otsu radial engine
38 Exhaust manifold
39 Unstepped nose glazing
40 Inner coaming
41 Fixed frame
42 Nose panels

43 Nose landing lamp
44 Starboard mainwheel
45 Nose access/(optional) camera hatch
46 Nose (optional) fuel tank
47 Fuselage forward frame
48 Rudder pedal assembly
49 Control column
50 Throttle quadrant
51 Seat adjustment lever
52 Control horn
53 Compass housing
54 Starboard electrics panel
55 Canopy sliding section
56 Pilot's headrest
57 Pilot's 13-mm back armour
58 Pilot's seat and harness
59 Oxygen hose
60 Seat support frame
61 Control rod linkage
62 Wing root fillet
63 Wing front spar/fuselage frame
64 Main spar centre-section carry-through
65 Wing control surface actuating rods
66 Canopy track
67 Canopy fixed aft glazing
68 Armoured headrest support
69 Aerial mast
70 Dorsal decking
71 Fuselage main (contoured cut-out) fuel tank
72 Spring-loaded hand/entry grips
73 Cockpit former longeron
74 Fuel feed lines
75 Centre-section camera mounting rings
76 Ventral sliding hatch

77 Hatch actuating lever
78 Ventral glazing
79 Centre-section compartment
80 Centre-section camera stowage
81 Support frame
82 Fuselage structure
83 Dorsal identification light
84 Aerial
85 Aerial lead-in
86 Radio installation
87 Anti-vibration mountings
88 Centre-section side window
89 Main reconnaissance camera installation
90 Aft cockpit
91 Fixed glazing
92 Canopy sliding section
93 Canopy frames
94 Aft bulkhead
95 Canopy track
96 Dorsal gun stowage trough (deleted)
97 Canopy end glazing
98 Fuselage panelling
99 Fuselage structure
100 Fuselage frames
101 Tail surface control lines
102 Lifting tube
103 Tailfin root fairing
104 Starboard tailplane
105 Elevator balance
106 Starboard elevator
107 Elevator hinge
108 Tailfin leading-edge

109 Tailfin forward spar
110 Tailfin structure
111 Aerial attachment
112 Rudder balance
113 Rudder upper hinge
114 Rudder frame
115 Rudder trim tab
116 Rudder actuating hinge
117 Rudder tab hinge fairing
118 Rudder post

119 Rudder contoured lower section
120 Tail navigation light
121 Elevator trim tab
122 Tab actuating hinge
123 Elevator frame
124 Elevator hinge
125 Elevator balance
126 Tailplane structure
127 Tailplane front spar
128 Control cables

SPECIFICATION

Mitsubishi Ki-46-III

Type

Two-seat reconnaissance aircraft

Powerplant

Two 1,500-hp (1119-kW) Mitsubishi Ha-112-II radial piston engines

Performance

Maximum speed 391 mph (630 km/h) at 19,685 ft (6000 m); service ceiling 34,450 ft (10500 m); range 2,485 miles (4000 km)

Weights

Empty 8,444 lb (3830 kg); maximum take-off 14,330 lb (6500 kg)

Dimensions

Wingspan 48 ft 2¾ in (14.70 m); length 36 ft 1 in (11.00 m); height 12 ft 8¾ in (3.88 m); wing area 344.46 sq ft (32.00 m2)

Armament

Ki-46-I and Ki-46-II had a single 7.7-mm (0.303-in) rear-firing machine-gun on a trainable mount; III Kai two 20-mm Ho-5 and oblique 37 Ho-203

The most obvious external change in the Ki-46-III was the distinctive redesign of the forward fuselage with a new canopy design.

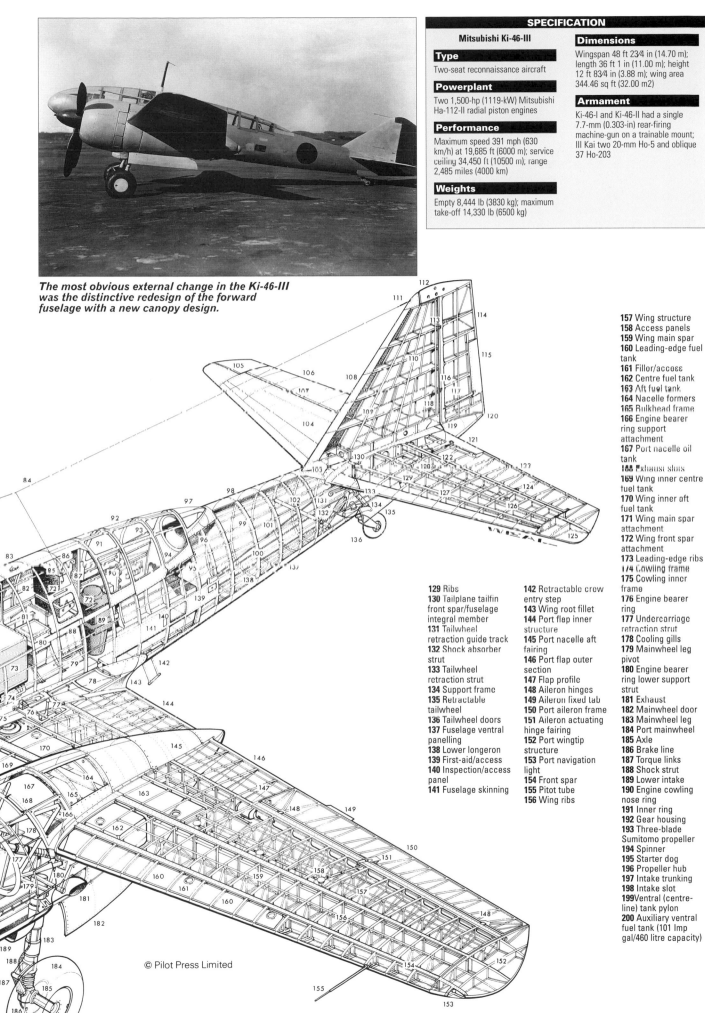

129 Ribs
130 Tailplane tailfin front spar/fuselage integral member
131 Tailwheel retraction guide track
132 Shock absorber strut
133 Tailwheel retraction strut
134 Support frame
135 Retractable tailwheel
136 Tailwheel doors
137 Fuselage ventral panelling
138 Lower longeron
139 First-aid/access
140 Inspection/access panel
141 Fuselage skinning
142 Retractable crew entry step
143 Wing root fillet
144 Port flap inner structure
145 Port nacelle aft fairing
146 Port flap outer section
147 Flap profile
148 Aileron hinges
149 Aileron fixed tab
150 Port aileron frame
151 Aileron actuating hinge fairing
152 Port wingtip structure
153 Port navigation light
154 Front spar
155 Pitot tube
156 Wing ribs

157 Wing structure
158 Access panels
159 Wing main spar
160 Leading-edge fuel tank
161 Filler/access
162 Centre fuel tank
163 Aft fuel tank
164 Nacelle formers
165 Bulkhead frame
166 Engine bearer ring support attachment
167 Port nacelle oil tank
168 Exhaust slots
169 Wing inner centre fuel tank
170 Wing inner aft fuel tank
171 Wing main spar attachment
172 Wing front spar attachment
173 Leading-edge ribs
174 Cowling frame
175 Cowling inner frame
176 Engine bearer ring
177 Undercarriage retraction strut
178 Cooling gills
179 Mainwheel leg pivot
180 Engine bearer ring lower support strut
181 Exhaust
182 Mainwheel door
183 Mainwheel leg
184 Port mainwheel
185 Axle
186 Brake line
187 Torque links
188 Shock strut
189 Lower intake
190 Engine cowling nose ring
191 Inner ring
192 Gear housing
193 Three-blade Sumitomo propeller
194 Spinner
195 Starter dog
196 Propeller hub
197 Intake trunking
198 Intake slot
199 Ventral (centre-line) tank pylon
200 Auxiliary ventral fuel tank (101 Imp gal/460 litre capacity)

Nakajima Ki-43

The Japanese puppet state of Manchukuo was supplied with Ki-43s for home defence. Here the Japanese equivalent of the British 'Hucks starter' is seen being employed to start a section of Hayabusas.

Nakajima Ki-43

Cutaway key
1 Starboard navigation light
2 Wingtip
3 Starboard fabric-covered aileron
4 Aileron actuating linkage
5 Aileron control rod
6 Control rod connecting fittings
7 Aileron tab
8 Flap outer cable drum
9 Flap travel
10 Flap control cables
11 Radio mast
12 Light alloy wing skinning
13 Starboard undercarriage fairing
14 Gun port fairings
15 Nose ring
16 Annular oil cooler
17 Two-blade two-pitch metal propeller
18 Spinner
19 Starter dog
20 Supercharger air intake
21 Intake fairing
22 Nakajima Ha-25 (Type 99) 14-cylinder two-row radial engine
23 Cowling gills
24 Exhaust collector ring
25 Exhaust outlet
26 Engine lower bearers
27 Oil regulator valve
28 Oil pressure tank
29 Engine accessories
30 Engine upper bearers
31 Cowling gill controls

32 Two 0.5-in (12.7-mm) Type 89 machine-guns
33 Gun gas outlet
34 Cartridge link ejection chute
35 Fireproof (No. 1) bulkhead
36 Ammunition magazine (500 rpg)
37 Cartridge ejection chute
38 Gun breech fairing
39 Telescopic gun sight
40 One-piece curved windscreen
41 Radio aerial
42 Aft-sliding cockpit canopy
43 Turnover structure
44 Seat back
45 Seat adjustment rails
46 Seat pan
47 Throttle quadrant
48 Instrument panel
49 Control column
50 Rudder pedals
51 Underfloor control linkage
52 Seat support frame
53 Control cable and rod bearings
54 Oxygen cylinders
55 Rudder cable pulleys
56 Transceiver
57 Type 96 Hi-3 radio installation
58 Receiver unit
59 Transmitter unit
60 Anti-vibration mounting slings
61 Fuselage construction break
62 Inspection/access panel
63 Fuselage stringers
64 Fuselage structure

65 Frame
66 Fuselage upper longeron
67 Elevator control cables
68 Fuselage skinning
69 Tailwheel shock strut
70 Tail unit attachment
71 Tailfin root fairing
72 Starboard tailplane
73 Elevator balance
74 Starboard elevator
75 Tailfin leading edge
76 Tailfin structure
77 Rear navigation light
78 Aerial attachment
79 Rudder upper hinge
80 Rudder post
81 Rudder frame
82 Rudder trim tab
83 Rudder middle hinge
84 Elevator control lever
85 Elevator trim tab
86 Elevator frame
87 Elevator balance
88 Tailplane structure
89 Rudder control lever
90 Non-retractable tailwheel

91 Cantilever tailwheel leg
92 Tailwheel leg/bulkhead attachment
93 Rudder cables
94 Fuselage skinning
95 Wing fillet
96 Flap inboard profiles
97 Flap actuating cylinder

SPECIFICATION

Nakajima Ki-43-IIb

Type
Single-seat fighter/fighter-bomber
Powerplant
one 1,150-hp (858-kW) Nakajima
Ha-115 radial piston engine

Performance
Maximum speed 329 mph (530
km/h) at 13,125 ft (4000 m); service
ceiling 36,745 ft (11200 m);
maximum range 1,988 miles (3200
km)

Weights
Empty 4,211 lb (1910 kg); maximum
take-off 5,710 lb (2590 kg)

Dimensions
Wingspan 35 ft 6¾ in (10.84 m);
length 29 ft 3¼ in (8.92 m); height
10 ft 8¾ in (3.27 m); wing area
230.36 sq ft (21.40 m2)

Armament
Two 0.50-in (12.5-mm) forward-
firing machine-guns, plus two
underwing racks each able to carry
a 551-lb (250-kg) bomb

*After participating in the Philippines campaign, the 50th Sentai
returned to Japan for conversion to Ki-43-Is for subsequent
operations in Burma. Photographed at Tokorozawa in June 1942,
these Ki-43-I-Hei belonged to either the unit's 1st Chutai (with
white lightning markings) or 3rd Chutai (yellow lightning).*

98 Rear
spar/fuselage
attachment
99 Mainspar/fuselage
attachment
100 Front
spar/fuselage
attachment
101 Port main fuel
tank (29.5 Imp gal/132
litre capacity)

102 Port overload fuel
tank (33 Imp gal/150
litre capacity)
103 Fuel filler caps
104 Main spar
105 Rear spar
106 Aileron control
rod
107 Flap inboard
travel
108 Flap pulley fairing
109 Fowler-type
'butterfly' combat flap

110 Flap outboard
travel
111 Aileron trim tab
112 Aileron inner
hinge
113 Aileron centre
hinge/control rod
attachment
114 Port aileron
115 Aileron outer
hinge
116 Port wingtip
117 Port navigation
light

118 Wing skinning
119 Pitot head
120 Leading edge ribs
121 Front spar
122 Landing light
123 Mainwheel leg
fairing
124 Torque links
125 Port mainwheel
126 Axle fork
127 Mainwheel oleo
128 Mainwheel leg
pivot
129 Gear support
bearer
130 Gear actuating
cylinder
131 Emergency
actuation cables
132 Leading edge rib
cut-outs
133 Mainwheel well
134 Underwing drop
tank pylon (mounted
aft and just inboard of
the main
undercarriage
attachment point)
135 Tank suspension
lugs
136 Air vent
137 Fuel pipe
connection
138 Tank fin
139 Sway brace
attachment points
140 Jettisonable 44-
Imp gal (200-litre) tank

*Shining under the Chinese sun, this Ki-43-II-Otsu of the 2nd Chutai (red
diagonal tail stripe), 25th Sentai, proves that the application of green mottle
over natural metal was less than effective.*

Nakajima Ki-84 Hayate

This is one of the initial pre-production batch of 83 Ki-84s, seen at Tachikawa in August 1943 from where it was flown by the Army Air Arsenal as a service trials aircraft.

Nakajima Ki-84

1 Starter dog
2 Spinner
3 Constant-speed electrically-operated Pe-32 propeller
4 Propeller reduction gear housing
5 Carburettor air intake
6 Starboard 20-mm Ho-5 cannon muzzle
7 Gun camera port
8 Starboard leading-edge fuel tank (14.7 Imp gal/67 litre capacity)
9 Mainspar
10 Starboard navigation light
11 Starboard wingtip
12 Fabric-covered aileron
13 Aileron control link fairing
14 Aileron trim tab
15 Flap track extension fairing
16 Starboard Fowler-type flap
17 Wing cannon ammunition box access
18 Wing cannon access covers
19 Carburettor intake trunking
20 Machine-gun blast tube
21 Machine-gun trough
22 Army Type 4 Model 21 (Nakajima Ha-45-21) 18-cylinder radial air-cooled engine
23 Cowling fasteners
24 Aluminium cylinder fans
25 Oil cooler intake
26 Starboard mainwheel

27 Oil cooler housing
28 Ejector exhaust stubs
29 Cowling gills
30 Engine bearers
31 Oil tank (11 Imp gal/50 litre capacity)
32 Vent
33 Gun cooling muffle
34 Firewall/bulkhead
35 Ho-103 machine-gun (two) of 13-mm calibre
36 Main fuel tank (47.7 Imp gal/217 litre capacity)
37 Port ammunition tank (350 rounds)
38 Fuel filler cap
39 Rudder pedals
40 Control column
41 Instrument panel
42 Fuselage flush-riveted stressed-skin panels
43 Reflector sight (offset to starboard)
44 Armourglass (65-mm) windscreen
45 Aft-sliding cockpit canopy
46 Canopy lock/release

47 Pilot's headrest
48 Pilot's head armour/turnover support
49 Canopy fixed aft glazing
50 Canopy track
51 Entry handgrip
52 Pilot's 13-mm back armour
53 Elevator trim handwheel
54 Pilot's seat (adjustable vertically)
55 Throttle quadrant
56 Flap setting lever
57 Undercarriage selector lever
58 Underfloor control runs
59 Flap-rod linkage
60 Water-methanol tank
61 Mid-fuselage construction break
62 Radio equipment tray
63 Type 4 Hi no.3 radio communications pack
64 Aerial lead-in
65 Aerial mast
66 Aerials

67 Light alloy semi-monocoque fuselage structure
68 Fuselage upper longeron
69 Oval section fuselage aft frames
70 Aft fuselage construction break
71 Starboard tailplane
72 Elevator balance
73 Starboard elevator (fabric covered)
74 Elevator trim tab

75 Tailfin leading edge
76 Tailfin structure
77 Rear navigation/formation light
78 Aerial stub attachment

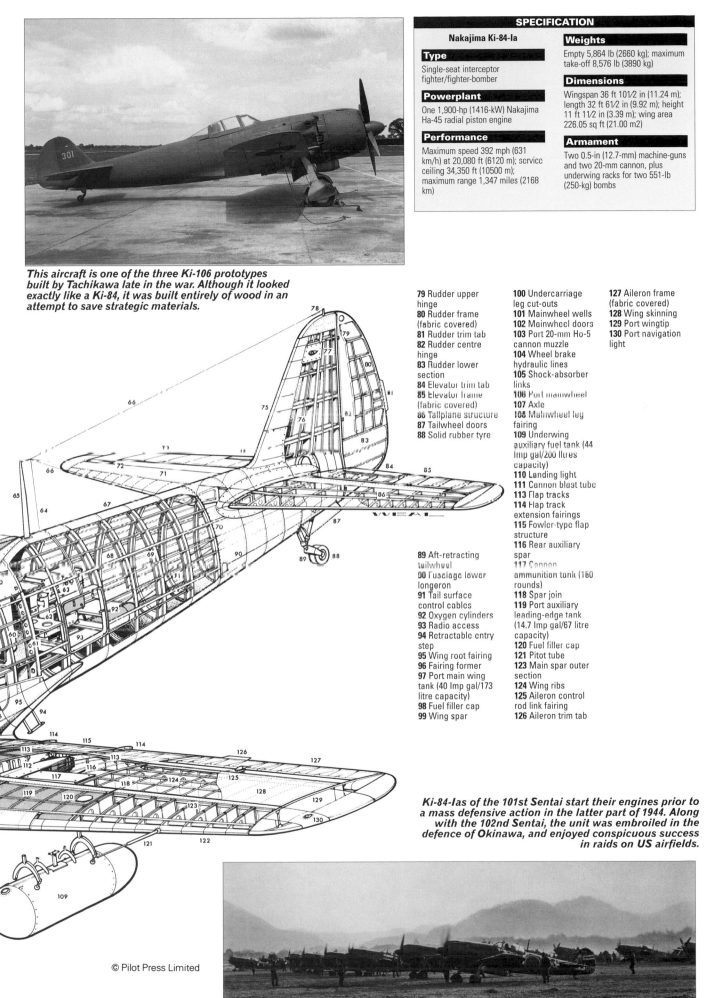

SPECIFICATION

Nakajima Ki-84-Ia

Type
Single-seat interceptor fighter/fighter-bomber

Powerplant
One 1,900-hp (1416-kW) Nakajima Ha-45 radial piston engine

Performance
Maximum speed 392 mph (631 km/h) at 20,080 ft (6120 m); service ceiling 34,350 ft (10500 m); maximum range 1,347 miles (2168 km)

Weights
Empty 5,864 lb (2660 kg); maximum take-off 8,576 lb (3890 kg)

Dimensions
Wingspan 36 ft 10½ in (11.24 m); length 32 ft 6½ in (9.92 m); height 11 ft 1½ in (3.39 m); wing area 226.05 sq ft (21.00 m2)

Armament
Two 0.5-in (12.7-mm) machine-guns and two 20-mm cannon, plus underwing racks for two 551-lb (250-kg) bombs

This aircraft is one of the three Ki-106 prototypes built by Tachikawa late in the war. Although it looked exactly like a Ki-84, it was built entirely of wood in an attempt to save strategic materials.

79 Rudder upper hinge
80 Rudder frame (fabric covered)
81 Rudder trim tab
82 Rudder centre hinge
83 Rudder lower section
84 Elevator trim tab
85 Elevator frame (fabric covered)
86 Tailplane structure
87 Tailwheel doors
88 Solid rubber tyre

89 Aft-retracting tailwheel
90 Fuselage lower longeron
91 Tail surface control cables
92 Oxygen cylinders
93 Radio access
94 Retractable entry step
95 Wing root fairing
96 Fairing former
97 Port main wing tank (40 Imp gal/173 litre capacity)
98 Fuel filler cap
99 Wing spar

100 Undercarriage leg cut-outs
101 Mainwheel wells
102 Mainwheel doors
103 Port 20-mm Ho-5 cannon muzzle
104 Wheel brake hydraulic lines
105 Shock-absorber links
106 Port mainwheel
107 Axle
108 Mainwheel leg fairing
109 Underwing auxiliary fuel tank (44 Imp gal/200 litres capacity)
110 Landing light
111 Cannon blast tube
113 Flap tracks
114 Flap track extension fairings
115 Fowler-type flap structure
116 Rear auxiliary spar
117 Cannon ammunition tank (150 rounds)
118 Spar join
119 Port auxiliary leading-edge tank (14.7 Imp gal/67 litre capacity)
120 Fuel filler cap
121 Pitot tube
123 Main spar outer section
124 Wing ribs
125 Aileron control rod link fairing
126 Aileron trim tab

127 Aileron frame (fabric covered)
128 Wing skinning
129 Port wingtip
130 Port navigation light

Ki-84-Ias of the 101st Sentai start their engines prior to a mass defensive action in the latter part of 1944. Along with the 102nd Sentai, the unit was embroiled in the defence of Okinawa, and enjoyed conspicuous success in raids on US airfields.

© Pilot Press Limited

North American P-51 Mustang

It is a tribute to the Mustang's popularity that today there are almost 150 airworthy examples. This aircraft represents 'Chuck' Yeager's Glamorous Glen III.

P-51B Mustang

Cutaway key

1 Plastic (Phenol fibre) rudder trim tab
2 Rudder frame (fabric covered)
3 Rudder balance
4 Fin front spar
5 Fin structure
6 Access panel
7 Rudder trim-tab actuating drum
8 Rudder trim-tab control link
9 Rear navigation light
10 Rudder metal bottom section
11 Elevator plywood trim tab
12 Starboard elevator frame
13 Elevator balance weight
14 Starboard tailplane structure
15 Reinforced bracket (rear steering stresses)
16 Rudder operating horn forging
17 Elevator operating horns
18 Tab control turnbuckles
19 Fin front spar/ fuselage attachment
20 Port elevator tab
21 Fabric-covered elevator
22 Elevator balance weight
23 Port tailplane
24 Tab control drum
25 Fin root fairing
26 Elevator cables
27 Tab control access panels
28 Tailwheel steering mechanism
29 Tailwheel mount
30 Tailwheel leg assembly
31 Forward-retracting steerable tailwheel
32 Tailwheel doors
33 Lifting tube
34 Fuselage aft bulkhead/break point
35 Fuselage break point

36 Control cable pulley brackets
37 Fuselage frames
38 Oxygen bottles
39 Cooling-air exit flap actuating mechanism
40 Rudder cables
41 Fuselage lower longeron
42 Rear tunnel
43 Cooling-air exit flap
44 Coolant radiator assembly
45 Radio and equipment shelf
46 Power supply pack
47 Fuselage upper longeron
48 Radio bay aft bulkhead (plywood)
49 Fuselage stringers
50 SCR-695 radio transmitter-receiver (on upper sliding shelf)
51 Whip aerial
52 Junction box
53 Cockpit aft glazing
54 Canopy track
55 SCR-552 radio transmitter-receiver
56 Battery installation
57 Radiator/ supercharger coolant pipes

58 Radiator forward air duct
59 Coolant header tank/radiator pipe
60 Coolant radiator ventral access cover
61 Oil-cooler air inlet door
62 Oil radiator
63 Oil pipes
64 Flap control linkage
65 Wing rear spar/ fuselage attachment bracket
66 Crash pylon structure
67 Aileron control linkage
68 Hydraulic hand pump
69 Radio control boxes
70 Pilot's seat
71 Seat suspension frame
72 Pilot's head/back armour
73 Rearward-sliding clear-vision canopy
74 External rear-view mirror
75 Ring and bead gunsight

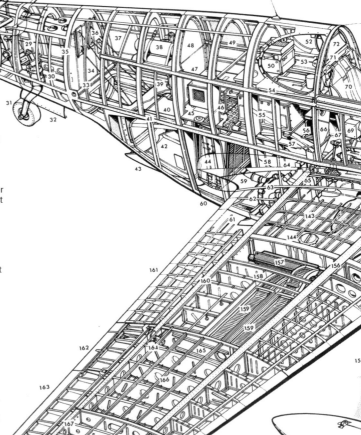

76 Bullet-proof windshield
77 Gyro gunsight
78 Engine controls
79 Signal-pistol discharge tube
80 Circuit-breaker panel
81 Oxygen regulator
82 Pilot's footrest and seat mounting bracket
83 Control linkage
84 Rudder pedal
85 Tailwheel lock control
86 Wing centre-section
87 Hydraulic reservoir
88 Port wing fuel tank filler point
89 Port Browning 0.5-in (12.7-mm) guns
90 Ammunition feed chutes
91 Gun-bay access door (raised)
92 Ammunition box troughs
93 Aileron control cables
94 Flap lower skin (Alclad)
95 Aileron profile (internal aerodynamic balance diaphragm)

96 Aileron control drum and mounting bracket
97 Aileron trim-tab control drum
98 Aileron plastic (Phenol fibre) trim tab
99 Port aileron assembly
100 Wing skinning
101 Outer section sub-assembly
102 Port navigation light
103 Port wingtip
104 Leading-edge skin
105 Landing lamp
106 Weapons/stores pylon
107 500-lb (227-kg) bomb
108 Gun ports
109 Gun barrels
110 Detachable cowling panels
111 Firewall/integral armour
112 Oil tank
113 Oil pipes
114 Upper longeron/engine mount attachment
115 Oil-tank metal retaining straps
116 Carburettor
117 Engine bearer assembly

118 Cowling panel frames
119 Engine aftercooler
120 Engine leads
121 Packard V-1650 (R-R Merlin) 12-cylinder liquid-cooled engine
122 Exhaust fairing panel
123 Stub exhausts
124 Magneto
125 Coolant pipes
126 Cowling forward frame
127 Coolant header tank
128 Armour plate
129 Propeller hub
130 Spinner
131 Hamilton Standard Hydromatic propeller
132 Carburettor air intake, integral with (133)
133 Engine-mount front-frame assembly
134 Intake trunk
135 Engine-mount reinforcing tie
136 Hand-crank starter
137 Carburettor trunk vibration-absorbing connection
138 Wing centre-section front bulkhead
139 Wing centre-section end rib
140 Starboard mainwheel well
141 Wing front spar/fuselage attachment bracket
142 Ventral air intake (radiator and oil cooler)
143 Starboard wing fuel tank
144 Fuel filler point
145 Mainwheel leg mount/pivot

146 Mainwheel leg rib cut-outs
147 Main gear fairing doors
148 Auxiliary fuel tank (plastic/pressed-paper composition, 108 US gal/409 litres)
149 Auxiliary fuel tank (metal 75 US gal/284 litres)
150 27-in (0.69-m) smooth-contour mainwheel
151 Axle fork
152 Towing lugs
153 Landing-gear fairing
154 Main-gear shock strut
155 Blast tubes
156 Wing front spar
157 Gun bay
158 Ammunition feed chutes
159 Ammunition boxes
160 Wing rear spar
161 Flap structure
162 Starboard aileron tab
163 Starboard aileron
164 Starboard aileron tab adjustment mechanism (ground setting)
165 Wing rib strengthening
166 Outboard section structure
167 Outer section single spar
168 Wingtip sub-assembly
169 Starboard navigation light
170 Detachable wingtip

SPECIFICATION

P-51D-5-NA Mustang

Dimensions

Fuselage length: 32 ft 3³⁄₁₆ in (9.84 m)
Wing span: 37 ft 0⁵⁄₁₆ in (11.27 m)
Wing aspect ratio: 4.46
Wing incidence: approx 1°
Wing dihedral angle: 5°
Wing sweepback angle: 3° 3' 32"
Tailplane span: 13 ft 2⅛ in (3.83 m)
Total wing area: 233.19 sq ft (21.66 m²)
Total aileron area: 12.64 sq ft (1.17 m²)
Total flap area: 32.60 sq ft (3.03 m²)
Total horizontal tail area: 27.85 sq ft (2.59 m²)
Total elevator area: 13.05 sq ft (1.21 m²)
Fin area: 8.83 sq ft (0.82 m²)
Rudder area: 10.25 sq ft (0.95 m²)
Overall height: 13 ft 8 in (4.16 m) (taxiing attitude, statically loaded)
Undercarriage track: 11 ft 10 in (3.61 m)
Maximum wing loading: 49.7 lb/sq ft (242.9 kg/m²)

Powerplant

One Packard-built Merlin V-1650-7 liquid-cooled 12-cylinder Vee inline piston engine with two-speed two-stage supercharger, driving an 11 ft 2-in (3.40-m) diameter Hamilton Standard constant-speed hydromatic four-bladed propeller
Take-off rating: 1,450 hp (1094 kW)
War emergency ratings: 1,695 hp (1264 kW) at 10,300 ft (3139 m) and 1,300 hp (1036 kW) at 24,000 ft (7315 m)
Military ratings: 1,550 hp (1156 kW) at 13,000 ft (3962 m) and 1,260 hp (940 kW) at 26,500 ft (8077 m)
Continuous ratings: 1,150 hp (858 kW) at 17,000 ft (5182 m) and 980 hp (731 kW) at 29,000 ft (8839 m)
Propeller pitch range: 23° - 65°

Weights

Empty operating: 7,125 lb (3232 kg)
Basic: 7,635 lb (3466 kg)
Combat weight (clean): 10,100 lb (4582 kg)
Maximum take-off: 11,600 lb (5262 kg) with two 108-US gal (409-litre) drop tanks

Fuel and load

Total internal fuel: 269 US gal (1018 litres), comprising total of 184 US gal (696 litres) in self-sealing wing fuel cells, plus 85 US gal (322 litres) in self-sealing fuselage tank
External fuel: provision for two 75-US gal (284-litre), 110-US gal (416-litre) or 108-US gal (409-litre) fuel tanks
Maximum weapon load: 2,000 lb (908 kg)

Performance

Maximum level speeds: (clean, no racks fitted) 395 mph (636 km/h) at 5,000 ft (1524 m), 413 mph (665 km/h) at 15,000 ft (4572 m), 437 mph (703 km/h) at 25,000 ft (7620 m) and 433 mph (697 km/h) at 30,000 ft (9144 m)
Maximum cruising speed: 362 mph (583 km/h)
Rate of climb: 3,475 ft (1059 m) per minute at 5,000 ft (1524 m)
Service ceiling: 41,900 ft (12771 m)
Time to climb: 20,000 ft (6096 m) in 7 minutes 20 seconds, 30,000 ft (9144 m) in 12 minutes 36 seconds
Landing speed: 100 mph (161 km/h)

Range

Range (clean): 825 nm (950 miles; 1529 km) at 25,000 ft (7620 m) at maximum cruise power
Maximum range (absolute): 1998 nm (2,304 miles; 3703 km) with two 108-US gal (409-litre) drop tanks, 1433 nm (1650 miles; 2655 km) at 25,000 ft (7620 m) at maximum cruise power
Operational radius with maximum fuel: 1129 nm (1,300 miles, 2092 km)

Armament

Fixed: six wing-mounted 0.50-in (12.7-mm) Colt-Browning M2 machine guns, with total 1880 rounds, comprising 400 rounds for each inboard gun and 270 rounds each for outboard pairs
External stores: two underwing hardpoints for two 500-lb (227-kg) or 1,000-lb (454-kg) free-fall general purpose bombs, plus bazooka-type tubes for six 4.5-in (114-mm) M-8 explosive rockets or (from P-51D-25-NA) six 5-in (127-mm) high-velocity aircraft rockets (HVARs) carried on zero-length launchers with tanks or bombs, or 10 HVARS without tanks or bombs

A pair of P-51Ds of the 458th Fighter Squadron, 506th Fighter Group, Seventh Air Force, are seen through the aft gun sight of a B-29 bomber while on an escort mission to Japan. This was only made possible by the taking of Iwo Jima in February 1945 which was achieved at bloody cost to the US Marines. No fewer than five airfields were built on the island which eventually became home for three Mustang fighter groups. These undertook escort missions as well as fighter-bomber sweeps over Japan.

P-51D Mustang

Li'l Butch was an Inglewood-built P-51D-20-NA assigned to the 47th Fighter Squadron, 15th Fighter Group, of the USAAF's Seventh Air Force in the Pacific. It wears the 47th Fighter Squadron's distinctive yellow-edged black wing and fuselage bands and fin triangle, and a black-banded yellow spinner. Other squadrons in the 15th FG used diagonal green stripes edged in black on wings, tail and fuselage, along with black and yellow fin, wing and tailplane tips. These large and prominent markings allowed easy differentiation between P-51s and Japanese fighters. Although it had Mustangs for only a relatively brief time (its aircraft arrived at Iwo Jima from 6 March 1945), the 15th FG notched up an impressive record. The 47th FS alone scored 36 kills during its brief Mustang era.

Engine supercharger and exhaust

The Merlin's two-speed, two-stage supercharger (reportedly designed by Wright) maintained pressures within the induction system equal to the pressures experienced at sea level. When any gas is compressed, its temperature rises. An intercooler is therefore used between the two supercharger compressors, giving a denser mixture of fuel and air in the cylinder. The supercharged Merlin produced more power at 26,000 ft (7925 m) than the Allison did on take-off. The Merlin's twelve cylinders exhausted through individual stub exhausts projecting from the sides of the cowling. These exhausts were often faired in, with a shroud, as seen here. They were usually of circular cross-section, unlike the flattened fish-tail exhausts fitted to many of the earlier Allison-engined aircraft. The later Twin Mustang (which was also Allison-powered) introduced flame-damping exhausts.

Propeller

Most examples of the P-51D were fitted with a J-6523A-24 or K-6523A-24 Hamilton Standard propeller, with drag reducing 'cuffs' at the roots. Such cuffs were often removed in service, especially after the war. The distinctive paddle-shaped blades were highly effective in the thin air found at high altitude. Some later aircraft used a square-tipped 'paddle-bladed' Model 6547A-6 Hamilton Standard prop, while P-51Ks used a four-bladed A20-156-24M Aeroproducts propeller.

Packard-Merlin engine

The P-51B and subsequent Mustang variants replaced the indigenously designed Allison engine with Packard-built versions of the Rolls-Royce Merlin. The Merlin (famously the powerplant for the Spitfire, Hurricane, Lancaster and Mosquito) was by 1942 a mature and reliable powerplant. A V-12 engine, the Merlin was, like the Allison, cooled by a mix of water and glycol, and was of similar overall dimensions. Compared to the American engine, it developed greater power at high altitudes, and promised superior range and endurance. It was a natural choice of engine for the Mustang. Rolls-Royce and North American started examining Merlin-engined Mustang versions virtually simultaneously, both opting to use the Packard-built V-1650-3 (equivalent to the Rolls-Royce Merlin 68) with two-stage supercharger and intercooler. The two programmes were soon merged, although two NAA and five Rolls-Royce prototypes were flown.

Colour scheme

Most USAAF P-51Ds wore an overall natural metal finish. European-based aircraft had camouflaged upper surfaces during 1944, but reverted to overall natural metal. Many P-51s had their wings painted silver, while the fuselages were left in bare metal finish. The top decking forward of the cockpit was painted matt olive drab to serve as an anti-dazzle panel. National markings were without red centre discs or stripes, in order to avoid any confusion with the Japanese 'meatball'. Various schemes were used to avoid misidentification – P-51s in Europe wore white (or black on silver aircraft) noses and stripes on wings and tails, while some aircraft in the Far East had equally prominent black bands.

Mustang canopies

The spacious cockpit of the P-51D was covered by an aft-sliding, blown, bubble canopy, which offered some improvement in all round visibility, by comparison with the standard canopy on the high-backed P-51B/C and earlier versions. The bubble canopy was produced in several versions, with a lower, reduced-drag canopy introduced from the middle of the P-51D-5-NA production run. The Dallas-built P-51Ks had a larger canopy, with a kinked 'trailing edge' just above the back of the canopy rail. The TF-51D conversions and Cavalier's post-war Mustangs each used yet another canopy shape. Various racing Mustangs use tiny 'pimple' canopies for the ultimate in drag reduction.

Fixed gun armament

In its primary fighter escort role, the P-51D relied on its internal armament of six Browning M2 0.50-in (12.7-mm) calibre machine-guns, three mounted side by side in each wing, together with 400 rounds for each inboard gun and 270 rounds each for the other four guns. Every fifth round was usually a tracer, but the mix of tracer and armour piercing or incendiary ammunition varied according to Command and even Group. Spent ammunition cases were ejected through rectangular ports on the underside of the wing. The guns were mounted upright, eliminating many of the jamming problems encountered in the four-gun P-51B and P-51C.

Intake

The liquid-cooled Merlin engine relied on a complex belly-mounted air-cooled radiator. Aspirated by a massive ventral airscoop, the radiator's location made it vulnerable to ground fire. The intake of the Merlin Mustang, like that of the A-36, was fixed, while the P-51 and P-51A had articulated intakes, with opening lips to admit more airflow under certain conditions, especially on the ground. All Mustangs had an opening rear vent, downstream of the radiator itself. In certain circumstances, the expulsion of hot air from this duct actually generated a small amount of thrust and thus gave a small improvement in performance.

Underwing stores

The Mustang also had underwing hardpoints for an external fuel tank or bomb of 500 lb (227-kg), or from the P-51D, 1,000 lb (454-kg) weight. This pylon could even mount a 'bazooka' type three-tube M10 launcher for 4.5-in (114-mm) rockets. The standard P-51D tank (seen here) was made of metal, and contained 75 US gal (284 litres), a larger tank of similar shape contained 110 US gal (416 litres). In an effort to save metal, and to avoid littering Germany with useful aluminium which could be recycled for its own war machine, a 108-US gal (409-litre) tank of impregnated paper construction was used by Eighth Air Force Mustang units. Redundant fuel tanks were often converted to serve as napalm containers. The P-51 could also be fitted with zero-length launchers for unguided 5-in (127-mm) rocket projectiles (seen here). These launchers were simple streamlined mini-pylons, to which rockets were clipped directly.

Northrop P-61 Black Widow

Above: This Saipan-based P-61A is seen cruising over the Pacific, some time during January 1945. The gun turrets' straight trailing edge indicates a fixed installation, although other P-61s, without the troublesome rotating unit, are known to have used the factory-produced 'teardrop'-shaped housing.

P-61B Black

Cutaway key
1 Starboard navigation light
2 Starboard formation light
3 Aileron hinge fairing
4 Conventional aileron
5 Aileron tab
6 Full-span flaps (Zapp type)
7 Retractable aileron (operable as spoiler)
8 Wing skinning
9 De-icer boot
10 Intercooler controllable shutters
11 Intercooler and supercharger induction
12 Fuel filler cap
13 Starboard outer wing fuel tank
14 Nacelle fairing
15 Cooling gills
16 Pratt & Whitney R-2800-65 engine
17 Nacelle ring
18 Starboard outer auxiliary tank
19 Four-bladed Curtiss Electric propeller
20 Propeller cuffs
21 Propeller boss
22 Heater air induction
23 Front spar
24 Plexiglas canopy
25 Cannon access bulkhead cut-out
26 Front gunner's compartment
27 Sighting station
28 Bullet-resistant windshield
29 Inter-cockpit/compartment armour (shaded)
30 Pilot's canopy
31 Pilot's seat
32 Control column
33 Gunsight (fixed cannon)
34 Bullet-resistant windshield
35 Fuselage structural joint (armour plate deleted for clarity)
36 Radar modulator
37 Dielectric nosecone
38 SCR-720 radar scanner
39 Gun camera (gunsight aiming point)
40 Mast
41 Pitot head
42 Radar equipment steel support tube
43 Bulkhead (centre joint)
44 Rudder pedals
45 Drag strut
46 Torque link
47 Towing eye
48 Nosewheel
49 Cantilever steel strut
50 Mud guard (often deleted)
51 Taxi lamp
52 Air-oil shock strut (shimmy damper on forward face)
53 Nosewheel door
54 Cockpit floor
55 Radar aerials
56 Gunner's compartment floor (stepped)
57 Gunner's seat-swivel mechanism
58 Cannon ports
59 Heater air induction
60 Cannon ammunition magazines
61 Ammunition feed chute
62 Four 20-mm cannon in ventral compartment
63 Magazine forward armour plate
64 Front spar fuselage cut-out
65 Magazine rear armour plate
66 Rear spar fuselage
67 Dorsal turret support/drive motor
68 Front spar carry-through
69 Turret support forward armour plate
70 Flush-riveted aluminium alloy skin

Four P-61Cs and an F-15 move out for a thunderstorm penetration mission in 1947 from the All-Weather Flying Center in Ohio. The aircraft would penetrate the storm at different intervals, recording temperatures and pressures and photographing cloud patterns. The nosecone of the lead Black Widow shows the battering caused by rain, hail and lightning.

SPECIFICATION

P-61B Black Widow

Dimensions

Length: 49 ft 7 in (15.11 m)
Wingspan: 66 ft 3/4 in (20.11 m)
Height: 14 ft 8 in (4.47 m)
Wing area: 662.36 sq ft (61.53 m²)

Powerplant

Two Pratt & Whitney R-2800-65 Double Wasp 18-cylinder radial engines with a 2,000-hp (1491-kW) military rating and a 2,250-hp (1678-kW) war emergency rating

Weights

Empty: 23,450 lb (10637 kg)
Maximum overload: 36,200 lb (16420 kg)

Performance

Maximum speed at war emergency engine rating: 366 mph (589 km/h)
Initial climb rate at military power: 2,090 ft (637 m) per minute
Range at long-range cruise power: 1,350 miles (2172 km)

Armament

Four 20-mm M2 cannon each with 200 rounds; (on some aircraft) dorsal turret with four 0.5-in (12.7-mm) Colt-Browning machine-guns each with 560 rounds; four external pylons each rated at up to 1,600 lb (726 kg) and able to carry bombs or other stores

F-15A Reporter

Dimensions

Same as P-61B except for
Length: 50 ft 4 in (15.34 m)

Powerplant

Two Pratt & Whitney R-2800-73 Double Wasp supercharged 18-cylinder radial engines with a 2,100-hp (1566-kW) military rating and 2,800-hp (2088-kW) maximum rating with water injection

Weights

Maximum take-off: 32,190 lb (16420 kg)

Performance

Maximum speed: 400 mph (708 km/h)
Service ceiling: 41,000 ft (12497 m)
Range: 4,000 miles (6437 km)

71 Gun mantle (four 0.50-in/12.7-mm machine- guns)
72 General Electric remote control power turret
73 Turret drive ring
74 Rear spar carry-through
75 Turret support rear armour plate
76 Radio operator/rear gunner's compartment
77 Gunner's seat-swivel mechanism
78 Plexiglas tailcone
79 Rear compartment glazing
80 Aerial attachment
81 Sighting station
82 Anti-collision beacon
83 Tailboom structure (inner stringers deleted for clarity)
84 Control runs
85 Tailboom/fin attachment
86 Fin spar attachment (inner face)
87 Rudder lower hinge
88 De-icer boot
89 Fin structure
90 Rudder upper hinge
91 Rudder
92 Rear navigation light
93 Rudder tab
94 Balance tab
95 Horizontal stabiliser structure
96 De-icer boot
97 Trim tab
98 Aerials
99 Elevator
100 De-icer boot
101 Port fin
102 Rudder
103 Rear navigation light
104 Rudder tab
105 Tab hinge fairing
106 Rudder lower hinge
107 Fin spar attachment (outer face)
108 Tailboom/fin attachment butt
109 Tailboom structure
110 Tailboom joint
111 Wing/boom fairing fillet
112 Mainwheel well
113 Port outer wing fuel tank
114 Spar dihedral-break attachment bolts
115 Cooling gills
116 Port inner auxiliary tank
117 Four-bladed Curtiss Electric propeller
118 Propeller boss
119 Nacelle construction
120 Port mainwheel
121 Hydraulic and airbrake pressure lines
122 Port outer auxiliary tank
123 Mainwheel leg (hydraulic shock strut)
124 Drag strut
125 Intercooler and supercharger induction trunking
126 Mainwheel flap
127 Mainwheel door
128 Radio antenna (port and starboard booms)
129 Wing flap lock
130 Full-span flaps (Zapp type)
131 Retractable aileron (operable as spoiler)
132 Front spar
133 De-icer boot
134 Wing structure
135 Rear spar
136 Aileron tab
137 Port aileron
138 Port formation light
139 Port wingtip
140 Port navigation light

P-61B Black Widow

The aircraft depicted here, 42-39404 *Midnite Madness II*, was the second of two P-61s with this name. Referred to as *Midnite Madness I* and *II*, their nose-art appears to have been identical, although the 'II' was added under the name on 239404 at some point. This aircraft was assigned to Captain James W. Bradford of the 548th NFS. Flying from le Shima on the night of 24 June 1945, Bradford, together with radar operator 1st Lieutenant Lawrence K. Lunt and gunner Master Sergeant Reno H. Sukow, destroyed a Mitsubishi G4M 'Betty' – one of only five victories credited to the squadron. That morning, a P-61 of the 548th's sister squadron, the 549th NFS, had destroyed another 'Betty' off Iwo Jima, for its only kill of the war. The fate of *Midnite Madness II* is unclear: it eventually either ended up in the 'boneyard' at Clark AB or was lost in an accident immediately after the war. James Bradford went on to become a group commander of the Instrument School (All Weather) at Moody AFB, did a tour with the Republic of Korea AF in F-86s as a senior advisor and was involved in an exchange tour with the RAF, flying Meteor T.Mk 7s. He became wing commander at the Training Base at Laredo, Texas and finished his career with a tour at the Pentagon, retiring as a full colonel.

Powerplant
The engines used on the P-61B were Pratt & Whitney R-2800-65 Double Wasp 18-cylinder radials rated at 2,000 hp (1491 kW). Late P-61s and the P-61B were fitted with water injection which provided war emergency power (also called combat emergency power). The application of water injection increased manifold pressure and therefore power. Two water tanks, each with a capacity of 26 US gal (98 litres), allowed war emergency power to be applied for up to 15 minutes.

Radio equipment
In addition to the SCR-720 radar set, nearly 30 other 'black boxes' were installed in the Black Widow. In reality, this number was mainly made up of control units and junction boxes for the main radar and communication sets. The principal items found in an early P-61B included SCR-522 VHF command radio (two sets), SCR-695 IFF, SCR-718 radar altimeter, AN/APS-13 tail-warning radar and SCR-729 IFF/beacon locater. By sending out pulses and 'interrogating' ground beacons, the SCR-729 could be used as a navigation aid.

Cannon armament
The four 20-mm Hispano M2 cannon were mounted in the P-61's belly in a staggered installation, with the two outboard guns located much further back, the breeches being mounted just forward of the centre-section trailing-edge flaps. Being located beneath the aircraft, the muzzle flash was not a threat to the crew's night vision. Containers for 200 rounds per gun were mounted fore and aft of the turret installation. The forward pair was accessible to the gunner in flight. To save on strategic materials, these boxes were initially made from a pressed fibre material that unfortunately broke down in humid conditions. Locally-made aluminium replacements had to be devised, and this material was later adopted for production. The pilot fired the cannon with a button on the right side of the control wheel and aimed with an LY-3N gunsight (L-1 on the P-61A). Microswitches prevented the activation of the guns with the nose gear down or the ladder in place. The nosewheel had to be raised and the fuselage supported to allow boresighting of the guns.

548th Night Fighter Squadron

The 548th NFS was assigned to the 301st Fighter Wing at this time. Unlike day-fighter units, the NFS squadrons did not belong to groups. Activated in Hawaii in September 1944, they were assigned to the 7th Fighter Wing of the 7th Air Force from October. The 548th was attached to the 301st Wing during May and June 1945 and was back under the 7th AF from July until December. Its sole commanding officer was Major Robert D. Curtis. As well as night-fighter patrols and the escort of night-bombing B-29s, the 548th engaged in a number of long-range interdiction missions, particularly against the Bonin Islands, for which the P-61s were fitted with 5-in (127-mm) HVAR rockets.

Plastics

The P-61 made extensive use of non-metallic components. The nosecone was originally frosted Plexiglas, later painted to reduce its visibility; the black coat caused the Plexiglas to sag in the heat. Eventually, a new nosecone made of resin-impregnated fibreglass was introduced on the production line; this did not suffer as much from the heat and could be left uncovered on the ground. Canopy sections were made of Lucite, manufactured by Dupont. The tailcone was made of two hemispheres of Lucite, cemented together along the vertical axis. After a number of these cones imploded at high speed, an aluminium reinforcing bar was added.

Dorsal turret

Due to the buffeting experienced when the General Electric A-4 turret was rotated or elevated, the bulk of P-61As and many P-61Bs, including the P-61B-1, were delivered from the factory without the unit. The need for additional firepower, and the crew composition of units already in the field, led some Pacific squadrons to accept aircraft with fixed installations, allowing forward-firing only. *Midnite Madness II* had such a fixed turret, allowing for the retention of a three-man crew who had been together since training. The original *Midnite Madness*, a P-61A-11, had been equipped with the fully-rotating turret, which weighed 1,600 lb (726 kg) and was the same model as that fitted to the B-29, which had a higher production priority – another reason why turrets were dropped from the P-61 line. The turret was fitted with four 0.50-in (12.7-mm) machine-guns, firing 800 rounds per minute. Each gun had 560 rounds of ammunition.

Polikarpov I-16

Created at a time when other manufacturers were still producing biplane fighters with fixed landing gear, the Polikarpov I-16 was a landmark in fighter design.

I-16 Type 10

Cutaway key
1 Rudder construction
2 Rudder upper hinge
3 Rudderpost
4 Fin construction
5 Rudder lower hinge
6 Fin auxiliary spar
7 Port tailplane
8 Rudder actuating mechanism
9 Tail cone
10 Rear navigation light
11 Elevator construction
12 Elevator hinge
13 Tailplane construction
14 Tailskid
15 Tailskid damper
16 Control linkage (elevator and rudder)
17 Tailplane filet
18 Fuselage half frames
19 Fin root fairing
20 Dorsal decking
21 Fuselage monocoque construction
22 Main upper longeron
23 Rudder control cable
24 Elevator control rigid rod
25 Main lower longeron
26 Control linkage crank
27 Seat support frame
28 Pilot's seat
29 Headrest
30 Cockpit entry flap (port)
31 Open cockpit
32 Rear-view mirror (optional)
33 Curved one-piece windshield
34 Tubular gunsight (PBP-1 reflector sight optional)
35 Instrument panel
36 Undercarriage retraction handcrank
37 Control column
38 Rudder pedal
39 Fuselage fuel tank, capacity 56 1 Imp gal (255 litres)
40 Fuel filler caps
41 Ammunition magazines
42 Machine-gun faring
43 Split-type aileron (landing flap)
44 Aileron hinge fairing
45 Fabric wing covering
46 Port navigation light
47 Aluminium alloy leading edge skin
48 Two-blade propeller
49 Conical spinner
50 Hucks-type starter dog
51 Hinged main wheel cover
52 Port main wheel
53 Lip intake
54 Adjustable (shuttered) cooling apertures

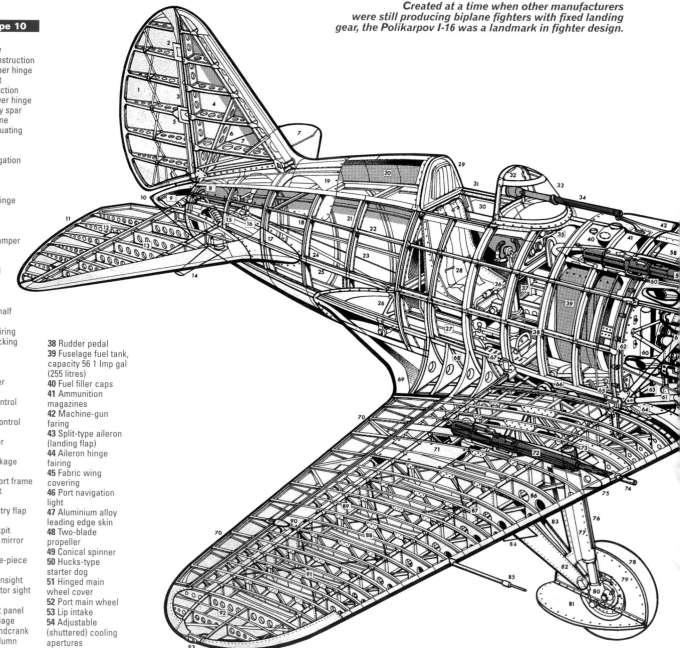

Above: The Soviets failed to capitalise on the lead they gained in fighter design with the I-16, a fact which saw the type committed to actions in 1941 in which it was at a considerable disadvantage. Even so, the I-16's contribution to Russia's defence cannot be underestimated.

SPECIFICATION

Polikarpov I-16 Type 24

Dimensions

Span: 29 ft 1.6 in (8.88 m)
Length: 19 ft 8.125 in (6.04 m)
Height: 7 ft 9.75 in (2.41 m)
Wing area: 160.06 sq ft (14.87 m²)

Powerplant

One Shvetsov M-62 nine-cylinder radial air-cooled engine rated at 1,000 hp (746 kW) at 2,000 rpm for take-off and 800 hp (597 kW) at 2,100 rpm at 13,780 ft (4200 m), driving an AV-2 two-bladed two-pitch propeller

Weights

Empty equipped: 3,252 lb (1475 kg)
Normal loaded: 4,215 lb (1912 kg)
Maximum take-off: 4,541 lb (2060 kg)

Performance

Maximum speed at sea level: 273 mph (440 km/h)
Maximum speed at 9,840 ft (3000 m): 304 mph (489 km/h)

Range (clean): 373 miles (600 km)
Range with external tanks: (600 miles (1100 km)
Rate of climb: 5.8 minutes to 16,405 ft (5000 m)
Service ceiling: 31,070 ft (9470 m)

Armament

Four 0.3in (7.62-mm) Shpital'ny-komaritsky ShKAS machine-guns (two synchronised in fuselage and two unsynchronised in wings) with 650 rounds per gun;
Alternatively, two fuselage-mounted ShKAS with 650 rpg and two wing-mounted 20-mm Shpital'ny-Viadimirov ShVAK cannon with 180 rpg
A Single 0.47-in (12.7-mm) Berezin UBK heavy machine-gun with 300 rounds, firing through the lower cowling, could be added, usually in place of the wing-mounted armament. Later model I-16s could carry two-220-lb (100-kg) bombs or six RS-82 rockets.

Right: The first UTI tandem trainers were produced in 1935. Later versions were fitted with a simple fixed undercarriage. The motto of the Soviet Air Force training schools was "If you can fly the I-16, you can fly anything."

63 Centre-section trussed-type spar carry-through
64 Wheel well
65 Fuselage/front spar attachment point
66 Retraction linkage
67 Fuselage/rear spar attachment point
68 Wingroot frames
69 Wingroot fillet
70 Aileron construction
71 Ammunition access panel
72 Starboard wing 7.62-mm ShKAS machine-gun
73 Undercarriage pivot point
74 Machine-gun muzzle
75 Centre/outer wing section break-point
76 Mainwheel leg
77 Leg cover
78 Starboard mainwheel
79 Mainwheel cover
80 Axle
81 Hinged cover flap
82 Actuating rod cover

83 Retraction actuating rod
84 Cover flap
85 Pitot head
86 Leading-edge construction
87 KhMA chrome-molybdenum steel alloy front spar
88 Alternate dural ribs/frames
89 KhMA chrome-molybdenum steel alloy rear spar
90 Aileron hinge fairing
91 Wire cross-bracing
92 Wingtip construction
93 Starboard navigation light
94 Wingtip edging

55 Propeller shaft support frame
56 Machine-gun muzzles
57 750-hp (559-kW) M-25V radial engine
58 Oil tank
59 Starboard synchronized 0.3-in (7.62-mm) ShKAS machine gun
60 Exhaust exit ports
61 Engine bearers
62 Firewall/bulkhead

Above: One of the most unusual variants of the I-16 was the **Sostavnoi pikiruyushchy bombardirovshchik – SPB** or composite dive bomber – in which two bomb-armed I-16 Type 5s were hung beneath the wings of an ANT-6 carrier aircraft. In August 1941 the combination was tested in action against oil and communications targets in Romania

I-16 Type 5

One of the great warplanes in history, the Polikarpov I-16 was the first low-winged monoplane with retractable landing gear to enter service with any air force. It saw its combat debut with republican forces in Spain, who knew the diminutive aircraft as the *Mosca*, or 'Fly'. Its nationalist opponents had a different name for the stubby fighter – they called it the *Rata* or 'Rat'. But to the majority of pilots who flew the I-16, the men of the Soviet air force who had to wrestle with its unruly handling, it was known as *Ishak* or 'Mule'. However, as they got to know its quirks, that was often contracted with back-handed affection as *Ishachka*, or 'Little Mule'. The example depicted here is a Polikarpov I-16 Type 5 Mosca, serving with the Aviación Militar Republicana during the Spanish Civil War.

Tail surfaces
The tail surfaces were necessarily large to counter the lack of stability caused by the short rear fuselage. In spite of the designers' best efforts, the I-16 had only limited stability longitudinally, and needed concentration from the pilot at all times. However, this instability brought great dividends in manoeuvrability at high speeds, where the rod-actuated elevators were noticeably effective. The rudder was actuated by pulley and cable.

Canopy
The canopy was another innovation, the whole unit, including windscreen, sliding forward on rails for ingress/egress. In practice the pilots were fearful of not being able to get out quickly in an emergency and the canopy was often locked in the open position. This led to later I-16s featuring a truncated canopy and partially open cockpit.

Markings
The entire rudder was taken up with the red, yellow and purple markings of the Republican air force. The 'Popeye' emblem was that of the 4a Escuadrilla de Moscas. Other squadron markings were the cartoon character Betty Boop (1a Escuadrilla de Moscas), a pelican on a crutch (2a Escuadrilla) and a double-six domino (3a Escuadrilla).

Wing structure
The I-16 had a metal two-spar wing structure, with trussed KhMA chrome-molybdenum steel alloy centre-section spars and tubular outer spars. Wing ribs were made of dural and skinning was aluminium inboard and fabric outboard The long ailerons were operated by rods and bell cranks. They could be drooped by 15° to act as flaps on landing, although this did little to reduce the high stalling speed of the I-16.

Fuel
The Mosca's fuel was housed in a single tank located in the central fuselage between the cockpit and engine installation. Total capacity was 56 Imp gal (255 litres). No fuel gauge was fitted in the cockpit, the pilot having to listen to the engine note to determine when fuel was low while keeping a close eye on his watch!

Fuselage structure
The fuselage structure was built in two halves, divided vertically. The main structure consisted of four longerons and eleven half-frames built of pine, to which was bonded a *shpon* skin – a kind of plywood made from long strips of birch glued together.

Cockpit
The cramped cockpit was equipped with only rudimentary instruments. No radio or oxygen equipment was fitted, and there was no indicator for the undercarriage. The pilot was provided with a control column with a yoke-type grip, and a cable-cutter for severing the undercarriage retraction cables if they became stuck partially open.

Gunsight
The Mosca was provided with a simple Aldis telescope sight which projected into the cockpit through the windscreen. Four magnification powers were provided, and the sight featured simple cross-hairs.

Powerplant
Power for the I-16 Type 5 was provided by a Shvetsov M-25 nine-cylinder radial, which was a 'Sovietised' version of the Wright Cyclone SR-1820-F-3. The heavy cowling completely enclosed the engine, with large apertures in the front to admit cooling air. These were shuttered to control the amount of air entering the engine compartments. The cylinders exhausted through individual ports arranged around the rear of the cowling.

Armament
The I-16 Type 5 featured a ShKAS 0.3-in (7.62-mm) machine-gun in each wing, known to the Spanish as the Rusa E rápida. The weapon weighed 22 lb (10 kg) and fired at a rate of 1,800 rpm. Each gun had 900 rounds, the 0.34-oz (9.6g) bullets being fired at a muzzle velocity of 2,706 ft/sec (825 m/sec). In spite of a tendency to jam, the highly accurate ShKAS was regarded in the early 1930s as the best aircraft gun in the world.

Undercarriage
The I-16 was innovative in the introduction of retractable main wheels. The pilot operated a crank in the cockpit which raised the undercarriage by cables, the wheels retracting inwards to lie in wells between the centre-section spars, covered by a hinged flap. The effort of retracting the undercarriage inevitably resulted in an erratic flight path after take-off as the crank was operated.

Propeller
The two-bladed AV-1 propeller was of metal construction, and had a diameter of 9 ft 2 in (2.80 m). It had two pitch options, and the large spinner was fitted with a Hucks starter dog.

Republic P-47 Thunderbolt

Ironically, the P-47, which developed as a light fighter for bomber interception, was first posted to Europe in the escort role supporting the USAAF's heavy bomber fleet, like this B-17.

P-47D

Cutaway key
1 Rudder upper hinge
2 Aerial attachment
3 Fin flanged ribs
4 Rudder post/fin aft spar
5 Fin front spar
6 Rudder trim tab worm and screw actuating mechanism (chain-driven)
7 Rudder centre hinge
8 Rudder trim tab
9 Rudder structure
10 Tall navigation light
11 Elevator fixed tab
12 Elevator trim tab
13 Starboard elevator structure
14 Elevator outboard hinge
15 Elevator torque tube
16 Elevator trim tab worm and screw actuating mechanism
17 Chain drive
18 Starboard tailplane
19 Tail jacking point
20 Rudder control cables
21 Elevator control rod and linkage
22 Fin spar/fuselage attachment points
23 Elevator
24 Aerial
25 Port tailplane structure (two spars and flanged ribs)
26 Tailwheel retraction worm gear
27 Tailwheel anti-shimmy damper
28 Tailwheel oleo
29 Tailwheel doors
30 Retractable and steerable tailwheel
31 Tailwheel fork
32 Tailwheel mount and pivot
33 Rudder cables
34 Rudder and elevator trim control cables
35 Lifting tube
36 Elevator rod linkage

37 Semi-monocoque all-metal fuselage construction
38 Fuselage dorsal 'razorback' profile
39 Aerial lead-in
40 Fuselage stringers
41 Supercharger air filter
42 Supercharger
43 Turbine casing
44 Turbosupercharger compartment air vent
45 Turbo-supercharger exhaust hood fairing (stainless steel)
46 Outlet louvres
47 Intercooler exhaust doors (port and starboard)
48 Exhaust pipes
49 Cooling air ducts
50 Intercooler unit (cooling and supercharged air)
51 Radio transmitter and receiver packs (Detrola)
52 Canopy track
53 Elevator rod linkage
54 Aerial mast
55 Formation light
56 Rearward-vision frame cut-out and glazing
57 Oxygen bottles
58 Supercharger and cooling air pipe (supercharger to carburettor) port
59 Elevator linkage
60 Supercharger and cooling air pipe (supercharger to carburettor) starboard
61 Central duct (to intercooler unit)
62 Wingroot air louvres
63 Wingroot fillet
64 Auxiliary fuel tank (100 US gal/379 litres)
65 Auxiliary fuel filler point
66 Rudder cable turnbuckle
67 Cockpit floor support
68 Seat adjustment lever

69 Pilot's seat
70 Canopy emergency release (port and starboard)
71 Trim tab controls
72 Back and head armour
73 Headrest
74 Rearward-sliding canopy
75 Rear view mirror fairing
76 'Vee' windshields with central pillar
77 Internal bulletproof glass screen

78 Gunsight
79 Engine control quadrant (cockpit port wall)
80 Control column
81 Rudder pedals
82 Oxygen regulator
83 Underfloor elevator control quadrant
84 Rudder cable linkage
85 Wing rear spar/fuselage attachment (tapered bolts/bushings)
86 Wing-supporting lower bulkhead section
87 Main fuel tank (205 US gal/776 litres)
88 Fuselage forward structure
89 Stainless steel/Alclad firewall bulkhead
90 Cowl flap valve
91 Main fuel filler point
92 Anti-freeze fluid tank
93 Hydraulic reservoir
94 Aileron control rod
95 Aileron trim tab control cables

96 Aileron hinge access panels
97 Aileron and tab control linkage
98 Aileron trim tab (port wing only)
99 Frise type aileron
100 Wing rear (No. 2) spar
101 Port navigation light
102 Pitot head
103 Wing front (No. 1) spar
104 Wing stressed skin
105 Four gun ammunition troughs (individual bays)
106 Staggered gun barrels
107 Removable panel
108 Inter spar gun bay access panel
109 Forward gunsight bead
110 Oil feed pipes
111 Oil tank (28.6 US gal/108 litres)
112 Hydraulic pressure line
113 Engine upper bearers
114 Engine control correlating cam

115 Eclipse pump (anti-icing)
116 Fuel level transmitter
117 Generator
118 Battery junction box
119 Storage battery
120 Exhaust collector ring
121 Cowl flap actuating
122 Exhaust outlets to collector ring
123 Cowl flaps
124 Supercharged and cooling air ducts to carburettor (port and starboard)
125 Exhaust upper outlets
126 Cowling frame
127 Pratt & Whitney R-2800-59 18-cylinder twin-row engine
128 Cowling nose panel
129 Magnetos
130 Propeller governor
131 Propeller hub

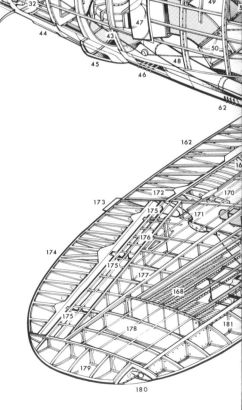

The first examples of the P-47 went into combat in April 1943. Designed as an interceptor, the P-47, as exemplified by this P-47D model, quickly found its niche as a long-range, hard-hitting ground attack platform. The long-legged P-47 was a credible escort aircraft too, drop tanks enabling it to fly from the UK as far as Berlin.

SPECIFICATION

Republic P-47N-1-RE Thunderbolt (unless otherwise stated)

Dimensions

Length: 36 ft 1¾ in (11.02 m)
Wingspan: 42 ft 6½ in (12.82 m)
Wing area: 322.2 sq ft (65.99 m²)
Height overall (unloaded): 14 ft 6 in (4.42 m)

Powerplant

One Pratt & Whitney R-2800-57 rated at 2,800 hp (2088 kW) with water injection
P-47B: one Pratt & Whitney R-2800-21 rated at 2,000 hp (1492 kW)
P-47C-5-RE: one Pratt & Whitney R-2800-21 rated at 2,000 hp (1492 kW)
P-47D-30-RA: one Pratt & Whitney R-2800-59 rated at 2,430 hp (1812 kW) with water injection
P-47M-1-RE: one Pratt & Whitney R-2800-57 rated at 2,800 hp (2088 kW) with water injection
Propeller: Curtiss Electric C642S-B40
Propeller diameter: 13 ft (3.96 m)

Weights

Empty weight: 10,988 lb (4984 kg)
Gross weight: 13,823 lb (6270 kg)
Maximum take-off weight: 21,200 lb (9616 kg)

Fuel load

Total fuel capacity: 1,270 US gal (4807 litres)

Total internal fuel capacity: 570 US gal (2157 litres)
Total external fuel capacity: 700 US gal (2650 litres)
Total wing fuel capacity: 186 US gal (704 litres)
Fuel consumption: 300 US gal (1136 litres) per hour

Performance

Maximum speed at altitude: 467 mph (752 km/h) at 32,000 ft (9754 m)
Cruising speed: 200 mph (322 km/h) with 300-US gal (1134-litre) underwing fuel tanks
Climb rate: 14.2 min to 25,000 ft (7620 m)
Landing speed: 98 mph (158 km/h)
Take-off run: 3,800 ft (1158 m) at gross weight
Maximum service ceiling: 43,000 ft (13106 m)

Range

Range with maximum fuel load: 2,000 miles (3219 km) at 25,000 ft (7620 m)
Normal operational range: 800 miles (1288 km) at 25,000 ft (7620 m)

Armament

Six or eight 0.5-in (12.7-mm) machine-guns in wing with 267- 500 rounds per gun; up to three 1,000-lb (454-kg) bombs, or up to eight rockets on underwing rails, or a combination of bombs and rockets

---

132 Reduction gear casing
133 Spinner
134 Propeller cuffs
135 Four blade Curtiss constant-speed electric propeller
136 Oil cooler intakes (port and starboard)
137 Supercharger intercooler (central) air intake
138 Ducting
139 Oil cooler feed pipes
140 Starboard oil cooler
141 Engine lower bearers
142 Oil cooler exhaust variable shutter
143 Fixed deflector
144 Excess exhaust gas gate
145 Belly stores/weapons shackles
146 Metal auxiliary drop tank (75 US gal/284 litres)
147 Inboard mainwheel well door
148 Mainwheel well door actuating cylinder
149 Camera gun port
150 Cabin air-conditioning intake (starboard wing only)
151 Wingroot fairing
152 Wing front spar/fuselage attachment (tapered bolts/bushings)
153 Wing inboard rib mainwheel well recess

154 Wing front (No. 1) spar
155 Undercarriage pivot point
156 Hydraulic retraction cylinder
157 Auxiliary (undercarriage mounting) wing spar
158 Gun bay warm air flexible duct
159 Wing rear (No. 2) spar
160 Landing flap inboard hinge
161 Auxiliary (No. 3) wing spar inboard section (flap mounting)
162 NACA slotted trailing-edge landing flaps
163 Landing flaps centre hinge
164 Landing flap hydraulic cylinder
165 Four 0.5-in (12.7-mm) Browning machine-guns
166 Inter-spar gun bay inboard rib
167 Ammunition feed chutes
168 Individual ammunition troughs
169 Underwing stores/weapons pylon
170 Landing flap profile
171 Flap door
172 Landing flap profile
173 Aileron fixed tab (starboard wing only)
174 Frise-type aileron structure
175 Aileron hinge/steel forging spar attachments
176 Auxiliary (No. 3) wing spar outboard section (aileron mounting)
177 Multi-cellular wing construction
178 Wing outboard ribs
179 Wingtip structure
180 Starboard navigation light
181 Leading-edge rib sections
182 Bomb shackles
183 500-lb (227 kg) M43 demolition bomb
184 Undercarriage leg fairing (overlapping upper section)
185 Mainwheel fairing (lower section)
186 Wheel fork
187 Starboard mainwheel
188 Brake lines
189 Landing gear air-oil shock strut
190 Machine-gun barrel blast tubes
191 Staggered gun barrels
192 Rocket launcher slide bar
193 Centre strap
194 Front mount (attached below front spar between inboard pair of guns)
195 Deflector arms
196 Triple tube 4.5-in (11.5-cm) rocket launcher (Type M10)
197 Front retaining band
198 4.5-in (11.5-cm) M8 rocket projectile

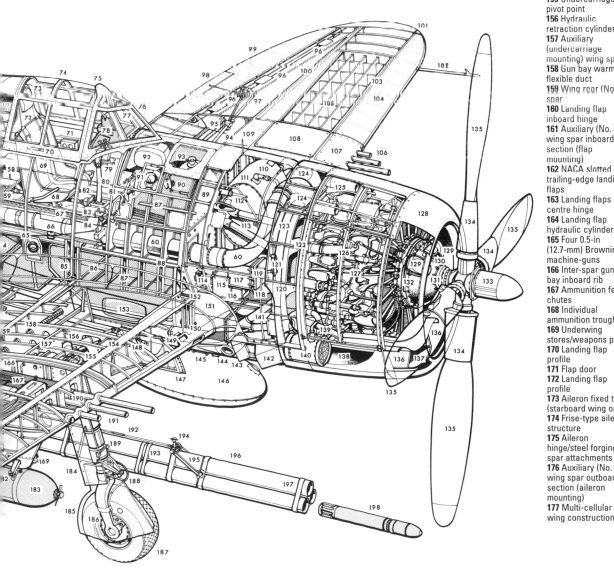

P-47D-25-RE Thunderbolt

David Carl Schilling flew 132 combat missions with the 56th Fighter Group, scoring 22½ kills. In the aircraft pictured, during 1943, Schilling shot down three Fw 190s (and one shared) and damaged a single Me 210. Based with the 8th Air Force in England, he was made CO of his Group during 1944. Post-war, he converted to the P-80 and, in 1948 in the F-84, became the first pilot to make a non-stop jet fighter flight across the Atlantic. Following his death in 1956, Smoky Hill AFB was renamed Schilling AFB in his honour.

Propeller

Most models in the P-47 series carried a characteristic large diameter four-bladed propeller, and the P-47D-22 introduced this giant 12.2-ft (3.71-m) diameter Hamilton Standard Hydromatic model, with paddle-blades. This was fitted to the aircraft along with other modifications and improvements, including a small dorsal fin in order to offset the loss of keel surface entailed after the introduction of the bubble canopy. These changes came as a result of extensive flight testing of the experimental XP-47K in July 1943, the first Thunderbolt to feature a cut-down rear fuselage and all-round vision canopy, as opposed to the framed aft-sliding canopy of earlier aircraft.

Powerplant

The Thunderbolt was powered by the Pratt & Whitney R-2800 series Double Wasp. A powerful and durable 18-cylinder radial air-cooled unit, the Double Wasp in the P-47 produced over 2,430 hp (1813 kW) at full power. Already immensely strong and fast, the P-47D-25 series was further advantaged by the addition of a rakish cut-down rear fuselage and streamlined teardrop canopy. Additional power was provided by a turbo-supercharger. The P-47D model illustrated introduced not only an improved system of turbocharger exhaust, but a new water injection system as standard for both the R-2800-21 and -59 engines. Later P-47D production models carried the improved R-2800-63 powerplant.

Rocket armament

A favourite weapon of the Thunderbolt pilots in Europe, particularly when engaging enemy armour, was the M-8 unguided rocket. Launched from triple-round M110 tube launchers underwing, the 4.5-in (11.5-cm) rockets could destroy the heavily-armoured Tiger or Panther tanks when used against them in low-level attacks. When the cloud base permitted, Thunderbolts would also knock out bridges, tanks and vehicles by dive-bombing from altitudes between 9,843 ft (3000 m) and 13,123 ft (4000 m), dropping high-explosive bombs, and pulling out at no lower than 820 ft (250 m). This was necessary in order to protect themselves from fragments from their own bombs. Known as 'jabos' (short for jagdbombers, or fighter-bombers), the P-47 attacks struck terror into the Axis troops below them.

Bubble canopy

From Block 25 onward, P-47Ds were fitted with a bubble cockpit canopy as standard. This feature provided the pilot with a superior all-round vision to that found on the 'razorback' models. This was a considerable advantage for both high- and low-level operations, but pilots were still vulnerable. After attacking ground targets, P-47s often returned with bomb casing and shrapnel lodged underwing and in the undercarriage bays. In one incident, a 3.2-ft (1-m)-long shard was found in the lower fuselage, just aft of the cockpit area.

'Dave' Schilling's P-47

Schilling's P-47D as seen here carries standard European theatre camouflage, although Thunderbolts were more regularly delivered in an unpainted bare metal finish. Schilling's aircraft carried his personal nose art as well as kill markings just below the cockpit. During the war, Schilling claimed 13½ Focke Wulf Fw 190s, plus three damaged; seven Bf 109s, plus one damaged; one He 111K; one Bf 110; one Junkers 34 damaged; and one Me 210 damaged. As well as helping to pioneer aerial refuelling post-war, Schilling's unit, flying F-84Gs, made ground-breaking flights across the Atlantic in 1953, testing new celestial navigation aids. In 1951 he received the Harmon International Trophy as the outstanding flier of the year, and the following year the Air Force Association presented him with the Flight Award as the man who had done the most for US air power during the year.

Wing-mounted guns

Mounted in a staggered formation in each wing of the P-47D were four 0.5-in (12.7-mm) machine-guns, reliable weapons with a good weight of fire, even if they lacked the destructive force of cannon. Pilots in the Thunderbolt realised that machine-guns could be used to destroy tanks when they carried extra cans of fuel tied to their sides. When the Germans realised the error of this ploy and removed their vehicles' external fuel, P-47 pilots were forced to attempt to strafe them. In this manner, bullets were intended to ricochet up under the tank, piercing their less heavily-armoured belly. This tactic was most effective against convoys on roads, maximising the effect of the ricochet.

Fuel capacity

The main fuel tank in the fuselage centre section was armoured, and augmented in this instance by a single 101-US gal (384-litre) drop-tank mounted under the centreline. When fully loaded, the bulky Thunderbolt could be as much as three times heavier than an early model Supermarine Spitfire, and in terms of range the P-47 was far superior to the Luftwaffe's Bf 109G fighter. The range of the P-47 made it a highly capable escort fighter for waves of bombers both over Europe, and later the Pacific. The endurance of the Thunderbolt originated from the fact that the aircraft had filled an initial requirement for a long-range bomber interceptor. By the time the P-47 entered the war, it was a long-range bomber escort as well as a capable ground-attack fighter.

Supermarine Spitfire Mk V

Built as a Spitfire Mk I and later modified to Mk VB standard, R6923 was shot down by a Bf 109 on 22 June 1941. The Spitfire was closely matched to the Bf 109 for much of World War II, with pilot skill often the deciding factor in a dogfight.

Spitfire Mk VB

Cutaway key
1 Aerial stub attachment
2 Rudder upper hinge
3 Fabric-covered rudder
4 Rudder tab
5 Sternpost
6 Rudder tab hinge
7 Rear navigation light
8 Starboard elevator tab
9 Rear navigation light
10 Elevator balance
11 Tailplane front spar
12 IFF aerial
13 Castoring non-retractable tailwheel
14 Tailwheel strut
15 Fuselage double frame
16 Elevator control lever
17 Tailplane spar/fuselage attachment
18 Fin rear spar (fuselage frame extension)
19 Fin front spar (fuselage frame extension)
20 Port elevator tab hinge
21 Port elevator
22 IFF aerial
23 Port tailplane
24 Rudder control lever
25 Cross shaft
26 Tailwheel oleo access plate
27 Tailwheel oleo shock-absorber
28 Fuselage angled frame
29 Battery compartment
30 Lower longeron
31 Elevator control cables
32 Fuselage construction
33 Rudder control cables
34 Radio compartment
35 Radio support tray
36 Flare chute

37 Oxygen bottle
38 Auxiliary long-range fuel tank
39 Dorsal formation light
40 Aerial lead-in
41 HF aerial
42 Aerial mast
43 Cockpit aft glazing
44 Voltage regulator
45 Canopy track

46 Structural bulkhead
47 Headrest
48 Plexiglass canopy
49 Rear-view mirror
50 Entry flap (port)
51 Air bottles (alternative rear fuselage stowage)
52 Sutton harness
53 Pilot's seat (moulded Bakelite)
54 Datum longeron
55 Seat support frame
56 Wingroot fillet
57 Seat adjustment lever
58 Rudder pedal frame
59 Elevator control connecting tube
60 Control column spade grip
61 Trim wheel
62 Reflector gunsight

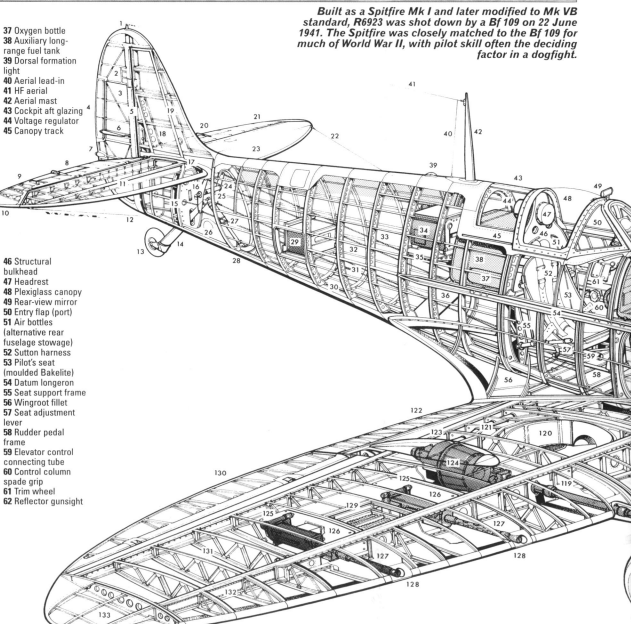

Above: With its underfuselage ferry tank and an additional 29 Imp gal (132 litres) of fuel in the rear fuselage tank, BR202 had a range of 1,450 miles (2334 km) at 15,000 ft (4572 m). The success of this installation led to 17 specially stripped-down aircraft being ferried from the UK to Gibraltar non-stop, and then on to Malta. Although one aircraft failed to complete the journey, the remaining 16 were soon rearmed and ready for action, long before any ship-delivered machines had arrived.

63 External windscreen armour
64 Instrument panel
65 Main fuselage fuel tank (48 Imp gal/218 litre)
66 Fuel tank/longeron attachment fittings
67 Rudder pedals
68 Rudder bar
69 King post
70 Fuselage lower fuel tank (57 Imp gal/160 litre)
71 Firewall/bulkhead
72 Engine bearer attachment

73 Steel tube bearers
74 Magneto
75 'Fishtail'/exhaust manifold
76 Gun heating intensifier
77 Hydraulic tank
78 Fuel filler cap
79 Air compressor intake
80 Air compressor accessories
81 Rolls-Royce Merlin 45 engine
82 Coolant piping
83 Port cannon wing fairing
84 Flaps

85 Aileron control cables
86 Aileron push tube
87 Bellcrank
88 Aileron hinge
89 Port aileron
90 Machine-gun access panels
91 Port wingtip
92 Port navigation light
93 Leading-edge skinning
94 Machine-gun ports (protected)
95 20-mm cannon muzzle

96 Three-blade constant-speed propeller
97 Spinner
98 Propeller hub
99 Coolant tank
100 Cowling fastening
101 Engine anti-vibration mounting pad
102 Engine accessories
103 Engine bearers
104 Main engine support member
105 Coolant pipe
106 Exposed oil tank

SPECIFICATION

Spitfire Mk V

Dimensions

Length: 29 ft 11 in (9.13 m); some late production aircraft 30 ft 2½ in (9.21 m)
Wing span: 36 ft 10 in (11.23 m); with clipped wings 32 ft 2 in (9.80 m)
Wing aspect ratio: 5.68
Wing area: 242 sq ft (22.45 m²); with clipped wings 231 sq ft (21.46 m²)
Total flap area: 15.6 sq ft (1.45 m²)
Total aileron area: 18.90 sq ft (1.76 m²)
Fin area: 4.61 sq ft (0.43 m²)
Rudder area: 8.23 sq ft (0.76 m²)
Tailplane area: 31.46 sq ft (2.92 m²)
Elevator area: 13.26 sq ft (1.23 m²)
Height: tail down with propeller vertical 11 ft 5½ in (3.49 m)
Wing loading: 36.0 lb/sq ft (175.8 kg/m²)
Wing section: root NACA 2213

Powerplant

Mk VA, VB and VC: one Rolls-Royce Merlin 45 liquid-cooled, 12-cylinder, single-stage supercharged, Vee-type piston engine rated at 1,230 hp (972 kW) for continuous operation or 1,515 hp (1130 kW) for five minutes of emergency combat power at 11,000 ft (3353 m); or one Merlin 46 rated at 1,190 hp (887 kW) continuous
Mk VC: one Merlin 50 rated at 1,230 hp (917 kW) continuous; or one Merlin 50A or 55 rated at 1,100 hp (820 kW) continuous; or one Merlin 56 rated at 1,580 hp (1178 kW) continuous
LF.Mk V: one Merlin 45M rated at 1,500 hp (1178 kW) at 2,600 ft (792 m); or one Merlin 50M rated at 1,230 hp (917 kW) continuous; or one Merlin 55M rated at 1,580 hp (1178 kW) continuous
Propeller: one de Havilland Type 5/29A or 5/39, or 45/1 or 45/4, Hydromatic three-bladed, constant-speed propeller of 10 ft 9 in (3.28 m) diameter; or one Rotol RX5/10 Jablo three-bladed, constant-speed propeller of 10 ft 3 in (3.12 m) diameter; or one RX5/14 or RS5/24 of 10 ft 9 in (3.28 m) diameter

Weights

Mk VA: empty 4,960 lb (2658 kg), normal loaded 6,237 lb (2829 kg), maximum loaded 6,700 lb (3039 kg)
Mk VB (with 30-Imp gal/136-litre auxiliary tank): empty 5,065 lb (2297 kg), normal loaded 6,630 lb (3007 kg), maximum loaded 6,700 lb (3039 kg)
Mk VC (with 30-Imp gal/136-litre auxiliary tank): empty 5,100 lb (2313 kg), normal loaded 6,785 lb (3078 kg), maximum loaded (with 'B' wing armament) 7,300 lb (3311 kg)
LF.Mk VB (with 30-Imp gal/136-litre auxiliary tank): empty 5,050 lb (2291 kg), normal loaded 6,615 lb (3000 kg)

Fuel and load

Total internal fuel: 85 Imp gal (386 litres), held as 48 Imp gal (218 litre) in upper fuselage tank and 37 Imp gal (168 litre) in lower fuselage tank (additional 29-Imp gal (132-litre) rear fuselage tank for ferry flights only)
External fuel: 30-Imp gal (136-litre), 90-Imp gal (409-litre) or 170-Imp gal (773-litre) underfuselage auxiliary tanks
Maximum external load (Mk VB and VC): 500 lb (227 kg)

Performance

Maximum speed: VA 376 mph (605 km/h) at 19,500 ft (5944 m); VB 369 mph (594 km/h) at 19,500 ft (5944 m); VC 374 mph (601 km/h) at 13,000 ft (3962 m); LF.Mk VB 357 mph (574 km/h) at 6,000 ft (1829 m)
Maximum diving speed: 450 mph (724 km/h)
Initial rate of climb: 4,740 ft (1445 m) per minute, 3240 ft (988 m) per minute at 5,000 ft (1524 m); 3,250 ft (1474 m) per minute at 15,000 ft (4572 m)
Maximum rate of climb at sea level (LF.Mk VB): 4,750 ft (2155 m) per minute
Service ceiling: 36,500 ft (11125 m)

Range

Maximum range: 470 miles (756 km) on internal fuel; 1,135 miles (1827 km) with 90-Imp gal (409-litre) external tank

Armament

VA: eight 0.303-in (7.7-mm) Browning machine-guns with 350 rpg (rounds per gun)
VB: four 0.303-in (7.7-mm) Browning machine-guns with 350 rpg, plus two 20 mm Hispano cannon with 60 rpg
VC: VA or VB armament, with the option of four 20-mm Hispano cannon with 120 rpg, plus one 500-lb (227-kg) bomb or two 250-lb (113-kg) bombs

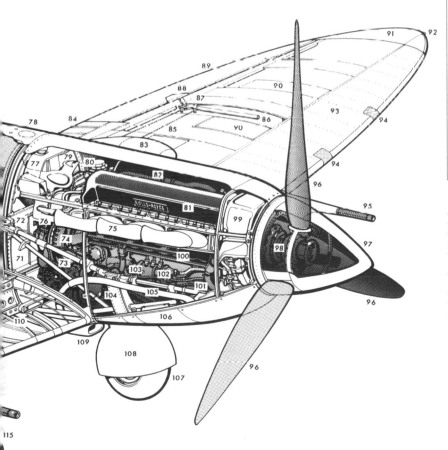

107 Port mainwheel
108 Mainwheel fairing
109 Carburettor air intake
110 Stub/spar attachment
111 Mainwheel leg pivot point
112 Main spar
113 Leading-edge ribs (diagonals deleted for clarity)
114 Mainwheel leg shock-absorber
115 Mainwheel fairing
116 Starboard mainwheel
117 Angled axle
118 Cannon barrel support fairing
119 Spar cut-out
120 Mainwheel well
121 Gun heating pipe
122 Flap structure

123 Cannon wing fairing
124 Cannon magazine drum (120 rounds)
125 Machine-gun support brackets
126 Gun access panels
127 0.303-in (7.7-mm) machine-gun barrels
128 Machine-gun ports
129 Ammunition boxes (350 rounds per gun)
130 Starboard aileron construction
131 Wing ribs
132 Single-tube outer spar section
133 Wingtip structure
134 Starboard navigation light

Spitfire Mk VC

In July 1943, No. 2 Squadron of No. 7 Wing, South African Air Force (SAAF), Desert Air Force, began relinquishing its Kittyhawks for the Spitfire Mk VC. Declared operational with its new machines in Sicily on 23 August, the unit moved to a newly captured airfield in Italy. Flying from a succession of Italian bases, No. 2 retained its Mk VCs until March 1944.

Merlin power

With the introduction of the 50-series Merlin to the Spitfire Mk V, a longstanding problem was eliminated. Previously, pilots flying negative-*g* manoeuvres found the engines of their Spitfires cutting out. Rolls-Royce devised a diaphragm-operated carburettor which eliminated the fuel starvation problem. The new carburettor was introduced on the 50-series powerplants, and transformed the fighting qualities of the Spitfire. Pilots were warned, however, that prolonged periods of negative-*g* or inverted flight could result in a catastrophic drop in engine oil pressure.

Engine and propeller

Engine efficiency was improved by the installation of a constant-speed propeller as standard. The pitch of the propeller blades was automatically adjusted according to the flight regime, ensuring that the engine always operating at its optimum level of about 3,000 rpm for maximum power delivery. Most Spitfire Mk Vs used Rotol three-bladed propellers.

Cockpit access

Entry to the Spitfire was gained via a downward-hinged door on the port side of the fuselage. The cockpit canopy slid backward along prominent rails running along the sides of the fuselage behind the cockpit. Extensive testing was carried out to ensure that the canopy would separate cleanly from the aircraft in the event of the pilot jettisoning it in flight. Tests revealed that the canopy could show an alarming tendency to rotate very slowly with minimum lift after separation if the aircraft's rate of descent were too high. This slow rotation caused the canopy to fly toward the fin, a problem which was solved by adjusting the centre of gravity of the canopy itself.

Tropical modifications

In order to cope with the harsh, sandy conditions of the Western Desert, and other tropical climates, a number of modifications were made to Spitfires destined for these regions. These 'tropicalised' aircraft were distinguished by the large Vokes Aero-Vee filter under the chin. This installation, plus more than 20 other modifications, were covered by the code Mod 411. Changes included fitting a larger oil tank, the addition of attachment points for three types of external fuel tank, replacement of a number of skin panels, provision of a desert survival kit and repainting of the aircraft in appropriate camouflage. The Vokes filter seriously reduced the Spitfire V's climb and speed performance. A comparison with a standard Mk VB showed that maximum speed at 20,000 ft (6096 m) was reduced by 11 mph (18 km/h). The Vokes filter was often replaced in service by the more compact Aboukir filter which caused less drag; it was designed by the RAF's No. 103 Maintenance Unit at Aboukir, Egypt.

Cannon armament

Early in the Spitfire's career, the lack of hitting power of its Browning machine-guns had been noted. It was remedied on the Mk IB, IIB and VB by the installation of two 20-mm Hispano cannon and four machine-guns. With the introduction of the 'universal' 'C' wing, it became possible to arm the Spitfire with four of the Hispano weapons, each supplied with 120 rounds of ammunition. This powerful internal armament, coupled with a respectable bombload, made the Spitfire Mk VC a potent fighter-bomber, especially when combined with the clipped wingtips which gave improved low-level manoeuvrability. Some Mk VBs and VCs were delivered to the Middle East with clipped wings, but many were modified in-theatre by No. 103 MU. Aircraft so-altered featured wooden wingtip fairings, which were of a slightly more rounded shape than those fitted to UK-based machines. In addition to its modification activities, which included various non-standard armament configurations, the MU was also responsible for reconditioning 140 aircraft per month.

No. 2 Squadron, SAAF

By mid-1944, No. 7 Wing, SAAF, whose springbok marking appears on the tail of this aircraft, formed part of the Desert Air Force with No. 3 Wing, SAAF and three RAF wings. As a component of No. 7 Wing, No. 2 Sqn received its Spitfire Mk Vs in July 1943, a month before it moved to Sicily. The squadron relocated again during September, moving onto the Italian mainland and occupying newly-captured Axis airfields. Though flown intensively during the squadron's time in Italy, the Spitfire Mk Vs were on charge with No. 2 for just eight months. Spitfire Mk IXs arrived in February 1944, and a few Mustang Mk IVs were taken 'on charge' in June 1945. On 12 July the squadron's personnel left Tissano airfield en route for South Africa.

Airframe variations

Apart from the three wing types fitted to the Spitfire Mk V, a host of other variations existed between individual aircraft. Many were the result of factory-fitted items, but many more resulted from field modifications. Tropicalisation resulted in reduced performance regardless of the filter type installed, but, beyond this, minor airframe modifications could amount to significant performance variations between airframes. In 1943 a thorough investigation into the effects of such minor changes was conducted at Farnborough, with startling results. A Spitfire Mk VB was subjected to modifications which ranged from minor engineering changes to gap-filling and simple polishing. Speed gained by each modification combined to give a 28.5-mph (45.9-km/h) increase in maximum speed.

Camouflage and markings

Very little variation from the standard RAF Middle East scheme was seen on the RAF, Commonwealth and USAAF Spitfires in the theatre. Most were finished with Dark Earth/Middle Stone top surfaces over Sky or Azure Blue below. The aircraft illustrated wears the 'DB' codes of No. 2 Sqn, along with the badge of No. 7 Wing on its fin. A somewhat heavy application of Dark Earth, apparently applied to cover an old code letter, has also obscured the serial number.

Fighter-bomber

With its strengthened structure, the Mk VC was the only Mk V version built to carry bombs. A pair of 250-lb (113-kg) bombs could be carried beneath the wings, or a single 500-lb (227-kg) weapon beneath the fuselage. On its arrival in Italy, No. 2 Sqn, SAAF provided top cover for Allied operations, but, as enemy air activity dwindled, the unit dedicated more of its time to fighter-bomber sorties. The stronger wing of the VC also freed pilots from the restrictions they had faced when flying earlier Mk Vs. Installing a more powerful engine into the basic Spitfire Mk II airframe had given pilots the potential for overstressing the aircraft's structure during high-g manoeuvres.

Undercarriage and wheels

Compared to the Spitfire Mk I, the Mk V's weight had increased considerably. With the wheels remaining unchanged in size, Dunlop was obliged to supply tyres of increased ply-rating. The tailwheel was a fixed castoring unit, Supermarine having retained the simple unit of the Mk II. A retractable tailwheel, as fitted to the Mk IV, did not appear on a production Spitfire until the Mk VII was introduced. Pilots always treated the Spitfire with respect on the ground, since the aircraft possessed less-than-ideal ground-handling characteristics, owing to the narrow track of its main landing gear. Aircraft operating in strong crosswinds, especially over rough ground or in slippery, muddy conditions, were easily ground looped (spun horizontally around their main wheels), a problem which also made Spitfires and Seafires tricky to operate from aircraft-carriers.

Several Spitfire Mk Vs were flown from carriers as the final leg of their delivery from the UK to Malta. In April and May 1942, the USS *Wasp* and HMS *Eagle* between them delivered 126 tropicalised Mk Vs to the island.

Supermarine Griffon Spitfire

Re-engining the Spitfire with the more powerful Griffon engine gave the aircraft a new lease of life. As well as increasing outright performance, the Griffon also allowed a considerable increase in weights, opening the door to a new period of Spitfire development. The aircraft illustrated is a Mk XIV.

Spitfire F.Mk 21

Cutaway key

1 Starboard elevator construction
2 Elevator tab
3 Tail navigation light
4 Rudder trim tab
5 Fabric-covered rudder construction
6 Sternpost
7 Rudder balance weight
8 Fin main spar
9 Tailfin construction
10 Tail ballast weights
11 Fin secondary spar
12 Rudder trim jack
13 Tailplane trim jack
14 Tailplane construction
15 Tailwheel doors
16 Mudguard
17 Tailwheel retraction jack
18 Elevator control rods
19 Tailwheel
20 Fuselage double bulkhead
21 Port elevator
22 Port tailplane
23 Finroot fillet fairing
24 Tail assembly joint frame
25 Oxygen cylinder
26 Six-cartridge signal flare launcher
27 Tailplane control cables
28 Access door
29 Fuselage ballast weights
30 Battery
31 R.3067 radio receiver
32 Radio access door
33 Whip aerial
34 Harness release
35 TR.1143 radio transmitter
36 Radio track
37 Fuselage frame and stringer construction
38 Wingroot trailing edge fillet
39 Control cable runs
40 Fuselage main longeron
41 Port side access door
42 Canopy aft glazing
43 Sliding canopy rail
44 Voltage regulator
45 Fuselage double frame
46 Seat support frame work
47 Back armour
48 Pilot's seat
49 Sutton harness
50 Head armour
51 Sliding cockpit canopy cover
52 Rear-view mirror
53 Windscreen framing
54 Bulletproof windscreen
55 Reflector gunsight
56 Port side entry hatch
57 Instrument panel
58 Control column
59 Compass mounting
60 Undercarriage control lever
61 Seat adjusting handle
62 Seat pan armour plate
63 Wingroot rib
64 Radiator shutter jack
65 Coolant radiator, oil cooler on port side
66 Gun heating duct
67 Wing rear spar
68 Flap hydraulic jack
69 Flap shroud ribs
70 Tubular flap spar
71 Starboard split trailing-edge flap
72 Aileron control bellcrank
73 Aileron hinge
74 Aileron tab
75 Aluminium skinned aileron construction
76 Wingtip fairing
77 Starboard navigation light
78 Wingtip construction
79 Aileron outer hinge rib
80 Wing rib construction
81 Main spar
82 Leading-edge nose ribs
83 Ammunition feed drums
84 Mainwheel fairing door
85 Ammunition feed drums
86 Blister fairings
87 Ammunition belt feed

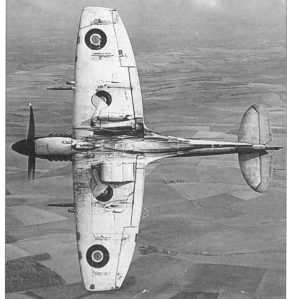

Clipped wings improved the Mk XII's speed and rate of roll at low altitudes. Up to 20,000 ft (6100 m), the Spitfire Mk XII was easily superior to the Mk IX, but above this altitude the earlier mark was faster.

Large numbers of surplus Griffon Spitfires became available in the immediate post-war period and the aircraft played an important role in the rebuilding of many European air arms. Such were the qualities of the Griffon Spitfires that many served on into the early jet era. These FR.Mk 14Es of the Force Aérienne Belge/Belgische Luchtmacht carry the 'IQ' codes of the Ecole de Chasse at Coxyde, which operated the variant between 1948 and 1954

SPECIFICATION

Spitfire F.Mk XII

Dimensions

Length: 30 ft 9 in (9.37 m)
Wingspan, clipped: 32 ft 7 in (9.93 m)
Wing area, clipped: 242 sq ft (22.45 m²)
Height: 11 ft (3.35 m)

Powerplant

One 1,735-hp (1294-kW) Rolls-Royce Griffon IIB, III or IV liquid-cooled, 12-cylinder inline piston engine with single-stage supercharging, driving a four-bladed Rotol propeller

Weight

Maximum loaded: 7,400 lb (3356 kg)

Performance

Maximum speed at 12,500 ft (3810 m): 389 mph (626 km/h)
Service ceiling: 37,350 ft (11387 m)

Armament

Two 20-mm British Hispano cannon and four 0.303-in (7.7-mm) Browning machine-guns

Spitfire F.Mk XIV

Dimensions

Length: 32 ft 0 in (9.96 m)
Wingspan: 36 ft 10 in (10.98 m)

Powerplant

One 2,050-hp (1529-kW) Rolls-Royce Griffon 65 liquid-cooled, 12-cylinder inline piston engine with two-stage supercharging, driving a five-bladed Rotol propeller

Weight

Empty: 6,376 lb (2892 kg)
Maximum loaded: 10,065 lb (4565 kg)

Performance

Maximum speed at 24,500 ft (7468 m): 439 mph (707 km/h)
Service ceiling: 43,000 ft (13110 m)

Armament

Two 20-mm British Hispano cannon and four 0.5-in (12.7-mm) Browning machine-guns plus (post-war only) one 500-lb (227-kg) bomb under the fuselage and two 250-lb (114-kg) bombs underwing, or up to 12 60-lb (27-kg) rocket projectiles underwing

Spitfire F.Mk 22

Dimensions

Length: 32 ft 11 in (10.03 m)
Wingspan: 36 ft 11 in (11.25 m)

Powerplant

As F.Mk XIV

Weight

Maximum loaded: 10,086 lb (4574 kg)

Performance

Maximum speed at 25,000 ft (7622 m): 449 mph (723 km/h)
Service ceiling: 45,500 ft (13872 m)

Armament

Four 20-mm Hispano Mk 5 cannon plus one 500-lb (227-kg) bomb under the fuselage and two 500-lb (227-kg) bombs underwing, or up to four 300-lb (136-kg) rocket projectiles underwing

---

88 20-mm British Hispano, Mk II cannon barrels
89 Cannon barrel support fairing
90 Recoil springs
91 Fuel filler cap
92 Leading-edge fuel tank, capacity 17 Imp gal (77 litres)
93 Main undercarriage wheel well
94 Mainwheel blister fairing
95 Undercarriage retraction link
96 Undercarriage leg pivot
97 Shock absorber leg strut
98 Hydraulic brake pipe
99 Starboard main wheel
100 Main wheel leg fairing door
101 Undercarriage torque scissors
102 Fuel pipe runs
103 Main spar stub attachment
104 Lower main fuel tank, capacity 48 Imp gal (218 litres)
105 Upper main fuel tank, capacity 36 Imp gal (164 litres)
106 Fuel filler cap
107 Oil tank vent
108 Oil tank, capacity 9 Imp gal (41 litres)
109 Oil tank access door
110 Engine compartment fireproof bulkhead
111 Port split trailing edge flap
112 Flap hydraulic jack
113 Flap synchronising jack
114 Port twin 20-mm British Hispano cannon
115 Spent cartridge case ejector chute

116 Ammunition feed drums
117 Ammunition belt feeds
118 Ammunition boxes, 150 rounds per gun
119 Aileron control bellcrank
120 Aileron tab
121 Port aileron
122 Wingtip fairing
123 Port navigation light
124 Pitot tube
125 Cannon barrel fairings
126 Cannon barrels
127 Port leading edge fuel tank, capacity 17 Imp gal (77 litres)
128 Upper engine cowling
129 Hydraulic fluid tank
130 Intercooler
131 Compressor intake
132 Generator
133 Heywood compressor
134 Engine bearer attachment
135 Hydraulic pump
136 Coolant pipes
137 Gun camera
138 Camera port
139 Engine air intake duct
140 Port mainwheel
141 Engine bearer
142 Cartridge starter
143 Exhaust stubs
144 2,035-hp (1517-kW) Rolls Royce Griffon 61 engine
145 Engine magnetos
146 Coolant header tank
147 Front engine mounting
148 Lower engine cowling
149 Spinner backplate
150 Propeller hub pitch change mechanism
151 Spinner
152 Rotol five-bladed constant speed propeller

For many years Spitfire PR.Mk 19 PS853 flew with the RAF's Battle of Britain Memorial Flight. The aircraft joined the RAF in 1945 for service with the Temperature and Humidity Flight (THUM) at Woodvale. PS853 was sold to Rolls-Royce in 1996, in order to supply funds for the rebuilding of BBMF Hurricane LF363.

Spitfire FR.Mk 18E

This aircraft, 'H' (serial unknown) of No. 28 Sqn, of the RAF's Far East Air Force, was based at Kai Tak, Hong Kong in late 1950. It is finished in the standard RAF fighter scheme of the day – Dark Green/Dark Sea Grey upper surfaces over Medium Sea Grey undersurfaces. National insignia consisted of Type D roundels of the type introduced in 1947. Squadron marks included a red spinner and a unit badge on the fin. The latter featured a demi-Pegasus, representing the white horse on the Downs near Yatesbury, Wiltshire where the squadron had received its fighters (Sopwith Camels) in 1917, after a period as a training unit. For the duration of the Korean War, Spitfires based in Hong Kong carried black and white recognition stripes on the rear fuselage (covering the serial number on the port side of this aircraft) and on both the upper and lower surfaces of each wing.

No. 28 in Hong Kong
Civil war in China and an increase in Nationalist movements in the Far East (often supported by Communist elements) brought a need for extra fighter reinforcement in the colony, and in May 1949 Spitfire FR.Mk 18s of No. 28 Sqn were deployed to Kai Tak from Malaya. At the same time, No. 80 Sqn with Spitfire F.Mk 24s left Germany for Hong Kong aboard HMS *Ocean*, arriving in August. Operational from September, No. 80 Sqn assumed daytime ground-attack and high- and low-level interception roles, with No. 28 Sqn covering medium-level interceptions. Other tasks included navy and army co-operation and anti-piracy patrols.

Development of the Griffon engine
The Rolls-Royce Griffon was a 12-cylinder, 60° Vee engine, with a bore and stroke of 6 in (15.24 cm) and 62⁄3 in (16.764 cm), respectively. This equated to a swept volume of 2,240 cu in (36.7 litres), some 35 per cent greater than that of the Merlin. Developed from the Buzzard via the 'R' racing engine (as fitted to the S.6 Schneider Trophy floatplanes), the Griffon was otherwise very much like an enlarged Merlin, incorporating many of the latter's features, but rotating in the opposite direction (anti-clockwise, from the pilot's point of view). A derated 'R' engine, known as the Griffon I, first ran in 1933 but was destined never to fly. Under pressure to develop a smaller engine (the Merlin), Rolls suspended Griffon development until 1939 and then carried out an extensive redesign to make the Griffon II a far more compact powerplant. As it was necessary to keep the engine's size and weight length within limits imposed by the configurations of existing fighter aircraft, much work went into keeping the Griffon's length to a minimum (centring on a redesign of the engine's supercharger drive system). Such was the success of these measures that the overall length of the Griffon was in the range 72-81 in (183-206 cm). For comparison, a Merlin with a single-speed supercharger measured 69 in (175 cm) in length, while a two-speed, two-stage Merlin was 88.7 in (225 cm) long.

Camera fit

Unlike that of its predecessor, the Mk 14, Spitfire Mk 18 production was almost entirely of the FR.Mk 18 fighter-reconnaissance variant, characterised by its cut-down rear fuselage, bubble canopy and oblique camera ports behind the cockpit, either side of the fuselage. The standard camera fit for the type consisted of three F.24 cameras with lenses of varying focal lengths – usually one 14-in (35.6-cm) and two 20-in (50.8-cm). One of these was fitted to look obliquely through one of the two oblique ports, while the other pair was positioned to look downwards through the lower fuselage. An alternate load was a single F.52 vertical camera in the same position.

Air-to-ground armament

Of the Griffon-engined Spitfire variants, the Mk XII was confined to an interception role, as was the Mk XIV in wartime RAF service. However, the latter variant was able to carry a 500-lb (227-kg) bomb under the fuselage and two 250-lb (114-kg) bombs underwing, as well as six rocket projectiles (RPs) (or 12 in pairs). The FR.Mk 18, effectively a strengthened late-production Mk XIV, was able to carry similar loads. Maximum loads quoted for the Mk 21, 22 and 24 appear to have been three 500-lb (227-kg) bombs or four 300-lb (136-kg) RPs, though in RAF service, the Mk 21 and 22 were confined to a fighter role. However, RPs were commonly seen fitted to Mk 24s, rocket-firing forming part of the training programme for No. 80 Sqn at Kai Tak.

The Spitfire Mk XVIII in RAF service

The first Spitfire Mk XVIII (NH872) flew in June 1945, the new mark being externally identical to a late production Mk XIV, with its bubble canopy and 'E' wing armament. Internally, the Mk XVIII had a stronger wing spar structure and two 31-Imp gal (141-litre) fuel tanks in the rear fuselage. Like the Mk XIV, there was a fighter-reconnaissance variant, the FR.Mk XVIII, with a single fuselage fuel tank and three cameras behind the cockpit. The Mk XVIII (known as the Mk 18 from 1947) joined RAF squadrons from August 1946, when No. 208 Sqn re-equipped in Palestine. Deliveries began in earnest in 1947; in January No. 60 Sqn re-equipped at Seletar, Singapore, followed by Nos 11 (with whom Mk 18s operated alongside Mk 14s), 28 (from February 1947) and 81 Sqns (from August, to augment the unit's PR.Mk 19s and Mosquito PR.Mk 34s). In the Middle East, No. 32 Sqn operated the new variant from April 1947.

Vought F4U Corsair

By far the most important operators of the Corsair in World War II were the fighter squadrons of the US Marine Corps, based on island airstrips in the Pacific. These aircraft were photographed leaving parking areas on Majuro Atoll, in the Marshalls, on 29 August 1944. The squadron belongs to the 4th Marine Air Wing.

F4U-1A Corsair

Cutaway key
1 Spinner
2 Three-bladed Hamilton Standard constant-speed propeller
3 Reduction gear housing
4 Nose ring
5 Pratt & Whitney R-2800-8W Double Wasp 18-cylinder two-row engine
6 Exhaust pipes
7 Hydraulically-operated cowling
8 Fixed cowling panels
9 Wing leading-edge unprotected integral fuel tank, capacity 62 US gal (235 litres)
10 Truss-type main spar
11 Leading-edge rib structure
12 Starboard navigation light
13 Wingtip
14 Wing structure
15 Wing ribs
16 Wing outer-section (fabric skinning aft of main spar)
17 Starboard aileron
18 Ammunition boxes (maximum total capacity 2,350 rounds)
19 Aileron trim tab
20 Aerial mast
21 Forward bulkhead
22 Oil tank, capacity 28 US gal (106 litres)
23 Oil tank forward armour plate

24 Fire suppressor cylinder
25 Supercharger housing
26 Exhaust trunking
27 Blower assembly
28 Engine support frame
29 Engine control runs
30 Wing main spar carry-through structure
31 Engine support attachment
32 Upper cowling deflection plate (0.1-in/ 0.25-cm aluminium)
33 Fuel filler cap
34 Fuselage main fuel tank, capacity 237 US gal (897 litres)
35 Upper longeron
36 Fuselage forward frames
37 Rudder pedals
38 Heelboards
39 Control column
40 Instrument panel
41 Reflector sight
42 Armoured-glass windshield
43 Rear-view mirror
44 Rearward-sliding cockpit canopy
45 Handgrip
46 Headrest
47 Pilot's head and back armour
48 Canopy frame
49 Pilot's seat
50 Engine control quadrant
51 Trim tab control wheels
52 Wing folding lever
53 Centre/aft fuselage bulkhead
54 Radio shelf

55 Radio installation
56 Canopy track
57 Bulkhead
58 Aerial lead-in
59 Aerial mast
60 Aerials
61 Heavy sheet skin plating
62 Dorsal identification light
63 Longeron
64 Control runs
65 Aft fuselage structure
66 Compass installation
67 Lifting tube
68 Access/inspection panels
69 Fin/fuselage forward attachment

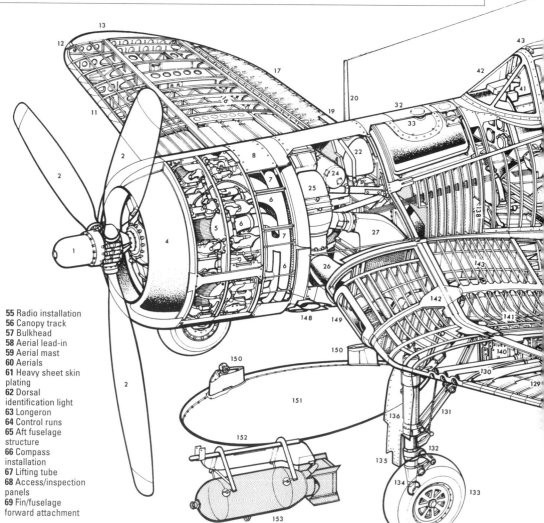

SPECIFICATION

F4U-1A Corsair

Dimensions
Length: 33 ft 4 in (10.16 m)
Height: 16 ft 1 in (4.9 m)
Wingspan: 41 ft (12.5 m)
Wing area: 314 sq ft (29.17 m²)

Powerplant
One 2,000-hp (1492-kW) Pratt & Whitney R-2800-8W Double Wasp 18-cylinder radial piston engine

Weights
Empty: 8,982 lb (4074 kg)
Loaded: 14,000 lb (6350 kg)

Fuel
External fuel: provision for one 175-US gal (662-litre) centreline tank

Performance
Maximum speed at 19,900 ft (6065 m): 417 mph (671 km/h)
Maximum speed at sea level: 316 mph (509 km/h)
Initial climb rate: 2,890 ft (881 m) per minute
Service ceiling: 36,900 ft (11247 m)

Range
Maximum range: 1,015 miles (1633 km)

Armament
Six 0.50-in (12.7-mm) Browning MG53-2 machine-guns in the folding outer wing section (replaced in the F4U-1C by four 20-mm cannon), and (F4U-1D/Corsair II and later models) provision for a bombload of 2,000 lb (908 kg), comprising bombs up to the weight of 1,000-lb (454-kg) or up to eight 5-in (127-mm) HVARs

During the Korean War, aircraft from both VF-92 (based aboard CVA-45 USS **Valley Forge** *from November 1952 to June 1953) and VF-94 (operating from CVA-47 USS* **Philippine Sea** *between December 1952 and August 1953) carried the tail code 'N'. The units' Corsairs shared their carrier decks with more modern F9F-2s and AD Skyraiders.*

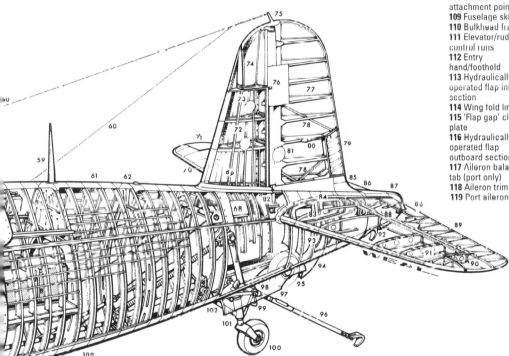

106 Tailwheel/arrester hook cylinder
107 Tailwheel retraction strut
108 Bulkhead attachment points
109 Fuselage skinning
110 Bulkhead frame
111 Elevator/rudder control runs
112 Entry hand/foothold
113 Hydraulically-operated flap inboard section
114 Wing fold line
115 'Flap gap' closure plate
116 Hydraulically-operated flap outboard section
117 Aileron balance tab (port only)
118 Aileron trim tab
119 Port aileron

120 Deck landing grip
121 Port wingtip
122 Port navigation light
123 Pitot head
124 Leading-edge ribs
125 Wing outer section structure
126 Ammunition boxes
127 Three 0.5-in (12.7-mm) Colt-Browning MG53-2 wing machine-guns with 400 rpg (inboard pair) and 375 rpg (outboard)
128 Wing fold outboard cylinder
129 Wing leading-edge unprotected integral fuel tank, capacity 62 US gal (235 litres), deleted from final 150 Corsair IIs
130 Machine-gun blast tubes
131 Mainwheel retraction strut
132 Torque links
133 Port mainwheel
134 Axle
135 Mainwheel leg fairing
136 Mainwheel oleo leg
137 Mainwheel leg pivot point

138 Undercarriage main spar attachment
139 Undercarriage actuating cylinder
140 Main spar fold point
141 Mainwheel well
142 Contoured main spar inboard section
143 All-aluminium wing centre section
144 Main spar/fuselage attachment
145 Blower radiator
146 Oil cooler
147 Engine supercharger intake duct
148 Exhaust stacks
149 Engine supercharger air intake
150 Auxiliary fuel tank centre line attachment points
151 'Duramold' auxiliary drop tank capacity 175 US gal (662 litres)
152 Bomb attachment shackle (underwing inner section, (F4U-1D and Corsair II only))
153 Bombload, up to 1,000 lb (454 kg) each side (F4U-1D and Corsair II only)

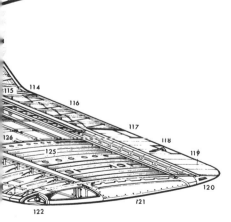

70 Starboard tailplane
71 Elevator balance
72 Fin structure
73 Inspection panels
74 Rudder balance
75 Aerial stub
76 Rudder upper hinge
77 Rudder structure
78 Diagonal bracing
79 Rudder trim tab
80 Trim tab actuating rod
81 Access panel
82 Rudder post
83 Tailplane end rib
84 Elevator control runs
85 Fixed fairing root
86 Elevator trim tabs (port and starboard)
87 Tail cone
88 Rear navigation light
89 Port elevator
90 Elevator balance

91 Port tailplane structure
92 Arrester hook (stowed)
93 Tail section frames
94 Fairing
95 Tailwheel (retracted)
96 Arrester hook (lowered)
97 Tailwheel/hook doors
98 Tailwheel/hook attachment/ pivot
99 Mooring/tie-down lug
100 Rearward-retracting tailwheel
101 Tailwheel oleo
102 Support strut
103 Arrester hook actuating strut
104 Aft/tail section bulkhead
105 Arrester hook shock absorber

A total of 312 USN F4Us was lost during the Korean conflict. The Corsair in its AU-1 guise soldiered on in US Navy Reserve service until 1957, and remained in Marines Reserve service a year longer. A small number of F4U-7 Corsairs remained in service with the Aéronavale until 1964.

F4U-5N Corsair

Wearing the 'WF' tailcode of VMF(N)-513 (nicknamed the 'Flying Nightmares') in white on top of overall midnight blue, and coded '4', this F4U-5N night-fighter carries colours and markings typical of fighters in the Korean theatre. The 'U-birds' of VMF(N)-513 played a vital role in the Korean War from an early stage. While the Pusan Perimeter was surrounded, the squadron's Corsairs helped other close support types to force the North Korean forces into resupplying their army by night. Then, augmenting a small number of F-82G Twin Mustangs, the Corsairs maintained their vigil under the cover of darkness, harassing enemy forces on the ground, and maintaining air superiority. The F4U-5N Corsairs were shorter-ranged than the first F-82 night-fighters to operate over Korea and, with no bases in Korea itself, the aircraft were initially forced to fly from Itazuke in Japan, their radius of action limited to just north of the Pusan Perimeter.

'Flying Nightmares' mission
A typical Korean operation for the F4U-5N pilot of VMF(N)-513 involved flying at tree-top height under the cover of darkness, following roads and other landmarks lit by moonlight. When a re-supply truck or convoy coming from the Chinese border was spotted, a quick wing-over would be followed by a strafing pass, attacking the target at close range due to the reduced visibility. The Corsairs often ran the gauntlet of heavy-calibre automatic AAA weapons, although tracer from these weapons on the ground also served to reveal targets to them.

Pusan Perimeter crossing
When the North Koreans crossed the 38th Parallel on the morning of Sunday 25 June 1950, the South Korean army quickly fell apart, with the hastily-assembled American reinforcements unable to stop the advancing troops. Falling back to the south coast, opposite southern Japan, the US and UN forces organised the defensive Pusan Perimeter. Aerial bombardment of the North Korean People's Army forced the enemy to operate during the night and in bad weather, when their activities began to come under attack from night-fighters, including Corsairs, behind the Perimeter.

Radar
The wing leading edge-mounted APS-19A radar superseded the crude APS-4 radar carried by the first F4U-2 night fighter. The APS-19A had an excellent range of some 80 miles (130 km) for ground-mapping, and an even longer range for picking up a ground beacon. In the interception role, the radar could pick up a fighter-sized target at ranges of up to three miles (4.8 km), although a detection range of two miles (3.2 km) was more usual. Initial problems were experienced when the radar sets were knocked out by the recoil from the wing cannon.

Cockpit and armament

The cockpit of the F4U-5N was covered by a bulged clear-view canopy, affording much better visibility than earlier Corsair variants, the first of which featured a lower 'birdcage' canopy. The raised clear-view canopy was first introduced on the Brewster-built F3A-1 and the Goodyear-built FG-1, and from the 689th F4U-1, although the latter retained two thin horizontal frames. Over Korea, the gloss midnight blue night-fighter finish with white codes worn by VMF(N)-513's Corsairs and Tigercats was later replaced with matt black and dull red codes in an effort to reduce conspicuity. The four wing-mounted 20-mm cannon carried a mixed load of 800 incendiary, high-explosive and armour-piercing rounds. Particularly effective weapons for attacks on resupply convoys were fragmentation bombs, six of which were typically carried on underwing racks. This example, however, carries a full load of eight 5-in (127-mm) HVARs. After this weapon was found to be too light to damage T-34 tanks, it was modified to 'Ram rocket' status, with 6.5-in (165-mm) anti-tank aerial rocket (ATAR) warheads.

Post-war improvements

Following the conclusion of the war in the Pacific theatre, development of the Corsair continued, with the first XF4U-5 (featuring uprated R-2800-32W powerplant and low-drag metal-skinned wings and tail) flying on 4 April 1946. Production F4U-5s and subsequent sub-variants also incorporated ailerons with spring tabs, and heated windshield, gun bays, and pitot head. A similar low-altitude version with the single row R-2800-83W engine and increased armour was the F4U-6, later designated AU-1.

GRANT RACE

Powerplant

The F4U-5 and F4U-5N were powered by a 2,850-hp (2126-kW) Pratt & Whitney R-2800-32W Double Wasp two-row 18-cylinder radial piston engine, with two-stage supercharger with twin supercharger inlets in the lower half of the cowling. Combined with aerodynamic improvements, the new engine gave the F4U-5 and F4U-5N dramatically improved performance, with a maximum speed of 470 mph (756 km/h) and a range of 1,120 miles (1802 km). In order to improve the pilot's visibility over the nose, the engine was drooped by 2.75°.

Yakovlev Yak-1/3/7/9

Yak-3

Cutaway key

1 Rudder trim tab
2 Rudder structure
3 Rudder post
4 Tail fin structure
5 Aerial attachment
6 Tail fin leading edge spar
7 Spar attachment points
8 Tail fin root fairing
9 Elevator control horns
10 Rudder lower hinge
11 Elevator torque tube
12 Rear navigation light
13 Elevator trim tab
14 Elevator structure
15 Tailplane construction
16 Tailwheel doors
17 Retractable tailwheel
18 Tailwheel oleo
19 Tailwheel well
20 Wheel-impact door-closure struts
21 Tailwheel retraction jack
22 Lifting tube

23 Tubular steel fuselage framework
24 Ventral former
25 Elevator control cables
26 Diagonal brace wires
27 Dorsal former
28 Decking
29 Aerial
30 Aerial attachment/lead-in
31 Canopy fixed aft glazing
32 Armourglass screen
33 Canopy track
34 HF (RSI-6M) radio equipment
35 Accumulator
36 Equipment rack
37 Hydraulic reservoir
38 Ventral coolant radiator housing
39 Control rod linkage
40 Radiator bath aft fairing
41 Radiator
42 Seat support frame
43 Pilot's seat pan
44 Trim tab control console (port)
45 Padded (armoured) seat back
46 Switchbox

47 Aft-sliding cockpit canopy
48 Reflector sight
49 One-piece moulded armourglass windscreen
50 Instrument panel coaming
51 Control column
52 Instrument panel starboard console
53 Control linkage
54 Rudder pedal bar
55 Bulkhead
56 Frame
57 Gun support tray
58 Bracket
59 0.5-in (12.7-mm) ShVAK machine-gun (port and starboard)
60 Port flap
61 Guide rollers
62 Aileron push-rod control linkage
63 Aileron trim tab
64 Port aileron
65 Port wingtip
66 Port navigation light
67 Pitot tube
68 Forward spar
69 Port outboard fuel tank
70 Fuel filler cap

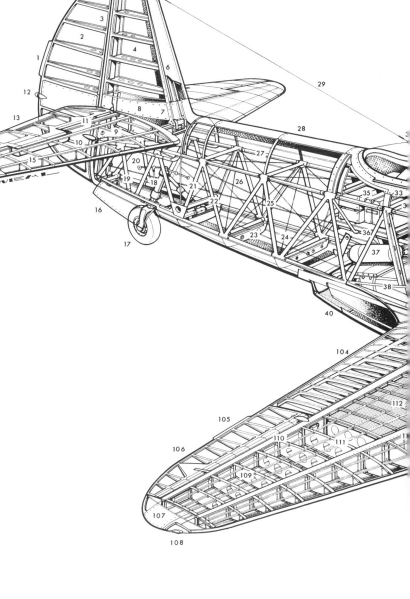

Although it introduced a number of refinements compared to the original Yak-7A fighter, the Yak-7B was still very much an interim machine. Problems afflicting the type ranged from the minor, including a slow climb rate; long take-off and landing runs and poor cockpit canopy; to the potentially lethal. In the latter category were the wing skins, which caused many crashes on separating from the wing.

SPECIFICATION

Yak-9

Dimensions

Length: 28 ft 5 in (8.66 m)
Height: 8 ft 7 in (2.60 m)
Wingspan: 31 ft 11½ in (9.74 m)
Wing area: 184.61 sq ft (17.15 m²)

Powerplant

One M-105PF-1 V-12 liquid-cooled piston engine rated at 1,260 hp (940 kW)

Weights

Empty: 5,066 lb (2298 kg)
Loaded: 6,669 lb (3025 kg)

Performance

Maximum speed at sea level: 331 mph (533 km/h)

Maximum speed at 13,123 ft (4000 m): 371 mph (597 km/h)
Range: 457 miles (735 km)
Climb to 16,404 ft (5000 m): 5 minutes 30 seconds
Service ceiling: 32,808 ft (10000 m)
Take-off run: 1,247 ft (380 m)
Landing run: 1,640 ft (500 m)

Armament

One 20-mm ShVAK cannon mounted to fire through tthe propeller hub and provided with 120 rounds and one 0.5-in (12.7-mm) UBS fixed forward-firing machine-gun mounted on the port side of the upper rear fuselage and provided with 200 rounds. Later aircraft were fitted with a similar UBS installation to starboard

Above: Yakovlev built and tested a single example of the Yak-9P (P – pushechnyi or cannon) in March 1945. The aircraft was lighter than the standard Yak-9, even though it had a 20-mm ShVAK cannon with 175 rounds of ammunition in place of the standard UBS machine-gun. The aircraft is shown here as it appeared during spin tests in the post-war period.

Left: Having entered production late in 1940, the Yak-1 was already struggling to match the Messerschmitt Bf 109F by June 1941. It formed the basis of suceeding designs, however, including the Yak-9 which matured as a superb multi-role fighter and the superlative Yak-3 dogfighter, which was able to meet the late-mark Bf 109 and formidable Fw 190A on more than equal terms.

Right: A distinctive feature of the Yak-1 and the Yak-1M was their overlapping two-part main undercarriage doors, those of the -1M being considerably larger. A further distinguishing feature between the two subvariants concerned their canopies, that of the Yak-1 fairing directly into the fuselage spine and that of the -1M being raised above the cut down rear fusleage decking to provide the pilot with an improved all-round view. The aircraft illustrated was the first Yak-1 to emerge from the GAZ-292 factory at Saratov.

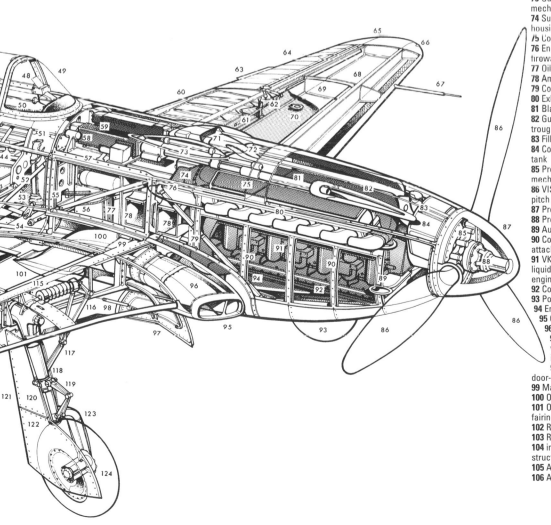

71 Supercharger intake scoop
72 Intake ducting
73 Gun cocking mechanism fairings
74 Supercharger housing
75 Cowling frame
76 Engine bearer/firewall attachment
77 Oil tank
78 Ammunition boxes
79 Cowling aft frame
80 Exhaust stubs
81 Blast tubes
82 Gun muzzle troughs
83 Filler cap
84 Coolant header tank
85 Propeller pitch mechanism
86 VISh-105 variable-pitch metal propeller
87 Propeller spinner
88 Propeller hub
89 Auxiliary intake
90 Cowling attachment frames
91 VK-105 12-cylinder liquid-cooled Vee engine
92 Coolant ducting
93 Port mainwheel
94 Engine bearer
95 Oil cooler intake
96 Ducting
97 Mainwheel well door inboard section
98 Wheel-impact door-closure struts
99 Main spar cut-out
100 Oil cooler housing
101 Oil cooler outlet fairing
102 Radiator intake
103 Radiator grill
104 inset flap structure
105 Aileron trim tab
106 Aileron frame

107 Starboard wingtip
108 Starboard navigation light
109 Outboard wing ribs
110 Rear spar
111 Stringers
112 Starboard outboard fuel tank
113 Front spar
114 Undercarriage/spar attachment plate
115 Undercarriage retraction cylinder
116 Mainwheel leg well
117 Undercarriage downlock strut
118 Brake lines
119 Torque links
120 Mainwheel oleo leg
121 Mainwheel leg fairing plate
122 Mainwheel fairing plate
123 Axle fork
124 Starboard mainwheel

Yak-3

General Major Georgii Nefedovich flew this Yak-3 while leading the 303rd IAD. He fought over Kursk and the 3rd Ukrainian Front with the unit and in 1945 moved into combat over East Prussia. Nefedovich began his combat career over Spain, having volunteered to fight on the Republican side during the Civil War. Flying an I-15, he scored six kills before returning to the Soviet Union. Nefedovich scored a further three victories over China in 1938 and by the end of the Great Patriotic War his personal total stood at 23 kills.

Cockpit and handling

The Yak-3 cockpit was a primitive affair compared to that of contemporary Allied or, indeed, Axis types. Blind flying had to be done on primary instruments alone, there being no gyroscopic instruments provided for this purpose. In general, the Yak-3 was a difficult aircraft to fly, especially for the novice pilot. The aircraft had a high stalling speed, which meant constant attention during slow-speed flight, and would willingly drop a wing on the approach if speed was allowed to drop. The tendancy to swing on landing and take-off was also a constant problem and ground-loops were relatively frequent. Nevertheless, in the hands of a competent pilot the Yak-3 was probably the most effective air combat fighter in the world at the time, having less than half the weight of the majority of its western counterparts and easily being able to out manoeuvre the best the Luftwaffe could offer in close-in, high-*g* dogfighting.

Powerplant

Although the Yak-3 was built in 18 versions, these can be broken down into two basic forms, the 'frontal' variants and the 'high-altitude' machines. The former, like that illustrated, were powered by variants of the VK-105PF liquid-cooled inline piston engine, typically driving a VISh-105SV three-bladed propeller. For high-altitude operations the Yak-3 was equipped with variants of the VK-105PD engine, which featured two-stage supercharging and, in its Yak-3 application, usually drove a three-bladed VISh-105L-2 propeller. All production variants of the Yak-3 dispensed with the distinctive undernose oil cooler air intake of the Yak-1, the radiator for this purpose having been moved to an intake in the port wing root. In air-to-air combat the Yak-3 was the most effective of the Yak-1/3/7/9 family, thanks to its light weight, small size and considerable agility, and the repositioned oil cooler intake provided a useful recognition aid for Luftwaffe fighter pilots, allowing them to judge the calibre of the opposition before engaging.

Armament

Since the Yak-3 was designed as a light-weight fighter, it was used exclusively in air-to-air roles and was never given provision for air-to-ground weapons. The earliest production Yak-3s were armed with a single engine-mounted 20-mm UBS cannon with 200 rounds and a single 0.5-in (12-7-mm) ShVAK machine-gun with 120 rounds synchronised to fire through the propeller disc, but pilot criticism soon led to a second ShVAK being added. Subsequent variants introduced a range of different gun combinations, the most powerful being the one engine-mounted 37-mm cannon and twin synchronised 20-mm cannon arrangement of the Yak-3T.

Stucture

In producing the Yak-3, Yakovlev combined a fuselage based
closely on that of the Yak-1, with the composite wing of the Yak-9.
Compared to the Yak-1, the fuselage of the Yak-3 had a lower rear
deck and the cockpit was covered by a canopy similar to that of
the Yak-1M. The fuselage retained the plywood skinning over steel-
tube framework construction of the Yak-1. The wing used a
considerable amount of steel and light alloy, replacing much of the
wood used in the Yak-1's wing, largely thanks to supplies of steel
becoming available from the US. This wing structure caused many
problems when first introduced into combat on the Yak-9, with the
plywood wing skins becoming loose and, on occasion ripping off
the airframe inflight. With much 'encouragement' from Stalin,
Yakovlev eventually traced the problem to the nitro-cellulose dope
used to protect the plywood from the elements: that being applied
by one of the factories was not waterproof and after just a short
time in the field the plywood had been weakened to the point
where it was no longer able to remain attached to the wing.

Undercarriage

The main undercarriage of all the World War II Yak piston-engined
fighters retracted inwards, that of the Yak-3 and Yak-9 being
enclosed by three doors on each side. The Yak-1 employed two
doors for each undercarriage unit, which left the retracted
mainwheels partly exposed in their bays, while the Yak-7's were
fully enclosed by pairs of doors of different design. A retractable
tailwheel was a standard feature on the Yak-1M, -3 and -9, while
the Yak-7 fighters progressed from having a semi- to a fully-
retractable tailwheel during the type's evolution.

Transport, Reconnaissance and Maritime Patrol Aircraft

Consolidated PBY Catalina

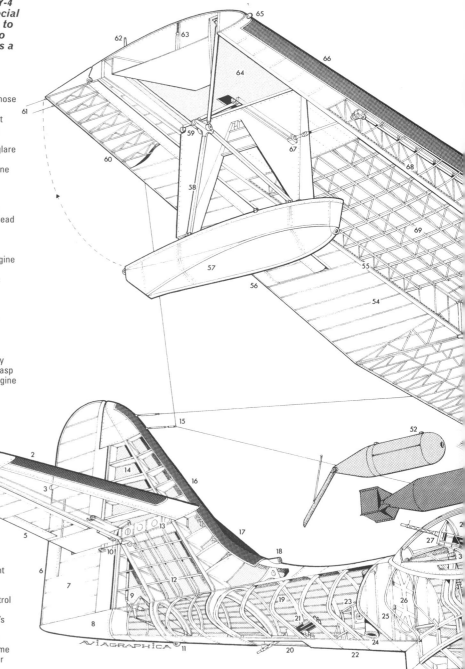

This is one of a small number of conversions of PBY-4 and PBY-5 Catalinas to the mine warfare role. A special electricity-generating plant supplied a large current to cables inside the ring, generating a magnetic field to explode magnetic mines. The mine warfare task was a dangerous one, the aircraft having to fly over the minefield at low level.

PBY-5A Catalina
Cutaway key

1 Starboard tailplane
2 Tailplane leading-edge de-icing
3 Tail navigation light
4 Starboard fabric-covered elevator
5 Elevator tab
6 Rudder trim tab
7 Fabric-covered rudder construction
8 Tailcone
9 Elevator push-pull control rod
10 Rudder control horn
11 Tail mooring point
12 Lower fin structure integral with tail fuselage
13 Tailplane centre-section attachment
14 Upper fin construction
15 Aerial cables
16 Fin leading-edge de-icing
17 Port tailplane
18 Cooling air intake
19 Rear fuselage frame and stringer construction
20 Ventral tunnel gun hatch
21 0.3-in (7.62-mm) machine-gun
22 Fuselage skin plating
23 Target-towing reel
24 Flare launch tube
25 Rear fuselage bulkhead
26 Bulkhead door
27 0.5-in (12.7-mm) beam machine-gun
28 Starboard beam gun cupola
29 Cupola opening side window
30 Flexible gun mounting
31 Port beam gun cupola
32 Gunner's folding seat
33 Semi-circular gun platform
34 Walkway
35 Hull bottom V-frames
36 Wardroom bulkhead
37 Crew rest bunks

38 Wardroom
39 Starboard mainwheel
40 Hull planing bottom step
41 Planing bottom construction
42 Fuselage skin planing
43 Mainwheel housing
44 Hydraulic retraction jack
45 Telescopic leg strut
46 Fore and aft wing support struts
47 Wing mounting centre pylon construction
48 Pylon tail fairing
49 Starboard wing integral fuel tank, capacity 875 US gal (3312 litres)
50 Fuel jettison pipe
51 1,000-lb (454-kg) bomb
52 Smoke generator tank
53 Trailing-edge ribs
54 Fabric-covered trailing edge
55 Rear spar
56 Aileron trim tab
57 Starboard retractable wingtip float
58 Float support struts
59 Retraction linkage
60 Fabric-covered starboard aileron
61 Static discharge wicks
62 Wingtip aerial mast
63 Float up-lock
64 Float leg housing
65 Starboard navigation light
66 Leading-edge de-icing boot
67 Float retracting gear
68 Front spar
69 Wing rib/stringer construction
70 ASV radar aerial
71 Outer wing panel attachment joint
72 Wing lattice ribs
73 Bomb-carrier and release unit
74 Two 500-lb (227-kg) bombs

75 Leading-edge nose ribs
76 Position of pitot tube on port wing
77 Landing lamp
78 Landing lamp glare shield
79 Starboard engine nacelle fairing
80 Hydraulic accumulator
81 Engine oil tank
82 Fireproof bulkhead
83 Exhaust stub
84 Engine bearer struts
85 Detachable engine cowlings
86 Curtiss Electric three-bladed constant-speed propeller, 12-ft (3.66-m) diameter
87 Propeller hub pitch-change mechanism
88 Pratt & Whitney R-1830-92 Twin Wasp two-row radial engine
89 Aerial cable lead-in
90 D/F loop aerial
91 Oil cooler
92 Control runs through pylon front fairing
93 Pylon step
94 Engineer's control panel
95 Flight engineer's seat
96 Wing mounting fuselage main frame
97 Radio and radar control units
98 Cabin heater
99 Front cabin walkway
100 Port main undercarriage leg strut

SPECIFICATION

Catalina Mk IB

Dimensions

Length: 65 ft 2 in (19.86 m)
Height: 17 ft 11 in (5.46 m)
Wingspan: 104 ft (31.70 m)
Wing area: 1,400 sq ft (130.06 m²)

Powerplant

Two 1,200-hp (895-kW) Pratt & Whitney R-1830 radial piston engines

Weights

Empty: 14,240 lb (6459 kg)
Maximum take-off: 27,080 lb (12283 kg)

Performance

Maximum speed at 10,500 ft (3200 m): 190 mph (306 km/h)
Cruising speed: 179 mph (288 km/h)
Service ceiling: 24,000 ft (7315 m)
Range: 4,000 miles (6437 km)

Armament

One 0.303-in (7.7-mm) machine-gun in bow and two 0.303-in (7.7-mm) machine-guns in each side blister and in ventral position, plus up to 4,000 lb (1814 kg) of bombs, torpedoes, smoke generators or depth charges

An original colour photograph taken early in the Aleutians campaign of 1942 shows a US Navy PBY-5 taking on supplies before slipping its moorings for a patrol. A pair of bombs can be seen under the wing (maximum load was four, each of 1,000 lb/ 454 kg). Defensive armament would be provided by two 0.3-in (7.62-mm) and two 0.5-in (12.7-mm) guns.

Painted black and tasked with harrying Japanese forces at night, the 'Black Cats' were specially selected Catalina squadrons. They were responsible for the sinking of thousands of tons of Japanese shipping during the Pacific War.

101 Torque scissor links
102 Port mainwheel
103 Mk 13-2 torpedo
104 450-lb (204-kg) depth charge
105 Forward fuselage frame construction
106 Navigator's seat
107 Radio/radar operator's seat
108 Radio rack
109 Cabin side window
110 Autopilot servo controller
111 Navigator's chart table
112 Fuselage chine member
113 Cockpit bulkhead
114 Co-pilot's seat
115 Pilot's seat
116 Pilot's electrical control panel
117 Sliding side window
118 Engine cowling cooling air
119 Port engine nacelle
120 Cockpit roof escape hatch
121 Overhead throttle and propeller controls
122 Windscreen wipers
123 Curved windscreens
124 Instrument panel
125 Control column yoke and handwheels
126 Rudder pedals
127 Cockpit flooring
128 Nose undercarriage hatch doors
129 Nosewheel bay
130 Port aileron
131 Nosewheel
132 Port retractable wingtip float
133 Float support struts
134 Port navigation light
135 Leading-edge de-icing boot
136 Nosewheel forks
137 Nose undercarriage retraction jack
138 Front gunner/bomb aimer's station
139 Curtained bulkhead
140 Gunner's footboards
141 Spare ammunition containers
142 Front rotating gun turret
143 0.3-in (7.62-mm) machine-gun
144 Bomb aimer's instrument panel
145 Drift sight
146 Bomb-aiming window with protective blind
147 Anchor cable

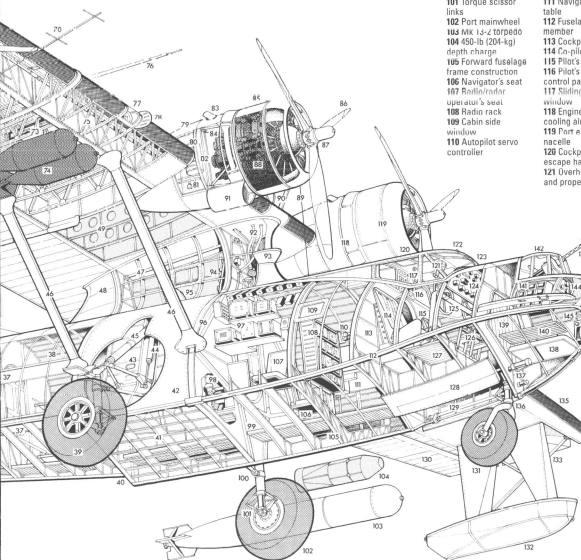

Catalina Mk IVA

No. 202 Sqn was formed in October 1914 as No. 2 Sqn, RNAS. For most of World War II, it was based at Gibraltar to secure the Strait and for patrols in the western Mediterranean and Atlantic. It moved to Ireland in September 1944 for anti-submarine patrols at night, maintaining a detachment at Sullom Voe in the Shetlands. Wartime equipment included the Saro London, Fairey Swordfish, Short Sunderland and the Catalina which, in Mk I, II and IV forms, served from May 1941 to June 1945. Today, the squadron flies Westland Sea King HAR.Mk 3As on search and rescue duties around the British coastline.

Leigh Light
An important aid for the Catalina's patrol duties was the high-illumination Leigh Light carried under the starboard wing – this denied surfacing submarines the cover of darkness. One notable attack took place in July 1944 when a Catalina of No. 210 Squadron operating out of Sullom Voe discovered U-boat *U-347*. As the Catalina made its first run over the U-boat, the depth charges failed to release. Flight Officer Cruickshank made a second pass, under intensive anti-aircraft fire, this time dropping the depth charges directly onto the U-boat, destroying it. However, the attack had been costly, with the navigator killed and Cruickshank badly injured. Nevertheless, he managed to return to base, where doctors treated him for 72 wounds. He was later awarded the VC for valour.

Armament
RAF Catalinas carried little in the way of defensive armament, and by the end of the war there was virtually no danger from enemy fighters, so guns could be dispensed with completely (as here). The standard fit was a Vickers K machine-gun in the bow turret and twin 0.303-in (7.7-mm) Brownings in the waist blisters. Offensive stores could be carried on four underwing hardpoints, each stressed for 1,000 lb (454 kg). Ordnance included bombs, torpedoes, smoke generators and depth charges (illustrated).

Flight deck
Pilot and co-pilot sat side-by-side on the flight deck and were provided with a roof escape hatch for emergency egress. The throttles and propeller controls were mounted in the overhead position.

Fuel

Fuel was held in integral tanks between the wing spars of the centre-section. This gave a range of around 2,350 miles (3780 km) with a full military load. Catalinas were renowned for their incredible endurance, which could be augmented in the Mk IVA with additional fuel tanks. Missions of up to 27 hours were undertaken.

Radar

The Catalina Mk IVA was fitted with ASV Mk II radar to spot surfaced U-boats. The antennas for this system were mounted under the wings. A centimetric surveillance radar was mounted in a large teardrop radome above the flight deck.

Wings

The broad wing was built around two main spars. The entire slab-like centre-section was built as one main structure and carried all the loads from the centre pylon, support struts, engine nacelles, weapon pylons and outer panels. The latter were tapered, and attached by a reinforced wing joint. The broad expanse of wing and slow flying speed of the Catalina meant that no flaps were required for landing or take-off. Fabric-covered ailerons were fitted to the outer sections, reaching out to the true wingtip (but inboard of the floats when retracted). The leading edges of the wings, tail and tailplanes were de-iced by a pneumatic boot.

Cabins

Immediately behind the flight deck was a cabin for the radio operator (starboard) and navigator (port). The latter had a large chart table, while the former had a large rack of radio equipment. Small windows gave some view of the outside world. A central walkway led through the entire hull from the flight deck to the rear, finally entering the aft cabin, where the gunners/observers worked. A semi-circular platform allowed these crewmen to swing guns through a wide arc, while the bulged waist blisters enabled them to carry out surveillance over a large area during patrols. The flight engineer's station was situated in the centre of the aircraft, projecting up into the wing support pylon. Small windows were incorporated into the pylon. Behind the flight engineer, under the wing trailing edge, was a wardroom, complete with crew rest bunks.

Hull

The stepped hull was all-metal, with one main deck and an unusual semi-circular upper section. The Catalina Mk IVA was the same as the US Navy's PBY-5, and was strictly a flying-boat. The Mk IIIA was a PBY-5A with amphibian gear, which retracted to a semi-enclosed position on the fuselage sides.

Douglas C-47 Skytrain/Dakota

South Africa's isolation during the years of apartheid meant that the SADF had to run its fleet of Dakotas long after other first line air forces had retired the type. But the tough and reliable Douglas design gave excellent service in the bush wars in Namibia and Angola.

Dakota Mk IV

Cutaway key

1 Hinged nose cone, access to instruments and controls
2 Rudder pedals
3 Instrument panel
4 Windscreen de-icing fluid spray nozzle
5 Starboard propeller
6 Windscreen panels
7 Co-pilot's seat
8 Engine throttles
9 Control column
10 Cockpit floor level
11 Access panels to control cable runs
12 Pilot static tubes
13 Aerial cables
14 Propeller de-icing fluid tank
15 Pilot's seat
16 Cockpit bulkhead
17 Cockpit roof escape hatch
18 Whip aerial
19 Starboard landing/taxiing lamp
20 Windscreen de-icing fluid tank
21 Starboard baggage compartment
22 Electrical fuse panel
23 Crew entry door
24 ADF loop aerial housing
25 Life raft stowage
26 Port baggage compartment
27 Main cabin bulkhead
28 Radio operator's seat
29 Air scoop
30 Heating and ventilating system heat exchangers
31 Astrodome observation hatch
32 Starboard outer wing panel
33 Pneumatic leading-edge de-icing boot
34 Starboard navigation light
35 Starboard aileron
36 Aileron cable controls
37 Trim tab
38 Trim tab control gear
39 Flap control shaft
40 Starboard outer flap

41 Fuselage frame and stringer construction
42 Centre fuselage main frames
43 Centre wing section corrugated inner skin
44 Port main fuel tank, capacity 210 US gal (794 litres)
45 Port auxiliary fuel tank capacity 201 US gal (761 litres)
46 Wing spar attachments
47 Flap hydraulic jack
48 Centre section flap
49 Floor beam construction

50 Cabin window panels
51 Window panel grommets for small arms attachments
52 Paratroop seating, 28 paratroops
53 Starboard emergency exit window
54 Port emergency exit window
55 Cabin lining panels
56 Overhead heating and ventilating duct
57 Rear cabin frames

58 Fuselage skin plating
59 Rear cabin bulkhead
60 First aid kit
61 Access door to tail controls
62 Fin root fillet
63 Starboard tailplane
64 Starboard elevator
65 Fin leading-edge pneumatic de-icing boot
66 Fin construction
67 Aerial cables
68 Rudder aerodynamic balance
69 Hinge post
70 Rudder construction

71 Fabric covering
72 Rudder trim tab
73 Trim tab control gear
74 Rudder and elevator control horns
75 Fuselage tail fairing
76 Elevator trim tab
77 Port elevator construction
78 Fabric covered elevator
79 Leading-edge pneumatic de-icing boot
80 Tailplane construction

81 Tailplane attachment joint
82 Rudder stop cables
83 Tailplane centre section
84 Tailwheel
85 Shock absorber leg strut
86 Tailwheel mounting plate
87 Tailwheel strut
88 Rudder and elevator control cables
89 Tail fuselage joint frame
90 Toilet
91 Rear freight door

92 Forward freight door
93 Paratroop/passenger door
94 Fuselage stringer construction
95 Freight floor
96 Wing root trailing-edge fillet
97 Inboard split trailing-edge flap
98 Flap shroud construction
99 Fuel filler caps

Central America is one of the last bastions of the C-47 in military service. Still capable of providing air forces like that of Honduras with effective service, it will soldier on well into the 21st Century, after more than 60 years in the front line.

SPECIFICATION

Douglas C-47A Skytrain

Dimensions

Wingspan: 95 ft 6 in (29.11 m)
Wing area: 987 sq ft (91.69 m²)
Length: 63 ft 9 in (19.43 m)
Height: 17 ft (5.18 m)

Powerplant

Two Pratt & Whitney R-1830-92 Twin Wasp 14-cylinder air-cooled two-row radial piston engines, each rated at 1,200 hp (895 kW)

Typical Weights

Empty: 17,865 lb (8103 kg)
Normal loaded: 26,000 lb (11793 kg)
Maximum take-off: 31,000 lb (14061 kg)
Maximum internal load: 10,000 lb (4536 kg)

Maximum fuel load: 4,824 lb (2188 kg)

Performance

Maximum speed: 230 mph (370 km/h) at 8,800 feet (2680 m)
Cruising speed: 185 mph (298 km/h) at 10,000 feet (3050 m)
Service ceiling: 24,000 ft (7315 m)
Maximum range: 1,600 miles (2575 km)
Rate of climb: 1,170 ft (357 m) per minute

Accommodation/Payload

Crew: three (pilot, co-pilot, radio operator/navigator)
Accommodation: 14 passengers as sleeper transport/ambulance; 21 passengers as standard airliner; 28 fully equipped troops; 31 passengers as high-density airliner

An Australian Dakota flies over the Straits of Malacca as it heads towards the RAAF base at Butterworth. The RAAF used Dakotas into the 1970s, until they were replaced by Lockheed C-130 Hercules and DHC-4 Caribou.

100 Outer wing panel bolted joint
101 Wing panel joint capping strip
102 Outer split trailing-edge flap
103 Port aileron
104 Aileron fabric covering
105 Detachable wingtip joint rib
106 Port navigation light
107 Leading-edge pneumatic de-icing boot

108 Wing stringer construction
109 Rear spar
110 Centre spar
111 Wing rib construction
112 Front spar
113 Leading-edge nose ribs
114 Leading-edge stringers
115 Port landing/taxiing lamp
116 Port mainwheel
117 Main undercarriage rear strut

118 Shock absorber leg struts
119 Undercarriage knee joints
120 Exhaust pipe
121 Undercarriage bungee cables
122 Engine nacelle fairing
123 Oil tank capacity 29.25 US gal (111 litres)
124 Undercarriage retraction jack
125 Mainwheel well
126 Engine fireproof bulkhead
127 Engine bearer struts
128 Oil cooler
129 Cooling air exit flaps

130 Exhaust collector pipe
131 Engine air intake
132 Engine cowlings
133 Pratt & Whitney R-1830-90C air-cooled 14-cylinder, two-row radial engine
134 Propeller hub pitch change mechanism
135 Hamilton Standard constant speed three-bladed propeller

South African 'Parabats' drop from a C-47. The SADF used its Dakotas in combat as late as 1987, dropping troops in support of operations against SWAPO guerrilla bases in southern Angola.

© 2001 Mike Badrocke/ Aviagraphica

C-47A Skytrain

The Douglas DC-3 has had a longer service history than any other aircraft. In its military form as the C-47, it contributed mightily to the Allied victory during World War II, and when large numbers of the ten thousand or more C-47s built came on to the market after the war they were quickly snapped up by civil and military operators alike. Simple, rugged and dependable, the C-47 has been in front-line service for more than fifty years: this example was flown by the Grupo de Transportes Aéreos Militares of the Fuerza Aérea Colombiana in the 1990s.

Cockpit and crew
The C-47 has a flight crew of two, though in military service it also carried a radio operator/ navigator in a compartment behind the cockpit. The sharply-angled windscreens contrast with the gentle curves elsewhere on the aircraft.

Powerplant and nacelle
This C-47 Skytrain is fitted with two Pratt & Whitney Twin Wasp R-1830-90C air-cooled, 14-cylinder two-row radial engines, developing 1,050 hp (783 kW) at 2,550 rpm. Some variants were fitted with Wright Cyclone nine-cylinder radials of similar size and power. The engines are mounted into streamlined nacelles, each of which also contains a 33.25 US gal (126-litre) oil tank. The wheels are retracted hydraulically into the rear of the nacelle, but are not fully enclosed when retracted. They can be raised or lowered in 15 seconds.

Colour scheme
Most Colombian C-47s flew in a natural metal finish, but the demands of the endless struggle against leftist guerrillas and the powerful drug lords of the cocaine cartels saw at least two aircraft painted in this two-tone camouflage scheme.

Rudder
The DC-3/C-47 has an unpowered rudder of extremely broad chord, which gives very good control authority at low speeds. This is essential when delivering troops or supplies by parachute, which is part of the reason that the C-47 remained a useful military aircraft for more than half a century. The rudder itself has a simple trailing-edge trim tab for fine control.

Cabin and exits
Military variants of the long-serving Douglas transport have stronger cabin floors and rear fuselages than their civil DC-3 counterparts, primarily to take heavier loads. Similarly, they are usually fitted with a large two-part cargo door at the port rear of the fuselage, with a smaller door in one leaf to allow the deployment of airborne troops. Airliner versions of the DC-3 were designed to carry between 18 and 21 passengers: the military C-47 could carry four and a half tonnes of cargo, or 28 fully-equipped paratroops in canvas or aluminium folding bucket seats mounted along the sides of the cabin.

Tail fairing
This Colombian C-47 would have been fitted with a glider towing hook in its earlier life as a World War II aircraft, but as with most such aircraft postwar the hook was removed and the space was faired over.

FAC 681

Horizontal tail
The C-47 has a large horizontal tail, fitted with simple fabric-covered trimming tabs on the ailerons. The leading edge of the tailplane is fitted with a de-icer boot – a rubber strip which can be inflated and deflated to dislodge any potentially dangerous build-up of ice.

Static line
There are two types of military parachutist. Special forces often jump from high altitude, pulling their own ripcords, but most paratroopers are dropped at very low level (under 975 ft/300 m). Their parachutes are opened automatically by a static line clipped to the aircraft, which is left streaming out of the door after the trooper has jumped.

Fieseler Fi 156 Storch

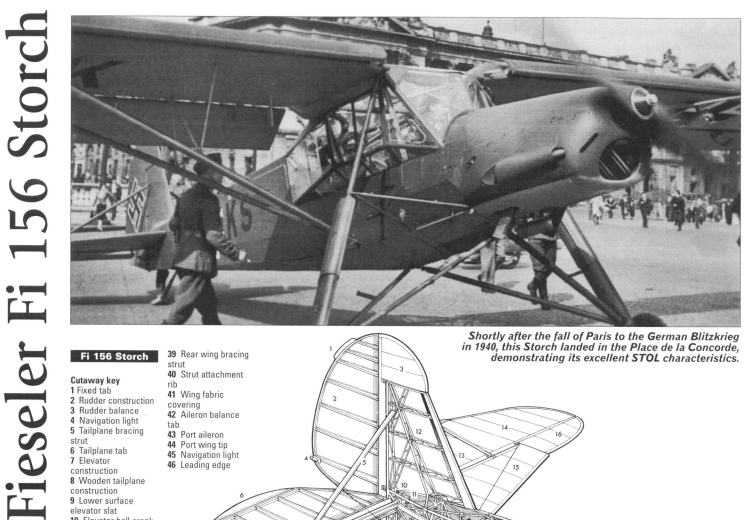

Shortly after the fall of Paris to the German Blitzkrieg in 1940, this Storch landed in the Place de la Concorde, demonstrating its excellent STOL characteristics.

Fi 156 Storch

Cutaway key
1 Fixed tab
2 Rudder construction
3 Rudder balance
4 Navigation light
5 Tailplane bracing strut
6 Tailplane tab
7 Elevator construction
8 Wooden tailplane construction
9 Lower surface elevator slat
10 Elevator bell crank
11 Tailplane pivot mounting
12 Fin construction
13 Fin leading edge
14 Elevator fabric covering
15 Port tailplane
16 Elevator balance
17 Tailplane trim jack
18 Tailskid strut cuff
19 Tailskid
20 Tailskid support strut
21 Welded steel-tube fuselage framework
22 Tailplane trim cables
23 Elevator push-pull control rods
24 Rudder push-pull control rod
25 Fuselage fabric covering
26 Zip-fastened access panel
27 Stowage locker door
28 Gun sight
29 7.9-mm MG 15 machine-gun (provision for three 50-round magazines)
30 LL-K machine-gun swivel mounting
31 Cartridge case collector box
32 Rear cabin bulkhead
33 Cabin roof construction
34 Radio aerial (for FuG XVII)
35 Stub wing spar attachment
36 Flap operating rod
37 Port flap
38 Wing root fuel tank (16.28 Imp gal/74 litre capacity)

39 Rear wing bracing strut
40 Strut attachment rib
41 Wing fabric covering
42 Aileron balance tab
43 Port aileron
44 Port wing tip
45 Navigation light
46 Leading edge fixed slat
47 Aileron control rod
48 Searchlight
49 Pitot head
50 Forward wing bracing strut
51 Flap operating jack
52 Port undercarriage framework
53 Access step
54 Windscreen

55 Compass
56 Downward vision windows
57 Trim control
58 Control column
59 Instrument panel shroud
60 Instrument access panel
61 Engine cowlings, detachable
62 Oil tank filler

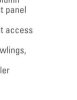

75

SPECIFICATION

Fieseler Fi 156C-2

Type

Two-seat army co-operation/reconnaissance aircraft

Powerplant

One 240-hp (179-kW) Argus As 10C-3 8-cylinder inverted Vee piston engine

Performance

Maximum speed 109 mph (175 km/h) at sea level, economical cruising speed 81 mph (130 km/h), service ceiling 15,090 ft (4600 m), range 239 miles (385 km)

Weights

Empty 2,050 lb (930 kg); maximum take-off 2,921 lb (1325 kg)

Dimensions

Wingspan 46 ft 9 in (14.25 m), length 32 ft 5¾ in (9.90 m), height 10 ft (3.05 m), wing area 279.87 sq ft (26.00 m2) Armament: one rear-firing 0.31-in (7.92-mm) machine-gun on pivoted mount

*Fi 156 V4 (the fourth prototype), **D-IFMR**, had ski undercarriage and a drop tank fitted for test purposes.*

63 Engine oil tank (2.42 Imp gal/11litre capacity)
64 Argus As 10C-3 engine
65 Engine mounting beam
66 Schwarz two-blade fixed-pitch wooden propeller
67 Propeller boss
68 Air intake
69 Exhaust pipe fairing duct
70 Starboard exhaust pipe
71 Port mainwheel
72 Main undercarriage side stay
73 Access step
74 Brake pipe
75 Starboard mainwheel
76 Main undercarriage leg
77 Shock absorber strut

78 Undercarriage mounting framework
79 Rudder pedal
80 Control rod linkage
81 Entry step
82 Cabin door
83 Pilot's seat
84 Observer's/gunner's seat
85 Ammunition magazines (two of 50-round capacity)
86 Starboard flap
87 Plywood flap construction
88 Flap hinge
89 Lattice ribs
90 Wing bracing Vee struts
91 Strut supporting framework
92 Leading edge fixed slat
93 Slat attachment
94 Leading edge construction
95 Aileron control rod linkage
96 Fabric bracing strips
97 Wooden main spar
98 Aileron hinge
99 Aileron balance weight
100 Balance tab
101 Starboard aileron

102 Plywood aileron construction
103 Aileron outer hinge
104 Wing tip construction
105 Navigation light

© Pilot Press Limited

A factory in liberated Czechoslovakia briefly built the Fi 156 prior to the Communist takeover, as the Mraz K.65 Cap. These aircraft are seen in northern Bohemia in 1957, apparently in use as glider tugs.

Focke Wulf Fw 200 Condor

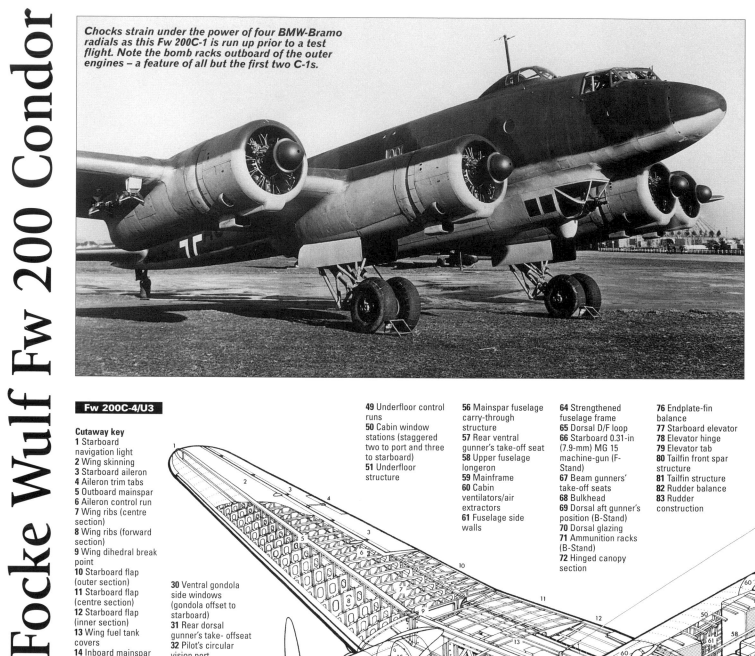

Chocks strain under the power of four BMW-Bramo radials as this Fw 200C-1 is run up prior to a test flight. Note the bomb racks outboard of the outer engines – a feature of all but the first two C-1s.

Fw 200C-4/U3

Cutaway key
1 Starboard navigation light
2 Wing skinning
3 Starboard aileron
4 Aileron trim tabs
5 Outboard mainspar
6 Aileron control run
7 Wing ribs (centre section)
8 Wing ribs (forward section)
9 Wing dihedral break point
10 Starboard flap (outer section)
11 Starboard flap (centre section)
12 Starboard flap (inner section)
13 Wing fuel tank covers
14 Inboard mainspar structure
15 Starboard outer oil tank
16 Multiple exhaust stubs
17 Cooling gills
18 Starboard outer nacelle (angled)
19 Three-blade VDM controllable-pitch metal-bladed propeller
20 Propeler boss
21 Carburettor air intake
22 Auxiliary fuel tank (66 Imp gal/300 litre capacity)
23 Starboard inner nacelle
24 FuG 200 Hohentwiel search radar array (port antenna omitted for clarity)
25 Nose D/F loop
26 Nose bulkhead
27 Rudder pedals
28 Hand-held 0.51-in (13-mm) MG 131 machine-gun (D-Stand)
29 Lotfe 7D bomb sight fairing

30 Ventral gondola side windows (gondola offset to starboard)
31 Rear dorsal gunner's take- offseat
32 Pilot's circular vision port
33 First pilot's seat
34 Sliding windscreen panel
35 Co-pilot's seat (co-pilot also served as bomb- aimer)
36 Flight deck entry
37 Arc-of-fire interrupter gate
38 Cabin air inlet (starboard side only)
39 Hydraulically-operated Fw 19 turret mounting single 0.31-in (7.9-mm) MG 15 machine-gun (A-Stand)
40 Gunner's seat
41 Ammunition racks (A-Stand)
42 Bulkhead
43 Radio operator's rectangular vision port
44 Ventral gondola entry hatch
45 Radio operator's station (A-Stand gunner's station)
46 Ammunition racks (D-Stand)
47 Ammunition racks (D-Stand)

48 Ventral gondola centre section (with maximum capacity of one 198- Imp gal/900-litre armoured fuel tank or 12 110-lb/50-kg bombs)

49 Underfloor control runs
50 Cabin window stations (staggered two to port and three to starboard)
51 Underfloor structure

52 Fuselage oil tank
53 De-icing fluid reservoir
54 Aerial mast
55 Five main fuselage fuel tanks (canted)

56 Mainspar fuselage carry-through structure
57 Rear ventral gunner's take- offseat
58 Upper fuselage longeron
59 Mainframe
60 Cabin ventilators/air extractors
61 Fuselage side walls

62 Ammunition racks (C-Stand)
63 Second radio operator's take-off seat

64 Strengthened fuselage frame
65 Dorsal D/F loop
66 Starboard 0.31-in (7.9-mm) MG 15 machine-gun (F-Stand)
67 Beam gunners' take-off seats
68 Bulkhead
69 Dorsal aft gunner's position (B-Stand)
70 Dorsal glazing
71 Ammunition racks (B-Stand)
72 Hinged canopy section

73 MG 15 machine-gun 0.31-in (7.9-mm calibre)
74 Rear fuselage frames
75 Starboard tailplane

76 Endplate-fin balance
77 Starboard elevator
78 Elevator hinge
79 Elevator tab
80 Tailfin front spar structure
81 Tailfin structure
82 Rudder balance
83 Rudder construction

84 Electrically-operated rudder trim tab (upper section)

A close-up view of an *Fw 200C-3/U2* shows details of the redesigned engine nacelles made necessary by the variant's new *BMW-Bramo Fafnir* engines, the *Fw 19* forward turret reintroduced in this variant and the Condor's complex main undercarriage. Also visible is the ventral gondola which, in the *C-3/U2*, housed a *Lotfe 7D* bomb sight and (though omitted from this aircraft) an *MG 131 0.51-in (13-mm)* machine-gun.

SPECIFICATION

Fw 200C-3/U4 Condor

Dimensions

Wing span: 107 ft 9 in (32.85 m)
Wing area: 1,290.10 sq ft (119.85 m²)
Length: 76 ft 11 in (23.45 m)
Height: 20 ft 8 in (6.30 m)

Powerplant

four BMW-Bramo 323R-2 Fafnir nine-cylinder radial piston engines, each rated at 1,200 hp (895 kW)

Typical weights

Empty: 37,490 lb (17005 kg)
Maximum take-off: 50,057 lb (24520 kg)

Performance

Maximum speed: 224 mph (360 km/h)
Cruising speed: 208 mph (335 km/h)
Service ceiling: 19,685 ft (6000 m)
Range: 2,212 miles (3560 km)
Endurance: 14 hours

Armament

four 13-mm (0.51-in) MG 131 machine-guns in dorsal and beam positions, and one MG 131 or one 20-mm MG 151 cannon in forward ventral gondola; maximum bomb load of 2100 kg (4,630 lb) comprising two 500-kg (1,102-lb), two 250-kg (551-lb) and 12 50-kg (110-lb) bombs

This was the fate which befell a number of *Condors* after months of punishing low-level flying and violent manoeuvres when avoiding *Flak* and/or fighters. The type's airframe was never sufficiently strengthened for the military role, an 'achilles heel' becoming apparent in the rear spar of the mainplane. This proved liable to catastrophic failure, resulting in wing failure (above) or a broken back on landing (below).

85 Electrically-operated rudder trim tab (lower section)
86 Rudderpost
87 Tail wheel mechanism access panel
88 Tail cone
89 Aft navigation light

93 Endplate-fin balance
94 Port tailplane
95 Elevator hinge
96 Tailplane
97 Forward-retracting tailwheel
98 Tailwheel retraction mechanism
99 Control runs
100 Oxygen bottles
101 Aft bulkhead
102 Chute for Schwan D/F buoys, Lux light-buoys or flares
103 Port 0.31-in (7.9-mm) MG 15 beam gun (F-Stand)

106 Aft 0.31-in (7.9-mm) MG 15 ventral gun (C-Stand)
107 Vontral gondola side windows
108 Main fuselage/wing attachment points
109 Ventral weapons/overload fuel bay
110 Port inner nacelle
111 Multiple exhaust stubs
112 Cooling gills
113 Engine mount
114 BMW-Bramo 323 R-2 Fafnir nine-cylinder radial air-cooled engine
115 Propeller pitch mechanism

117 Carburettor air intake
118 Twin mainwheels
119 Forward-retracting hydraulically-operated main undercarriage member
120 Retraction jack
121 Mainwheel well
122 Mainwheel door
123 Wing structure
124 Main spar
125 Wing fuel tanks
126 Flap structure
127 Port flap (centre section)
128 Wing dihedral breakpoint
129 Port outer oil tank
130 Port outer nacelle (angled)

133 Position of 1102-lb (500-kg) bomb on outboard nacelle rack (external)
134 Port underwing bomb rack
135 551-lb (250-kg) bomb
136 Pitot head
137 Wing skinning
138 Port aileron
139 Aileron trim tabs
140 Electrically-operated aileron trim tab (port only)

90 Elevator tab
91 Port elevator
92 Electrically-operated elevator tab (port only)

104 Ammunition racks (F-Stand) – starboard racks identical
105 Entry door

116 Three-blade VDM controllable-pitch metal-bladed propeller

131 Propeller boss
132 Semi-recessed 551-lb (250-kg) bomb beneath outboard nacelle

The Fw 200C-4/U1 was a one-off armed VIP transport version employed by SS commander Heinrich Himmler. Equipped to accommodate 11 passengers, the aircraft had a private compartment for Himmler with an armour-plated seat and an escape hatch in the floor. The aircraft is seen here in RAF markings during post-war evaluation at RAE Farnborough.

Fw 200C-1 Condor

F8+AH of I./KG 40, IV Fliegerkorps, Luftflotte 3, was based at Bordeaux-Mérignac, France, in 1940. In addition to KG 40s' badge, this Condor carries a name in white on its nose cone and kill markings on its fin. This particular aircraft was flown by Obertleutnant Edgar Petersen, the commander of KG 40 and architect of much of the Condor's considerable success over British shipping during its first month of maritime operations.

Radar
Early Fw 200C-4s had FuG Rostock search radar, served by antennas on the nose and outer wings, but this was soon replaced by FuG 200, with the nose antenna arrays. A few aircraft had both Rostock and Hohentwiel, the Rostock having greater range and wider search angle but longer minimum range.

Crew
The addition of an extra gunner in the Fw 200C-3/U4 and subsequent versions brought the crew complement to seven, having been raised from five in the Fw 200C–1 and C-2 to six in the C-3. The basic five-man crew consisted of a pilot and co-pilot, with a flight engineer/gunner, a navigator/bombardier (who also doubled as radio operator/gunner) and a rear dorsal gunner

Bombload
The Fw 200C-1 carried four 250-kg (551-lb) SC 250 bombs on its armed reconnaissance missions. These were carried externally, two under the outboard engine nacelles and two on racks under the wings. The gondola accommodated a similar-sized cement bomb, which was used for calibrating the bombsight or assessing ballistics immediately before the main weapons were released.

Defensive armament
The first four basic Fw 200C-0s were unarmed transports, but the next six had defensive armament and bomb racks for the maritime reconnaissance role. The defensive armament consisted of a single 0.31-in (7.9-mm) MG 15 machine-gun in the vestigial turret above and behind the flight deck, with two similar weapons firing from a downward hatch and from the glazed fairing above the rear fuselage. The C-1 replaced the ventral MG 15 with an offset gondola, in the nose of which was a 20-mm MG FF on a flexible mounting, and with an MG 15 in its tail. The turret above the fuselage was replaced by a fixed cupola with an MG 15 on a flexible mounting. The C-3 replaced the cupola with a powered turret, and introduced two MG 15s behind sliding beam panels, while the C-3/U1 introduced an HDL 151 turret with a 15-mm MG 151 cannon. The gondola's MG FF was replaced by another MG 151. The C-3/U2 and U4 reintroduced the Fw 19 forward upper turret, while the C-3/U3 had an EDL 131 turret with a 0.51-in (13-mm) MG 131, and with another MG 131 in the aft dorsal position. The C-4, C-6 and C-8 reintroduced the high drag HDL 151 turret and had MG 131s in the aft dorsal and beam positions.

Powerplants

The Fw 200C was powered by the same 830-hp (620-kW) BMW 132H air-cooled, nine-cylinder piston engines as its airline progenitor, the Fw 200B-2, although the nacelles were lengthened and the aircraft received long-chord cowlings. The Fw 200C-3 and subsequent versions were powered by the BMW-Bramo 323R-2 Fafnir, rated at 1,000 hp (745 kW) for take off, or 1,200 hp (894 kW) with water-methanol injection. The Fw 200C-2 introduced low drag, cut-down outboard engine nacelles, although C-6 and C-8 missile carriers had deeper outboard nacelles.

Focke Wulf Fw 189 Uhu

Everything about the Fw 189 was slender, especially the wings and tail booms. Despite this, it was an immensely strong aircraft, able to take large amounts of battle damage. The latter was a vital asset in the low-level, over the battlefield environment in which the Uhu operated.

Fw-189 Uhu

Cutaway key
1 Starboard navigation light
2 Aileron control linkage (outer and inner)
3 Starboard aileron
4 Aileron tab
5 Starboard outer flap control linkage
6 Pitot tube
7 ETC 50/VIIId underwing rack fairings
8 Two 50-kg (110-lb) SC 50 bombs
9 Papier-maché 'screamers' attached to bomb fins
10 Wing centre/outer section join
11 Starboard engine nacelle
12 Air intake
13 Argus two-bladed controllable-pitch propeller
14 Pitch control vanes
15 Oil cooler intake
16 Engine air intake

17 FuG 212 Lichtenstein C-1 radar array (fitted to night fighter adaptation)
18 Starboard mainwheel
19 Ventral radio mast
20 Optically flat nose panels
21 Rudder pedals
22 GV 219d bomb sight
23 Control column
24 Bomb switch panel
25 Pilot's ring-and-bead sight (for fixed wing-root machine-guns)
26 Padded overhead instrument panel
27 Navigator's swivel seat
28 Throttle levers
29 Pilot's seat
30 Mainspar carry-through
31 Centre-hinged two-piece canopy hatch
32 Turnover bar with attached plasticised anti-glare curtain
33 Radio equipment

34 Shell collector box
35 Centre-section camera well (one RB 20/30, RB 50/30, RB 21/18 or RB 15/18 camera)
36 Canvas shell collection chute
37 Dorsal turret
38 MG 81Z twin 7.9-mm machine-gun
39 MG 151 (15-mm) fixed cannon in 'schräge Musik' installation (fitted to night fighter adaptation)
40 Starboard tailboom
41 Rudder and elevator control cables
42 Ammunition stowage (dorsal position)
43 Entry handholds
44 Centre-section flap below crew nacelle
45 Wing-root gun access panel (raised)
46 Rear turret-cone drive motor
47 Rear gunner's two-

piece quilted pad
48 Ammunition stowage (rear position)
49 Rear canopy opening
50 MG 81Z twins 7.9-mm machine-guns (trunnion mounted)
51 Revolving Ikarin powered cone turret
52 Field or fire cut out
53 Aft glazing
54 Tailboom mid-section strengthening frame
55 Starboard tailfin
56 Starboard rudder
57 Rudder tab
58 Elevator construction
59 Tailplane forward spar
60 Elevator tab
61 Tailplane construction
62 Tailwheel hinged (two piece) door
63 Tailwheel (swivelling)
64 Tailwheel retraction mechanism

With a completely redesigned fuselage nacelle, the Fw 189B was intended as a five-seat trainer. Ten of the Fw 189B-1 production aircraft were delivered before Fw 189A production began.

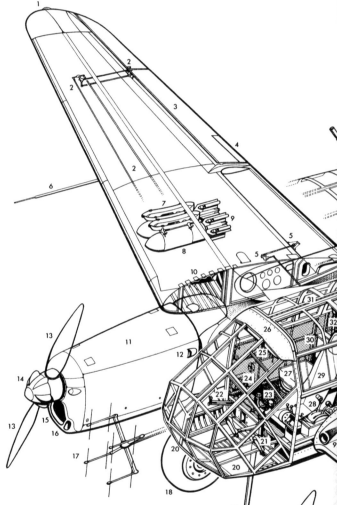

65 Tailwheel well (offset to port)
66 Tailfin construction
67 Rudder tab
68 Rear navigation light
69 Tail bumper
70 Tailboom frames
71 Tailboom upper longeron
72 Mid-section strengthening frame
73 Tail surface control cables
74 External stiffening strake (upper and lower)
75 Master compass
76 Wing-root fairing
77 Port outer flap construction
78 Aileron tab

79 Aileron construction
80 Port navigation light
81 Wing stringers (upper shell)
82 Lower shell wing inner skin stringers
83 Two-piece shaped wing ribs
84 Mainspar structure
85 Mainspar/boom attachment point
86 Rear spar/boom attachment point
87 Port fuel tank (24.2 Imp gal/110 litres)
88 Centre section one-piece flap
89 Wing walkway
90 Fixed 7.9-mm MG 17 machine-gun

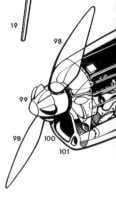

SPECIFICATION	
Focke-Wulf Fw 189A-1	**Weights**
Type	Empty 6,185 lb (2805 kg); maximum take-off 8,708 lb (3950 kg)
Two-seat short-range reconnaissance aircraft	**Dimensions**
Powerplant	Wingspan 60 ft 4½ in (18.40 m); length 39 ft 5½ in (12.03 m); height 10 ft 2 in (3.10 m); wing area 409.04 sq ft (38.00 m2)
Two 465-hp (347-kW) Argus As 410A-1 12-cylinder inverted Vee piston engines	Armament: two flexible 0.31-in (7.92-mm) MG 15 machine-guns, two 0.31-in (7.92-mm) MG 17 machine-guns and four 110-lb (50-kg) bombs
Performance	
Maximum speed 208 mph (335 km/h); cruising speed 196 mph (315 km/h); service ceiling 22,965 ft (7000 m); range 416 miles (670 km)	

The first V1 prototype took to the air in July 1938, with Kurt Tank himself at the controls. The aircraft, registered D-OPVN, differed little from the production aircraft which followed.

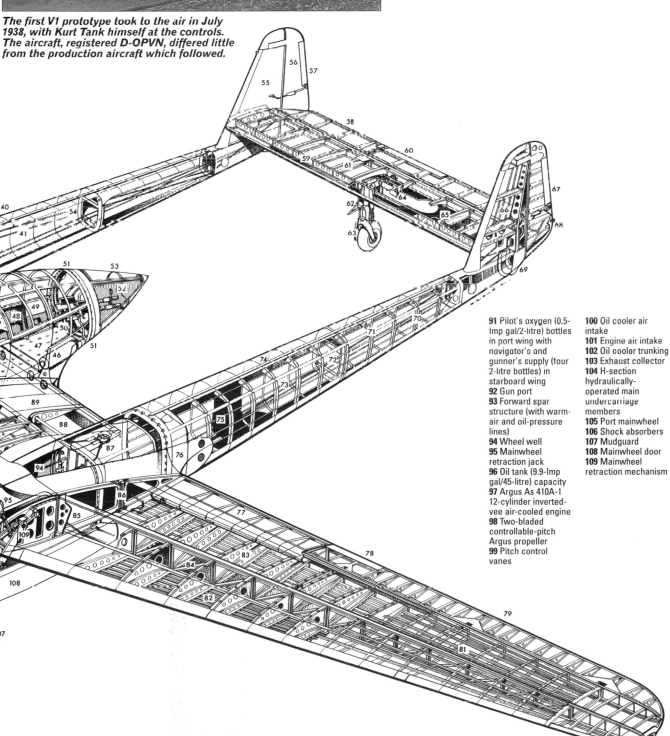

91 Pilot's oxygen (0.5-Imp gal/2-litre) bottles in port wing with navigator's and gunner's supply (four 2-litre bottles) in starboard wing
92 Gun port
93 Forward spar structure (with warm-air and oil-pressure lines)
94 Wheel well
95 Mainwheel retraction jack
96 Oil tank (9.9-Imp gal/45-litre) capacity
97 Argus As 410A-1 12-cylinder inverted-vee air-cooled engine
98 Two-bladed controllable-pitch Argus propeller
99 Pitch control vanes
100 Oil cooler air intake
101 Engine air intake
102 Oil cooler trunking
103 Exhaust collector
104 H-section hydraulically-operated main undercarriage members
105 Port mainwheel
106 Shock absorbers
107 Mudguard
108 Mainwheel door
109 Mainwheel retraction mechanism

Junkers Ju 52

Although it was the best transport type the Luftwaffe possessed, the Ju 52/3m was slow, lacked manoeuvrability and defensive armament and was an easy target for marauding Allied fighters.

Junkers Ju-52

Cutaway key
1 Starboard navigation light
2 Drooping aileron section of Junkers 'double wing'
3 Aileron hinge fairings
4 Control linkage
5 Underwing inspection panels
6 Corrugated wing skin
7 Aerial mast
8 Wing strut diagonal bracing
9 Starboard oil filler cap
10 House-flag mast
11 Starboard engine cowling (NACA cowling)
12 Junkers metal two-blade propeller
13 Centre BMW 132A radial engine (in Townend ring)
14 Exhaust
15 Filter intakes
16 Engine bearers
17 Bulkhead
18 Centre oil tank
19 Oil filler cap
20 Flat windscreen panels
21 Co-pilot's seat
22 Radio-operator's jump-seat
23 Pilot's seat
24 Control column
25 Rudder pedals
26 Raised cockpit floor level
27 Control linkage
28 Control lines
29 Port BMW 132A radial engine (in NACA cowling)
30 Bulkhead
31 Engine bearers
32 Engine oil tank

33 Oil filler cap
34 Fuel filler cap
35 Mainwheel support strut
36 Mainwheel spat
37 Exhaust
38 Port mainwheel
39 Corrugated wing skin
40 Multi-spar wing structure
41 Diagonal cross-brace members
42 Pitot head
43 Port navigation light
44 Drooping aileron section of Junkers 'double wing'
45 Aileron hinge fairings
46 Trim tab
47 Tab control
48 Control runs
49 Inner section trailing-edge flap
50 Control linkage
51 Port wing fuel tanks
52 Fuselage/wing ball-and-socket attachment points
53 Centre aisle
54 Single-seat cabin arrangement (17 maximum)
55 Upper fuselage longeron
56 Luggage rack
57 Ceiling lights
58 Aerial
59 Two-seat rear bench
60 Passenger entry door
61 Underfloor control lines
62 Entry vestibule
63 Entry steps attachment
64 Toilet compartment
65 Rear cabin bulkhead
66 Cabin ventilation

67 Cargo compartment
68 Luggage loading hatch
69 Baggage shelves
70 Aft fuselage frames
71 Inspection walkway
72 Lower fuselage longeron
73 Fuselage construction
74 Control lines
75 Rear fuselage frame
76 Fin/fuselage attachment
77 Tailskid spring
78 Tailskid
79 Port tailplane structure
80 Port elevator
81 Lower rudder hinge

82 Control linkage
83 Multi-spar tailplane construction
84 Elevator corrugated skin
85 Fin construction
86 Rudder control linkage
87 Rudder post
88 Rudder structure
89 Corrugated skin
90 Rear navigation light

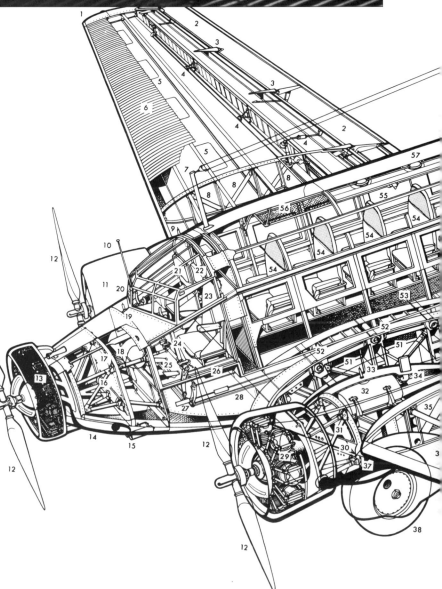

German forces in North Africa relied heavily on supplies and reinforcements delivered by Ju 52/3ms. These aircraft are seen in April 1941 shortly before the German invasion of Crete which saw the Ju 52/3m in its other major role – as a paratroop assault transport.

SPECIFICATION

Junkers Ju 52/3mg3e

Type

Medium bomber and troop transport

Powerplant

Three 725-hp (541-kW) BMW 132A-3 radial piston engines

Performance

Maximum speed 171 mph (275 km/h) at 2,955 ft (900 m); service ceiling 19,360 ft (5900 m); range with auxiliary fuel 808 miles (1300 km)

Weights

Empty 12,610 lb (5720 kg); maximum take-off 23,149 lb (10500 kg)

Dimensions

Wingspan 95 ft 11½ in (29.25 m); length 62 ft (18.90 m); height 18 ft 2½ in (5.55 m); wing area 1,189.45 sq ft (110.50 m2)

Armament

Two 0.31-in (7.92-mm) MG15 machine-guns, plus up to 1,102 lb (500 kg) of bombs

Close-up of the Ju 52/3m's engine arrangement. Essentially similar to the single-engined variant from which it was developed, the prototype flew in April 1932, powered by three Pratt & Whitney Hornet radials.

Junkers Ju 52

Development of the basic single-engined Ju 52 design led the Junkers firm to produce a three-engined version, the Ju 52/3m. The prototype, coded 4007, flew in April 1932, powered by three licence-built Pratt & Whitney Hornet nine-cylinder radials. The Ju 52/3mg5e, seen here, was powered by three BMW 132T-2 radials. The two outboard engines faced slightly outwards to reduce yaw should one of them fail. The exhaust gases were collected by annular ducts, which gave the aircraft its distinctive appearance.

Radio equipment
The Ju 52 had a loop antenna for direction-finding equjipment, and an aerial mast mounted behind the cockpit. Radio equipment was constantly improved, and several Ju 52s were fitted with specialist equipment of one kind or another. This included a large-diameter duralumin hoop which, when energized by a small auxiliary motor, was used for detonating magnetic mines. Aircraft carrying this device were used by the Minensuchgruppe based at Cognac, Le Leu and Biarritz. Later versions of the Ju 52 wre fitted with an automatic pilot.

Undercarriage
The Ju 52's undercarriage had to be very robust to cope with repeated landings on rough fields. Spats were issued to reduce the drag created by the wheels, but on operations these would clog up with mud and debris, and were rarely fitted. Many aircraft were fitted with floats in place of the wheeled undercarriage. The first Ju 52/3m floatplanes were operated by Aero O/Y, a Finnish company, and Sweden's AB Aerotransport. One Lufthansa Ju 52 was used to fly the Olympic Torch from Greece to Berlin for the 1936 Olympic Games.

Armament

The dorsal hatch had a mounting for a 0.31in (7.92mm) MG 15 machine gun. A transparent fairing was fixed in front of it to give the gunner some protection from the slipstream in flight. The first Ju 52 variant for the Luftwaffe, the Ju 52mg3e, was designed as a heavy bomber with a crew of four and armed with two MG 15 machine guns, one mounted in the dorsal position and the other carried in a retractable 'dustbin' suspended under the fuselage. The Ju 52 was soon superseded by more modern types of bomber aircraft.

Construction

The corrugated fuselage was a common feature of many early Junkers designs. The metal skin was load-bearing, and the corrugation gave it immense strength for little weight penalty. The first aircraft to use this type of skin was the Junkers J4 of 1917, and the Ju 52 was the last. The first Junkers all-metal monoplane was the J1, completed in 1915; it was developed via the Junkers D1 monoplane fighter into the F13 four-passenger transport, which was one of the most advanced aircraft if its time. The prototype flew on 25 June, 1919.

Operations

When fitted with seats the Ju 52 could carry up to 18 passengers, sitting in single rows separated by an aisle. The aircraft's value as a military transport was first demonstrated during the Spanish Civil War, when 20 Ju 52/3ms were used to ferry 10,000 colonial troops from Morocco to Spain in support of General Franco's nationalist uprising. The Ju 52s then carried out many bombing operations in support of the land battle around Madrid in November 1936. The Spanish nicknamed the Ju 52 Pava (Turkey).

Savoia Marchetti SM.79 Sparviero

One of the highly successful torpedo-bomber units equipped with the Sparviero, 278ª Squadriglia, 132° Gruppo was based in Sicily and Sardinia for much of 1942/43, operating against Allied shipping in the Mediterranean.

SM.79-I Sparviero

Cutaway key

1 Starboard pitot tube
2 Starboard navigation light
3 Three-spar wing structure
4 Aileron mass balance
5 Starboard aileron
6 Aileron control rods
7 Flap linkage
8 Starboard slotted flap
9 Starboard outer fuel tank, capacity 33 Imp gal (150 litres)
10 Flap rod
11 Wing skinning
12 Leading-edge slot
13 Starboard engine nacelle
14 Propeller
15 Exhaust collector ring
16 Three-bladed propeller
17 Spinner
18 Engine cowling ring
19 Alfa Romeo 126 radial engine
20 Exhaust
21 Engine bearers
22 Firewall bulkhead
23 Oil filter
24 Starboard mainwheel
25 Ventral landing lamp
26 Undercarriage cylinders
27 Nose compartment access panel
28 Intake
29 Centre engine oil tank
30 Undercarriage warning horns
31 Fire extinguisher
32 Instrument panel
33 Control column
34 Rudder pedals
35 Main fuel filter
36 Flap control linkage
37 Oil cooler intakes
38 Front spar/fuselage frame pick-up
39 Pilot's seat
40 Central control console

41 Pilot's seat
42 Windscreen panels
43 Roof panels
44 Fixed forward-firing 12.7-mm (0.5-in) Breda-SAFAT machine-gun
45 Dorsal fairing frame
46 Ammunition tank
47 Link collector box
48 Radio transmitter/receiver
49 Radio operator's position
50 Main spar carry-through
51 Central forward fuel tank, capacity 46 Imp gal (210 litres)
52 Port forward fuel tank, capacity 44 Imp gal (200 litres)
53 Port aft fuel tank, capacity 111 Imp gal (505 litres)
54 Main spar/fuselage frame pick-up
55 Rear spar/fuselage frame pick-up
56 Central aft fuel tank, capacity 128 Imp gal (580 litres)
57 Oxygen cylinder
58 Crew compartment entry steps
59 Flight mechanic's seat
60 Bulkhead partition
61 Ammunition tanks
62 Link collector box
63 Radio operator's seat
64 Fixed window
65 Flexible link chute
66 Dorsal blister
67 Dorsal glazing
68 Dorsal flexible 12.7-mm (0.50-in) Breda-SAFAT machine-gun
69 Gun support bracket
70 Sliding fairing
71 Bomb bay support frame

72 Bomb vertical stowage attachment lugs
73 Twelve 100-kg (220-lb) bombs (alternatives: five 250-kg (550-lb) or two 500 kg (1,100 lb) bombs
74 Bomb magazine (offset to starboard)
75 Bomb bay doors
76 Fuselage frames
77 Crew entry catwalk
78 OMI vertical camera installation
79 Ventral gondola
80 Jozza bombsight
81 Bomb-aimer's rudder control handwheel

82 Starboard side windows (three)
83 Radio receiver
84 Fuel header tank, capacity 8.8 Imp gal (40 litres)
85 Dorsal fairing fixed aft section
86 Plywood dorsal skinning
87 D/F loop
88 Starboard waist position
89 Waist gun mounting bar
90 Verey cartridge stowage boxes
91 Crew entry doorway
92 Bomb-aimer's sliding knee supports

93 Flexible link chute
94 Ventral gondola fairing
95 Ventral flexible 12.7-mm (0.50-in) Breda-SAFAT machine-gun
96 Gondola hinged aftersection
97 Port side windows (two)
98 Ammunition feed
99 Waist machine gun
100 Ammunition tank
101 Mist window frame

102 Elevator control linkage
103 Control rods
104 Fuselage structure
105 Fabric side covering
106 Fin/fuselage attachment
107 Fin spar
108 Starboard tailplane
109 Elevator balance
110 Starboard elevator
111 Fin structure

112 Rudder upper hinge
113 Rudder torque tube
114 Rudder frame
115 Rudder tab
116 Rudder lower hinge
117 Tailplane brace strut
118 Rudder tab control link
119 Port elevator

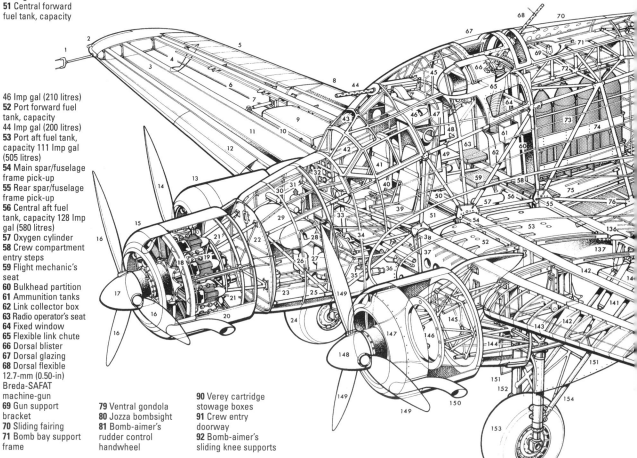

SPECIFICATION

SM.79-I Sparviero

Dimensions

Length: 51 ft 2 in (15.60 m)
Height: 15 ft 1 in (4.60 m)
Wingspan: 69 ft 6¾ in (21.20 m)
Wing area: 664.2 sq ft (61.70 m²)

Powerplant

Three Alfa Romeo 126 RC.34 nine-cylinder radial piston engines, each rated at 780 hp (582 kW) for take off

Weights

Empty: 15,322 lb (6950 kg)
Maximum take-off: 23,655 lb (10730 kg)

Performance

Maximum speed at 13,125 ft (4000 m): 267 mph (430 km/h)
Climb to 13,125 ft (4000 m): 13 minutes 15 seconds
Maximum range at 211 mph (340 km/h): 2,050 miles (3300 km)
Service ceiling at maximum take-off weight: 21,325 ft (6500 m)

Armament

One fixed 12.7-mm (0.5-in) machine-gun firing forward over cabin roof, guns of the same calibre in dorsal position and in rear of ventral position, one 7.7-mm (0.303-in) machine-gun for beam defence, plus a maximum bomb load of five 250-kg (551-lb) or one 45-cm (17.70-in) torpedo

An experimental twin-torpedo installation was tested at Gorizia in the spring of 1938. As it caused a marked deterioration in aircraft performance, the modification was abandoned.

This SM.79-II was seized by the Luftwaffe after the Armistice and employed as a transport. Note that it retains its defensive armament.

155 Leading-edge slot
156 Wooden wing structure
157 Slotted flap
158 Aileron frame
159 Wing skinning
160 Port wingtip structure
161 Port navigation light
162 Port pitot tube

120 Elevator balance
121 Tailplane structure
122 Non-retracting tailwheel
123 Tailwheel steering mechanism
124 Tailwheel shock absorber
125 Rudder control links
126 Elevator control horn

127 Tailplane inboard end rib
128 Tailplane spar attachment
129 Tailplane lower struts attachment bracket
130 Fuselage lower frame
131 Crew hinged entry door (integral steps)
132 Door fully extended position
133 Bomb-aimer's ventral position
134 Wingroot strut
135 Fixed inboard trailing-edge section
136 Rearspar
137 Mainwheel well
138 Rear nacelle fuel tank, capacity 106 Imp gal (480 litres)
139 Port outer fuel tank, capacity 33 Imp gal (150 litres)

140 Undercarriage retraction strut attachment
141 Retraction jack
142 Main spar
143 Undercarriage mounting bracket
144 Nacelle support frame
144 Engine bearer assembly
146 Engine mounting ring
147 Exhaust collector ring
148 Spinner
149 Three-bladed propeller
150 Exhaust
151 Mainwheel doors
152 Mainwheel oleo legs
153 Port mainwheel
154 Retraction struts

Sparvieros in Spain

From the outset the Regia Aeronautica test pilots expressed enthusiasm for the SM.79, and production orders were placed, before the end of 1935. Early aircraft, SM.79-Is, with three 780-hp (582-kW) Alfa Romeo 126 RC.34 radials, entered service with the 8' and 11P Stormi Bombardamento Veloce (fast bomber groups) in 1936. In 1937 these units were sent to Spain to serve with the Aviacion del Tercio, flying during the Spanish Civil War as the 27º and 28º Gruppi (Falchi delle Baleari, Hawks of Balearics, based in the Balearic Islands), and the 29º and 30º Gruppi (Sparvieri, or Sparrows). These units, together with two of SM.81s, flew 5,318 sorties, dropped 11,850 tons of bombs and scored 224 direct hits on government vessels. At the end of the Civil War the new Spanish government took over 80 SM.79s and these came to provide a major portion of the Spanish air force's bombing arm for many years to come. Pictured are SM.79-I bombers of XXVII Gruppo Bombardamento Terrestre, Aviacion del Tercio during the Spanish Civil War. Note the green blotching on sand camouflage of the nearest aircraft, which contrasts with the brown and sand schemes of the other aircraft.

SM.79-II Sparviero

This 'sparrowhawk' of 283ª Squadriglia, 130° Gruppo Autonomo Aerosiluranti was based at Gerbini, Sicily during 1942. During this period the 280° and 283° Squadriglie concentrated on attacking the Malta convoys, most notably 'Harpoon' during June. By the beginning of January 1943 the Gruppo had just nine serviceable aircraft and withdrew to Italy to reform and retrain.

Armament

Above the cockpit was a single Breda-SAFAT 12.7-mm (0.5-in) machine-gun, fixed in the roofing and fired by the pilot. A similar weapon on a flexible mount was situated in the rear of the blister, covered by a panel when not in use. Protection to the rear and sides was provided by a 7.7-mm (0.303-in) machine-gun for the waist position, and a Breda-SAFAT 12.7-mm (0.5-in) gun in the rear of the ventral gondola. The waist gun was mounted on a lateral bar so that it could fire out of either beam window.

Powerplant

Early versions of the SM.79 featured only two engines, but the major production for the Regia Aeronautica and Aerosiluranti were three-engined. The SM.79-II was the major production version, and featured the Piaggio P.XI RC.40 radial, rated at 1,000 hp (746 kW). The central engine was mounted externally on bearers attached to a firewall bulkhead. The gap between the cowling and the fuselage was partially filled with a secondary cowl which still allowed the passage of cooling air through the engine itself. The oil tank was mounted behind the bulkhead.

Camera

To provide a limited reconnaissance capability, the SM.79 could be fitted with an OMI vertical camera, situated in the rear fuselage forward of the ventral gondola and peering through a flat pane in the cabin floor.

Bomb load

The SM.79 carried its bombs vertically, stowed in a bay offset to starboard aft of the rear spar. A maximum load was five 250-kg (551-lb) weapons, with two 500-kg (1,102-lb) bombs or 12 100-kg (220-lb) bombs as common alternatives. The SM.79 scored its greatest successes as a torpedo-bomber with the Gruppi Aerosiluranti (specialist torpedo-bombing units). These carried one or two weapons under the fuselage, usually a 45-cm (17.70-in) weapon.

Fuel

The S.M.79 carried its fuel in 11 tanks. Six were inboard of the nacelles located between the spars, comprising port and starboard forward (44 Imp gal/200 litres each), port and starboard aft (111 Imp gal/505 litres each), central forward (46 Imp gal/210 litres) and central aft (128 Imp gal/580 litres). A further tank of 33 Imp gal (150 litres) was located between the central and rear spars outboard of each engine nacelle, while the rear of each nacelle had a 106-Imp gal (480-litre) tank. A small (8.8-Imp gal/40-litre) header tank in the upper rear fuselage brought the internal capacity to 770 Imp gal (3500 litres).

Fuselage and wing structure

The fuselage was built on a traditional frame structure, the main members running along the four corners of the fuselage and forming a rectangular frame work. The curved upper decking was a secondary structure, skinned in plywood. The fuselage sides were fabric-covered. The Sparviero had a three-spar wing, the spars carrying through the lower fuselage and the top of each engine nacelle. The structure was of wood.

Camouflage and markings

This SM.79 has the standard presentation of its squadriglia number ('283') on the rear fuselage, followed by the individual aircraft number. The white cross on the fin constituted national markings, as did the fasces symbol on the nose and underwing. This symbol was a bundle of rods with a protruding axe, a Roman symbol of state power adopted by Mussolini's Fascist movement. SM.79s were flown wearing many different camouflage patterns, but most featured the 'sand-and-spinach' style finish. This consisted of a basic sandcoloured base, with mottles of two tones of green applied on top. In common with Luftwaffe aircraft in the Mediterranean, white theatre bands were worn around the rear fuselage and engine cowlings.

Ventral gondola

In addition to housing the rear-facing gun, the gondola provided a bomb-aiming station, the bomb-aimer being provided with forward-and downward-facing flat panes. At his side was a small wheel with which he made minute corrections to the aircraft's path by controlling the rudder. The rear of the gondola was a hinged fairing which retracted to allow the gun to fire.

Short Sunderland

BOAC Sunderland Mk III G-AGIA started life as RAF aircraft ML728 and joined the airline in July 1943 for use on priority passenger and mail services to West Africa, India and (after VJ-Day) Burma. Twenty-four aircraft were converted for use on these routes, all military equipment and armament being removed and basic bench-and-mattress seating being fitted.

Sunderland Mk

Cutaway key
1 Twin Vickers 0.303-in (7.7-mm) machine-guns
2 Bomb aiming window, retractable
3 Bomb aimers station
4 Retractable nose turret
5 Front entry/mooring hatch
6 Mooring cable stowage
7 Hull planing bottom
8 Anchor
9 Parachute stowage
10 Anchor winch
11 Dinghy
12 Front turret rails
13 Cockpit bulkhead
14 Mooring ladder
15 Toilet compartment door, starboard side
16 Nose gun turret hydraulic reservoir
17 Instrument panel
18 Windscreens
19 Cockpit roof glazing
20 Overhead control panels
21 Co-pilot's seat
22 Signal cartridge rack
23 Pilot's seat
24 Control column
25 Raised cockpit floor level
26 Autopilot controllers
27 Stairway between upper and lower decks
28 Front entry door
29 Fuselage chine member
30 Crew luggage locker
31 Rifle rack
32 Wardroom door
33 Planing bottom hull construction
34 Wardroom bunks
35 Window panes
36 Folding table
37 Upper deck floor level
38 Parachute stowage
39 Fire extinguisher
40 Navigator's seat
41 Chart table
42 Forward ASV radar aerial mast

43 Navigator's instrument panel
44 Flight engineer's aft facing seat
45 Radio operator's station
46 Air intake duct
47 Wing/fuselage attachment main frames
48 Wing root rib cut-outs
49 Air conditioning plant
50 Engineer's control panels
51 Carburettor de-icing fluid tank
52 D/F loop aerial
53 Astrodome observation hatch
54 Auxiliary Power Unit
55 Forward inner fuel tank, 529-Imp gal (2405-litre) capacity
56 Fold-down, leading-edge maintenance platform
57 Starboard inner engine nacelle
58 Cowling air flaps
59 Detachable engine cowlings
60 Flame suppressor exhaust pipe
61 Forward inner fuel tank, 325-Imp gal (1477-litre) capacity
62 Oil coolers
63 Forward outer fuel tank, 132-Imp gal (600-litre) capacity
64 Starboard wing tip float
65 de Havilland three-bladed, constant-speed propeller, 12ft 9in (3.89 m) diameter
66 Propeller hub pitch change mechanism
67 Engine reduction gearbox
68 Bristol Pegasus XVIII, nine-cylinder radial engine, 1065 hp (794 kW)
69 Exhaust collector ring
70 Oil filter
71 Oil tank, 32-Imp gal (145-litre) capacity
72 Flame suppressor exhaust pipe
73 Leading edge de-icing

74 Starboard ASV aerial array
75 Starboard navigation light
76 Aileron hinges
77 Starboard aileron
78 Fixed tab
79 Aileron control horns
80 Control cable runs
81 Starboard 'Gouge-type' trailing-edge flap
82 Flap guide rails
83 Rear outer fuel tank, 147-Imp gal (668-litre) capacity
84 Flap jack
85 Rear inner fuel tank, 111-Imp gal (505-litre) capacity
86 Pitot tubes
87 Aerial mast
88 Observation window
89 Propeller de-icing fluid tank
90 Windscreen de-icing fluid tank
91 Bomb carriage traversing drive motor
92 Smoke floats and flame floats
93 Tailplane control cable runs
94 Reconnaissance flares
95 Turret fairing

96 Mid-upper gun turret, offset to starboard
97 Twin Browning 0.303-in (7.7 mm) machine guns
98 Fuselage skin plating

99 Spare propeller blade stowage
100 Fire extinguisher
101 Rear entry door
102 Maintenance platform stowage
103 Observation window

104 Fuselage frame and stringer construction
105 ASV Mk II search radar aerial array
106 Leading edge de-icing
107 Starboard tailplane

108 Starboard elevator
109 Fin root attachments
110 Fin construction
111 Leading edge de-icing
112 Fin tip construction

The Sunderland's flight deck was relatively spacious and provided an excellent all-round view for its pilots. The covered buttons on the pilot's control wheel (left) are for bomb release and firing the four forward-firing, nose-mounted guns.

SPECIFICATION

Sunderland Mk III

Dimensions

Wing span: 112 ft 9½ in (34.38 m)
Wing area: 1,487 sq ft (119.85 m²)
Length: 85 ft 4 in (26.01 m)
Height (on beaching chassis): 32 ft 2 in (9.79 m)

Powerplant

Four Bristol Pegasus XVIII nine-cylinder radial piston engines, each rated at 1,065 hp (794 kW)

Typical weights

Empty: 33,000 lb (14969 kg)
All-up: 58,000 lb (26308 kg)

Performance

Maximum speed: 212 mph (341 km/h)

Initial climb rate: 790 ft (241 m) per minute
Service ceiling: 15,000 ft (4570 m)
Range: 3,000 miles (4828 km) at 145 mph (233 km/h)
Endurance: 20 hours

Armament

One 0.303-in (7.7-mm) Vickers GO machine-gun in nose turret, two 0.303-in (7.7-mm) Browning machine-guns in mid-upper turret, four similar Brownings in tail turret; optional second nose turret gun, four fixed Brownings firing ahead and twin 0.5-in (12.7-mm) Brownings fired from waist hatches; assorted ordnance to total weight of 4,960 lb (2250 kg) housed in hull and cranked out under wings prior to attack

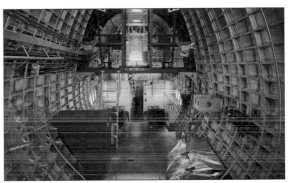

Above: This view of a Sunderland Mk I's interior, looking forward towards the cockpit, gives an impression of the spaciousness of the aircraft's fuselage, with its double-deck layout.

Below: WAAFs service a Sunderland's Bristol 'Peggies' between sorties from a Coastal Command base. The Sunderland was always considered underpowered until the Mk V entered service.

© 2001 Mike Badrocke/Aviagraphica

113 Fabric covered rudder construction
114 Rudder tabs
115 Tail gun
116 Four Browning 0.303-in (7.7-mm) machine guns
117 Elevator tab
118 Fabric-covered elevator construction
119 Port tailplane construction
120 Leading edge de-icing
121 Tailplane spar fixing fuselage double frames
122 Tail fuselage fabric draught screen
123 Smoke and flame floats
124 Handrail
125 Tail fuselage walkway
126 Reconnaissance flare chute, stowed
127 Mooring shackle
128 Tow bar
129 Rear beaching trolley

130 Camera stowage
131 Dinghy paddles
132 Distress flares
133 Emergency ration container
134 Dinghy stowage
135 Crew luggage locker
136 Tool locker
137 Bilge keel construction
138 Rear fuselage deck level
139 Crew rest bunks
140 Trailing-edge wing root fillet
141 Reconnaissance camera mounting
142 Ditching flare chutes
143 Ladder to upper deck level
144 Rear wardroom
145 Twin bunks
146 Fuselage bomb door, open
147 Retractable bomb carriage
148 Four 100-lb (45.4-kg) bombs

149 Bomb store and loading room maximum bomb load, 2000 lb (907 kg)
150 Port flap shroud
151 Port 'Gouge-type' trailing-edge flap
152 Fabric-covered aileron construction
153 Aileron tab, fixed
154 Trailing-edge lattice ribs
155 Wing tip construction
156 Port navigation light
157 Rearspar
158 Wing rib construction
159 Front spar
160 Leading-edge de-icing
161 Port ASV radar aerial
162 Wing-tip float construction
163 Float support struts
164 Diagonal wire bracing

165 Wing spar girder construction
166 Landing lamps
167 Leading-edge rib construction
168 Diagonal wire-braced wing ribs
169 Fold-down, leading-edge maintenance platform
170 Engine nacelle construction
171 Engine mounting ring
172 Port outer engine nacelle
173 Oil cooler intakes
174 Oil coolers

175 Exhaust shroud heat exchangers
176 Port inner engine nacelle
177 Emergency escape hatch
178 Ice chest
179 Drogue container
180 Galley compartments, port and starboard
181 Watertight trailing aerial socket
182 Main beaching gear leg strut
183 Twin beaching wheels

Sunderland Mk II

Sunderland Mk II T9087 was an aircraft of No. 201 Squadron, Coastal Command, based on Lough Erne, Northern Ireland from September 1941 until March 1944. One of 20 Sunderland IIs built by Blackburn, in Dumbarton, it is depicted as it would have appeared during 1942, with the unit's 'ZM' codes and typical 'early war' Coastal Command camouflage of Dark Slate Grey, Extra Dark Sea Grey extending well down the sides of the hull and with Sky lower surfaces.

Powerplant

Early Sunderlands, like this aircraft, had 1,010-hp (753-kW) Bristol Pegasus XXII engines, but after the 35th airframe had been completed, 1,065-hp (794-kW) Pegasus XVIIIs, with two-speed superchargers, had been substituted. It was not until the Mk V the 1,200-hp (865-kW) Pratt & Whitney Twin Wasps were adopted, the last giving Short's airframe sufficient power to compensate for its increased weight.

Flight deck

The two pilots sat side-by-side with full dual controls, with the navigator and wireless operator behind them facing to starboard and port respectively. The flight engineer sat further back, facing aft. Because the Air Ministry distrusted the optical qualities of the curved windscreen of the Empire, the windscreen and canopies consisted of flat Triplex panels.

Hull

By comparison with the 'Empire'-class flying boat from which it was derived, the Sunderland had a cleaner hull, with a rear step tapering to a vertical knife edge. The Mk III introduced a fully faired step, which reduced drag, but caused bounce-porpoising or skipping in the water.

Twin-deck layout

Forward of the entrance door on the lower deck was the dinghy and anchor stowage (and the bomb-aimers compartment with its hinging bomb-aimers window), while the wardroom with its folding bunks and tables was situated aft. Behind this was a small workshop, and aft of the rear step was a walkway to the tail gunner's compartment. The upper deck began with the spacious flight deck, with the galley between the main frames under the wing and the bomb room aft.

Fuel tanks

The Sunderland had three drum-like fuel tanks in the inner part of each wing, aft of the leading edge. The innermost of these contained 529 Imp gal (2405 litres), the next 325 Imp gal (1477 litres) and the outermost 132 Imp gal (600 litres). Aft of these were box-like tanks containing 147 Imp gal (668 litres, outer) and 111 Imp gal (505 litres, inner).

D/F loop aerial and aerial mast

A streamlined fairing contained the direction finding (D/F) loop antenna, and was located adjacent to the navigator's astrodome, which itself was used for taking sun and star shots with an old-fashioned sextant. A huge aerial mast above the centre fuselage also served as a mounting point for twin pitot tubes.

Mid-upper turret

In all but the first few Mk IIs, a pair of open K-gun mountings (with streamlined metal slipstream protectors) in the upper fuselage were replaced by a power-operated Frazer Nash FN.7 mid-upper turret offset to starboard. This was similar to the unit used in the Blackburn Botha, and contained a pair of 0.303-in (7.7-mm) machine-guns.

Radar

Most Mk II Sunderlands were fitted with ASV Mk II radar, which necessitated the fitting of four vertical dipole mast antennas above the fuselage and 16 transmitter loops on masts projecting horizontally from the rear fuselage in two fore-and-aft rows of four masts. Yagi homing aerials were carried below the outer wings and above the flight deck. The Germans eventually developed radar warning gear capable of detecting the ASV Mk II's 4.92-ft (1.5-m) transmissions. This was countered by ASV Mk III, which incorporated Bomber Command's H_2S.

Depth charges

The ineffective 100-lb (45-kg) depth charges were soon replaced by 250-lb (113-kg) charges filled with Torpex. Stored in a bomb room aft of the wing, these were moved electrically out below the wing through hinged drop panels in the fuselage.

De-icing

Pneumatic rubber 'pulsating' de-icer boots were fitted to the leading edges of the wings, tailplanes and tailfins on all but the earliest Sunderlands.

Defensive armament

The Sunderland's generous array of defensive armament, which the Luftwaffe believed to include 20-mm cannon, resulted in it being nicknamed the *Fliegende Stachelschwein* ('Flying Porcupine'). While it is true that in several incidents, lone Sunderlands shot down several attacking fighters, the aircraft's 0.303-in (7.7-mm) machine-gun armament often proved insufficiently light to inflict decisive damage on an attacking aircraft.

Index